WEBSTER'S
UNIVERSAL

MEDICAL
DICTIONARY

**GEDDES &
GROSSET**

The material contained in this book is set out in good faith for general guidance only. Whilst every effort has been made to ensure that the information in this book is accurate, relevant and up to date, this book is sold on the condition that neither the author nor the publisher can be found legally responsible for the consequences of any errors or omissions.

Diagnosis and treatment are skilled undertakings which must always be carried out by a doctor and not from the pages of a book.

This edition published 2007
by Geddes & Grosset,
David Dale House, New Lanark,
ML11 9DJ, Scotland

Copyright © 2004 Geddes & Grosset

ISBN 978-1-84205-629-5

Printed and bound in India

A

abdomen the region of the body that lies below the THORAX, being divided from it by the DIAPHRAGM, and above the PELVIS. The abdominal cavity contains the DIGESTIVE ORGANS (e.g. the STOMACH and INTESTINES), the excretory ORGANS (BLADDER and KIDNEYS) and, in females, the reproductive organs (UTERUS and OVARIES).

ablation the surgical removal (i.e. by cutting) of any part of the body.

ABO system a BLOOD GROUP classification.

abortifacient one of a number of drugs used to bring about an induced ABORTION.

abortion the removal of an EMBRYO or FOETUS from the UTERUS, either by natural expulsion or by human intervention, before the foetus is VIABLE. An abortion may be spontaneous or induced. Spontaneous abortion (MISCARRIAGE) is commonest during the first three months of PREGNANCY and is thought to be most often associated with abnormalities in the foetus. Induced abortion, also described as therapeutic or elective or as a termination of pregnancy, is carried out for medical or social reasons. Most induced abortions are carried out in the first trimester of pregnancy.

A threatened abortion occurs when the foetus is alive but there is bleeding from the uterus and/or pain. If the foetus has died, the abortion is referred to as inevitable. An incomplete abortion describes the situation where some of the foetal material is left behind in the uterus. Habitual abortion is where a woman loses each foetus in three consecutive pregnancies before the 20th week. The foetus weighs less than 500 grams, and an abnormality in the uterus is one of the reasons why this occurs.

abrasion or **graze** a superficial injury caused by the mechanical rubbing off of the SKIN surface or outer layer of a MUCOUS MEMBRANE.

abruptio placentae The partial or complete detachment of the PLACENTA from the wall of the UTERUS in the later stages

3

of PREGNANCY. Symptoms include abdominal and/or back pain and vaginal bleeding. Bleeding into the uterus may not be visible externally and there is a danger of foetal distress and maternal SHOCK. In severe cases, there is a risk of foetal and (more rarely) maternal death. Risk factors include alcohol and drug abuse, high BLOOD PRESSURE and DIABETES MELLITUS. If the degree of detachment is relatively small, with medical care and rest for the mother the pregnancy may continue to full term. If there are signs of foetal distress, the baby may be delivered by emergency CAESAREAN SECTION.

abscess a collection of PUS at a localized site anywhere in the body resulting from an INFECTION caused by BACTERIA. Treatment is by the surgical opening of the abscess and by the administration of ANTIBIOTICS.

abscission the surgical removal of TISSUE by cutting.

absence seizure formerly known as petit mal, a form of generalized epileptic seizure (*see* EPILEPSY). There are no convulsions, but the sufferer will lose consciousness for a number of seconds, staring blankly and not responding to outside stimuli. This form of epilepsy appears in childhood and can be hard to diagnose because the 'absences' are brief and may go unnoticed. The absences, or 'blanks', can be misconstrued as inattentiveness, and unless the condition is recognized and treated, children who suffer from this form of epilepsy may have difficulties with learning because of frequent seizures.

acetabulum *see* HIP JOINT.

acetonuria *see* KETONURIA.

acetylcholine an important organic chemical substance that is present in the body and is known as a NEUROTRANSMITTER. It is involved in the transmission of electrical impulses along NERVES.

acetylsalicylic acid the chemical name for ASPIRIN.

achalasia a failure to relax, usually referring to a condition called achalasia of the cardia. It describes the situation where the MUSCLE fibres surrounding the opening of the OESOPHAGUS (gullet) into the STOMACH do not relax properly and hinder the passage of swallowed food. Symptoms include difficulty with swallowing, chest pain and weight loss.

Achilles tendon a large, thick TENDON present in the lower leg that attaches the calf MUS-CLES to the heel BONE, enabling this to be moved. It is prone to damage during the playing of energetic sports.

achondroplasia a genetic disorder characterized by abnormal BONE growth and the commonest cause of DWARF-ISM. The long bones of the FOETUS fail to develop properly, resulting in short arms and legs. Another typical physical characteristic of the condition is a large head, with a prominent forehead. In some cases, HYDROCEPHALUS may be present. Achondroplasia can be inherited and if one or both parents have achondroplasia, there is a 50% chance that their children will be born with the condition. In most instances however, the condition is not inherited and results instead from a mutation, before the EMBRYO is formed, in either SPERM cell or OVUM.

acidosis a condition in which the acidity of the BLOOD and body fluids rises to an abnormally high level as a result of a failure in the mechanisms that regulate the acid/base balance in the body. It is commonly caused by a faulty ME-TABOLISM, as in DIABETES MELLITUS, or during starvation and excessive VOMITING.

It may also have a respiratory origin, e.g. during drowning, when a higher than normal level of carbon dioxide is retained in the body. It also occurs as a result of KID-NEY failure (renal acidosis), when too much sulphuric and phosphoric acid are retained within the body or an excess of bicarbonate is excreted.

acini (*sing* **acinus**) *see* PAN-CREAS.

acne a disorder of the SKIN, the commonest of which is acne vulgaris in adolescents, characterized by the presence of PUSTULES and blackheads on the face and also on the shoulders, back and chest. SEBA-CEOUS GLANDS in the skin become overactive (because of hormonal influence) and there is a greater production of SEBUM and proliferation of BACTERIA, which cause infection. The hair follicles become blocked and pustules form, which eventually turn black. Severe acne can leave scars. The condition usually resolves with time but can be eased with creams and sometimes ANTIBIOTICS. Other forms of acne also occur, *see* ROSACEA.

acquired a term used to describe a condition or malady that is not CONGENITAL but arises after birth.

acromegaly an abnormal growth of BONES and TISSUES in the hands, head, feet and CHEST, caused by excessive secretion of GROWTH HORMONE by the PITUITARY GLAND, commonly as a result of a TUMOUR.

acrosome *see* SPERM.

ACTH *see* ADRENOCORTICO-TROPHIC HORMONE.

action potential *see* NERVE IMPULSE.

acupuncture a method of Chinese traditional healing involving the insertion of fine steel needles at various points beneath the SKIN. The needles may, if necessary, be stimulated manually or by electric current. Acupuncture stimulates the NERVES and can affect the functioning of the systems of the body as well as the body's response to pain. It has been proved to be effective in the relief of a variety of conditions, including musculoskeletal pain, MIGRAINE, di-

gestive problems, menstrual problems and allergies and is now widely accepted by the medical profession as a useful adjunct to orthodox medicine. Acupuncturists do not need to be medically trained in order to practise, but a growing number of physicians undergo training to practise as medical acupuncturists.

acute a term used to describe a disease or condition that is short-lived and starts rapidly with severe symptoms.

Adam's apple a projection of the thyroid CARTILAGE of the LARYNX, which is visible beneath the skin of the THROAT.

addiction a broadly used term that describes a state of physical and psychological dependence on a substance or DRUG.

Addison's disease *or* **adrenal insufficiency** a hormonal disorder caused by the failure of the ADRENAL GLANDS to secrete the adrenocortical HORMONES, most commonly as a result of damage to the adrenal cortex, which may be caused by AUTOIMMUNE DISEASE or TUBERCULOSIS. The symptoms of the disease are wasting, weakness, low BLOOD PRESSURE and dark PIGMENTATION of the skin. The disease is treated by replacing the hormones that are not being produced (cortisol, aldosterone).

adenine *see* NUCLEOTIDE.

adenitis INFLAMMATION of one or more GLANDS or LYMPH NODES.

adenoidectomy the removal, by surgery, of the ADENOIDS.

adenoids a clump of lymphoid TISSUE situated at the back of the NOSE (in the NASOPHARYNX). The adenoids may become swollen as a result of persistent throat INFECTIONS and obstruct breathing through the nose.

adenohypophysis *see* PITUITARY GLAND.

adenosine triphosphate *see* ATP.

adhesion the joining together of two surfaces that should normally be separate as a result of severe INFLAMMATION. Bands of FIBROUS TISSUE are formed that join the structures together. Adhesions may form within a damaged JOINT or following abdominal surgery, when they may form between loops of the INTESTINE, etc. Adhesions at a joint restrict its movement (ANKYLOSIS) and can sometimes be resolved by manipulation.

Adhesions within the ABDOMEN or involving the LUNGS (resulting from PLEURISY) may require surgery.

adipose tissue a type of loose, fibrous, CONNECTIVE TISSUE containing a mass of fat CELLS. It is a reserve energy store and has an insulating function.

adrenal gland *or* **suprarenal gland** each of the two KIDNEYS within the body bears an adrenal GLAND on its upper surface. The adrenal glands are important ENDOCRINE organs, producing HORMONES that regulate various body functions. Each adrenal gland has two parts, an outer cortex and an inner medulla, which secrete a variety of hormones. Two of the most important ones are ADRENALINE and CORTISONE.

adrenaline *or* **epinephrine** a very important HORMONE produced by the MEDULLA of the ADRENAL GLANDS, which, when released, prepares the body for 'fright, flight or fight' by increasing the depth and rate of RESPIRATION, raising the heartbeat rate and improving MUSCLE performance. It also has an inhibitive effect on the processes of DIGESTION and EXCRETION. It can be used medically in a variety of ways, for instance in the treatment of bronchial ASTHMA, where it relaxes the airways, and also to stimulate the heart when there is CARDIAC ARREST. *See* ADDISON'S DISEASE.

adrenocorticotrophic hormone (ACTH) an important substance produced and stored by the anterior PITUITARY GLAND. It regulates the release of CORTICOSTEROID hormones from the ADRENAL GLANDS and is used medically, by INJECTION, to test their function. It is also used in the treatment of ASTHMA and rheumatic disorders.

adsorbent a substance, such as KAOLIN, that is capable of absorbing gas, liquid, etc.

adult respiratory distress syndrome a condition of severe respiratory failure brought about by a number of different disorders. There is a lack of oxygen in the blood, which exhibits itself by imparting a blue tinge to the skin (CYANOSIS) and rapid breathing and heartbeat. The syndrome may be caused by physical damage to the LUNGS, by INFECTION or by an adverse reaction following surgery or BLOOD TRANSFUSION. It is often fatal.

aerosol a suspension of fine solid or liquid particles in gas.

aetiology *or* **etiology** the scientific study of the causes of disease.

afferent a term meaning 'inwards to an ORGAN, etc', especially the BRAIN or SPINAL CORD, e.g. an afferent NERVE. *Compare* EFFERENT.

African trypanosomiasis *see* SLEEPING SICKNESS.

afterbirth a mass of TISSUE that consists of the PLACENTA, UMBILICAL CORD and membranes, detached and expelled from the womb (UTERUS) during the third stage of LABOUR following a birth.

afterpains pains following a birth, caused by uterine contractions that help to restore the UTERUS to its normal size. They may also indicate that a piece of PLACENTA has been retained, which the uterus is trying to expel.

agglutinin, agglutinogen *see* BLOOD GROUPS.

agonist *see* FLEXOR.

agoraphobia an abnormal fear of public places or open spaces.

AID *see* ARTIFICIAL INSEMINATION.

AIDS the acronym for Acquired Immune Deficiency Syndrome, which was first recognized in Los Angeles in the USA in 1981. The causal agent was identified in 1983 as being the human immunodeficiency VI-RUS, known as HIV, a ribonucleic acid (RNA) RETROVIRUS. The virus has been found in BLOOD, other body fluids, SE-MEN and cervical secretions. It can be transmitted by sexual activity, or through blood contact with an infected person—e.g. by using contaminated hypodermic syringes. The virus can also pass from mother to child during birth or through BREAST feeding. Routine screening for HIV antibodies in DONOR blood now prevents transmission through transfusion of blood or blood products. The HIV virus affects the T-LYMPHOCYTES of the immune system (*see* IM-MUNITY) and leaves the patient increasingly unable to resist opportunistic INFECTIONS and TUMOURS that are particularly associated with Aids. At the present time there is no known cure for Aids, but the development of several antiretroviral drugs has brought significant improvements in the treatment of patients and prolonged life expectancy for those treated.

AIH *see* ARTIFICIAL INSEMINA-TION.

air embolism a bubble of air in a BLOOD VESSEL that interferes with the outward flow of blood from the right VENTRI-CLE of the heart. The air may enter the CIRCULATION after an injury, surgery or infusion into a VEIN. The symptoms are CHEST pain and BREATH-LESSNESS, leading to acute HEART FAILURE.

air passages *or* **airway** all the openings and passages through which air enters and is taken into the LUNGS. These are the NOSE, PHARYNX (throat), LAR-YNX, TRACHEA (windpipe) and bronchial tubes (BRONCHI and BRONCHIOLES). Air entering via this route has dust particles removed, and is warmed and moistened before entering the lungs.

albinism an inherited disorder in which there is a lack of pigmentation in the SKIN, HAIR and EYES. The PIGMENT involved is MELANIN.

albino an individual affected by ALBINISM who typically has pink SKIN and EYES and white hair. The pink colour is imparted by BLOOD in the blood vessels in the skin, which, in a normal person, is masked by the presence of the pigment MELANIN. Albino people additionally suffer from poor eyesight and have increased sensitivity to sunlight, tending to burn easily.

albumin a water-soluble PROTEIN that coagulates when heated and is found in PLASMA, egg white, etc.

alimentary canal or **gastrointestinal tract** the whole of the passage along which food is passed, starting at the MOUTH and ending at the ANUS.

alkalosis an abnormal rise in the alkalinity (a decrease in pH) of the BLOOD and body fluids because of a failure or swamping of the mechanisms that regulate the acid-base balance in the body. It may arise through acid loss following prolonged VOMITING or occur in a patient who has been treated for a GASTRIC ULCER with a large amount of alkalis. Respiratory alkalosis may arise if breathing is too deep for the amount of physical exertion being undertaken. The symptoms of alkalosis include muscular CRAMPS and fatigue.

allotransplant see TRANSPLANTATION.

allele one of several forms of a GENE at a given place on the CHROMOSOME. They are usually present on different chromosomes and are responsible for certain characteristics of the PHENOTYPE. It is the dominance of one allele over another that determines the phenotype of the individual.

allergen any substance, usually a PROTEIN, that causes a hypersensitive (allergic) reaction in a person who is exposed to the allergen. There is a great variety of allergens, which cause reactions in different TISSUES and body functions. The RESPIRATORY SYSTEM and SKIN are often affected.

allergy a state of hypersensitivity in an affected individual to a particular ALLERGEN, which produces a characteristic response whenever the person is exposed to the substance. In an unaffected person, antibodies present in the bloodstream destroy their particular antigens. However, in an affected individual this reaction causes some CELL damage and there is a release of substances, such as HISTAMINE and BRADYKININ, which cause the allergic reaction. Examples of allergies are DERMATI-

TIS, HAY FEVER, ASTHMA and the severe response known as ANAPHYLAXIS.

alopoecia loss of HAIR, baldness. Androgenic alopoecia (male and female pattern baldness) is the most common form of baldness. It is hormone-related and hereditary. Alopoecia areata is a patchy baldness of the scalp that can affect other areas of the body. Alopoecia universalis is total loss of head and body hair. Alopoecia may be a symptom of some diseases, e.g. SYPHILIS, MYXOEDEMA and ANAEMIA, and can also be caused by inflammatory skin conditions, such as SEBORRHOEIC ECZEMA, which causes hair FOLLICLES to lose their capacity to produce hair in the natural cycle of replacement.

alpha fetoprotein a type of PROTEIN formed in the LIVER and gut of the FOETUS, detectable in the AMNIOTIC FLUID and maternal BLOOD. It is normally present in small amounts, but when the foetus has a neural tube defect (SPINA BIFIDA, ANENCEPHALY) this level rises higher in the first six months of pregnancy. *See* AMNIOCENTESIS.

alpha wave *see* ELECTROENCEPHALOGRAM.

alternative medicine *or* **complementary medicine** forms of healing other than orthodox medical practice, including ACUPUNCTURE, HOMEOPATHY, OSTEOPATHY, naturopathy, faith healing and herbal remedies.

alveolus (*pl* **alveoli**) a small sac or cavity that in numbers forms the alveolar sacs at the end of the BRONCHIOLES in the LUNGS. Each alveolus is fed by a rich blood supply via capillaries (*see* CAPILLARY) and is lined with a moist MEMBRANE where oxygen and carbon dioxide, the respiratory gases, are exchanged. The alveolar sacs provide an enormous surface area for efficient RESPIRATION.

Alzheimer's disease the commonest cause of DEMENTIA, afflicting those in middle or old age, and a degenerative disease of the CEREBRAL CORTEX for which there is no cure. Symptoms include gradual but progressive loss of memory and speech, confusion, increasing problems with coordination and decreasing mobility. The average length of of survival from diagnosis is approximately 8–10 years, but the rate at which the disease progresses is very variable. In the earlier stages of the illness, drugs can be prescribed to stall the progression of symptoms for some time. The cause is not understood but is the subject of ongoing research.

amenorrhoea an absence of MENSTRUATION, which is normal before PUBERTY, during PREGNANCY and while breast-feeding is being carried out, and following the MENO-PAUSE. Primary amenorrhoea describes the situation where the menstrual periods do not begin at puberty. This occurs if there is a chromosome abnormality (such as TURNER'S SYNDROME) or if some reproductive organs are absent (*see* REPRODUCTIVE SYSTEM). It can also occur where there is a failure or imbalance in the secretion of HORMONES. In secondary amenorrhoea, the menstrual periods stop when they would normally be expected to be present. There are a variety of causes, including hormone deficiency, disorders of the HYPOTHALA-MUS, psychological and environmental stresses, during

starvation, ANOREXIA nervosa or DEPRESSION.

amfetamines (*formerly* **amphetamines**) a group of drugs that are chemically similar to ADRENALINE and have a stimulating effect on the CENTRAL NERVOUS SYSTEM. They act on the SYMPATHETIC NERVOUS SYSTEM and produce feelings of mental alertness and wellbeing, eliminating tiredness. They are highly addictive and dangerous, and their medical use is very strictly controlled.

amines naturally occurring compounds found in the body which have an important role in a variety of functions. They are derived from AMINO AC-IDS and ammonia and include such substances as ADRENA-LINE and HISTAMINE.

amino acids the end products of the digestion of PROTEIN foods and the building blocks from which all the protein components of the body are built up. They all contain an acidic carboxyl group (-COOH) and an amino group (-NH$_2$), which are both bonded to the same central carbon atom. Some can be manufactured within the body whereas others, the ESSENTIAL AMINO

ACIDS, must be derived from protein sources in the diet.

amnesia loss of memory, which may be partial or total. Anterograde amnesia is the loss of memory of recent events following a TRAUMA of some kind. Retrograde amnesia is the inability to remember events that preceded a trauma. Other types of amnesia are post-traumatic and hysterical and more than one kind may be experienced by an individual.

amniocentesis a procedure carried out to sample the AMNIOTIC FLUID surrounding a FOETUS. A fine needle is inserted through the abdominal wall of the mother and the amniotic sac is pierced so that a small quantity of fluid can be drawn off. The amniotic fluid contains ALPHA FETOPROTEIN and CELLS from the EMBRYO, and various disorders such as DOWN'S SYNDROME and SPINA BIFIDA can be detected. It is usually carried out between the 16th and 20th week of pregnancy if a foetal abnormality is suspected.

amnion a fibrous, tough, membranous sac that lines the womb in PREGNANCY and encloses the FOETUS floating within it surrounded by AMNIOTIC FLUID. A CAUL is a piece of the amnion.

amnioscopy the procedure by which an examination of the FOETUS in the UTERUS is carried out, using an ENDOSCOPE. The procedure may be performed through a small incision in the mother's abdominal wall, using a transabdominal endoscope (FOETOSCOPE), or through the mother's CERVIX, using a transcervical endoscope (amnioscope).

amniotic cavity the cavity, filled with fluid, that is enclosed by the AMNION and surrounds the FOETUS.

amniotic fluid the liquid in the AMNIOTIC CAVITY, which is clear and composed mainly of water containing foetal CELLS, lipids and URINE from the FOETUS. At first it is produced by the AMNION, but its volume is supplemented by urine from the KIDNEYS of the foetus. It is circulated by being swallowed by the foetus and excreted by the kidneys back into the cavity and has an important protective function. The amniotic fluid ('waters') is released when the MEMBRANES rupture during LABOUR.

amniotomy *or* **artificial rupture of membranes (ARM)** The rupture of the foetal membranes (AMNION), in order to induce the onset of LABOUR. It is carried out using instrument called an amnihook which is inserted into the VAGINA.

amoeba (*pl* **amoebae**) a microscopic invertebrate that consists of a gelatinous mass which constantly alters its state. It is found in freshwater ponds and ditches and in soil. It is parasitic in humans and animals and can cause amoebic DYSENTERY and AMOEBIASIS.

amoebiasis an intestinal INFECTION caused by AMOEBAE.

amoxicillin an antibiotic that is similar to PENICILLIN and can be used to treat a broad spectrum of bacterial INFECTIONS.

amphetamines *see* **amfetamines.**

ampicillin a type of semisynthetic PENICILLIN which is used to treat various bacterial INFECTIONS and usually given by mouth or by INJECTION.

ampoule a small plastic or glass bubble that is sterile and sealed, usually containing one dose of a DRUG to be administered by INJECTION.

ampullae (*sing* **ampulla**) *see* BREAST.

amputation the surgical removal of any body part but generally referring to a LIMB.

amylase *see* DIASTASE; ENZYME; PANCREAS.

anabolic steroid a synthetic male sex HORMONE (that mimics ANDROGEN) used to enhance TISSUE growth by promoting the build-up of PROTEIN, e.g. to enhance MUSCLE bulk. Anabolic steroids are used medically to aid weight gain after wasting illnesses and to promote growth in children with certain types of DWARFISM. They may also be used in the treatment of OSTEOPOROSIS. They should not be taken by healthy people as they have serious SIDE EFFECTS, especially after prolonged use, and have been misused by athletes.

anabolism *see* CATABOLISM; METABOLISM.

anaemia a decrease in the ability of the BLOOD to carry oxygen because of a reduction in the number of red blood cells (ERYTHROCYTES) or in the amount of HAEMOGLOBIN that they contain. Haemoglobin is the PIGMENT within the red blood cells that binds to oxygen. There are a number of different types of anaemia and a variety of reasons for it, and treatment depends on the underlying cause.

anaesthesia a loss of sensation or feeling in the whole or part of the body, usually relating to the administration of ANAES-THETIC drugs so that surgery can be performed without pain. *See also* EPIDURAL ANAESTHE-SIA; SPINAL ANAESTHESIA.

anaesthetic a substance that, when administered, produces a loss of sensation in the whole body (general anaesthetic) or part of it (local anaesthetic). A general anaesthetic results in a loss of CONSCIOUSNESS, and usually a combination of drugs is used to achieve an optimum effect. These drugs act to de-press the activity of the CEN-TRAL NERVOUS SYSTEM, have an ANALGESIC effect and relax MUSCLES, enabling surgical procedures to be carried out with no awareness on the part of the patient. A local anaes-thetic blocks the transmission of NERVE impulses in the area where it is applied so that no pain is felt. Commonly used local anaesthetics are COCAINE and LIDOCAINE, and they are also used for minor surgical

procedures and in dentistry. *See* EPIDURAL ANAESTHESIA, SPINAL ANAESTHESIA.

anaesthetist a doctor who is medically specialized in the administration of ANAES-THETICS.

analgesia a state of reduced re-action to pain, but without loss of CONSCIOUSNESS. It may be because of drugs (ANALGESICS) or it may happen accidentally should NERVES become dis-eased or damaged.

analgesic a DRUG or substance that relieves pain, varying in potency from mild, such as PARACETAMOL, IBUPROFEN and ASPIRIN, to very strong, e.g. PETHIDINE and MORPHINE.

anaphase *see* MEIOSIS.

anaphylaxis a response exhib-ited by a hypersensitive indi-vidual when exposed to a particular ANTIGEN. It results from the release of HISTAMINE in body TISSUES following the ANTIGEN-antibody reaction within CELLS. An allergic re-action is an example of mild anaphylaxis. Anaphylactic SHOCK is a less common but significantly more serious condition that can follow the injection of DRUGS or VAC-CINES, the ingestion of certain foods or a sting from a bee or wasp, to which the individual is hypersensitive. Its onset is immediate and results from a widespread release of histamine in the body. The symptoms include severe breathing difficulties, swelling (OEDEMA), a fall in BLOOD PRESSURE, acute URTICARIA and HEART FAILURE. Death may follow if the individual is not soon treated with ADRENALINE by injection.

anaplasia the condition in which CELLS and TISSUES become less differentiated and distinctive and revert to a more primitive form. This state is typical in TUMOURS that are MALIGNANT and growing very rapidly.

anastomosis 1. in surgery, the artificial joining together of two or more tubes that are normally separate, e.g. between parts of the INTESTINE or BLOOD VESSELS. **2.** in ANATOMY, the area of communication between the end branches of adjacent blood vessels.

anatomy the scientific study of the body structure of human beings and animals.

androgen one of a group of HORMONES that is responsible for the development of the sex organs (*see* REPRODUCTIVE SYSTEM) and also the SECONDARY SEXUAL CHARACTERISTICS in the male. Androgens are steroid HORMONES, and the best-known example is TESTOSTERONE. They are mainly secreted by the testes (*see* TESTICLE) in the male but are also produced by the adrenal cortex (*see* ADRENAL GLAND) and by the ovaries (*see* OVARY) of females in small amounts.

anencephaly a failure in the development of a FOETUS, resulting in the absence of the cerebral hemispheres of the BRAIN and some skull BONES. If the PREGNANCY goes to term, the infant dies soon after birth, but spontaneous ABORTION occurs in about 50 per cent of affected pregnancies. Anencephaly is often associated with SPINA BIFIDA and is the most common developmental defect of the CENTRAL NERVOUS SYSTEM. Anencephaly can be detected during pregnancy by measuring the amount of ALPHA FETOPROTEIN present. *See* AMNIOCENTESIS.

aneuploidy a condition in which an abnormal number of CHROMOSOMES are present in the CELLS of an affected individual. The number of chromosomes is either more or less than the normal exact multiple of the HAPLOID number (half the full complement) and is characteristic of DOWN'S SYNDROME and TURNER'S SYNDROME. *See* EUPLOID.

aneurysm a balloon-like swelling in the wall of an artery that occurs when it becomes weakened or damaged in some way. There may be a congenital weakness in the muscular wall of the artery involved, as is often the case within the BRAIN. Damage may also be the result of INFECTION, particularly SYPHILIS, or degenerative conditions, e.g. ATHEROMA.

angina a suffocating, choking pain, usually used in reference to angina pectoris, which is felt in the CHEST. The pain is felt or brought on by exercise and relieved by rest, and occurs when the blood supply to the HEART muscle is inadequate. During exercise the demand for BLOOD (supplied by the coronary arteries) is increased and if the supply is insufficient, because the arteries are damaged, chest pain results. The coronary arteries may be damaged by ATHEROMA, the most common cause.

Angina pectoris is usually first treated with drugs but if the condition worsens, coronary artery bypass surgery may need to be performed. *See* CORONARY BYPASS GRAFT.

angiocardiography an X-RAY examination of the activity of the HEART, and its blood supply, following the injection of a radio-opaque substance.

angiography (angiogram) an examination technique of BLOOD VESSELS using X-RAYS, made possible by first injecting a radio-opaque substance. If the blood vessels being examined are arteries, it is called ARTERIOGRAPHY and if they are veins, VENOGRAPHY or phlebography. Angiography is used for diagnosis and in ANGIOPLASTY.

angioma a growth formed from a cluster of distended BLOOD VESSELS. Angiomas can occur at various sites on the body, e.g. on the SKIN (cherry angioma, spider angioma), and are usually non-malignant, but can bleed profusely if damaged. An angioma sited in or on the surface of the BRAIN may cause neurological problems, e.g. EPILEPSY and occasionally a vessel may burst to cause a cerebral HAEMORRHAGE.

angioplasty 1. a surgical method used to widen or re-open a narrowed or blocked BLOOD VESSEL or HEART valve (transluminal angioplasty, balloon angioplasty). A balloon is inserted and then inflated to clear the obstruction. **2.** Surgery to repair a blood vessel. *See also* ANGIOGRAPHY.

angitis *or* **vasculitis** a condition in which there is INFLAMMATION of the walls of small BLOOD VESSELS, usually in patches.

animal starch *see* GLYCOGEN.

ankle joint the JOINT between the leg and the foot. It is a hinge joint, where the TIBIA and FIBULA of the leg articulate with the TALUS.

ankylosing spondylitis *see* SPONDYLITIS.

ankylosis stiffness, restricted mobility or immobility of a JOINT, caused by ADHESIONS following surgery, injury or INFLAMMATION.

anorexia literally, a loss of appetite. Anorexia nervosa is a psychological disorder that is commonly associated with young women and girls. Sufferers have a false and distorted image of themselves as being fat. They develop a fear or PHOBIA relating to OBESITY and an aversion to food and consequently can eat very little. They may exercise excessively, take LAXATIVES or induce VOMITING, as well as starving themselves, in order to lose weight. Accompanying symptoms include AMENORRHEA in female sufferers, low BLOOD PRESSURE, ANAEMIA and a risk of sudden death from heart damage. *See also* BULIMIA NERVOSA.

anoxia the condition in which the body TISSUES do not receive sufficient oxygen. It may be caused by high altitudes (and thus lower atmospheric pressure), a lack of red blood cells (ERYTHROCYTES), or by a disease such as PNEUMONIA in which the amount of oxygen reaching the surfaces of the LUNGS is limited and therefore the amount available for transfer to the BLOOD is reduced.

antacid a substance that neutralizes acidity, usually hydrochloric acid in the digestive juices of the STOMACH. An example is sodium bicarbonate.

antagonistic action an action in which systems or processes act against each other so that the activity of one reduces that of the other. Two

MUSCLES may operate in this way, the contraction of one necessitating the relaxation of the other, as in the movement of a LIMB (*see also* VOLUNTARY MUSCLE). In addition, some HORMONES and DRUGS act antagonistically, the release of one limiting the effect of the other.

antenatal before birth. Pregnant women attend antenatal clinics, which monitor the health of both mothers and their unborn babies.

antepartum anoxia *see* PERINATAL MORTALITY.

anterior a term meaning 'situated towards the front or at the front', the opposite of POSTERIOR.

anthracosis *see* PNEUMOCONIOSIS.

anthrax a serious infectious disease of cattle and sheep, which can be transmitted to humans and is caused by a BACILLUS, *B. anthracis*. The spores of the bacillus remain viable for many years and are resistant to destruction. People can be infected by handling contaminated skins, fleeces and bones, and the spores may either be inhaled or enter through a cut in the SKIN. The danger is increased

if the infected skins are dry so that spores and dust are inhaled. The disease takes two forms in human beings, either affecting the LUNGS (if the spores are inhaled), causing PNEUMONIA (woolsorter's disease), or the skin (if infected through a cut), known as malignant PUSTULE, a severe ulceration.

antibiotic a substance, derived from a microorganism, that kills or inhibits the multiplication of other microorganisms, usually BACTERIA or fungi. Well-known examples are PENICILLIN and STREPTOMYCIN.

antibodies PROTEIN substances of the GLOBULIN type which are produced by the lymphoid TISSUE and circulate in the BLOOD. They react with their corresponding ANTIGENs and neutralize them, rendering them harmless. Antibodies are produced against a wide variety of antigens and these reactions are responsible for IMMUNITY and ALLERGY.

anticoagulant a drug that delays or tends to prevent BLOOD CLOTting, examples of which are warfarin and heparin. Anticoagulants are used in the treatment of EMBOLISM and

THROMBOSIS, to disperse clots in BLOOD VESSELS.

anticonvulsant a drug that is used to reduce the severity of epileptic SEIZURES or to prevent them from occurring.

antidepressant a drug that is administered in order to alleviate DEPRESSION and its accompanying symptoms.

antidiuretic hormone *see* VASOPRESSIN.

antidote a substance that counteracts the effect of a particular poison.

antiemetic a drug or substance that prevents VOMITING, e.g medications taken to counteract travel sickness (*see* MOTION SICKNESS) and VERTIGO.

antigen any substance that causes the formation by the body of ANTIBODIES to neutralize their effect. Antigens are often PROTEIN substances, regarded as 'foreign' and 'invading' by the body, and elicit the production of antibodies against them. *See* ALLERGEN; ALLERGY; ANAPHYLAXIS.

antihaemophilic factor *see* FACTOR VIII.

antihistamines drugs that counteract the effects of HISTAMINE release in the body. They are widely used to treat allergic reactions of various sorts (*see* ALLERGY), particularly to relieve skin conditions and allergic RHINITIS. Those taken by mouth have a SEDATIVE effect and so care must be taken when they are used.

anti-inflammatory anything that reduces INFLAMMATION. Typical anti-inflammatory drugs are the ANTIHISTAMINES and NON-STEROIDAL ANTI-INFLAMMATORY DRUGS (used especially in the treatment of ARTHRITIS and RHEUMATISM).

antimetabolite one of a group of DRUGS, used particularly in the treatment of certain CANCERS, that mimic substances (metabolites) present in the CELLS. The antimetabolites combine with ENZYMES that would otherwise use the metabolites for cell growth. Hence they reduce the growth of cancer cells but also have attendant SIDE EFFECTS, which can be severe.

antiperistalsis *see* PERISTALSIS.

antiretroviral *see* RETROVIRUS; AIDS.

antiseptic a substance that prevents the growth of disease-causing microorganisms, such as BACTERIA, and is applied to the SKIN to prevent INFECTION and to cleanse wounds. Examples are iodine and crystal violet.

antiserum a SERUM that contains a high concentration of ANTIBODIES against a particular ANTIGEN. It is injected to give IMMUNITY against a particular disease or TOXIN.

antitoxin *see* TOXIN; TOXOID.

antiviral a word used to describe a substance or DRUG that inhibits the growth of VIRUSES.

antrum (*pl* **antra**) a natural CAVITY or SINUS, particularly in a BONE, e.g. the MASTOID antrum.

anuria a failure of the KIDNEYS to produce URINE, which may result from a disorder that causes a prolonged drop in BLOOD PRESSURE. Anuria is typical of increasing URAEMIA, and HAEMODIALYSIS may be necessary.

anus the opening of the ALIMENTARY CANAL, at the opposite end from the MOUTH, through which FAECES are voided. The anus is at the lower end of the bowel and its opening is controlled by two MUSCLEs, the internal and external SPHINCTERS.

aorta the major large ARTERY of the body, which arises from the left VENTRICLE of

the HEART and which carries BLOOD to all areas. The other arteries of the body are all derived from the aorta.

aortic relating to do with the AORTA, e.g. the aortic VALVE.

aortic stenosis a narrowing of the opening of the aortic VALVE, resulting in the obstruction of BLOOD flow from the left VENTRICLE to the AORTA. This is commonly caused by calcium deposits formed on the valve, associated with ATHEROMA, or damage may have been caused by previous RHEUMATIC FEVER. The condition may also arise CONGENITALLY. The effect is that the left ventricle MUSCLE has to work harder in order to try to maintain the blood flow and becomes thicker as a result. The symptoms of aortic stenosis include ANGINA pectoris and breathlessness, and the condition is treated surgically by valve replacement.

apgar score a method of assessing the health of an infant immediately after birth, carried out at one minute and five minutes after delivery. Five physical signs are observed: A—activity (MUSCLE tone), P—PULSE, G—grimace (response to stimuli), A—appearance (SKIN colour), R—RESPIRATION. The signs are scored individually on a scale from 0–2 then the scores are added to give a total out of ten.

aphasia speechlessness caused by disease or injury to those parts of the BRAIN that govern the activities involved in speech-making. It is caused by THROMBOSIS, EMBOLISM or HAEMORRHAGE of a BLOOD VESSEL within the brain, as in a STROKE, or by a TUMOUR or trauma. It may be temporary if the blood supply is not permanently damaged, but often the power of speech continues to be impaired and may be associated with other intellectual disorders.

aphonia loss of the voice, which may be caused by disease or by damage to the LARYNX or mouth or to NERVES controlling throat MUSCLES, or may be the result of HYSTERIA.

aplasia a complete or partial failure in the correct development of an ORGAN or TISSUE.

apnoea a temporary halt in breathing, which may result from a number of different causes. Apnoea is quite common in newborn infants and

can be registered by an apnoea monitor, which sounds an alarm if the baby ceases to breathe. Sleep apnoea in adults is a problem commonly associated with OBESITY and chronic SNORING. The soft TISSUES at the back of the THROAT relax and collapse and cause temporary obstruction until the person wakes briefly and starts breathing again. The main symptom of sleep apnoea is excessive daytime sleepiness.

apocrine the term for SWEAT GLANDS that occur in hairy parts of the body. The odours associated with sweating are the result of bacterial action on the sweat produced. *See also* PERSPIRATION.

apoplexy *see* STROKE.

appendicectomy *or* **appendectomy** the surgical operation to remove the vermiform APPENDIX.

appendicitis INFLAMMATION of the vermiform APPENDIX, which, in its acute form, is the most common abdominal emergency in the western world, usually requiring treatment by APPENDICECTOMY. It is most common in young people during their first 20 years, and the symptoms include severe pain in the lower ABDOMEN, particularly on the right side, appetite loss, VOMITING and DIARRHOEA. If not treated the appendix can become the site of an ABSCESS, or gangrenous, which eventually may result in PERITONITIS. This arises because infected material spreads from the burst appendix into the peritoneal cavity.

appendix a blind-ended tube that is an appendage of various organs within the body. It normally refers to the vermiform appendix, which is about 9 to 10cm long and projects from the CAECUM of the large INTESTINE. It has no known function and can become the site of INFECTION, probably as the result of obstruction. *See* APPENDICITIS.

aqueous humour *see* EYE and GLAUCOMA.

arachidonic *see* ESSENTIAL FATTY ACID.

arachnodactyly *see* MARFAN'S SYNDROME.

arachnoid mater the enveloping MEMBRANE of the BRAIN and SPINAL CORD, between the dura mater and the pia mater. *See also* MENINGES.

arch a part or structure of the body that is curved, e.g. the

vault formed by the TARSUS and METATARSAL BONES of the foot. *See also* FLAT FOOT.

areola (*pl* **areolae**) the brown-coloured, PIGMENTed ring around the nipple of the BREAST.

arginine *see* ESSENTIAL AMINO ACID.

ARM *see* AMNIOTOMY.

arrhythmia any disturbance in the normal rhythm of heartbeat. The built-in PACEMAKER of the HEART is the SINO-ATRIAL NODE situated in the wall of the right ATRIUM, which itself is regulated by the AUTONOMIC NERVOUS SYSTEM. The electrical impulses produced by the pacemaker control the rate and rhythm of heartbeat. Arrhythmias occur when these electrical impulses are disturbed.

arteriectomy the surgical removal of a part or the whole of an ARTERY.

arteriography (arteriogram) the X-ray examination of an ARTERY following the injection of a radio-opaque substance. Arteriography can be used as a diagnostic tool to detect abnormalities (e.g. ANEURYSM) or blockages in the arteries supplying various parts of the body, including the HEART, KIDNEYS, LUNGS and limbs. It is also used as an aid to ARTERIOPLASTY.

arteriole a small branch of an ARTERY leading to a CAPILLARY.

arterioplasty surgery to reconstruct an ARTERY, which is carried out especially in the treatment of ANEURYSMS.

arteriosclerosis hardening of the arteries. *See also* ATHEROMA, ATHEROSCLEROSIS and HYPERTENSION.

arteritis INFLAMMATION of an ARTERY.

artery a BLOOD VESSEL that carries blood away from the HEART. Oxygenated (bright red) blood is carried by the arteries to all parts of the body. However, the pulmonary arteries carry dark, unoxygenated blood from the heart to the LUNGS. An artery has thick, elastic walls that are able to expand and contract, and contain smooth MUSCLE fibres. This smooth muscle is under the control of the SYMPATHETIC NERVOUS SYSTEM.

arthritis INFLAMMATION of the JOINTS or SPINE, the symptoms of which are pain and swelling, restriction of movement, redness and warmth of the skin. There are many different causes of arthritis, including OSTEOARTHRITIS, RHEUMATOID ARTHRITIS, TUBERCULOSIS and RHEUMATIC FEVER.

arthropathy any JOINT disorder or disease.

arthroplasty surgery to repair a diseased JOINT by constructing a new one, often involving the insertion of artificial materials.

artificial insemination SEMEN collected from a DONOR is inserted by means of an instrument into the VAGINA of a woman in the hope that she will conceive. The semen may be from her husband or partner (AIH) or from an anonymous donor (AID) and is introduced near the time of OVULATION. Usually AIH is used where the partner is impotent (*see* IMPOTENCE) and AID when he is sterile or has a very low SPERM count.

artificial respiration an emergency procedure carried out when normal respiration has ceased in order to ventilate the lungs artificially, either mouth-to-mouth or using a hand-held, self-reinflatable bag and mask. In hospital, where a seriously ill person is unable to breathe unaided, artificial respiration is achieved by means of a machine known as a RESPIRATOR. *See also* CARDIOPULMONARY RESUSCITATION.

asbestosis a disease of the lungs caused by the inhalation of asbestos dust. Asbestos dust causes scarring of the lungs. There is a serious risk of MESOTHELIOMA or cancer of the lung.

ascorbic acid *see* VITAMIN C.

asphyxia the state of suffocation during which breathing eventually stops and oxygen fails to reach tissues and organs. It occurs as a result of drowning, strangulation and inhaling poisonous fumes. It can also result from obstruction of the air passages either by a foreign body lodged at the opening (e.g. a piece of food) or swelling as a result of a wound or infection.

aspiration the process of removing fluid or gases from cavities in the body by means of suction. The instrument used is called an aspirator, and various types exist depending on site of use.

aspirin a type of drug in widespread use that is correctly called acetylsalicylic acid. It is used to relieve mild pain, e.g. headache, neuralgia and

that associated with rheumatoid arthritis. It is used to combat fever and is also helpful in the prevention of CORONARY THROMBOSIS. In susceptible individuals it may cause irritation and bleeding of the stomach lining and is not normally given to children under the age of 12 years. High doses will cause dizziness and possibly mental confusion.

asthma a condition characterized by breathing difficulties caused by narrowing of the airways (BRONCHI) of the lung. Asthma may occur at any age but usually begins in early childhood and is a hypersensitive response that can be brought on by exposure to a variety of ALLERGENS, exercise, stress or infections. An asthma sufferer may have other hypersensitive conditions, such as ECZEMA and HAY FEVER, and it may be prevalent within a family. Treatment involves the use of drugs to dilate the airways (BRONCHODILATORS) and also inhaled CORTICOSTEROIDS.

astigmatism a defect in vision that results in sight being blurred and distorted. It is caused by abnormal curvature of the CORNEA, and possibly the LENS, of the EYE.

ataxia a loss of coordination in the limbs as a result of a disorder of the CENTRAL NERVOUS SYSTEM. There may be a disease of the SENSORY nerves (sensory ataxia) or of the CEREBELLUM (cerebellar ataxia). An ataxic person produces clumsy movements and lacks fine control.

atheroma a degenerative condition of the arteries (*see* ARTERY). The inner and middle coats of the arterial walls become scarred, and fatty deposits (CHOLESTEROL) are built up at these sites. Blood CIRCULATION is impaired, and it may lead to such problems as ANGINA pectoris, stroke and MYOCARDIAL INFARCTION. The condition is associated with the western lifestyle, i.e. lack of exercise, smoking, obesity and too high an intake of animal fats.

atherosclerosis similar to ATHEROMA, being a degenerative disease of the arteries (*see* ARTERY) associated with fatty deposits on the inner walls, leading to reduced blood flow.

athetosis *see* CEREBRAL PALSY.

athlete's foot a fungal infection of the skin, particularly between the toes and often caused by RINGWORM.

atlas the first cervical VERTEBRA of the SPINAL COLUMN, which articulates with the OCCIPITAL BONE.

ATP (adenosine triphosphate) an important molecule found in MITOCHONDRION, that is synthesized or broken down to produce energy to drive metabolic processes.

atrial the term used to describe anything relating to the ATRIUM.

atrial septal defect *see* MARFAN'S SYNDROME.

atrium (*pl* **atria**) **1.** one of the two thin-walled, upper chambers of the HEART, which receive BLOOD from major VEINS. The right atrium receives (deoxygenated) blood from the venae cavae (*see* VENA CAVA) and the left atrium is supplied with (oxygenated) blood from the PULMONARY vein. **2.** a chamber in various other parts of the body.

atrophy the wasting of a body part because of lack of use, malnutrition or as a result of ageing. The ovaries of women atrophy after the menopause, and muscular atrophy accompanies certain diseases. *See* POLIOMYELITIS.

aural a term used to describe anything relating to the ear.

auricle 1. the external part of the EAR flap, the pinna. **2.** an ear-shaped appendage of the ATRIUM of the heart.

autism a severe mental disorder of childhood in which there is a failure in emotional development and an inability to communicate. There are accompanying behavioural problems, and autism may be caused by brain damage and genetic factors. Autistic individuals exhibit stereotyped patterns of behaviour and may or may not be intellectually impaired. They require intensive and prolonged education in order to progress.

autoantibody an antibody produced by the body against one of its own tissues, a feature of AUTOIMMUNE DISEASE.

autoclave equipment used to sterilize surgical equipment and dressings, etc, by means of steam at high pressure. It is one of the most important methods of sterilization.

autograft a graft of skin or tissue taken from one part of a person's body and transferred to another region. The graft is 'self' and is therefore not rejected by the body's IMMUNE system.

autoimmune disease one of a number of conditions resulting from the production of antibodies by the body that attack its own tissues. For reasons that are not yet understood the immune system (*see* IMMUNITY) loses the ability to distinguish between 'self' and 'non-self'. Autoimmune disease is currently thought to be the cause of a number of disorders, including acquired haemolytic ANAEMIA and HYPOTHYROIDISM.

autoimmunity a failure of the immune system (*see* IMMUNITY) in which the body develops ANTIBODIES that attack components or substances belonging to itself. *See* AUTOANTIBODY, AUTOIMMUNE DISEASE.

autonomic nervous system the part of the NERVOUS SYSTEM that controls body functions that are not under conscious control, e.g. the heartbeat and other smooth muscles and glands. It is divided into the SYMPATHETIC and PARASYMPATHETIC NERVOUS SYSTEMS.

autopsy *or* **post mortem** the examination and dissection of a body after death.

autotransplant *see* TRANSPLANTATION.

avian influenza *or* **bird flu** a type A INFLUENZA virus that can spread rapidly among birds kept in captivity, causing large numbers of deaths. Some strains of the VIRUS have spread to humans. There have been a number of outbreaks of avian influenza in Hong Kong and China since 1997, giving rise to fears of an imminent PANDEMIC.

avidin *see* BIOTIN.

axon one of numerous long threadlike extensions of a NERVE cell that conduct NERVE IMPULSES from the CELL body. *See also* MOTOR NEURON; NEURON.

AZT *or* **azidothymidine** *or* **zidovudine** *or* **ZDV** an antiretroviral drug (trade name Retrovir) used in the treatment of HIV and AIDS. When taken by pregnant women who are HIV positive, AZT reduces the likelihood of transmitting the virus to their baby during pregnancy or birth.

B

Babinski reflex a REFLEX ACTION response of the foot. When the sole is stroked, the big toe turns up and the others fan out. This is normal for infants up to two years but abnormal thereafter.

bacillus (*pl* **bacilli**) **1.** a bacterium (*see* BACTERIA) that is rod-shaped. **2.** a genus of Gram-positive (*see* GRAM'S STAIN) bacteria that includes *B. anthracis*, the cause of ANTHRAX.

Bacillus Calmette-Guérin vaccine *see* BCG VACCINE.

backache pain in the back, which may vary in intensity, sharpness and cause. Much back pain is the result of mechanical/structural problems, including fractures, muscle strain or pressure on a NERVE. Other causes may include TUMOURS, BONE disease (such as OSTEOPOROSIS) referred pain from an ULCER or INFLAMMATIONS, e.g. SPONDYLITIS. Treatment is varied and may be surgical, by heat, ULTRASOUND, medication, PHYSIOTHERAPY, etc.

backbone *see* SPINAL COLUMN.

bacteria (*sing* **bacterium**) single-celled organisms that underpin all life-sustaining processes. GRAM'S STAIN is a test used to distinguish between the two types (Gram positive and Gram negative). They are also identified by shape: spiral, (spirilli), rod-like (bacilli), spherical (cocci), comma-shaped (vibrios) and the spirochaetal, which are corkscrew-like. Bacteria are the key agents in the chemical cycles of carbon, oxygen, nitrogen and sulphur.

bactericide something that kills BACTERIA, used especially when referring to DRUGS and ANTISEPTICS.

bacteriology the study of BACTERIA.

bacteriophage *or* **phage** a VIRUS that attacks BACTERIA. The phage replicates in the host, which is ultimately destroyed as new phages are released. Each phage is specific to a certain bacterium and uses are found in GENETIC ENGINEERING, in cloning and certain manufacturing processes.

baldness *see* ALOPECIA

ballottement a technique in which a floating structure in the body, e.g. a FOETUS, moves when it is gently pushed and then rebounds.

bandage a material pad or strip wrapped around a part of the body to cover a wound, hold a dressing in place, immobilize a limb or maintain pressure on a compress.

barbiturate a drug derived from barbituric acid that has ANAESTHETIC, hypnotic or SEDATIVE effects. Barbiturates reduce BLOOD PRESSURE and body TEMPERATURE and depress the CENTRAL NERVOUS SYSTEM and RESPIRATION. Prolonged use can result in dependence. TRANQUILLIZERS are replacing barbiturates to lessen drug abuse.

barium sulphate a chemical powder used in X-RAY examinations. Because of its opaque nature (to X-rays), it forms a shadow in whatever cavity it lies. It is used in the examination of the STOMACH and INTESTINES and can be used to trace a meal through the digestive tract.

bartonellosis *see* SANDFLY FEVER.

basal ganglion (*pl* **basal glanglia**) GREY MATTER at the base of the CEREBRUM that is involved in the subconscious control of voluntary movement.

B-cell *see* LYMPHOCYTE.

BCG vaccine *or* **Bacillus Calmette-Guérin vaccine** a VACCINE named after the two French bacteriologists who first introduced it in France in 1908. It is used as a vaccine against TUBERCULOSIS, usually administered intradermally, and although a localized skin reaction is common, serious complications are rare. It is administered to people of all ages who are at risk of coming into contact with the disease and is also routinely given to children between the ages of ten and fourteen. A tuberculin skin test is performed a few days beforehand and those with a negative result are immunized.

bed sores *or* **pressure sores** *or* **decubitus ulcers** areas of sore and ulcerated skin caused by constant pressure on an area of the body. Bedridden patients are at risk, particularly those who are unconscious or paralysed and their position has to be changed at regular intervals to relieve pressure on areas prone to skin breakdown: heels, buttocks, elbows, lower back, etc. The best action is preventative because healing may be slowed by reduced blood supply.

Bell's palsy a PARALYSIS of the facial MUSCLES on either or both sides of the FACE, caused by INFECTION or INFLAMMATION, when it may be temporary. Permanent paralysis may result from a basal skull FRACTURE, STROKE, etc. The paralysis results in an inability to open and close the eye or to smile or close the mouth on the side that is affected.

B endorphin a painkiller released by the PITUITARY in response to pain and stress.

bends *or* **compressed air illness** *or* **caisson disease** *or* **decompression sickness** a condition that may affect workers operating in high pressure in diving bells or at depth underwater if they surface too rapidly. Pain in the JOINTS (the bends), HEADACHE, dizziness and PARALYSIS may be caused by the formation of nitrogen bubbles in the BLOOD, which then accumulate in different parts of the body. Death may occur.

Benedict's test a test for detecting glucose and reducing sugars in URINE. A solution of copper sulphate, sodium carbonate and sodium citrate is added to a sample of urine. The solution is boiled, and sugar is indicated by a rust-coloured precipitate. The test is used if DIABETES MELLITUS is suspected.

benign a term used most frequently to refer to TUMOURS, meaning not harmful, the opposite of MALIGNANT.

benzocaine a local ANAESTHETIC for relief of painful SKIN conditions, including those within the mouth, used in various forms.

benzodiazepines a group of drugs that act as TRANQUILLIZERS (e.g. diazepam), HYPNOTICS (flurazepam) and ANTICONVULSANTS, depending on the duration of action.

benzoic acid an ANTISEPTIC used to preserve certain pharmaceutical preparations and foodstuffs. It is also used in treating fungal INFECTIONS of the SKIN and urinary tract infections.

benzoin a resin used in the preparation of compounds (e.g. FRIAR'S BALSAM) that are inhaled in the treatment of colds, bronchitis, etc.

benzothiadiazine a DIURETIC compound, taken orally, that reduces the reabsorption of chloride and sodium ions in the renal tubules of the KIDNEY. It lowers the BLOOD PRESSURE and relieves OEDEMA in HEART FAILURE.

benzoyl peroxide a bactericidal agent used as a bleach in the food industry and also as a treatment for ACNE.

beriberi a disease that causes INFLAMMATION of the NERVES because of a dietary lack of VITAMIN B1 (thiamine) and results in FEVER, PARALYSIS, palpitations and occasionally HEART FAILURE. It occurs mainly in countries where the staple diet is polished rice, although similar symptoms are displayed by some people suffering from alcoholism.

beta-blocker a drug used to treat ANGINA, reduce high BLOOD PRESSURE and manage abnormal HEART rhythms. Certain receptors of nerves in the SYMPATHETIC NERVOUS SYSTEM are blocked, reducing heart activity. A notable SIDE EFFECT is constriction of bronchial passages (see BRONCHI), which may adversely affect some patients.

biceps a MUSCLE that is said to have two heads, e.g. the biceps of the upper arm (biceps brachii) and the biceps on the back of the thigh (biceps femoris).

bicuspid valve *see* MITRAL VALVE.

bifurcation the branching of, for example, a BLOOD VESSEL into two. Also the TRACHEA where it forms two BRONCHI.

biguanide a substance, taken orally, that reduces blood sugar level by reducing the amount of glucose produced by the LIVER. It is used in the treatment of type 2 DIABETES MELLITUS.

bile a viscous, bitter fluid produced by the LIVER and stored in the GALL BLADDER. It is an alkaline solution of bile salts, pigments, some mineral salts and CHOLESTEROL, which aids in fat digestion and absorption of nutrients. Discharge of bile into the INTESTINE is increased after food, and of the amount secreted each day (up to one litre), most is reabsorbed with the food, passing into the blood to circulate back to the liver. If the flow of bile into the intestine is restricted, it stays in the blood, resulting in JAUNDICE.

bile duct a duct that carries BILE from the liver. The main duct is the hepatic, which joins the cystic duct from the GALL BLADDER to form the common bile duct, which drains into the small INTESTINE.

bilharziasis *see* SCHISTOSOMIASIS.

bilirubin one of the two important BILE pigments, formed primarily from the breakdown of HAEMOGLOBIN from red blood cells (ERYTHROCYTES). Bilirubin is orange-yellow in colour while its oxidized form, BILIVERDIN, is green. The majority of bile produced daily is eventually excreted and confers colour to the stools.

biliuria *see* **choluria.**

biliverdin *see* JAUNDICE.

bioassay the determination of a drug's activity or potency by comparing its effects on a living organism with that of a reference sample of known strength.

biochemistry the study of the chemistry of biological processes and substances in living organisms. Such studies contribute to the overall understanding of CELL metabolism, diseases and their effects.

biopsy an adjunct to DIAGNOSIS that involves removing a small sample of living TISSUE from the body for examination under the microscope. The technique is particularly important in differentiating between benign and malignant TUMOURS. A biopsy can be undertaken with a hollow needle inserted into the relevant ORGAN.

biotin a B-complex VITAMIN that is synthesized by BACTERIA in the INTESTINE. A biotin deficiency can occur only if large amounts of egg white are ingested because a constituent, avidin, binds to the biotin.

bipolar disorder *or* **manic depressive psychosis** a form of severe mental illness in which there are alternating bouts of MANIA and severe DEPRESSION. While manic, the person may be incoherent, outrageous or violent. Drug treatment is required for both phases of the illness, and there seems to be an inherited tendency towards acquiring it. Drugs are also helpful in reducing the frequency of attacks, between which the person is normally quite well.

bird flu *see* AVIAN INFLUENZA.

birthmark *or* **naevus** an agglomeration of dilated BLOOD VESSELS that creates a malformation of the SKIN and is present at birth. It may occur as a large port-wine stain, which can now be treated by laser, or a strawberry mark, which commonly fades in early life. *See also* MOLE.

blackwater fever a severe and sometimes fatal form of MALARIA.

bladder a SAC of fibrous and muscular TISSUE that contains secretions and can increase and decrease in capacity. Discharge of the contents is through a narrow opening (*see for example* GALL BLADDER *and* URINARY ORGANS).

blindness the inability to see, a condition that may vary from a complete lack of light perception (total blindness) through degrees of visual impairment. Causes of blindness include GLAUCOMA, CATARACT, vitamin A deficiency (night blindness) and DIABETES MELLITUS.

blister a thin VESICLE on the skin containing watery matter or SERUM.

blood a suspension of red blood cells (or corpuscles) called ERYTHROCYTES, white blood cells (LEUCOCYTES) and platelets (small disc-shaped CELLS involved in BLOOD CLOTting) in a liquid medium, blood PLASMA. The circulation of blood through the body provides a mechanism for transporting substances. Its functions include:

1 carrying oxygenated blood from the HEART to all TISSUES via the arteries while the veins return deoxygenated blood to the heart.

2 carrying essential nutrients, e.g. glucose, fats and AMINO ACIDS to all parts of the body.

3 removing the waste products of METABOLISM—ammonia and carbon dioxide—to the LIVER, where UREA is formed and then transported by the blood to the KIDNEYS for excretion.

4 carrying important molecules, e.g. HORMONES, to their target cells.

The red blood cells, produced in the BONE MARROW, are HAEMOGLOBIN-containing discs, while the white varieties vary in shape and are produced in the marrow and lymphoid tissue. The plasma comprises water, PROTEINS and ELECTROLYTES and forms approximately half the blood volume.

blood clot a hard mass of blood PLATELETS, trapped red blood cells (ERYTHROCYTES) and FIBRIN. After TISSUE damage, blood vessels in the area are constricted and a plug forms to seal the damaged area. The plug formation is initiated by an ENZYME released by the damaged blood vessels and platelets.

blood count *or* **complete blood count** (**CBC**) a count of the numbers of red and white blood CELLS per unit volume of BLOOD. The count may be performed on samples of blood manually, using a microscope, or electronically.

blood groups the division and classification of people into one of four main groups based on the presence of ANTIGENS on the surface of the red blood cells (ERYTHROCYTES). The classifying reaction depends on the SERUM of one person's blood agglutinating (clumping together) the red blood cells of someone else. The antigens, known as agglutinogens, react with antibodies (agglutinins) in the serum. There are two agglutinogens termed A and B and two agglutinins called anti-A and anti-B. This gives rise to four groups: corpuscles with no agglutinogens, group O; with A; with B; with both A and B (hence blood group

AB). The agglutinin groups match those of the agglutinogens. thus a person of blood group B has anti-A serum in his or her blood. It is vital that blood groups are matched for transfusion because incompatibility will produce blood clotting.

The rhesus factor or Rh factor is another antigen (named after the rhesus monkey, which has a similar antigen), those with it being Rh-positive and those without Rh-negative. About 85 per cent of people are Rh-positive. If a Rh-negative person receives Rh-positive blood, or if a Rh-positive foetus is exposed to antibodies to the factor in the blood of the Rh-negative mother, then HAEMOLYSIS occurs in the FOETUS and newborn child. This may cause the stillbirth of the child or JAUNDICE after birth. Testing of pregnant women is thus essential.

blood poisoning *see* SEPTICAEMIA.

blood pressure the pressure of the blood on the HEART and BLOOD VESSELS in the system of circulation. Also, the pressure that has to be applied to an ARTERY to stop the PULSE beyond the pressure point. Blood pressure peaks at a heart beat (SYSTOLE) and falls in between (DIASTOLE). The systolic pressure in young adults is equivalent to approximately 120 mm mercury (and 70 mm in diastole). The pressure also depends on the hardness and thickness of vessel walls, and blood pressure tends to increase with age as arteries thicken and harden. A temporary rise in blood pressure may be precipitated by exposure to cold; a permanent rise by KIDNEY disease and other disorders. A lower blood pressure can be induced by a hot bath or caused by exhaustion. The instrument used to measure blood pressure is the SPHYGMOMANOMETER.

blood sugar glucose concentration in the BLOOD for which the typical value is 3.5 to 5.5 mmol/l (millimoles per litre). *See also* HYPOGLYCAEMIA and HYPERGLYCAEMIA.

blood transfusion the replacement of BLOOD lost because of injury, surgery, etc. A patient may receive whole blood but more commonly or a component, e.g. packed red cells (red blood cells separated from the PLASMA, used to counteract ANAEMIA and restore HAEMOGLOBIN levels). Blood from DONORS is matched to the recipient for BLOOD GROUP. Donor blood can be stored for three weeks before use if kept just a few degrees above freezing, after which the PLATELETS, LEUCOCYTES and some red blood cells (ERYTHROCYTES) become non-viable. PLASMA and SERUM are also transfused, and in dried form plasma can be stored for up to five years.

blood vessel the veins and arteries (*see* VEIN; ARTERY) and their smaller branchings, venules and arterioles, through which BLOOD is carried to and from the HEART.

blue baby the condition whereby an infant is born with CYANOSIS because of a CONGENITAL malformation of the HEART. The result is that deoxygenated BLOOD does not go through the LUNGS to be oxygenated but is pumped around the body. Surgery can usually be performed to correct the condition.

boil *or* **furuncle** a skin INFECTION in a hair FOLLICLE or GLAND that produces INFLAMMATION and PUS. The infection is often caused by the bacterium *Staphylococcus*, but healing is generally quick upon release of the pus or administration of ANTIBIOTICS. Frequent occurrence of boils is usually investigated to ensure the patient is not suffering from DIABETES MELLITUS.

bolus 1. a chewed lump of food ready for swallowing. **2.** a large pill. **3.** a method of drug delivery in which a small quantity of a drug is injected into a VEIN or directly into an ORGAN where a maximum concentration is required.

bonding the creation of a link between an infant and its parents, particularly the mother. Factors such as eye to eye contact, soothing noises, etc, are part of the process.

bone the hard CONNECTIVE TISSUE that, with CARTILAGE, forms the SKELETON. Bone has a matrix of COLLAGEN fibres with bone salts (crystalline calcium phosphate or hydroxyapatite, in which are the bone CELLS, OSTEOBLASTS and OSTEOCYTES). The bone cells form the matrix. There are two types of bone: compact or dense, forming the shafts of long bones, and spongy or cancellous, which occurs on the inside and at the ends of long bones and also forms the short bones. Compact bone is a hard tube covered by the periosteum (a membrane) and enclosing the BONE MARROW and contains very fine canals (*see* HAVERSIAN CANALS) around which the bone is structured in circular plates. *See also* SKULL.

bone diseases *see* OSTEOMY-ELITIS, OSTEOCHONDRITIS, OSTEOSARCOMA and ACHON-DROPLASIA.

bone marrow a soft TISSUE found in the spaces of BONES. In young animals, all bone marrow, the red marrow, produces blood CELLS. In older animals the marrow in long bones is replaced by yellow marrow, which contains a large amount of fat and does not produce blood cells. In mature animals, the red marrow occurs in the ribs, sternum, vertebrae and the ends of the long bones (e.g. the femur). The red marrow contains MYELOID tissue with ERYTHROBLASTS from which red blood cells (ERYTHROCYTES) develop. LEUCOCYTES also form from the myeloid tissue and them-selves give rise to other cell types.

botulism the most dangerous type of food poisoning, caused by the anaerobic bacterium *Clostridium botulinum*. The bacterium is found in oxygen-free environments, e.g. in contaminated food in bottles or tins. During growth it releases a TOXIN of which one component attacks the NERVOUS SYSTEM. It has a very small lethal dose, and symptoms commence with a dry mouth, CONSTIPATION and blurred vision, and worsen to MUSCLE weakness. Death is caused by PARALYSIS of the muscles involved in RESPIRATION.

bovine spongiform encephalopathy (BSE) a disease of cattle that proves fatal and is similar to scrapie in sheep and CREUTZFELDT-JAKOB DISEASE in humans. *See also* VARIANT CJD.

bowel the large INTESTINE.

bow legs *or* **genu varum** a deformity in which the legs curve outwards, producing a gap between the knees when standing. Small children may exhibit this to some degree but continuance into adult life or its later formation is the result of abnormal growth of the EPIPHYSIS.

Bowman's capsule *see* KID-NEY.

brachial a term used to describe the upper arm, hence brachial ARTERY, etc.

brachiocephalic trunk *see* INNOMINATE ARTERY.

bradycardia slowness of the heartbeat and PULSE to below 60 per minute.

bradykinesia the condition in which there is abnormally slow movement of the body and limbs and slowness of speech, as may be caused by PARKINSON'S DISEASE.

bradykinin a polyPEPTIDE derived from plasma PROTEINS that causes smooth MUSCLE to contract. It is also a powerful dilator of BLOOD VESSELS.

brain the part of the CENTRAL NERVOUS SYSTEM contained within the CRANIUM that is connected via the SPINAL CORD to the remainder of the NERVOUS SYSTEM. The brain interprets information received from sense organs and emits signals to control MUSCLES. The brain comprises distinct areas: the CEREBRUM, CEREBELLUM, PONS, MEDULLA OBLONGATA and mid-brain or MESENCEPHALON. GREY MAT-TER and WHITE MATTER make up the brain, in different arrangements, and a dense network of blood vessels supplies the grey matter, and both blood vessels and nerve CELLS are supported by a fibrous network, the NEUROGLIA.

The average female brain weighs 1.25kg, and the male 1.4kg and the maximum size occurs around the age of 20, whereupon it decreases gradually. Three membranes (the MENINGES) separate the brain from the skull, and between each pair is a fluid-filled space to cushion the brain. There are twelve NERVES connected to the brain, mainly in the region of the brain stem, and four arteries carrying blood to the brain. Two veins drain the central portion and many small veins open into venous SINUSES that connect with the internal jugular vein.

brain death *see* BRAIN-STEM DEATH.

brain diseases disorders, either CONGENITAL or ACQUIRED (e.g. through INFECTION) that affect the functioning of the BRAIN. Many brain diseases are indicated by some impairment of a facility, e.g. a loss of sensation or an alteration in behaviour. Some result in permanent brain damage and consequent loss of physical and/or mental function to varying degrees. *See, amongst others,* APHASIA, CONCUSSION, EPILEPSY, HYDROCEPHALUS *and* MENINGITIS.

brain-stem death *or* **brain death** a complete and continuous absence of the vital reflexes controlled by centres in the brain stem (breathing, pupillary responses, etc). Tests are performed by independent doctors, repeated after an interval, before brain-stem death is formally confirmed.

breast the MAMMARY GLAND that produces milk. Each breast has a number of compartments with lobules surrounded by fatty TISSUE and MUSCLE fibres. Milk formed in the lobules gathers in branching tubes or DUCTS that together form lactiferous ducts. Near the nipple the ducts form ampullae (small 'reservoirs') from which the ducts discharge through the nipple.

breastbone *see* STERNUM.

breast cancer a CARCINOMA or SARCOMA, which is the commonest cancer in women. Risk factors include immoderate alcohol consumption and obesity and the likelihood of developing breast cancer increases with age. It has also been discovered that some women with a history of breast cancer in the family have a genetic predisposition to the disease. The first sign may be a lump in the breast or armpit (the latter being caused by spread to the LYMPH NODES). There may also be puckering or dimpling of the skin and inversion of, or discharge from the nipple. Diagnosis can be confirmed after MAMMOGRAPHY, and BIOPSY of the breast tissue. A localized TUMOUR may be removed surgically (lumpectomy). More radical surgical treatment involves removal of the whole breast (MASTECTOMY), sometimes with associated lymph nodes. In addition, RADIOTHERAPY, CHEMOTHERAPY and HORMONE therapy can form part of the treatment.

breast screening procedures adopted to detect breast cancer as early as possible. In addition to self-examination, mammography (particularly for the post-menopausal woman) is a valuable diagnostic tool.

breathlessness is caused fundamentally by any condition

that depletes blood oxygen resulting in excessive and/or laboured breathing to gain more air. The causes are numerous, ranging from lung diseases or conditions (PNEUMONIA, EMPHYSEMA, BRONCHITIS) to heart conditions and OBESITY. In children, narrowing of the air passages is a cause, as is ASTHMA.

breech presentation the position of a baby in the UTERUS whereby it would be delivered buttocks first instead of the usual head-first delivery. The baby, and possibly the mother, may be at risk in such cases.

brittle bone disease *see* OSTEOGENESIS IMPERFECTA.

bronchi (*sing* **bronchus**) air passages supported by rings of CARTILAGE. Two bronchi branch off from the TRACHEA, and these split into further bronchi. The two main bronchi branch to form five lobar bronchi, then twenty segmental bronchi, and so on. *See* LUNGS; RESPIRATION.

bronchial the term used to describe the BRONCHI and BRONCHIOLES.

bronchiectasis *see* CYSTIC FIBROSIS.

bronchioles very fine tubes occurring as branches of the BRONCHI in the LUNGS. The bronchioles end in alveoli (*see* ALVEOLUS) where carbon dioxide and oxygen are exchanged.

bronchitis INFLAMMATION of the BRONCHI, which occurs in two forms, acute and chronic. BACTERIA or VIRUSES cause the acute form, which is initially typified by the symptoms of the common COLD but develops, with painful coughing, wheezing, throat and chest pains and the production of purulent (PUS-containing) MUCUS. If the infection spreads to the BRONCHIOLES (bronchiolitis) the consequences are more serious as the body is deprived of oxygen. ANTIBIOTICS and EXPECTORANTS can relieve the symptoms. Chronic bronchitis is identified by an excessive production of mucus and may be the result of recurrence of the acute form. It is a common cause of death among the elderly, and there are several parameters of direct consequence to its cause: excessive smoking of cigarettes; cold, damp climate; OBESITY; respiratory infections. Damage to the bronchi and other complications may occur, giving rise to constant BREATHLESSNESS.

bronchodilator a drug used to relax the smooth MUSCLE of the BRONCHIOLES, thus increasing their diameter and the air supply to the LUNGS. Bronchodilators are used in the treatment of e.g ASTHMA and EMPHYSEMA. Depending on the drug, bronchodilators may be administered orally, by injection or through an inhaler or NEBULIZER.

bronchopneumonia *see* PNEUMONIA.

brown fat *see* ADIPOSE TISSUE.

brucellosis a disease of farm animals (pigs, cattle, goats) caused by a species of a Gram-negative bacillus, *Brucella* (*see* GRAM'S STAIN). It may be passed to humans through contact with an infected animal or by drinking contaminated, untreated, milk. In cattle the disease causes contagious ABORTION, but in humans it is characterized by FEVER, sweats, joint pains, backache and headache.

bruise an injury without an open wound, where the skin has become discoloured by leakage of blood into an area of TISSUE. In the simplest case, minute BLOOD VESSELS rupture at the point of injury and

blood leaks into the immediate area. A larger injury may be accompanied by swelling.

BSE the abbreviation of BOVINE SPONGIFORM ENCEPHALOPATHY.

bubonic plague *see* PLAGUE.

buffer a chemical compound that is added to a solution to minimize changes in acidity.

buccal a term used generally to pertain to the mouth, specifically the inside of the cheek or the gum next to the cheek.

bulimia an insatiable craving for food.

bulimia nervosa an eating disorder, characterized by repeated episodes of uncontrolled binge-eating (large quanities of food over short periods of time), followed by 'purging'—misuse of LAXATIVES or induced VOMITING to avoid weight gain. Sufferers have a distorted body image and a fear of obesity. There is an attempt to hide the condition as it is psychological in origin. People suffering from ANOREXIA NERVOSA may demonstrate similar behaviours.

bunion *see* CORN.

burns damage to SKIN and TISSUE caused by heat. Burns and scalds show similar symptoms and require similar treatment, the former being caused by dry heat, the latter by moist heat. Burns may also be caused by electric currents and chemicals. The severity of burns is assessessed by degrees (1st—4th, according to depth of injury) and by the estimated percentage of body surface affected. Severe injuries can prove life-threatening because of SHOCK as a result of fluid loss from damaged TISSUE.

bursa (*pl* **bursae**) a small fluid-filled fibrous SAC that reduces friction between parts of the body, especially at the JOINTS.

bursitis *see* HOUSEMAID'S KNEE.

C

caecum (*pl* **caeca**) an expanded, blind-ended SAC at the start of the large INTESTINE between the small intestine and COLON. The small intestine and vermiform APPENDIX open into the caecum.

Caesarean section a surgical operation to deliver a baby by means of an INCISION through the ABDOMEN and UTERUS. It is performed when there is a risk to the health of the baby or mother in normal delivery, both as a planned and as an emergency procedure. It can be performed under general, spinal or epidural ANAESTHETIC.

caisson disease *see* BENDS.

calamine zinc carbonate, which is a mild astringent and is a component of lotions used to relieve itchy, painful skin conditions such as ECZEMA, URTICARIA and SUNBURN.

calcaneus (*pl* **calcanei**) *see* FOOT; HEEL; TALUS.

calciferol a form of VITAMIN D that is manufactured in the SKIN in the presence of sunlight or derived from certain foods (e.g. liver and fish oils). Its main role is in calcium METABOLISM, enabling CALCIUM to be absorbed from the gut and laid down in BONE. A deficiency of vitamin D leads to the bone disease OSTEOLAMACIA and also RICKETS.

calcification the deposition of calcium salts, which is normal in the formation of BONE but may occur at other sites in the body. *See* OSSIFICATION.

calcitonin *see* PAGET'S DISEASE OF BONE.

calcium a metallic element that is essential for normal growth and functioning of body processes. It is an important component of BONES and teeth and has a role in vital metabolic processes, e.g. muscle contraction, passage of nerve impulses and blood clotting. Its concentration in the BLOOD is regulated by various THYROID HORMONES.

calcium-channel blocker *or* **calcium antagonist** a drug that inhibits the movement of calcium ions into smooth MUSCLE and cardiac muscle CELLS. Their effect is to relax the muscle and reduce the strength of contraction and to cause VASODILATION. They are used in the treatment of high BLOOD PRESSURE and ANGINA.

calculi *see* CONCRETIONS.

callus material that forms around the end of a broken BONE containing bone-forming CELLS, CARTILAGE and CONNECTIVE TISSUE. Eventually this tissue becomes calcified.

calorie a term applied to a unit of energy, which is the heat required to raise the temperature of one gram of water by one degree Celsius.

canaliculi (*sing* **canaliculus**) *see* HAVERSIAN CANAL; LACRIMAL GLAND.

cancer a widely used term for any form of malignant TUMOUR. It is characterized by an uncontrolled and abnormal growth of cancer CELLS, which invade surrounding TISSUES and destroy them. Cancer cells may spread throughout the body via the bloodstream or LYMPHATIC SYSTEM, a process known as METASTASIS, and set up secondary growths elsewhere. There are known to be a number of different causes or risk factors, including smoking, diet, radiation, ultraviolet light, some VIRUSES and genetic factors. Treatment depends on the site of the cancer but involves RADIOTHERAPY, CHEMOTHERAPY and surgery. GENE THERAPY is also being researched for its uses in combating the disease.

candidiasis *see* THRUSH.

canine *see* TOOTH.

cannula *or* **canula** a narrow tube that is inserted into a body cavity to drain off fluid or insert medication.

capillary a fine BLOOD VESSEL that communicates with an ARTERIOLE or VENULE. Capillaries form networks in most TISSUES and have walls that are only one CELL thick. There is a constant exchange of substances (oxygen, carbon dioxide, nutrients, etc) between the capillaries, arterioles and venules, supplying the needs of the surrounding tissues.

capsule 1. a sheath of CONNECTIVE TISSUE or MEMBRANE surrounding an ORGAN. The ADRENAL GLAND, KIDNEY and SPLEEN are all housed within a capsule. **2.** a FIBROUS TISSUE sheath surrounding various JOINTS. **3.** a small, gelatinous pouch containing a DRUG, which can be swallowed.

carbamazepine see TRIGEMINAL NEURALGIA.

carbohydrates organic compounds, which include sugars and starch and contain carbon, hydrogen and oxygen. They are the most important source of energy available to the body and are an essential part of the diet. They are eventually broken down in the body to the simple sugar, glucose, which can be used by CELLS in numerous metabolic processes.

carbolic acid phenol derived from coal tar and the forerunner of modern ANTISEPTICS. A strong disinfectant, it is used in lotions and ointments such as CALAMINE lotion, but is highly poisonous if ingested.

carbon dioxide or **carbonic acid** (formula CO_2) a gas formed in the TISSUES as a result of metabolic processes within the body. Medically, carbon dioxide is used combined with oxygen during ANAESTHESIA.

carbon monoxide (formula CO) an odourless and colourless gas that is highly dangerous when inhaled, leading to carbon monoxide poisoning. In the BLOOD it has a very great affinity for oxygen and converts HAEMOGLOBIN into carboxyhaemoglobin. When carbon monoxide is inhaled, the TISSUES of the body are quickly deprived of oxygen because there is no free haemoglobin left to pick it up in the LUNGS. Carbon monoxide is present in coal gas fumes and vehicle exhaust emissions. The symptoms of poisoning include giddiness, flushing of the SKIN (because of carboxyhaemoglobin in the blood, which is bright red), NAUSEA, headache, raised respiratory and PULSE rate and eventual COMA, respiratory failure and death. An affected person must be taken into the fresh air and given oxygen and ARTIFICIAL RESPIRATION if required.

carboxyhaemoglobin *see* CARBON MONOXIDE.

carcinogen any substance that causes damage to tissue CELLS likely to result in CANCER. Various substances are known to be carcinogenic, including tobacco smoke, asbestos and ionizing radiation.

carcinoma a CANCER of the EPITHELIUM, i.e. the TISSUE that lines the body's internal ORGANS and SKIN.

cardia the opening of the OE-SOPHAGUS into the STOMACH.

cardiac arrest the cessation of the pumping action of the HEART. There is a loss of consciousness and breathing and the PULSE ceases. Death follows very rapidly unless the heartbeat can be restored, and methods of achieving this include external CARDIAC MASSAGE, ARTIFICIAL RESPIRATION, DEFIBRILLATION and direct CARDIAC MASSAGE. *See also* CARDIOPULMONARY RESUSCITATION.

cardiac cycle the whole sequence of events that produces a heartbeat and normally takes place in less than one second. The atria (*see* ATRIUM) contract together and force the BLOOD into the VENTRICLES (DIASTOLE). These then also contract (SYSTOLE), and blood exits the HEART and is pumped around the body. As the ventricles are contracting, the atria relax and fill up with blood once again.

cardiac massage a means of restoring the heartbeat if this has suddenly ceased. Direct cardiac massage, which is only feasible if the person is in hospital, involves massaging the HEART by hand through an INCISION in the chest wall. External cardiage massage, which is used in conjunction with ARTIFICIAL RESPIRATION in emergency CARDIOPULMO-NARY RESUSCITATION, involves rhythmic compression of the chest wall, with hands placed at the lower end of the person's sternum, while the person is laid on his or her back.

cardiac muscle specialized MUSCLE unique to the HEART, consisting of branching, elongated fibres possessing the ability to contract and relax continuously.

cardiac pacemaker *see* PACE-MAKER; SINOATRIAL NODE.

cardiology the area of medicine concerned with the study of the structure, function and diseases of the HEART and circulatory system.

cardiomyopathy any disease or disorder of the CARDIAC MUSCLE that may arise from a number of different causes, including viral infections, congenital abnormalities and chronic alcoholism.

cardiopulmonary bypass an artificial mechanism for maintaining the body's CIRCULATION while the HEART is intentionally stopped in order to carry out cardiac surgery. A pump oxygenator, or heart-lung machine, carries out the circulatory function of the heart and the oxygenating function of the lungs until surgery is completed.

cardiopulmonary resuscitation (CPR) restoration of breathing and circulation when they have ceased, using a combination of external CARDIAC MASSAGE and ARTIFICIAL RESPIRATION. Where the heart has not stopped but is fibrillating, a defibrillator (*see* DEFIBRILLATION; FIBRILLATION) may be used to restore a normal rhythm.

cardiovascular system the HEART and the whole of the circulatory system, which is divided into the systemic (arteries and veins of the body) and pulmonary (arteries and veins of the LUNGS). (*See* ARTERY; VEIN.) The cardiovascular system is responsible for the transport of oxygen and nutrients to the TISSUES, and for removing waste products and carbon dioxide from them, taking these to the ORGANS from which they are eventually eliminated.

carditis INFLAMMATION of the HEART.

carotid artery either of the two large arteries (*see* ARTERY) in the neck that branch and provide the BLOOD supply to the head and neck. The paired common carotid arteries arise from the AORTA on the left side of the HEART and from the innominate artery on the right. These continue up on either side of the neck and branch into the internal CAROTID BODY and the external carotid body.

carotid body a small area of specialized reddish-coloured TISSUE situated one on either side of the neck where the common CAROTID ARTERY branches to form the internal and external carotids. It is sensitive to chemical changes in the BLOOD, containing CHEMORECEPTORS that respond to oxygen, carbon dioxide and hydrogen levels. If the oxygen level falls, impulses are transmitted to the respiratory centres in the BRAIN, resulting in an increase in the rate of RESPIRATION and heartbeat.

carpus the Latin word for the WRIST, which consists of eight small BONES that articulate with the ULNA and RADIUS of the forearm on one side and with the METACARPAL BONES (of the hand) on the other.

cartilage a type of firm CONNECTIVE TISSUE that is pliable and forms part of the SKELETON. There are three different kinds: hyaline cartilage, fibrocartilage and elastic cartilage. Hyaline cartilage is found at the JOINTS of movable BONES and in the TRACHEA, NOSE, BRONCHI and as costal cartilage joining the RIBS to the STERNUM. Fibrocartilage, which consists of cartilage and CONNECTIVE TISSUE, is found in the INTERVERTEBRAL DISCS of the SPINAL COLUMN and in TENDONS. Elastic cartilage is found in the external part of the EAR (pinna).

cast *see* PLASTER OF PARIS.

castration *see* ORCHIDECTOMY.

catabolism the biochemical processes within the body (METABOLISM) are divided into two different sorts— those that build up or produce (synthesize) substances, which is anabolism, and those that break down material (LYSIS), known as catabolism. In catabolism, more complex materials are broken down into simpler ones with a release of energy, as occurs during the digestion of food.

catalepsy a mental disorder in which the person enters a trance-like state. The body becomes rigid, like a statue, and the LIMBs, if moved, stay in the position in which they are placed. There is no sense of recognition or sensation and there is a loss of voluntary control. The vital body functions are shut down to a minimum level necessary for life although heartbeat and breathing continue. The condition is brought on by severe mental TRAUMA, either as a result of a sudden shock or by a more prolonged DEPRESSION. It may last for minutes or hours or, rarely, for several days.

cataract a condition in which the LENS of the EYE becomes opaque, which results in a blurring of VISION. It may arise from a number of different causes, including injury to the eye, as a CONGENITAL condition or as a result of certain diseases, such as DIABETES MELLITUS. However, the commonest cause is advancing age, during which changes naturally take place in the lens involving the PROTEIN components.

catarrh inflammation of the MUCOUS MEMBRANES, particularly in the NOSE and THROAT, causing excess production of mucus. Catarrh may be caused by ALLERGY, e.g. hay fever, or by INFECTION.

catatonia when a patient becomes statue-like, remaining rigid. It is a symptom of mental disease and is often a feature of catatonic SCHIZOPHRENIA.

catecholamine *see* DOPAMINE.

catheter a fine flexible tube that is passed into various ORGANS of the body either for diagnostic purposes or to administer some kind of treatment. One of the commonest kinds is the urethral catheter, which is inserted into the BLADDER to clear an obstruction, draw off URINE or wash out this organ. *See* FOLEY CATHETER.

CAT scan *or* **computerised axial tomography** a diag-nostic technique in radiology whereby images of cross-sectional 'slices' of the body are recorded using a special X-RAY scanner known as a CAT or CT scanner. The information is integrated by computer to build up a three-dimensional picture of the TISSUE under investigation. The technique is commonly used for investigations of the BRAIN, e.g. if a TUMOUR, HAEMATOMA or ABSCESS is present. Whole-body scans may be required for a number of conditions, but are particularly useful when malignancy is present, supplying information about the position and outline of a tumour and the extent of spread of CANCER.

caul a piece of MEMBRANE (part of the AMNION) that sometimes partly covers a newborn baby.

cautery 1. a heated instrument, a laser or a caustic substance, e.g silver nitrate, that is applied to skin, etc, to destroy or remove living TISSUE or to seal BLOOD VESSELS and stop bleeding. 1. The procedure, also known as cauterization, of using heated instruments or caustic substances in this way.

Cautery is commonly used in the treatment of WARTS and other small growths.

cavernous sinus one of a pair of cavities located on either side of the SPHENOID BONE behind the eye sockets at the base of the SKULL. Venous blood drains into it from the BRAIN, part of the cheek, EYE and NOSE and leaves through the facial VEINS and internal JUGULAR.

cavity a hollow space within the body, e.g. the abdominal cavity or a dental cavity.

CBC (complete blood count) *see* BLOOD COUNT.

cell the basic building block of all life and the smallest structural unit in the body. Human body cells vary in size and function and number several billion. Each cell consists of a cell body surrounded by a MEMBRANE. The cell body consists of a substance known as cytoplasm, containing various ORGANELLES and also a nucleus. The nucleus contains the CHROMOSOMES, composed of the genetic material, the DNA. Most human body cells contain 46 chromosomes (23 pairs), half being derived from the individual's father and half from the mother. Cells

are able to make exact copies of themselves by a process known as MITOSIS, and a full complement of chromosomes is received by each daughter cell. However, the human sex cells (SPERM and ova) differ in always containing half the number of chromosomes. At fertilization, a sperm and OVUM combine and a complete set of chromosomes is received by the new embryo. *See also* MEIOSIS.

cells of Leydig *see* TESTICLE.

cementum a thin hard substance resembling BONE that covers the root of a TOOTH.

central nervous system the BRAIN and the SPINAL CORD, which receive and integrate all the nervous information from the PERIPHERAL NERVOUS SYSTEM.

cephalosporin one of a group of semi-synthetic ANTIBIOTICS derived from a mould called *Cephalosporium*. They are effective against a broad spectrum of micro-organism and are used to treat a variety of bacterial INFECTIONS. They are sometimes able to destroy organisms that have become resistant to PENICILLIN.

cerebellum the largest part of the hind BRAIN, consisting of a pair of joined hemispheres. It has an outer grey cortex, which is a much folded layer of GREY MATTER, and an inner core of WHITE MATTER. The cerebellum coordinates the activity of various groups of voluntary MUSCLES and maintains posture and balance.

cerebral cortex the outer layer of GREY MATTER of the cerebral hemispheres of the CEREBRUM. It is highly folded and contains many millions of nerve CELLS and makes up about 40 per cent of the BRAIN by weight. The cerebral cortex controls intellectual processes such as thought, perception, memory and intellect, and is also involved in the senses of sight, touch and hearing. It also controls the voluntary movement of MUSCLES and is connected with all the different parts of the body.

cerebral palsy an abnormality of the BRAIN that usually occurs before or during birth. It may arise as a development defect in the FOETUS because of genetic factors or as the result of a (viral) INFECTION during PREGNANCY. A lack of oxygen during a difficult LABOUR or other TRAUMA to the infant can also result in cere-

bral palsy. After birth, the condition can result from HAEMOLYTIC DISEASE OF THE NEWBORN or infection of the brain, e.g. MENINGITIS. It can also be caused by cerebral THROMBOSIS or trauma. The condition is characterized by spastic PARALYSIS of the limbs, the severity of which is variable. Also, there may be involuntary writhing movements, called athetosis, and balance and posture are also affected. Children born with cerebral palsy may have some degree of learning difficulty and/or speech impairment and may suffer from EPILEPSY.

cerebrospinal fluid a clear, colourless fluid with a similar composition to LYMPH. It fills the ventricles and cavities in the CENTRAL NERVOUS SYSTEM and bathes all the surfaces of the BRAIN and SPINAL CORD. The brain floats in it, and it has a protective function, acting as a shock absorber and helping to prevent mechanical injury to the central nervous system. The cerebrospinal fluid is secreted by the CHOROID PLEXUSes in the ventricles of the brain, and it contains some white blood cells (LEUCOCYTES), salts, glucose and enzymes. It is reabsorbed by veins back into the bloodstream.

cerebrovascular accident *see* STROKE.

cerebrum the largest and most highly developed part of the BRAIN, consisting of a pair of cerebral hemispheres divided from each other by a longitudinal FISSURE. The cerebral hemispheres are covered by the CEREBRAL CORTEX, below which lies WHITE MATTER in which the BASAL GANGLIA are situated. The cerebrum controls complex intellectual activities and also all the voluntary responses of the body.

cervical a term meaning relating to the neck and often used in connection with the CERVIX, the neck of the womb (UTERUS).

cervical cancer CANCER of the neck or CERVIX of the womb. In the precancerous stage, readily detectable changes occur in the CELLS lining the surface of the cervix. These can be identified by means of a CERVICAL SMEAR test and, if treated at this stage, the prevention and cure rates of the cancer are very high. Infection with some types of human papilloma VIRUS is linked to the disease. The sexual behaviour of a woman influences her risk of developing cervical cancer. Early sexual intercourse and numerous different partners are now recognized to increase the risk. Cigarette smoking is another risk factor.

cervical smear a simple test, involving scraping off some CELLS from the CERVIX and examining them microscopically. The test is routinely carried out every three years on women over the age of eighteen to detect early indications of CERVICAL CANCER and is a form of PREVENTIVE MEDICINE.

cervix a neck-like structure, especially the cervix uteri or neck of the womb, which is partly above and partly within the VAGINA, projecting into it and linking it with the cavity of the UTERUS via the cervical canal.

Chagas' disease a form of SLEEPING SICKNESS that is found in South and Central America.

cheloid *see* KELOID.

chemoreceptor a CELL (present in the NOSE and TASTE BUDS) that detects the presence of specific chemical compounds. An electrical impulse is then sent to the BRAIN. *See also* CAROTID BODY.

chemotherapy the treatment or control of any disorder or disease by the administration of chemical substances or DRUGS. The term is now most commonly used to refer to the treatment of many different forms of CANCER with ANTIMETABOLITE drugs.

chest *or* **thorax** the upper part of the body cavity, separated from the lower ABDOMEN by the DIAPHRAGM. The chest cavity is enclosed within the rib cage. The thoracic skeleton consists of the RIBS and COSTAL CARTILAGES attached to the STERNUM (breastbone) at the front. At the back, the ribs join the thoracic VERTEBRAe of the spine. The thorax contains the LUNGS, HEART and OESOPHAGUS and above it lie the neck and head.

chickenpox a highly infectious disease that mainly affects children and is caused by the *Varicella zoster* VIRUS. There is an INCUBATION period of two to three weeks and then usually a child becomes slightly feverish and unwell. Within 24 hours an itchy rash appears on the SKIN, which consists of fluid-filled BLISTERS. Eventually these dry up and form SCABS. Infected children should be isolated from others until the blisters have dried and crusted over (about one week). Cool baths and the application of CALAMINE lotion can soothe the itching. In some cases, where the disease is caught early, ANTIVIRAL medication may be helpful. The disease is uncommon in adults as a childhood attack gives lifelong IMMUNITY and most children are exposed to chickenpox at some stage. However, the virus may remain within the system and become active later as shingles (HERPES zoster).

chilblain a round, itchy INFLAMMATION of the SKIN that usually occurs on the toes or fingers during cold weather and is caused by a ocalized deficiency in the CIRCULATION. Chilblains may sometimes be an indication of poor health or inadequate clothing and nutrition.

china clay *see* KAOLIN.

chiropody the branch of medicine concerned with the health of the FOOT, including its normal structure and development, diseases and their treatment.

chiropractor a person who practises chiropractic, which is a system of manipulation, mainly of the VERTEBRAE of the SPINAL COLUMN, to relieve stress on NERVES, which might be causing pain.

chlamydia a sexually transmitted INFECTION caused by the microorganism *chlamydia trachomatis*. It is commonly symptomless in both men and women. Symptoms, if they appear, include discharge of PUS from the PENIS or the VAGINA and pain on urination. The throat and EYES may also be affected. If left untreated, chlamydia can lead to PELVIC INFLAMMATORY DISEASE and sterility in women. It can be passed from mother to child during birth, causing CONJUNCTIVITIS and PNEUMONIA in the newborn child, and pregnant women are routinely screened for infection. It can be cured with ANTIBIOTICS.

chloral hydrate a type of SEDATIVE drug that is given mainly to elderly people and children. Within half an hour of being taken by mouth (usually as a SYRUP), it induces sleep and its effects last for about eight hours. It is useful when used sparingly but harmful in large doses, causing toxic effects and addiction.

chloramphenicol *see* TYPHOID FEVER.

chlordiazepoxide *see* TRANQUILLIZER.

chlorhexidine *or* **hibitane** an ANTISEPTIC substance that is used in preparations to cleanse the SKIN. It is also used in LOZENGES for mild INFECTIONS of the mouth and throat. Dilute solutions are effective as a mouthwash.

chlorpromazine a major TRANQUILLIZER, used widely in the treatment of PSYCHOSIS, e.g. SCHIZOPHRENIA. It is also used in the treatment of RADIATION SICKNESS.

chloroform a volatile and colourless liquid that is a compound of carbon, hydrogen and chlorine ($CHCl_3$). It was once widely in use as a general ANAESTHETIC, but it affects the rhythm of the HEART and also causes LIVER damage. It is little used today, except in very low concentrations as a preservative and in some LINIMENTS.

choking violent coughing and interference in breathing caused by an obstruction in the airway in the region of the LARYNX. If the obstruction is large, there is a danger of suffocation. If the coughing fails to dislodge the obstruction, it is necessary to use other methods to aid a choking person. With adults it may be necessary to use the HEIMLICH'S MANOEUVRE. There are also specific first aid procedures for dealing with choking babies and children.

cholecalciferol *see* VITAMIN D.

cholecystectomy the surgical operation to remove the GALL BLADDER. A cholecystectomy may be carried out using LAPOROSCOPY, but where there are complications, e.g. bleeding, open surgery may be required.

cholecystitis inflammation of the GALL BLADDER, which is caused in the majority of cases by GALLSTONES, but may be caused by other factors, e.g. alcohol abuse.

cholera an infection of the small INTESTINE caused by the bacterium *Vibrio cholerae*. It varies in degree from very mild cases to extremely severe illness and death. During EPIDEMICS of cholera, which are associated with conditions of poor sanitation and overcrowding, the death rate can be over 50 per cent. The disease is spread through contamination of drinking water by FAECES of those affected and also by flies landing on infected material and then crawling on food. Epidemics are rare in conditions of good sanitation, but when cholera is detected, extreme attention has to be paid to hygiene, including treatment and scrupulous disposal of the body waste of the infected person. TETRACYCLINE or other SULPHONAMIDE drugs are given to kill the BACTERIA. The death rate is markedly reduced given proper and prompt treatment, but the risk is greater in children and the elderly. VACCINATION against cholera can be given but it is effective for only about 6 months.

cholesterol a fatty insoluble molecule (sterol), which is widely found in the body and is synthesized from saturated FATTY ACIDS in the LIVER. It is an important substance in the body, being a component of CELL membranes and a precursor in the production of STEROID hormones (SEX HORMONES) and BILE salts. An elevated level of BLOOD cholesterol is associated with ATHEROMA, which may result in high BLOOD PRESSURE and CORONARY THROMBOSIS, and this is seen in the disease DIABETES MELLITUS. It is recommended that people should reduce their consumption of saturated fat and look for an alternative in the form of unsaturated fat, which is found in vegetable oils.

choluria *or* **biliuria** BILE in the URINE, which occurs when there is an elevated level of bile in the BLOOD. This may result from the condition known as obstructive JAUNDICE, when the bile ducts become obstructed so that bile manufactured in the LIVER fails to reach the INTESTINE. The urine is dark coloured and contains bile salts.

chondromalacia patellae *see* CREPITUS.

chorda tympani *see* EAR.

chorea a disorder of the NERVOUS SYSTEM, characterized by involuntary jerky movements of the MUSCLES, mainly of the face, shoulders and hips. Sydenham's chorea (or Saint Vitus' Dance) is a disease that mainly affects children and is associated with acute RHEU-MATISM. About one-third of affected children develop rheumatism elsewhere in the body, often involving the HEART, and the disease is more common in girls than in boys. If the heart is affected, there may be problems in later life. The condition usually subsides over a period of a few months. Huntington's chorea is a fatal, inherited condition that does not appear until after the age of 40 and is accompanied by DEMENTIA. Senile chorea afflicts some elderly people but there is no dementia. *See also* RHEUMATIC FEVER.

chorionic gonadotrophic hormone *or* **human chorionic gonadotrophin** (**HCG**) a HORMONE produced during PREGNANCY by the PLACENTA, large amounts of which are present in the URINE of a pregnant woman. The presence of this hormone is the basis of most pregnancy tests. It is given by injection to treat cases of delayed PUBERTY and, with another hormone, called follicle-stimulating hormone (*see* GONADOTROPHINS), to women who are sterile because of a failure in OVULATION. It may also be used to treat PREMENSTRUAL TENSION.

chorionic villus sampling (CVS) a test carried out between the 10th and 12th week of pregnancy, whereby a sample of PLACENTA is taken to test for fetal abnormality or inherited disease. The test carries a small risk of MISCARRIAGE and is not carried out unless GENETIC SCREENING or maternal blood testing has identified that there is a risk of the FOETUS having specific problems.

choroid *see* RETINA; DETACHED RETINA.

choroid plexus an extensive network of BLOOD VESSELS present in the VENTRICLES of the BRAIN and responsible for the production of the CEREBROSPINAL FLUID.

Christmas factor *see* HAEMOPHILIA.

chromatin *see* NUCLEUS.

chromosomes the rod-like structures, present in the nucleus of every body CELL, that carry the genetic information or GENES. Each human body cell contains 23 pairs of chromosomes, apart from the SPERM and ova (*see* OVUM), half derived from the mother and half from the father. Each chromosome consists of a coiled double filament (double helix) of DNA, with genes carrying the genetic information arranged linearly along its length. The genes determine all the characteristics of each individual. Of the pairs of chromosomes, 22 are the same in males and females. The 23rd pair are the SEX CHROMOSOMES, and males have one X-CHROMSOME and one Y-CHROMSOME, whereas females have two X-chromosomes. *See also* SEX-LINKED INHERITANCE.

chyle *see* DIGESTION; LACTEAL VESSELS.

chyme the partly digested food that passes from the STOMACH into the INTESTINE. It is produced by the mechanical movements of the stomach and the acid secretions present in the GASTRIC JUICE.

chymotrypsin *see* PANCREAS.

cilia (*sing* **cilium**) fine hair-like projections which line the EPITHELIUM of the upper respiratory tract (*see* RESPIRATORY SYSTEM). These beat and help to maintain the flow of air and remove and trap particles of dust.

ciliary body *see* EYE.

circulation of the blood the basic circulation is as follows: all the BLOOD from the body returns to the HEART via the

VEINS, eventually entering the right ATRIUM through the inferior and superior venae cavae (*see* VENA CAVA). This contracts and forces the blood into the right VENTRICLE, and from there it is driven to the LUNGS via the pulmonary ARTERY. In the lungs, oxygen is taken up and carbon dioxide is released, and the blood then passes into the pulmonary veins and is returned to the left atrium of the heart. Blood is forced from the left atrium into the left ventricle and from there into the AORTA. The aorta branches, giving off the various arteries that carry the blood to all the different parts of the body. The blood eventually enters the fine network of arterioles and capillaries and supplies all the TISSUES and ORGANS with oxygen and nutrients. It passes into the venules and veins, eventually returning to the right atrium through the vena cavae to complete the cycle.

circumcision a surgical removal of the FORESKIN (or prepuce) of the PENIS in males and part or all of the external GENITALIA (CLITORIS, labia minora, labia majora) in females. Male circumcision may be carried out for religious reasons but may also be required in the medical conditions known as PHIMOSIS and PARAPHIMOSIS. Female circumcision is carried out for cultural reasons only. It has no medical benefits and can severely damage a woman's health. It is illegal in many western countries.

cirrhosis a disease of the LIVER in which FIBROUS TISSUE resembling SCAR tissue is produced as a result of damage and death to the CELLS. The liver becomes yellow-coloured and nodular in appearance, and there are various types of the disease, including alcoholic cirrhosis and postnecrotic cirrhosis caused by viral HEPATITIS. The cause of the cirrhosis is not always found (cryptogenic cirrhosis), but the progress of the condition can be halted if this can be identified and removed. This particularly is applicable in alcoholic cirrhosis where the consumption of alcohol has to cease.

CJD *see* CREUTZFELD-JAKOB DISEASE.

clavicle the collar BONE forming a part of the shoulder girdle of the SKELETON. It is the most commonly fractured bone in the body.

cleft palate a developmental defect in which a FISSURE is left in the midline of the PALATE as the two sides fail to fuse. It may also involve the lip (HARELIP), and the condition is corrected by surgery.

climacteric *see* MENOPAUSE.

clitoris a small ORGAN present in females, situated at the front of the VULVA where the labial folds meet below the pubic bone. It contains erectile TISSUE that enlarges and hardens with sexual stimulation.

clone a group of CELLS that are derived from one cell (by asexual division) and are genetically identical.

clonic phase *see* TONIC-CLONIC SEIZURE.

clostridium one of a group of BACTERIA that are present in the INTESTINES of humans and animals. Some species are responsible for diseases such as BOTULISM, TETANUS and GAS GANGRENE.

clot a semi-solid lump of BLOOD or other fluid in the body. A blood clot consists of a fine network of FIBRIN in which blood corpuscles are caught. *See* COAGULATION.

coagulation (of the blood) the natural process in which BLOOD is converted from a liquid to a semi-solid state to arrest bleeding (HAEMORRHAGE). A substance known as prothrombin and calcium are normally present in the blood, and the ENZYME thromboplastin is present in the PLATELETS. When bleeding occurs, thromboplastin is released and prothrombin and calcium are converted by the enzyme into thrombin. A soluble PROTEIN called FIBRINOGEN is always present in the blood and is converted by thrombin into FIBRIN, which is the final stage in the coagulation process. A fibrous meshwork or CLOT is produced, consisting of fibrin and blood CELLS, which seals off the damaged blood vessel. The coagulation or clotting time is the time taken for blood to clot and is normally between three and eight minutes.

coagulation factors substances present in PLASMA that are involved in the process of blood COAGULATION. They are designated by a set of Roman numerals, e.g. factor VIII, and a lack of any of them means that the blood is unable to clot. *See* HAEMOPHILIA.

coarctation a narrowing, especially of the AORTA. *See also* MARFAN'S SYNDROME.

cobalamin *see* HYDROXOCOBALAMIN.

cocaine an alkaloid substance, derived from the leaves of the coca plant, that is used as a local ANAESTHETIC and a vasoconstrictor (*see* VASOCONSTRICTION) in nose, throat, ear and eye surgery. It has a stimulating effect on the CENTRAL NERVOUS SYSTEM when absorbed, in which fatigue and breathlessness (caused by exertion) disappear. However, it is highly addictive and damaging to the body if it is used often and hence it is very strictly controlled.

coccyx the end of the backbone (SPINAL COLUMN), which consists of four fused and reduced VERTEBRAE and corresponds to the tail of other mammals. The coccyx is surrounded by MUSCLE and joins with the SACRUM, a further group of fused vertebrae, which is part of the PELVIS.

cochlea a spiral-shaped ORGAN, resembling a snail shell, forming a part of the inner EAR and concerned with hearing. It consists of three fluid-filled canals with receptors that detect pressure changes caused by sound waves. NERVE impulses are sent to the BRAIN where the information is received and decoded.

codeine a substance, derived from MORPHINE, that is used for pain relief and as a cough suppressant.

cod-liver oil oil derived from the pressed fresh liver of cod, which is a rich source of VITAMINS D and A and is used as a dietary supplement.

codon *see* GENETIC CODE.

coeliac pertaining to the CAVITY of the ABDOMEN.

coeliac disease *or* **gluten enteropathy** a wasting disease of childhood in which the INTESTINES are unable to absorb fat. The intestinal lining is damaged because of a sensitivity to the PROTEIN gluten, which is found in wheat and rye flour. An excess of fat is excreted, and the child fails to grow and thrive. Successful treatment is by adhering strictly to a gluten-free diet throughout life.

cold *or* **common cold** a widespread and mild INFECTION of the upper RESPIRATORY TRACT caused by a VIRUS. There is INFLAMMATION of the MUCOUS MEMBRANES, and symptoms include FEVER, COUGHing, sneezing, runny nose, sore THROAT, HEADACHE and sometimes face ache as a result of CATARRH in the SINUSES. The disease is spread by coughing and sneezing, and treatment is by means of bed rest and the taking of mild ANALGESICS.

cold sore *see* HERPES.

colectomy surgical removal of the COLON.

colic spasmodic, severe abdominal pain that occurs in waves with brief interludes in between. Intestinal colic is usually the result of the presence of some indigestible food, which causes the contraction of the intestinal muscles. Infantile colic, common in young babies, is caused by wind associated with feeding. An attack of colic is generally not serious but can result in a twisting of the BOWEL, which must receive immediate medical attention. Colic-type pain may also be caused by an obstruction in the bowel, such as a TUMOUR, which again requires early medical treatment. *See also* RENAL COLIC.

colitis INFLAMMATION of the COLON, the symptoms of which include abdominal pain and DIARRHOEA, sometimes blood-stained. Colitis may be a symptom of IRRITABLE BOWEL SYNDROME or may be the result of INFECTIONS caused by the organism *Entamoeba histolytica* (amoebic colitis) or by BACTERIA (infective colitis). It also occurs in CROHN'S DISEASE. Ulcerative colitis is a serious and chronic disease that tends to affect young adults and usually occurs periodically over a number of years. It occurs most commonly in the large INTESTINE, where ULCERS form with associated bleeding and inflammation There is abdominal discomfort and pain, FEVER, frequent, watery diarrhoea containing MUCUS and blood, and ANAEMIA. The condition can be fatal but usually there is a gradual recovery. Treatment is by means of bed rest, drug treatment with CORTICOSTEROIDS and iron supplements, and a bland, low roughage diet. In severe cases, surgery may be necessary to remove the affected part of the bowel.

collagen a PROTEIN substance that is widely found in the body in CONNECTIVE TISSUE, TENDONS, SKIN, CARTILAGE, BONE and LIGAMENTS. It plays a major part in conferring tensile strength to various body structures.

collar bone *see* CLAVICLE.

colon the main part of the large INTESTINE, which removes water and salts from the undigested food passed into it from the small intestine. When water has been extracted, the remains of the food (FAECES) are passed on to the RECTUM.

colostomy a surgical operation to produce an artificial opening of the COLON through the abdominal wall. The colostomy may just be temporary, as part of the management of a patient's condition, e.g. to treat an obstruction in the colon or RECTUM. However, if the rectum or part of the colon has been removed because of CANCER, the colostomy is permanent and functions as the ANUS.

colostrum the first fluid produced by the MAMMARY GLANDS. It is a fairly clear fluid containing antibodies, SERUM and white blood cells (LEUCOCYTES) and is produced during the first two or three days prior to the production of milk.

colour blindness a general term for a number of conditions in which there is a failure to distinguish certain colours. It is more prevalent in males than in females and is usually inherited. The most common form is Daltonism, in which reds and greens are confused. This is a SEX-LINKED DISORDER, the recessive gene responsible being carried on the X-CHROMOSOME and hence more likely to be present in males. The cause of colour blindness is thought to be a failure in the operation of the CONES, which detect colours.

coma a state of deep unconsciousness from which a person cannot be roused. There may be an absence of pupillary and corneal reflexes and no movements of withdrawal when painful stimuli are applied. It may be accompanied by deep, noisy breathing and strong HEART action, and is caused by a number of conditions. These include STROKE, high FEVER, BRAIN injury, DIABETES MELLITUS, carbon monoxide poisoning and drug overdose. A comatose person may eventually die but can recover, depending on the nature of the coma and its cause.

comminuted fracture a serious injury to a BONE in

which more than one break occurs accompanied by splintering and damage to the surrounding TISSUES. It usually results from a crushing force, with damage to NERVES, MUSCLES and BLOOD VESSELS, and the bone is difficult to set.

commissure a joining or connection of two similar structures on either side of a mid-line. It is usually applied to bundles of NERVE fibres connecting the right and left side of the BRAIN and SPINAL CORD.

common cold *see* COLD.

complementary medicine *see* ALTERNATIVE MEDICINE.

complete blood count (CBC) *see* BLOOD COUNT.

compress a pad soaked in hot or cold water, wrung out and applied to an inflamed or painful part of the body. A hot compress is called a fomentation.

compressed air illness *see* BENDS.

computerized axial tomography *see* CAT SCAN.

conception the first formation of an EMBRYO, when an OVUM in the FALLOPIAN TUBE is fertilized by a SPERM followed by implantation in the womb.

concretions *or* **calculi** (*sing* **calculus**) hard, stony masses of various sizes formed within the body.

concussion a loss of consciousness caused by a blow to the head. The sudden knock to the head causes a compression wave, which momentarily interrupts the BLOOD supply to the BRAIN. The unconsciousness may last for seconds or hours, and when the person comes round there may be some HEADACHE and irritability, which can last for some time. A mild case of concussion may not involve complete loss of consciousness but be marked by giddiness, confusion and headache. In all cases, the person needs to rest and remain under observation.

conduction anaesthesia *see* NERVE BLOCK.

condyle a rounded knob that is found at the ends of some BONES, e.g. on the FEMUR and HUMERUS, and that articulates with an adjacent bone.

cone a type of photoreceptor (light-sensitive CELL) found in the RETINA of the EYE, which detects colour. Cones contain the PIGMENT retinene and the PROTEIN opsin, and there are three different types which react to light of differing wave-lengths (blue, green and red).

congenital a term used to describe a disease or condition that is present at birth, the opposite of ACQUIRED.

congenital hyperthyroid-ism *see* CRETINISM.

conjoined twins *or* **Siamese twins**. MONOZYGOTIC TWINS who are joined together physically at birth. The condition varies from superficial joining, e.g. by the umbilical vessels, to major fusion of head, torso and internal organs. The latter cases are inevitably very much more difficult to separate. The condition is caused by FOETUSES developing from the same OVUM where complete division into two EMBRYOS does not occur.

conjunctivitis inflammation of the MUCOUS MEMBRANE (conjunctiva) that lines the inside of the eyelid and covers the front of the EYE. The eyes become pink and watery, and the condition is usually caused by an INFECTION that may be bacterial, viral or caused by the microorganism *Chlamydia*. Treatment depends on the cause, but a number of drugs are used, often in the form of eyedrops.

connective tissue supporting or packing TISSUE within the body that holds or separates other tissues and ORGANS. It consists of a ground material composed of substances called mucopolysaccharides. In this, certain fibres such as yellow elastic, white collagenous and reticular fibres are embedded along with a variety of other cells, e.g MAST CELLS, MACRO-PHAGES, fibroblasts and fat cells. The constituents vary in proportions in different kinds of connective tissue to produce a number of distinct types. Examples are ADIPOSE TISSUE, CARTILAGE, BONE, TENDONS and LIGAMENTS.

consensual pupillary stim-ulation *see* LIGHT REFLEX.

constipation the condition in which the BOWELS are opened too infrequently and the FAE-CES become dry and hard and difficult and painful to pass. The frequency of normal bowel opening varies from person to person but when constipation becomes a problem, it is usually· a result of inattention to this habit or to the diet. To correct the condition, a change of lifestyle may be needed, including taking more exercise and increasing fluids and roughage in the diet. LAXATIVES and ENEMAS are also used to alleviate the condition. Constipation is also a symptom of the more serious condition of blockage of the bowel (by a TUMOUR), but this is less common.

consumption *see* TUBERCULOSIS.

contraception prevention of CONCEPTION. Pregnancy can be prevented by barrier methods, in which there is a physical barrier to prevent the SPERM from entering the CERVIX.The condom (sheath) and DIAPHRAGM (cap) are both barrier methods. The sheath also reduces the risk of either partner contracting a sexually transmitted disease (*see* VENEREAL DISEASE), including HIV infection. Non-barrier methods, used by women, include the INTRAUTERINE DEVICE (coil) and oral contraceptives (the Pill), which are hormonal preparations. DEPOT PREPARATIONS are hormonal drugs given by INJECTION, in subcutaneous IMPLANTS or released from intrauterine devices or intravaginal rings. HORMONE implants and injections for men are the most recent development in contraceptive products. STERILIZATION of either a man or a woman provides a means of permanent contraception. It is also possible to give a high dose of oral contraceptives within 72 hours of unprotected intercourse, to prevent implantation of a fertilized ovum, but this is regarded as an emergency method. The rhythm method of contraception involves restricting sexual intercourse to certain days of a woman's monthly cycle when conception is least likely to occur. *See* SAFE PERIOD.

controlled drug any drug that, in the UK, is subject to the restrictions of the Misuse of Drugs Act 1971. Controlled drugs are classified into three categories. Class A includes LSD, MORPHINE, COCAINE and PETHIDINE. Class B includes oral AMFETAMINES and BARBITURATES, and Class C comprises cannabis (reclassified from class B to class C in 2004), amfetamine-related drugs and some others.

contusion a severe BRUISE on the body, a hurt or injury to the flesh or some part of the body without breaking the SKIN, as caused by a blunt instrument or by a fall.

convalescence the gradual recovery of a person's health and strength after a disease or operation.

convulsions involuntary, alternate, rapid, muscular contractions and relaxations that throw the body and limbs into contortions, sometimes accompanied by temporary loss of consciousness. They are caused by a disturbance of BRAIN function, and in adults usually result from EPILEPSY, although not all types of epileptic SEIZURE are accompanied by convulsions. In babies and young children they occur quite commonly but, although alarming, are generally not serious. Causes include a high FEVER (febrile convulsions) because of INFECTION, brain diseases such as MENINGITIS, and breath-holding, which is quite common in infants and very young children. They are thought to be more common in the very young because the NERVOUS SYSTEM is immature. Unless they are caused by a disease or INFECTION that requires treatment, they are rarely life-threatening.

Cooley's anaemia see THALASSAEMIA.

corn *and* **bunion** a corn is a small, localized cone-shaped portion of hardened, thickened SKIN occurring on or between the toes. The point of the cone, known as 'the eye', points inwards and causes pain. It is caused by pressure from poorly-fitting shoes. A bunion is found over the JOINT at the base of the largest toe and is also caused by tight-fitting footwear. With a bunion, the joint between the toe and the first METATARSAL BONE becomes swollen and forms a lump beneath the thickened skin because of bending caused by the shoe. A hammer toe is similar but involves the second toe, which becomes bent at the joint to resemble a hammer because shoes or boots are too tight or pointed.

cornea the outermost, exposed layer of the EYE, which is transparent and lies over the IRIS and LENS. It refracts light entering the eye, directing the rays to the lens and thus acting as a coarse focus. It is a layer of CONNECTIVE TISSUE that has no BLOOD supply of its own but is supplied with nutrients from the aqueous humour within the eye. It is highly sensitive to pain, and presence or absence of response if the cornea is touched is used as an indicator of a person's condition, e.g. in a comatose patient.

corneal graft *or* **keratoplasty** a surgical procedure to replace a damaged or diseased CORNEA with one from a donor. Sometimes only the outer layers of the cornea are replaced (lamellar keratoplasty) or the whole structure may be involved (penetrating keratoplasty).

coronary angioplasty *see* ANGIOPLASTY.

coronary arteries the arteries (*see* ARTERY) that supply blood to the HEART and arise from the AORTA.

coronary artery disease any abnormal condition that affects the arteries (*see* ARTERY) of the heart. The commonest disease is coronary ATHEROSCLEROSIS, which is more prevalent in those populations with high fat, saturated fat, refined CARBOHYDRATES, etc, in their diet. ANGINA is a common symptom of such diseases.

coronary bypass graft a surgical operation that is carried out when one or more of the coronary arteries have become narrowed by disease (ATHEROMA). A section of VEIN from a leg is grafted in to bypass the obstruction, and this major operation is usually successful and greatly improves a person's quality of life. In most cases, the heart is put on bypass (*see* CARDIOPULMONARY BYPASS) while surgery is performed.

coronary care unit (CCU) a section of a hospital specially equipped and staffed for the intensive care and monitoring of patients with life-threatening heart conditions.

coronary thrombosis a sudden blockage of one of the coronary arteries by a BLOOD CLOT or THROMBUS that interrupts the blood supply to the heart. The victim collapses with severe and agonizing chest pain, often accompanied by vomiting and NAUSEA. The skin becomes pale and clammy, the temperature rises and there is difficulty in breathing. Coronary thrombosis generally results from ATHEROMA, and the part of the heart MUSCLE that has its blood supply disrupted dies, a condition known as MYOCARDIAL INFARCTION. Treatment consists of giving strong pain-relieving drugs, e.g. MORPHINE. Specialist care in a

CORONARY CARE UNIT is also usually required to deal with ARRHYTHMIA, heart failure and CARDIAC ARREST, which are the potentially fatal results of coronary thrombosis.

corpuscle *see* BLOOD.

corpus luteum the TISSUE that forms within the OVARY after a Graafian follicle (the structure that contains the egg) ruptures and releases an ovum at the time of OVULATION. It consists of a mass of CELLS containing yellow, fatty substances and secretes the hormone PROGESTERONE, which prepares the UTERUS to receive a fertilized egg. If the egg is not fertilized and no implantation of an EMBRYO takes place, the corpus luteum degenerates. However, if a PREGNANCY ensues, the corpus luteum expands and secretes progesterone until this function is taken over by the PLACENTA at the fourth month.

cortex (*pl* **cortices**) the outer part of an ORGAN situated beneath its enclosing capsules or outer MEMBRANE. Examples are the adrenal cortex of the ADRENAL GLANDS, renal cortex of the KIDNEYS and cerebral cortex of the BRAIN.

cortico- a prefix indicating the CORTEX.

corticosteroid any steroid HORMONE manufactured by the adrenal cortex, of which there are two main types. Glucocorticosteroids, such as cortisol and CORTISONE, are required by the body mainly for glucose metabolism and for responding to stress. Mineralocorticosteroids, e.g. aldosterone, regulate the salt and water balance. Both groups are manufactured synthetically and used in the treatment of various disorders.

cortisone a glucocorticosteroid (*see* CORTICOSTEROID) hormone produced by the adrenal cortex. It is used medically to treat deficiency of CORTICOSTEROID hormones. Deficiency occurs in ADDISON'S DISEASE and if the ADRENAL GLANDS have had to be surgically removed for some reason. Its use is restricted because it causes severe SIDE EFFECTS, including damage to the MUSCLE and BONE, eye changes, GASTRIC ulcers and bleeding, as well as nervous and hormonal disturbances.

cosmetic surgery *see* PLASTIC SURGERY.

costal cartilage a type of CARTILAGE connecting the RIBS to the sternum (breastbone).

cot death *see* SUDDEN INFANT DEATH SYNDROME.

cough a deep inspiration of air followed by a spasmodic and noisy expiration, caused by some irritation in the air passages (dry cough) or to expel MUCUS (wet cough). *See also* EXPECTORANT.

Coxsackie virus *see* ENTEROVIRUS.

CPR *see* CARDIOPULMONARY RESUSCITATION.

cradle cap a form of SEBORRHOEA or DERMATITIS of the scalp, which affects young babies and responds to an ointment containing white soft paraffin, salicylic acid and sulphur.

cramp a prolonged and painful spasmodic muscular contraction that often occurs in the limbs but can affect certain internal ORGANS (*see* COLIC and GASTRALGIA). Cramp may result from a salt imbalance, as in heat cramp. Working in high temperatures causes excessive sweating and consequent loss of salt. It can be corrected and prevented by an increase of the salt intake. Occupational cramp results from continual repetitive use of particular muscles, e.g. WRITER'S CRAMP. Night cramp occurs during sleep and is especially common among elderly people, diabetics (*see* DIABETES MELLITUS) and pregnant women. The cause of night cramp is not known.

cranial nerves 12 pairs of NERVES that arise directly from the BRAIN, each with dorsal and ventral branches known as roots. Each root remains separate and is assigned a Roman numeral as well as a name. Some cranial nerves are mainly SENSORY while others are largely MOTOR, and they leave the SKULL through separate apertures. The cranial and spinal nerves (*see* SPINAL CORD) are an important part of the PERIPHERAL NERVOUS SYSTEM, which comprises all parts lying outside the brain and SPINAL CORD.

cranium the part of the SKULL that encloses the BRAIN, formed from eight fused and flattened BONES that are joined by immovable suture JOINTS.

creatinine *see* URINE.

crepitus 1. the grating sound heard when the ends of fractured BONES rub together and also from arthritic JOINTS. **2.** the grating sound and pain in chondromalacia patellae (degeneration of the cartilage of the kneecap). **3.** the sound heard by means of a STETHO-SCOPE from an inflamed lung when there is fluid in the alveoli (*see* ALVEOLUS).

cretinism *or* **congenital hypothyroidism** a syndrome caused by lack of THYROID hormone, which is present before birth. It is characterized by DWARFISM, mental RETAR-DATION and coarseness of SKIN and hair. Early diagnosis and treatment with thyroid extract (thyroxine) are vital as this treatment greatly improves a child's intellectual and other abilities. In the UK, blood SERUM from newborn babies is tested for thyroxine level in order to detect this condition.

Creutzfeldt-Jakob disease (CJD) *or* **spongiform encephalopathy** a fatal disease of the BRAIN, thought to be caused by a SLOW VIRUS. There is a spongy degeneration of the brain and rapid progressive DEMENTIA. It usually strikes in middle and early old age and is usually fatal within a year. Similar diseases in animals are BOVINE SPONGIFORM ENCEPHALOPATHY (BSE) in cattle and scrapie in sheep. *See also* NEW VARIANT CJD.

Crohn's disease chronic IN-FLAMMATION of the bowel, especially the ILEUM. *See also* ILEITIS. Symptoms are similar to those of other bowel conditions and include abdominal pain, DIARRHOEA, bleeding and in more severe cases, ANAEMIA and nutritional deficiencies. Diagnosis is confirmed by endoscopic examination (*see* ENDOSCOPE) of the bowel. Children with Crohn's disease may have restricted growth. The disease can often be managed with a combination of diet and drugs and sufferers may experience lengthy periods when symptoms subside. Surgery may be necessary if the bowel is perforated or becomes blocked by scar TISSUE, or if FISTULAS form, causing INFECTION.

croup a group of diseases characterized by a swelling, partial obstruction and IN-FLAMMATION of the entrance to the LARYNX, occurring in young children. The breathing is harsh and strained, producing a typical crowing sound, accompanied by coughing and FEVER. DIPH-THERIA used to be the most common cause of croup, but it now usually results from a viral INFECTION of the RESPIRATORY TRACT (LARYNGOTRACHEOBRONCHITIS). The condition is relieved by inhaling steam (a soothing preparation such as tincture of BENZOIN is sometimes added to the hot water) and also by mild SEDATIVES and/or ANALGESICS. Rarely, the obstruction becomes dangerous and completely blocks the larynx, in which case emergency TRACHEOSTOMY or nasotracheal INTUBATION may be required. Usually, the symptoms of croup subside, but the child may have a tendency towards future attacks.

crown see TOOTH.

cryosurgery the use of extreme cold to perform surgical procedures, usually on localized areas to remove unwanted TISSUE. The advantages are that there is little or no bleeding or sensation of pain, and scarring is very much reduced. An instrument called a cryoprobe is used, the fine tip of which is cooled by means of a coolant substance contained within the probe. The coolants used are carbon dioxide and nitrous oxide gas and liquid nitrogen. Cryosurgery is used for the removal of CATARACTS, WARTS and to destroy some bone TUMOURS.

CT scanner see CAT SCAN.

culture a population of bacteria viruses, other microorganisms or CELLS grown in the laboratory on a nutrient base known as a culture medium.

curette a surgical instrument that is used to remove growths, dead TISSUE, etc, from the wall of a body cavity.

Cushing's syndrome a metabolic disorder that results from excessive amounts of CORTICOSTEROIDS in the body because of an inability to regulate cortisol or ADRENOCORTICOTROPIC HORMONE (ACTH). The commonest cause is a TUMOUR of the PITUITARY GLAND (producing secretion of ACTH) or a malignancy elsewhere, e.g. in the LUNG or ADRENAL GLAND, requiring extensive therapy with corticosteroid drugs. Symptoms include obesity, reddening of face and neck, growth of body and facial hair, OSTEOPOROSIS, high blood pressure and possible mental disturbances.

cutaneous a term used to describe anything belonging to the SKIN or existing on or affecting the skin.

cuticle 1. a name for the outer layer or EPIDERMIS of the SKIN. **2.** the outer layer of CELLS covering a HAIR.

CVS *see* CHORIONIC VILLUS SAMPLING.

cyanide poisoning poisoning with any salts of hydrocyanic acid, which paralyses the NERVOUS SYSTEM and is usually fatal within minutes.

cyanocobalamin *see* VITAMIN B12.

cyanosis a blue appearance of the SKIN because of insufficient oxygen within the BLOOD. It is first noticeable on the lips, tips of the ears, cheeks and nails and occurs in HEART FAILURE, lung diseases, ASPHYXIA and in 'BLUE BABIES' who have CONGENITAL heart defects.

cyst a small, usually benign, TUMOUR containing fluid (or soft secretions) within a membranous sac. Examples are SEBACEOUS CYSTS, cysts in the BREASTS (caused by blocked milk ducts), and ovarian cysts, which may be large and contain a clear, thick liquid. Dermoid cysts are congenital and occur at sites in the body where embryonic clefts have closed up before birth. These may contain fatty substances, hair, skin, fragments of bone and even teeth. Hydatid cysts are a stage in the life cycle of certain PARASITES (tapeworm) and may be found in humans, especially in the LIVER.

cystic fibrosis a genetic disease, the defective gene responsible for it being located on human CHROMOSOME no. 7. The disease affects all the MUCUS-secreting GLANDS of the LUNGS, PANCREAS, MOUTH and gastrointestinal tract and also the SWEAT GLANDS of the skin. A thick mucus is produced, which affects the production of pancreatic ENZYMES and causes the BRONCHI to widen (bronchiectasis) and become clogged. Respiratory infections are common, and the sweat contains abnormally high levels of sodium and chloride. The FAECES also contain a lot of mucus and have a foul smell. The disease varies in degree of severity but is chronic and progressive. The average life expectancy for sufferers is approximately thirty years. There is hope that treatment of the disease can be significantly improved with GENE THERAPY. If both parents are identified as carriers, prenatal testing either by AMNIOCENTESIS or CHORIONIC

VILLUS SAMPLING can identify whether their baby will be affected.

cystitis INFLAMMATION of the bladder, normally caused by bacterial INFECTION, the causal organism usually being ESCHERICHIA coli. It is marked by the need to pass URINE frequently, accompanied by a burning sensation. The condition is common in females and is usually not serious but there is a danger that the infection may spread to the KIDNEYS. The prevalence of the condition in women is because the URETHRA is much shorter than in men and the BACTERIA (which are present and harmless in the bowel) are more likely to gain access to both the urinary tract and the VAGINA. Treatment is by means of ANTIBIOTICS and also by drinking a lot of fluid.

cystocele prolapse of the BLADDER into the VAGINA which may cause problems with urination, including stress INCONTINENCE (leakage of URINE when coughing, sneezing, running, etc) and difficulty emptying the bladder.

cytogenetics see DROSOPHILA.

cytokine see INTERLEUKIN.

cytoplasm the substance within the CELL wall that surrounds the NUCLEUS and contains a number of ORGANELLES. See also MAST CELL.

cytosine see NUCLEOTIDE.

cytotoxic a term used to describe a substance that damages or destroys CELLS. Cytotoxic drugs are used in the treatment of various forms of CANCER and act by inhibiting cell division. They also damage normal cells and their use has to be carefully regulated in each individual patient. They may be used in combination with RADIOTHERAPY or on their own.

D

Daltonism see COLOUR BLINDNESS.

D and C see DILATATION AND CURETTAGE.

dead space the volume of air, primarily in the TRACHEA and BRONCHI, that does not take part in the oxygen/carbon dioxide exchange. In each breath taken into the LUNGS, this proportion does not contribute directly to the respiratory process.

deafness a partial or complete loss of hearing. The deafness may be temporary or permanent, conductive or sensory, congenital or acquired. Congenital hearing loss is not a common cause. In many cases, the loss is because of a problem in the COCHLEA, the auditory nerve or BRAIN-nerve deafness. This is a common condition in the elderly although no particular cause can be identified. Other causes include exposure to industrial noise or explosions. Conductive hearing loss is the result of poor transmission of sound waves to the inner ear, possibly because of OTITIS, which can cause middle ear INFLAMMATION and perforation of the eardrum. This latter condition can be treated by surgery or helped by the use of a hearing aid. *See also* RINNE'S TEST; WEBER'S TEST.

decidua the soft epithelial TISSUE that forms a lining to the UTERUS during PREGNANCY and is shed in birthing. *See also* EPITHELIUM.

decubitus ulcers *see* BED SORES.

defibrillation the application of a large electric shock to the chest wall of a patient whose heart is fibrillating (*see* FIBRILLATION). The delivery of a direct electric countershock should allow the PACEMAKER to set up the correct rhythm again.

deficiency disease a disease that is caused by a lack of VITAMINS or other essential dietary items. Examples include BERIBERI, PELLAGRA and SCURVY.

degeneration the deterioration over time of body TISSUES or an ORGAN, resulting in a lessening of its function. The changes may be structural or chemical, and there are a number of types: fatty, FIBROID, calcareous (as with CONCRETIONS), mucoid, and so on. Degeneration may the result of ageing, heredity or poor nutrition. Poisons such as alcohol also contribute to degeneration, as with CIRRHOSIS.

dehydration the removal of water. More specifically, the loss of water from the body through DIURESIS, sweating, DIARRHOEA, etc., or a reduction in water content because of a low intake. Essential body ELECTROLYTES (such as sodium chloride and potassium) are disrupted, and after the first symptom, thirst, irritability and confusion follow.

delirium a mental disorder typified by confusion, agitation, fear, anxiety, illusions and sometimes HALLUCINATIONS. The causal cerebral dysfunction may be deficient nutrition, stress, toxic poisoning, high FEVER or mental shock.

delirium tremens a form of DELIRIUM, often caused by partial or total withdrawal of alcohol after a period of excessive intake. Symptoms are varied and include INSOMNIA, agitation, confusion and FEVER, often with vivid HALLUCINATIONS. Severe cases can be fatal if untreated. The treatment involves lessening and removing the dependence on alcohol, which is accompanied by sedation with drugs such as BENZODIAZEPINE. Fluid replacement therapy and nutritional supplements may also be required.

delta wave one of the four types of BRAIN waves and the slowest of the four. Delta waves are associated with deep sleep. If delta waves are seen in the ELECTROENCEPHALOGRAM of a waking adult, brain damage is indicated, e.g. as with epileptics and around brain TUMOURS.

deltoid the MUSCLE, triangular in shape, that covers the shoulder and is attached to the CLAVICLE, SCAPULA and HUMERUS. It enables the arm to be raised from the side.

delusion a false belief, that is maintained in spite of evidence to the contrary. Delusions, eg of grandeur or persecution, are a common symptom of PSYCHOSIS.

dementia a mental disorder typified by confusion, disorientation, memory loss, personality changes and a lessening of intellectual capacity. Dementia occurs in several forms: SENILE DEMENTIA, ALZHEIMER'S DISEASE and multi-infarct dementia. The causes are various and include vascular disease, brain TUMOUR, SUBDURAL HAEMATOMA, HYDROCEPHALUS and HYPERTHYROIDISM.

demyelination the process whereby the MYELIN sheath surrounding a NERVE fibre is destroyed, resulting in impaired nerve function. This is associated with MULTIPLE SCLEROSIS but can also happen after a nerve has been injured.

denaturation the disruption, usually by heat, of the weak bonds that hold a PROTEIN together. Extremes of temperature are fatal to most animals because the ENZYMES (which are proteins) that perform essential catalytic functions in life-sustaining biochemical processes are irreversibly denatured.

dendrite one of numerous thin branching extensions of a NERVE cell. The dendrites are at the 'receiving end' of the nerve cell (NEURON), and they form a network that increases the area for receiving impulses from the terminals of AXONS of other neurons at the SYNAPSE.

dengue fever a tropical disease that is caused by a VIRUS that is transmitted by mosquitoes.

dentine the material that forms the bulk of a TOOTH, lying between the pulp cavity and the enamel. It is similar to BONE in composition but contains blood capillaries, NERVE fibres and extensions of odontoblasts (CELLS producing the dentine).

deoxyribonucleic acid *see* DNA.

depot preparation a DRUG, usually hormonal, in a medium like oil or wax that is injected deeply and INTRA-MUSCULARly. The medium then allows the slow release of the drug over days, weeks or months.

depressant a DRUG that is used to reduce the functioning of a system of the body, e. g. a respiratory depressant. Drugs such as OPIATES, general ANAESTHETICS, etc, are depressants.

depression a mental state of extreme sadness dominated by pessimism, in which normal behaviour patterns (sleep, appetite, etc) are disturbed. Causes are varied: upsetting events, loss, etc, and treatment involves the use of therapy and drugs.

dermatitis an INFLAMMATION of the SKIN that is similar in many respects to, and often interchanged with, ECZEMA. It is characterized by ERYTHEMA, pain and PRURITIS. Several forms can be identified: contact dermatitis is caused by the skin coming into contact with a substance to which it is sensitive. A large range of compounds and materials may cause such a reaction. Treatment usually involves the use of a CORTICOSTEROID. Light dermatitis manifests itself as a reddening and blistering of skin exposed to sunlight, and this occurs on hands, face and neck, usually during the summer months. Some individuals become sensitized by drugs or perfumes in cosmetics, while others have an innate sensitivity. Erythroderma or exfoliative dermatitis involves patches of reddened skin that thicken and peel off. It is often associated with other skin conditions, e.g. PSORIASIS. Corticosteroids form a central part of the treatment in this case.

dermis *see* EPIDERMIS; SKIN.

desensitization 1. the technique whereby an individual builds up resistance to an ALLERGEN by taking gradually increasing doses of the substance over a period of time. **2.** in the treatment of PHOBIAS, when a patient is gradually faced with the thing that is feared and concurrently learns to relax and reduce anxiety.

detached retina the condition when the RETINA of the EYE becomes detached from the choroid (a layer of the eyeball with BLOOD VESSELS and PIGMENT that absorbs excess light, preventing blurred VISION). The detachment may be caused by a TUMOUR or INFLAMMATION or by the leaking of VITREOUS HUMOUR through holes in the retina to fill the space between the retina and choroid, thus disrupting the fine attachments. The condition can be corrected by surgery, whereby heat binds the retina and choroid together using scarred TISSUE.

dhobi itch *see* RINGWORM.

diabetes insipidus a rare condition that is completely different from DIABETES MELLITUS and is characterized by excessive thirst (*see* POLYDIPSIA) and POLYURIA. It is caused by a lack of antidiuretic HORMONE or the inability of the KIDNEY to respond to the hormone.

diabetes mellitus a complex metabolic disorder involving CARBOHYDRATE, fat and PROTEIN. It results in an accumulation of sugar in the BLOOD and URINE and is the result of a lack of INSULIN produced by the PANCREAS, so that sugars are not broken down to release energy. Fats are thus used as an alternative energy source. Symptoms include thirst, POLYURIA and loss of weight, and the use of fats can produce KETOSIS and KETONURIA. In its severest form, CONVULSIONS are followed by a diabetic COMA. Treatment relies on dietary control with doses of insulin or drugs. Long-term effects include thickening of the arteries, and in some cases, the EYES, KIDNEYS, NERVOUS SYSTEM, skin and circulation may be affected (*see also* HYPOGLYCAEMIA and HYPERGLYCAEMIA).

diagnosis (*pl* **diagnoses**) the process whereby a particular disease or condition is identified after consideration of the relevant parameters, i.e. symptoms, physical manifestations, results of laboratory tests, etc. In many instances the diagnosis requires greater skills than does the treatment.

dialysis (*pl* **dialyses**) the use of a semipermeable MEMBRANE to separate large and small molecules by selective diffusion. Starch and PROTEINS are large molecules while salts, glucose and AMINO ACIDS are small molecules. If a mixture of large and small molecules is separated from distilled water by a semipermeable membrane, the smaller molecules diffuse into the water, which is itself replenished. This principle is the basis of the artificial KIDNEY, which, because a patient's blood is processed, is known as HAEMODIALYSIS.

diamorphine hydrochloride *see* HEROIN.

diaphragm 1. a MEMBRANE of MUSCLE and TENDON that separates the CHEST and abdominal cavities. It is covered by a SEROUS MEMBRANE and attached at the lower RIBS, breastbone (STERNUM) and backbone (SPINAL COLUMN). The diaphragm is important in breathing, when it bulges up to its resting position during exhalation. It flattens during inhalation and in so doing it reduces pressure in the thoracic cavity and helps to draw air into the lungs. **2.** a rubber bowl-shaped cap used as a CONTRACEPTIVE with spermicidal cream. It fits inside the VAGINA over the neck of the UTERUS.

diaphysis (*pl* **diaphyses**) the central part or shaft of a long BONE.

diarrhoea increased frequency and looseness of bowel movement, involving the passage of unusually soft or fluid FAECES. Diarrhoea can be caused by FOOD POISONING, COLITIS, IRRITABLE BOWEL SYNDROME,

DYSENTERY, etc. A severe case can be life-threatening, particularly in young children and the elderly and will result in the loss of water and salts, which must be replaced, and antidiarrhoeal drugs are used in certain circumstances.

diastase (amylases) ENZYMES that break down starch into sugar. Diastase is used to help in the digestion of starch in some digestive disorders.

diastasis the separation of a growing BONE from the shaft.

diastole the point at which the HEART relaxes between contractions, when the VENTRICLEs fill with blood. This usually lasts about half a second, at the end of which the ventricles are about three-quarters full.

diathermy the use of high-frequency non-lethal electric currents to produce heat in a part of the body. The heat generated increases BLOOD flow and is used for the relief of deep-seated pain such as NEURITIS, SCIATICA and particularly painful rheumatic conditions. The use of currents in this way can be adapted to cauterize tissues (*see* CAUTERY) and small BLOOD VESSELS (the latter because the

blood coagulates on contact with the heated element).

diazepam *see* TRANQUILLIZER.

dietetics the study and application of the science of nutrition to all aspects of food and feeding for individuals and groups in health and disease.

diethylcarbamazine *see* TOXOCARIASIS.

digestion the process of breaking down food into substances that can be absorbed and used by the body. Digestion begins with the chewing and grinding of food, at which point it is mixed with SALIVA to commence the process of breakdown. Most digestion occurs in the STOMACH and small INTESTINE. In the stomach the food is subjected to GASTRIC JUICE, which contains PEPSINS, to break down PROTEINS, and hydrochloric acid. The food is mixed and becomes totally soluble before passing into the small intestine as CHYME, where it is acted on by pancreatic juice, BILE, BACTERIA and succus entericus (intestinal juices).

Water is absorbed in the intestine in a very short time, while the bulk of the food may take several hours to be processed. The chyme forms chyle because of the action of BILE and pancreatic juice. Fats are removed from this in emulsion form into the lymph vessels (*see* LACTEAL VESSELS) and then into the blood. Sugars, salts and AMINO ACIDS move directly into the small blood vessels in the intestine, and the whole process is promoted by microfolding of the intestine wall producing finger-like projections (villi). The food passes down the intestine as a result of muscular contractions of the intestine wall (PERISTALSIS), and ultimately the residue and waste are excreted.

digit a finger or toe.

digitalis a powder derived from the leaf of the wild foxglove (*Digitalis purpurea*), which is used in cases of HEART disease. It acts in two ways: strengthening each heartbeat and increasing each pause (DIASTOLE) so that the damaged heart MUSCLE has longer to rest. It also has a DIURETIC effect. Digitalis poisoning may occur with prolonged use or an overdose. Symptoms include NAUSEA, VOMITING, blurred vision, irregular heartbeat and possibly breathing difficulties and unconsciousness.

dilatation and curettage (D and C) the technique whereby the CERVIX is opened using DILATORS and then the lining is scraped using a CURETTE. Such sampling is performed for the removal of incomplete ABORTIONS and TUMOURS, to diagnose disease of the UTERUS or to correct bleeding, etc.

dilator 1. an instrument that is employed to increase the opening of an orifice, e.g the CERVIX. **2.** a MUSCLE that increases the diameter of a vessel or ORGAN. **3.** a drug that is used to achieve a similar effect.

dipeptide *see* PEPTIDE.

diphtheria an infectious disease caused by the bacterium *Corynebacterium diphtheriae* and commonest in children. The infection causes a membranous lining on the THROAT, which can interfere with breathing and eating. The TOXIN produced by the bacterium damages HEART tissue and the CENTRAL NERVOUS SYSTEM and can be fatal if not treated. The infection is countered by injection of antitoxin with PENICILLIN or

ERYTHROMYCIN given to kill the bacterium. It can be prevented by VACCINATION.

diplegia PARALYSIS on both sides of the body.

diplopia double vision caused by dysfunction in the MUSCLES that move the eyeballs so that rays of light fall in different places on the two RETINAE. The condition can be caused by a nervous disease, intoxication or certain diseases such as DIPHTHERIA.

disc a flattened circular structure, such as the CARTILAGE between VERTEBRAE. *See also* INTERVERTEBRAL DISC.

disinfection the process of killing PATHOGENIC organisms (not spores) to prevent the spread of INFECTION. Compounds appropriate to the surface being disinfected are used.

dislocation an injury to a JOINT in which BONES are displaced from their normal, respective positions. Associated effects include bruising of the surrounding TISSUES and tearing of the LIGAMENTS that hold the bones together. Most dislocations are simple rather than compound (the latter being where the bone punctures the SKIN) and ACQUIRED rather

than CONGENITAL. Immediate treatment involves the application of a splint or bandage to render the joint stable. Repositioning the bone (REDUCTION) requires skill, after which the LIMB must be fixed to avoid a repetition. Even after some time, care is necessary when using the limb.

diuresis an increase in URINE production as a result of disease, drugs, hormone imbalance or increased fluid intake.

diuretic a substance that increases URINE formation and excretion and may work specifically within the KIDNEY, e.g. by prevention of sodium, and therefore water, reabsorption or outside the kidney.

diverticulitis INFLAMMATION of diverticula (*see* DIVERTICULUM) in the large INTESTINE. During the condition, there are cramp-like pains in the left side of the ABDOMEN, possibly with CONSTIPATION and FEVER. Treatment normally involves complete rest with no solid food, and ANTIBIOTICS.

diverticulosis the condition in which there are diverticula (*see* DIVERTICULUM) in the large INTESTINE, occurring primarily in the lower COLON. They are caused by the MUS-

CLES of the BOWEL forcing the bowel out through weak points in the wall. It is thought that it may be related to diet but symptoms are not always produced.

diverticulum (*pl* **diverticula**) in general, a pouch extending from a main cavity. Specifically, in the INTESTINE, a SAC-like protrusion through the wall, many of which usually develop later in life and are thought to be related to dietary factors. The formation of diverticula is called DIVERTICULOSIS, and their INFLAMMATION (causing pain, FEVER and CONSTIPATION) is called DIVERTICULITIS.

DNA (**deoxyribonucleic acid**) a nucleic acid and the primary constituent of CHROMOSOMES. It transmits genetic information from parents to offspring in the form of GENES. It is a very large molecule comprising two twisted NUCLEOTIDE chains that can store enormous amounts of information in a stable but not rigid way, i.e. parental traits and characteristics are passed on but evolutionary changes are allowed to occur.

donor a person who donates part of his/her body for use in other people. BLOOD is the most common donation, but many TISSUES and ORGANS are now used, including KIDNEYS, LIVERS, HEARTS, SKIN, CORNEAS, BONE MARROW, etc. Almost all organ donations occur when the donor has been certified as BRAIN-STEM dead, although in exceptional cases, a patient may receive a kidney from a live donor, usually a family member.

donor insemination *see* ARTIFICIAL INSEMINATION.

dopa an AMINO ACID compound that is formed from tyrosine (an amino acid synthesized in the body) and is a precursor of DOPAMINE and NORADRENALINE. A drug form, levodopa or l-dopa, is used to treat PARKINSON'S DISEASE, as it can increase the concentration of dopamine in the BASAL GANGLIA.

dopamine a catecholamine derived from DOPA and an intermediate in the synthesis of NORADRENALINE. (Catecholamines comprise benzene, hydroxyl groups and an amine group and are physiologically important in the functioning of the NERVOUS SYSTEM, mainly as NEUROTRANSMITTERS.) It is found mainly in the BASAL GANGLIA of the BRAIN and a deficiency is typical in PARKINSON'S DISEASE.

dorsal the term used to describe anything relating to the back or SPINAL COLUMN or the posterior part of an ORGAN.

dosage the overall amount of a DRUG administered, determined by body size, frequency and number of doses and taking into account the patient's age, weight and possible allergic reactions (*see* ALLERGY). Modern techniques enable controlled dosage using transdermals (drugs absorbed from a plaster on the SKIN) and IMPLANT devices. The latter are polymeric substances that contain the drug and are placed just beneath the skin to deliver the correct dose at a predetermined rate.

Down's syndrome a syndrome created by a CONGENITAL chromosome disorder that occurs as an extra CHROMOSOME 21, producing 47 in each body cell. Characteristic facial features are produced—a shorter, broader face with slanted eyes. It also results in a shorter stature, weak MUSCLES and the possibility of HEART defects and respiratory problems. The syndrome

also confers mental RETARDATION. Down's syndrome occurs once in approximately 600 to 700 live births, and although individuals may live beyond middle age, life expectancy is reduced and many die in infancy. The incidence increases with the age of the mother. It is therefore likely that pregnant women over 35 will be offered an AMNIOCENTESIS test.

drosophila a fruit fly of the genus *Drosophila* that is used a great deal in genetic research because it breeds easily and quickly and has just four pairs of CHROMOSOMES which are visible under the microscope. It is used to study LINKAGE and cytogenetics (inheritance related to all structure and function).

drug any substance, vegetable, animal or mineral, used in the composition or preparation of medicine.

drug binding when a drug is attached to a PROTEIN, fat or component of TISSUES.

drug clearance the volume of BLOOD that in one minute is completely cleared of a drug.

drug interaction when a patient is prescribed several drugs, there is the possibility for interactions between some or all of the medications. There are several ways in which the interaction may occur, e.g. one drug displacing another at the site of action thus affecting its effectiveness, or alteration in the rate of destruction of one drug by another (by altering the activity of liver ENZYMES), and also by prevention of absorption.

drug metabolism the process by which a drug is altered by the body into a metabolite (i.e. necessary for metabolic action), which may be the active agent. It is the process that ultimately results in the removal of the drug and thus determines the length of time during which it is active.

duct a narrow tube-like structure joining a GLAND with an ORGAN or the body surface, through which a secretion passes, e.g. sweat ducts opening on to the SKIN.

ductless gland a GLAND that releases its secretion directly into the BLOOD for transport around the body, e.g. the PITUITARY and THYROID. Some glands, such as the PANCREAS, operate as a ductless gland (for INSULIN) but secrete a di-

gestive juice via ducts into the small INTESTINE.

ductus arteriosus when a FOETUS is in the UTERUS, the LUNGS do not function and the foetal BLOOD bypasses the lungs by means of the ductus arteriosus, which takes blood from the pulmonary ARTERY to the AORTA. The vessel stops functioning soon after birth.

dullness *see* RESONANCE.

duodenal ulcer the commonest type of PEPTIC ULCER. Duodenal ulcers may occur after the age of 20 and are more common in men. The bacterium HELICOBACTER PYLORI has been identified as a cause of most duodenal ulcers and can be detected with a breath test. Long-term use of NON-STEROIDAL ANTI-INFLAMMATORY DRUGS can also cause duodenal ulcers. The condition is aggravated by spicy food, strong tea and coffee and stress. Smoking and alcohol are also contributory factors. If *helicobacter pylori* has been identified as the causative agent, ANTIOBIOTIC therapy will eradicate the problem.

The ulcer manifests itself as an upper abdominal pain roughly two hours after a meal and also occurs during the night. Bland food (e.g. milk) relieves the SYMPTOMS, and a regime of frequent meals and milky snacks, with little or no fried food and spices and a minimum of strong tea and coffee, is usually adopted. Some drug treatments enable the acid secretion to be reduced, thus allowing the ulcer to heal. If *Helicobacter pylori* is the causative agent, ANTIBIOTIC therapy is effective both in healing the ulcer and preventing a recurrence of the problem. Surgery is required only if there is no response to medical treatment, if the PYLORUS is obstructed or if the ulcer becomes perforated. The last is treated as an emergency. *See also* GASTRIC ULCER.

duodenum the first part of the small INTESTINE where food (CHYME) from the stomach is subject to action by BILE and pancreatic ENZYMES. The duodenum also secretes a HORMONE secretion that contributes to the breakdown of fats, PROTEINS and CARBOHYDRATES. In the duodenum, the acid conditions pertaining from the stomach are neutralized and rendered al-kaline for the intestinal enzymes to operate.

dura mater *see* BRAIN; MENINGES.

dwarfism an abnormal under-development of the body manifested by small stature. There are several causes, including incorrect functioning of the PITUITARY or THYROID GLANDS. Pituitary dwarfism produces a small but correctly proportioned body and, if diagnosed sufficiently early, treatment with growth HORMONE can help. A defect in the thyroid gland may result in CRETINISM or disturbance in the activity of digestive organs and their secretions. RICKETS may also be responsible for dwarfism.

dysarthria poorly articulated speech that sounds weak or slurred because of impairment in the control of the MUSCLES that effect speech. The cause may be damage in the BRAIN or to the muscles themselves. Dysarthria occurs with STROKES, in MULTIPLE SCLEROSIS, CEREBRAL PALSY, and so on.

dysentery an INFECTION and ulceration of the lower part of the BOWELS that causes severe DIARRHOEA with the passage of MUCUS and BLOOD. There are two forms of dysentery caused by different organisms. Amoebic dysentery is caused by *Entamoeba histolytica*, which is spread via infected food or water and occurs mainly in the tropics and subtropics. The appearance of symptoms may be delayed, but in addition to diarrhoea there is indigestion, ANAEMIA and weight loss. Drugs are used in treatment. Bacillary dysentery is caused by the bacterium *Shigella* and spreads by contact with a carrier or contaminated food. Symptoms appear from one to six days after infection and include diarrhoea, CRAMP, NAUSEA aned FEVER. The severity of the attack varies.

dyslexia a disorder that renders reading or learning to read difficult. There is usually an associated problem in writing and spelling correctly and there may also problems with mathematics and short-term memory. The condition tends to run in families and varies in severity. Boys are more prone to it than girls by a factor of three.

dyspepsia *or* **indigestion** discomfort in the upper AB-DOMEN or lower chest after eating, with HEARTBURN, NAUSEA and FLATULENCE accompanying a feeling of fullness. The causes are numerous and include GALLSTONES, PEPTIC ULCER, HIATUS HERNIA and diseases of the LIVER or PANCREAS.

dysphasia a general term for an impairment of speech, whether it is manifested as a difficulty in understanding language or in self-expression. There is a range of conditions with varying degrees of severity. Global aphasia is a total inability to communicate, but some individuals partially understand what is said to them. Dysphasia is when thoughts can be expressed up to a point. Non-fluent dysphasia represents poor self-expression but good understanding while the reverse is called fluent dysphasia. The condition may be caused by a STROKE or other BRAIN damage and can be temporary or permanent.

E

ear the sense organ used for detection of sound and maintenance of balance. It comprises three parts: the external or outer, the middle and the inner ear, the first two acting to collect sound waves and transmit them to the inner ear, where the hearing and balance mechanisms are situated. The outer ear (auricle or pinna) is a CARTILAGE and SKIN structure that is not actually essential to hearing in humans. The middle ear is an air-filled cavity that is linked to the PHARYNX via the EUSTACHIAN TUBE. Within the middle ear are the ear (or auditory) ossicles, three BONES called the incus, malleus and stapes (anvil, hammer and stirrup respectively). Two small MUSCLES control the bones and the associated NERVE (the chorda tympani). The ossicles bridge the middle ear, connecting the eardrum with the inner ear and, in so doing, convert sound (air waves) into mechanical movements that then impinge on the fluid of the inner ear. The inner ear lies within the temporal bone of the SKULL and contains the apparatus for hearing and balance. The COCHLEA is responsible for hearing, and balance is maintained by the semicircular canals.

These are made up of three loops positioned mutually at right angles, and in each is the fluid endolymph. When the head is moved, the fluid moves accordingly, and sensory CELLS produce impulses that are transmitted to the BRAIN.

earache pain in the EAR that may be caused directly by INFLAMMATION of the middle ear but is often referred pain from other conditions, e.g. INFECTIONS of the NOSE or LARYNX or tooth decay.

eating disorders *see* ANOREXIA and BULIMIA NERVOSA.

ECG *see* ELECTROCARDIOGRAM.

echinococcosis the condition created when CYSTS from the larval stages of a tapeworm create malignant TUMOURS in the BRAIN, LUNGS or LIVER. Those in the brain can cause blindness and EPILEPSY.

echocardiography the use of ULTRASOUND to study the heart and its movements.

echography *or* **ultrasonography** the use of sound waves (ULTRASOUND) to create an image of the deeper structures of the body, based on the differences in reflection of the sound by various parts of the body.

echovirus a VIRUS that can cause symptoms of the common COLD, mild MENINGITIS and intestinal and respiratory INFECTIONS.

eclampsia CONVULSIONS, sometimes leading to COMA, that occur during PREGNANCY, usually at the later stages or during delivery. Eclampsia is a complication of PRE-ECLAMPSIA. Although the cause is not known, the start of convulsions may be associated with cerebral OEDEMA or a sudden rise in BLOOD PRESSURE. KIDNEY function is usually badly affected. The condition is often preceded for days or weeks by symptoms such as headache, dizziness and VOMITING, and seizures follow. The seizures differ in severity and duration, and in severe cases, there may be a cerebral HAEMORRHAGE, PNEUMONIA or the breathing may gradually fade, resulting in death. The condition requires immediate treatment as it threatens both mother and baby. Treatment is by drugs and reduction of outside stimuli, and a CAESAREAN SECTION is needed.

E. coli *see* ESCHERICHIA.

ECT *see* ELECTROCONVULSIVE THERAPY.

ectopic a term used to refer to something or some event that is not in its usual place or occurring at its usual time, e.g. an ectopic PREGNANCY is one in which the fertilized egg implants outside the UTERUS.

ectopic beat *see* EXTRASYSTOLE.

eczema an INFLAMMATION of the SKIN that causes itching, a red RASH and often small BLISTERS that weep and become encrusted. This may be followed by the skin thickening and then peeling off in scales. There are several types of eczema, atopic, the hereditary tendency to form allergic reactions because of an ANTIBODY in the skin, being one of the most common. A form of atopic eczema is infantile eczema, which starts at three or four months, and it is often the case that eczema, HAY FEVER and ASTHMA are found in the family history. However, many children improve markedly as they approach the age of 10 or 11. The treatment for such conditions usually involves the use of EMOLLIENTS, HYDROCORTISONE and other

STEROID creams and ointments.

EEG *see* ELECTROENCEPHALOGRAM.

effector a motor or sensory NERVE ending that terminates in a MUSCLE, GLAND or ORGAN and stimulates contraction or secretion.

efferent a term meaning 'outwards from an ORGAN, etc', especially the BRAIN or SPINAL CORD, e.g. an efferent NERVE. *Compare* AFFERENT.

ejaculation the emission of SEMEN from the PENIS via the URETHRA. It is a REFLEX ACTION produced during copulation or masturbation, and the sensation associated with it is ORGASM.

elastin *see* FIBROUS TISSUE.

Electrocardiogram (ECG) a record of the changes in the HEART's electrical potential made on an instrument called an electrocardiograph. The subject is connected to the equipment by leads on the chest and legs or arms. A normal trace has one wave for the activity of the atria and others relating to the ventricular beat. Abnormal heart activity is often indicated in the trace and it therefore forms a useful diagnostic aid.

electrocautery CAUTERY, using an electrically heated wire or needle or an instrument which passes an electric current into small areas of TISSUE.

electroconvulsive therapy (ECT) a treatment for severe DEPRESSION and sometimes SCHIZOPHRENIA. An electric current is passed through the brain, producing an epileptic CONVULSION that is controlled by administering an ANAESTHETIC and a muscle relaxant. There is no memory of the shock, and there may be temporary AMNESIA with headache and confusion—symptoms that usually dissipate within a few hours. It is a treatment that is used much less now than formerly.

electroencephalogram (EEG) a record of the BRAIN's electrical activity measured on an electroencephalograph. Electrodes on the scalp record the charge of electric potential—or brain waves. There are four main types of waves: alpha, beta, theta and delta. Alpha waves, with a frequency of ten per second, occur when the person is awake and DELTA WAVES (seven or fewer per second) occur in sleeping adults. The occurrence of delta waves in wakeful adults indicates brain damage or cerebral TUMOURS.

electrolyte strictly, a compound that dissolves in water to produce a solution, containing ions, that is able to conduct an electrical charge. In the body, electrolytes occur in the blood PLASMA, all fluid and interstitial fluid, and correct concentrations are essential for normal metabolic activity (*see* METABOLISM). Some diseases alter the electrolyte balance, either through VOMITING or DIARRHOEA or because the KIDNEY is malfunctioning. The correct balance can be restored through oral or intravenous dosage or by DIALYSIS.

elephantiasis a dramatic and debilitating enlargement of SKIN and underlying CONNECTIVE TISSUE because of INFLAMMATION of the skin, subcutaneous tissue and the blocking of LYMPH vessels, preventing drainage. Inflammation and blocking of vessels is caused by parasitic worms (filariae), which are carried to humans by mosquitoes. The parts of the body most commonly affected are the legs, scrotum and breasts, in some cases to enormous proportions. Associated MUSCLES of a limb may degenerate as a result of the abnormal pressure on them, and eventually overall health suffers. Prevention is the key, by eradication of the mosquitoes, but some relief is gained by using certain drugs early in the disease.

emaciation particularly severe leanness caused by lack of nourishment or disease. It tends to be assocated with diseases such as TUBERCULOSIS or CANCER or those producing DIARRHOEA over a long period of time.

embolectomy the surgical, and often emergency, removal of an EMBOLUS or CLOT to clear an obstruction in a BLOOD VESSEL.

embolism the state in which a small BLOOD VESSEL is blocked by an EMBOLUS. This plug may be fragments of a CLOT, a mass of BACTERIA, air bubbles that have entered the system during an operation or a particle of a TUMOUR. The blockage leads usually to the destruction of that part of the ORGAN supplied by the vessel. The most common case is a PULMONARY EMBOLISM. Treatment utilizes an ANTICOAGULANT drug such as warfarin or heparin, EMBOLECTOMY or STREPTOKINASE, an ENZYME capable of dissolving blood clots.

embolus (*pl* **emboli**) material carried by the BLOOD which then lodges elsewhere in the body (*see* EMBOLISM). The material may be a blood CLOT, fat, air, a piece of TUMOUR, etc.

embryo the first stage of development of a FOETUS after the fertilized OVUM is implanted in the UTERUS until the second month.

embryology the study of the EMBRYO, its growth and development from FERTILIZATION to birth.

embryo transfer the FERTILIZATION of an OVUM by SPERM and its development into an early EMBRYO, outside the mother, and its subsequent implantation in the mother's UTERUS. Such procedures result in what is popularly termed a 'test-tube baby'. *See also* IN VITRO FERTILIZATION.

emesis the medical term for VOMITING.

emetic a substance that causes VOMITING. Direct emetics, such as mustard in water, copper sulphate, alum or a lot of salty water, irritate the STOMACH while indirect emetics, such as apomorphine and ipecacuanha, act on the centre of the BRAIN that controls the act of vomiting. Tickling the THROAT is also classed as an emetic (indirect). Emetics tend to be used little nowadays, but great care must be exercised if their use is advocated.

emollient a substance that softens, soothes and moisturizes the SKIN, often used in the treatment of ECZEMA. Examples are aqueous cream, olive oil and glycerin.

emphysema in the main, an abnormal condition of the LUNGS in which the walls of the alveoli (*see* ALVEOLUS) are over-inflated and distended and changes in their structure occur. This destruction of parts of the walls produces large air-filled spaces that do not contribute to the respiratory process. Acute cases of emphysema may be caused by WHOOPING COUGH or bronchOPNEUMONIA, and chronic cases often accompany chronic BRONCHITIS, which itself is caused in great part by tobacco smoking. Emphysema is also developed after TUBERCULOSIS, when the lungs are stretched until the fibres of the alveolar walls are destroyed. Similarly, in old age, the alveolar MEMBRANE may collapse, producing large air sacs, with decreased surface area.

enamel *see* TOOTH.

encephalin a PEPTIDE that acts as a NEUROTRANSMITTER. Two have been identified, both acting as ANALGESICS when their release controls pain. They are found in the BRAIN and in nerve cells of the SPINAL CORD.

encephalitis INFLAMMATION of the BRAIN. It is a life-threatening condition, usually caused by viral INFECTION and sometimes occurs as a complication of some common infectious diseases, e.g. MEASLES (herpes encephalitis) or CHICKENPOX. There are several forms of the disease, including encephalitis lethargica (SLEEPING SICKNESS or epidemic encephalitis), which attacks and causes swelling in the basal ganglia, cerebrum and brain stem that may result in TISSUE destruction. Other forms are Japanese encephalitis, which is caused by a VIRUS carried by mosquitoes, and tick-borne encephalitis, which occurs in Europe and Siberia. There is a vaccine available for Japanese encephalitis, and herpes encephalitis, if diagnosed early, can respond to antiviral drugs. In other cases the treatment is for symptoms only.

encephalography any technique that is used to record BRAIN structure or activity, e.g. electroencephalography (*see* ELECTROENCEPHALOGRAM).

encephaloid the term given to a form of CANCER that superficially resembles BRAIN tissue.

encephalomyelitis INFLAMMATION of the BRAIN and SPINAL CORD, typified by headaches, FEVER, stiff neck and back pain, with VOMITING. Depending on the extent of the inflammation and the patient's condition, it may cause PARALYSIS, personality changes, COMA or death.

encephalopathy any disease affecting the BRAIN or an abnormal condition of the brain's structure and function. It refers in particular to degenerative and chronic conditions such as Wernicke's encephalopathy, which is caused by a thiamine deficiency (*see* VITAMIN B) and associated with alcoholism.

endemic the term used to describe, for example, a disease that is indigenous to a certain area.

endocarditis INFLAMMATION of the ENDOCARDIUM, heart valves and MUSCLE, caused by BACTERIA, VIRUS or RHEUMATIC FEVER. Those at greatest risk are patients with some damage to the endocardium from a CONGENITAL deformity or alteration of the immune system by drugs. Patients suffer FEVER, HEART FAILURE and/or EMBOLISM. Large doses of an ANTIBIOTIC are used in treatment, and surgery may prove necessary to repair heart valves that become damaged. If not treated, the condition is fatal.

endocardium a fine MEMBRANE lining the HEART, which forms a continuous membrane with the lining of VEINS and arteries (*see* ARTERY). At the cavities of the heart it forms cusps on the valves, and its surface is very smooth to facilitate blood flow.

endocrine glands DUCTLESS GLANDS that produce HORMONES for secretion directly into the bloodstream (or lymph). Some ORGANS, e.g. the PANCREAS, also release secretions via a DUCT. In addition to the pancreas, the major endocrine glands are the THYROID, PITUITARY, PARATHYROID, OVARY and TESTIS. Imbalances in the secretions of endocrine glands produce a variety of diseases (*see individual entries*).

endocrinology the study of the ENDOCRINE GLANDS, the HORMONES secreted by them and the treatment of any problems.

endogenous a term used to refer to what is within the body, whether growing within, originating from within or the result of internal causes.

endolymph *see* EAR.

endometriosis the occurrence of ENDOMETRIUM in other parts of the body, e.g. within the muscle of the UTERUS, in the OVARY, FALLOPIAN TUBES, PERITONEUM and possibly the BOWEL. Because of the nature of the TISSUE, it acts in a way similar to that of the uterus lining and causes pelvic pain, bleeding and painful MENSTRUATION. The condition occurs between PUBERTY and the MENOPAUSE and ceases during PREGNANCY. The treatment required may include total HYSTERECTOMY, but occasionally the administration of a STEROID hormone will alleviate the symptoms.

endometritis INFLAMMATION of the ENDOMETRIUM caused most commonly by BACTERIAl infection, but also sometimes by VIRUS, PARASITE or foreign body. It is associated with FEVER and abdominal pain and occurs mainly after ABORTION or childbirth or in women with an INTRAUTERINE DEVICE.

endometrium the MUCOUS MEMBRANE lining of the UTERUS that changes in structure during the menstrual cycle, becoming thicker with an increased blood supply later in the cycle. This is in readiness for receiving an EMBRYO, but if this does not happen, the endometrium breaks down and most is lost in MENSTRUATION.

endorphin one of a group of PEPTIDES that occur in the BRAIN and have pain-relieving qualities similar to MORPHINE. They are derived from a substance in the PITUITARY and are involved in endocrine control. In addition to their OPIATE effects, they are involved in URINE output, depression of RESPIRATION, sexual activity and learning (*see also* ENCEPHALIN).

endoscope the general term for an instrument used to inspect the interior of a body cavity or ORGAN, e.g. the gastroscope is for viewing the STOMACH. The instrument is fitted with lenses and a light source and is usually inserted through a natural opening although an incision can be used. *See also* FIBREOPTIC ENDOSCOPY.

endotoxin *see* TOXIN.

endotracheal tube (ET tube) a flexible tube that is passed through the nose or mouth into the TRACHEA, then attached to a RESPIRATOR, to enable a patient with breathing difficulties or undergoing ANESTHESIA to be artificially ventilated.

enema the procedure of putting fluid into the RECTUM for purposes of cleansing or therapy. An evacuant enema removes FAECES and consists of soap in water or olive oil, while a barium enema is given to permit an X-RAY of the colon to be taken. The compound BARIUM SULPHATE is opaque to X-rays. The insertion of drugs into the rectum is a therapeutic enema.

engagement the stage in a PREGNANCY when the presenting part of the FOETUS, which is usually the head, descends into the PELVIS of the mother.

enteral a term meaning relating to the INTESTINE.

enteral feeding the procedure of feeding a patient who is very ill through a tube via the nose to the STOMACH. Through the tube is passed a liquid, low-waste food, and there are a number of proprietary brands, some containing whole PROTEINS and some AMINO ACIDS.

enteric fevers see TYPHOID FEVER and PARATYPHOID FEVER.

enteritis INFLAMMATION of the INTESTINE, usually caused by a viral or bacterial INFECTION, resulting in DIARRHOEA.

enterocele bulging of the INTESTINE through the posterior wall of the upper VAGINA, which has become weakened.

enteropeptidase see TRYPSIN.

enterovirus a VIRUS that enters the body via the gut, where it multiplies and from where it attacks the CENTRAL NERVOUS SYSTEM. Examples are POLIOMYELITIS and the Coxsackie viruses (the cause of severe throat INFECTIONS, MENINGITIS and INFLAMMATION of heart TISSUE, some MUSCLES and the BRAIN).

enzyme any PROTEIN molecule that acts as a catalyst in the biochemical processes of the body. They are essential to life and are highly specific, acting on certain substrates at a set temperature and pH. Examples are the digestive enzymes amylase, lipase and TRYPSIN. Enzymes act by providing active sites (one or more for each enzyme) to which substrate molecules bind, forming a short-lived intermediate. The rate of reaction is increased, and after the product is formed, the active site is freed. Enzymes are easily rendered inactive by heat and some chemicals. They are vital for the normal functioning of the body, and their lack or inactivity can produce metabolic disorders.

epicardium *see* MYOCARDIUM.

epidemic a disease that affects a large proportion of the population at the same time, usually an infectious disease that occurs suddenly and spreads rapidly, e.g. an INFLUENZA epidemic.

epidemiology the study of EPIDEMIC disease. It involves aspects such as occurrence and distribution, causes, control and prevention. Included are the obvious epidemics such as CHOLERA and SMALLPOX and also others associated with more recent times (e.g. related to diet, lifestyle, etc). Thus, the links between smoking and cancer, diet and coronary disease are also included.

epidermis the outer layer of the SKIN, which comprises four layers and overlies the dermis. The top three layers are continually renewed as CELLS from the innermost germinative layer (called the Malpighian layer or stratum germinativum), which are pushed outwards. The topmost layer (stratum corneum) is made up of dead cells where the CYTOPLASM has been replaced by KERATIN. This layer is thickest on the palms and on the soles of the feet.

epididymis (*pl* **epididymides**) *see* TESTICLE.

epidural anaesthesia ANAESTHESIA in the region of the PELVIS, ABDOMEN or genitals produced by local anaesthetic injected into the epidural space of the SPINAL COLUMN (the epidural space being that space between the vertebral canal and the dura mater of the spinal cord). Epidural anaesthesia is commonly used to relieve maternal pain in chidbirth.

epiglottis situated at the base of the tongue, a thin piece of CARTILAGE enclosed in MUCOUS MEMBRANE that covers the LARYNX. It prevents food from passing into the larynx and TRACHEA when swallowing. The epiglottis resembles a leaf in shape.

epiglottitis INFLAMMATION of the MUCOUS MEMBRANE of the EPIGLOTTIS. Swelling of the TISSUES may obstruct the airway and swift action may be necessary, i.e. a TRACHEOSTOMY, to avoid a fatality. The other symptoms of epiglottitis are sore THROAT, FEVER and a croup-like cough, and it occurs mainly in children, usually during the winter. Epiglottitis can also occur as an allergic reaction (*see* ALLERGY) to something ingested or inhaled.

epilepsy a neurological disorder involving periodical, sudden disruption in BRAIN activity. The disruptions cause SEIZURES which may be convulsive (*see* CONVULSIONS) and sometimes result in loss of consciousness. There are many different types of epileptic seizure. Sufferers may experience a variety of symptoms ranging from strange sensations (eg abnormal smells, unexplained fear) while conscious, to TONIC CLONIC SEIZURES. The type of seizure depends on the area of the brain that is affected and its particular function. If all of the brain is involved (generalized seizure), motor and sensory function and consciousness will all be affected to some degree. There are several different types of generalized seizure. If part of the brain is involved (partial seizure), there may be motor or sensory disfunctions without loss of consciousness. The most common kind of partial seizure originates in the TEMPORAL LOBE, but partial seizures can occur in any part of the brain. Complex partial seizures involve some alteration of consciousness. In some cases a seizure may begin in one part of the brain and spread to involve all of the brain. This is known as a partial seizure evolving to a secondary generalized seizure. Most epileptic attacks occur without warning, although some people experience a variety of sensations beforehand (an 'aura'). Epileptic attacks may be 'triggered' by a number of factors, e.g. stress, bright or flashing lights and alcohol. Epilepsy may be caused by trauma or disease, e.g. cerebral TRAUMA, brain TUMOUR, cerebral HAEMORRHAGE, metabolic disorder or drug or alcohol abuse, but in the majority of cases, the exact cause is unknown. Most forms of epilepsy can be controlled successfully with drugs. Surgery is only an option in a minority of cases, where the cause is known. *See also* ABSENCE SEIZURE; STATUS EPILEPTICUS; TONIC-CLONIC SEIZURE.

epineurium *see* NERVE.

epiphysis (*pl* **epiphyses**) the softer end of a long BONE that is separated from the shaft by a plate (the epiphyseal plate) of CARTILAGE. It develops separately from the shaft, but when the bone stops growing it disappears as the head and shaft fuse. Separation of the epiphysis is a serious FRACTURE because the growing bone may be affected.

epinephrine *see* ADRENALINE.

episiotomy the process of making an incision in the PERINEUM to enlarge a woman's VAGINAl opening to facilitate delivery of a child. The technique is used to prevent tearing of the perineum.

epithelioma an epithelial (*see* EPITHELIUM) TUMOUR used formerly to describe any CARCINOMA.

epithelium (*pl* **epithelia**) TISSUE made up of CELLS packed closely together and bound by connective material. It covers the outer surface of the body and lines vessels and ORGANS in the body. One surface is fixed to a basement MEMBRANE and the other is free, and it provides a barrier against injury, microorganisms and some fluid loss. There are various types of epithelium in single and multiple (or stratified) layers and differing shapes, namely, cuboidal, squamous (like flat pads) and columnar. The shape suits the function, so the SKIN is formed from stratified squamous (and KERATINIZED) epithelium while columnar epithelia, which can secrete solutions and absorb nutrients, line the INTESTINES and STOMACH.

Epstein-Barr virus a virus, similar to HERPES, that causes infectious mononucleosis (GLANDULAR FEVER) and is implicated in HEPATITIS.

erection the condition in which erectile tissue in the PENIS (and to some degree in the CLITORIS) is engorged with blood, making it swell and become hard. It is the result primarily of sexual arousal, although it can occur during sleep because of physical stimulation. It also occurs in young boys. It is a prerequisite of VAGINAl penetration for emission of SEMEN.

eruption an outbreak or RASH on the SKIN, usually in the form of a red and raised area, possibly with fluid-containing BLISTERS or scales/crusts. It may be associated with a disease such as MEASLES or CHICKENPOX, a drug reaction or a physical or short-lived occurrence, e.g. nettle rash (URTICARIA).

erysipelas an infectious disease, caused by *Streptococcus pyogenes*. It produces an INFLAMMATION of the SKIN with associated redness. Large areas of the body may be affected, and other symptoms may include BLISTERS, FEVER and pain with a feeling of heat and a tingling sensation. In addition to being isolated, patients are given PENICILLIN.

erythema an INFLAMMATION or redness of the SKIN in which the tissues are congested with BLOOD. The condition may be accompanied by pain or itching. There are numerous causes, some infectious (bacterial or viral), and others physical, e.g. mild SUNBURN.

erythroblast a CELL occurring in the red BONE MARROW that develops into a red blood cell (ERYTHROCYTE). The cells are colourless at first but accumulate HAEMOGLOBIN and become red. In mammals, the NUCLEUS is lost.

erythrocyte the red blood CELL that is made in the BONE MARROW and occurs as a red disc, concave on both sides, full of HAEMOGLOBIN. These cells are responsible for carrying oxygen to TISSUES and carbon dioxide away. The latter is removed in the form of the bicarbonate ion (HCO_3^-), in exchange for a chloride ion (Cl^-).

erythroderma *see* DERMATITIS.

erythromycin an ANTIBIOTIC used for bacterial and mycoplasmic INFECTIONS. It is similar to PENICILLIN in its activity and can be taken for infections that penicillin cannot treat.

eschar a SCAB or slough formed after living tissue has been destroyed by a BURN, CAUTERY or GANGRENE.

Escherichia a group of Gram-negative (*see* GRAM'S STAIN) rod-shaped BACTERIA (*E. coli*) normally found in the INTESTINES and common in water, milk, etc. *E. coli*, which was first described by a German physician, Theodor Escherich, is a common cause of INFECTIONS of the URINARY TRACT. *E. coli* is also a common cause of food poisoning. Symptoms vary from mild (abdominal pain, DIARRHOEA) to very severe, with complications such as KIDNEY failure, and it can result in death, with the elderly and the very young being especially at risk.

essential amino acid of the 20 AMINO ACIDS required by the body, a number are termed essential because they must be included in the diet as they cannot be synthesized in the body. The essential ones are: isoleucine, leucine, lysine, methionine, phenylalanine, threonine, tryptophan and valine. In addition, infants require arginine and histidine. A lack leads to PROTEIN deficiency, but they are available in meat, cheese and eggs, and all eight would be obtained if the diet contained corn and beans.

essential fatty acid there are three polyunsaturated acids in this category, which cannot be produced in the body—arachidonic, linoleic and linolenic. These compounds are found in vegetable and fish oils and are vital for the proper functioning of the METABO-LISM. A deficiency may cause such symptoms as allergic conditions, skin disorders, poor hair and nails, and so on.

essential hypertension high BLOOD PRESSURE with no identifiable cause. ARTERIOSCLE-ROSIS is a complication of, and often associated with, essential hypertension. Other complications include cerebral HAEM-ORRHAGE, HEART FAILURE and KIDNEY failure. There are now several drugs that reduce blood pressure, including BETA-BLOCKERS and METHYL-DOPA. Lifestyle is an important factor for some sufferers: excessive weight should be lost, excess salt intake avoided, alcohol consumption reduced and strain of all types lessened. *See also* HYPERTENSION.

ET tube *see* ENDOTRACHEAL TUBE.

etiology *see* AETIOLOGY.

eugenics the study of how the inherited characteristics of the human population can be improved by GENETICS or selective/controlled breeding.

euploid a term used to describe a CHROMOSOME number that is an exact multiple of the normal (HAPLOID) number.

Eustachian tube one of two tubes, one on each side, that connect the middle EAR to the PHARYNX. The short (about 35–40 mm) tube is fine at the centre and wider at both ends and is lined with MUCOUS MEMBRANE. It is normally closed but opens to equalize air pressure on either side of the eardrum. It was named after the 16th-century Italian anatomist Eustachio.

euthanasia the intentional hastening of the death of someone who is suffering from a disease that is painful, incurable and inevitably fatal.

Ewing's sarcoma a form of bone CANCER that develops from the BONE MARROW in the pelvis or long BONES. It occurs in young adults and children and soon spreads around the body. It is uncommon but very aggressive, although recent use of anticancer drugs has prolonged the life expectancy of sufferers. The cancer was named after the American pathologist James Ewing.

excision in general terms, a cutting out. More specifically, removal of, for example, a GLAND or TUMOUR from the body.

excoriation injury of the surface of the SKIN (or other part of the body) caused by the ABRASION or scratching of the area.

excreta waste material discharged from the body. The term is often used specifically to denote FAECES.

excretion the removal of all waste material (EXCRETA) from the body, including

URINE and FAECES, the loss of water and salts through SWEAT GLANDS, and the elimination of carbon dioxide and water vapour from the LUNGS.

exhalation *see* RESPIRATION.

exocrine gland a GLAND that discharges its secretions through a DUCT, e.g. SALIVARY GLANDS and SWEAT GLANDS. *Compare* ENDOCRINE GLAND. *See also* PERSPIRATION.

exogenous a term used to describe something originating outside the body, including an outside ORGAN of the body.

expectorant one of a group of DRUGS that are taken to help in the removal of secretions from the LUNGS, BRONCHI and TRACHEA. The drugs work in one of several ways or can be used to combine their effects. Some dry up excess MUCUS and SPUTUM while others render these secretions less viscous to promote their removal. There are other varieties that work in still different ways.

expiration *see* RESPIRATION.

extensor *or* **antagonist** a MUSCLE that extends or stretches to cause an arm, leg, etc, to move (*compare* FLEXOR).

extrasystole *or* **ectopic beat** a heartbeat that is outside the normal rhythm of the HEART and is the result of an impulse generated outside the SINOATRIAL NODE. It may go unnoticed or it may seem that the heart has missed a beat. Extrasystoles are common in healthy people, but they may result from heart disease or nicotine from smoking, or caffeine from excessive intake of tea and coffee. Drugs can be taken to suppress these irregular beats.

eye the complicated ORGAN of sight. Each eye is roughly spherical and contained within the bony ORBIT in the skull. The outer layer is fibrous and comprises the opaque SCLERA and transparent CORNEA. The middle layer is vascular and is made up of the choroid (the blood supply for the outer half of the retina), ciliary body (which secretes AQUEOUS HUMOUR) and the IRIS. The inner layer is sensory, the RETINA. Between the cornea and the LENS is a chamber filled with liquid aqueous humour, and behind the lens is a much larger cavity with jelly-like VITREOUS HUMOUR. Light enters the eye through the cornea and thence via the aqueous humour to the lens, which focuses the light on to the retina. The latter contains CONE and ROD cells that are sensitive to light, and impulses are sent to the visual cortex of the BRAIN via the optic nerve to be interpreted.

F

face the front-facing part of the head, which extends from the chin to the forehead. There are 14 bones in the SKULL, supporting the face, and numerous fine MUSCLES are responsible for movements around the EYES, nose and mouth, producing expression. These are under the control of the seventh cranial nerve, which is a mixed sensory and motor nerve known as the FACIAL NERVE.

facial nerve a CRANIAL NERVE that has a number of branches and supplies the MUSCLEs that control facial expression. It also has branches to the middle EAR, TASTE BUDS, SALIVARY GLANDS and lacrimal glands. Some branches are MOTOR and others SENSORY in function.

facial paralysis PARALYSIS of the FACIAL NERVE, which leads to a loss of function in the

MUSCLES of the face, producing a lack of expression in the affected side. It occurs in the condition known as BELL'S PALSY, in which there may also be a loss of taste and inability to close the eye. The condition is often temporary, if caused by INFLAMMATION, and recovers in time. If the nerve itself is damaged by injury, however, or if the person has suffered a STROKE, the condition is likely to be permanent.

factor VIII *or* **antihaemophilic factor** one of the COAGULATION FACTORS normally present in the BLOOD. If the factor is deficient in males, it results in HAEMOPHILIA.

factor IX *see* HAEMOPHILIA.

faeces *or* **stools** the end waste products of DIGESTION, which are formed in the COLON and discharged via the ANUS. They consist of undigested food, BACTERIA, MUCUS and other secretions, water and BILE pigments, which are responsible for the colour. The condition and colour of the faeces are indicators of general health; e.g. pale stools are produced in JAUNDICE and COELIAC DISEASE and black stools often indicate the presence of bleeding in the digestive tract.

fainting *or* **syncope** a temporary and brief loss of consciousness caused by a sudden drop in the blood supply to the BRAIN. It can occur in perfectly healthy people, brought about by prolonged standing or emotional shock. It may also result from an INFECTION or severe pain or loss of blood through injury and may occur during pregnancy. Fainting is often preceded by giddiness, blurred vision, sweating and ringing in the ears. Recovery is usually complete, producing no lasting ill-effects, although this depends upon the underlying cause.

Fallopian tubes a pair of tubes, one of which leads from each OVARY to the UTERUS. At the ovary, the tube is expanded to form a funnel with finger-like projections, known as fimbriae, surrounding the opening. This funnel does not communicate directly with the ovary but is open to the abdominal cavity. However, when an egg is released from the ovary, the fimbriae move and waft it into the Fallopian tube. The tube is about 10 to 12cm long and leads directly into the womb at the lower end through a narrow opening.

false rib *see* RIB.

familial adenomatous polyposis (FAP) a rare hereditary condition affecting the COLON, in which multiple POLYPS (adenomas) develop on the mucosal surface of the large INTESTINE. Symptoms, if present, include abdominal pain, DIARRHOEA and rectal bleeding. There is a risk that one or more of the adenomas may become cancerous and once the condition has been diagnosed, surgery to remove the colon is generally recommended to prevent this. *See* ILEO-ANAL POUCH.

farmer's lung an allergic condition caused by sensitivity to inhaled dust and the fungal spores that are found in mouldy hay or straw. It is a form of allergic alveolitis (INFLAMMATION of the alveoli of the lungs, *see* ALVEOLI), characterized by increasing BREATHLESSNESS. The condition may be treated by CORTICOSTEROID drugs but can be cured only by avoidance of the ALLERGEN.

FAS *see* FOETAL ALCOHOL SYNDROME.

fascioliasis a disease of the LIVER and BILE ducts caused by the organism *Fasciola hepatica* or liver fluke. Human beings and animals are hosts to the adult flukes, and the eggs of the PARASITE are passed out in FAECES. These are taken up by a certain species of snail, which forms an intermediate host for the parasite and from which the larval stages are deposited on vegetation, especially wild watercress. Human beings are then infected, especially by eating wild watercress, which should always be avoided. Symptoms include FEVER, loss of appetite, indigestion, NAUSEA and VOMITING, DIARRHOEA, abdominal pain, severe sweating and coughing. In severe cases the liver may be damaged, and there may be JAUNDICE and even death. CHEMOTHERAPY is required to kill the flukes, the principal drugs being chloroquine and bithionol.

fat *see* ADIPOSE TISSUE.

fatigue physical or mental tiredness following a prolonged period of hard work. MUSCLE fatigue resulting from hard exercise is caused by a build-up of lactic acid. Lactic acid is produced in muscles (as an end product of the breakdown of GLYCOGEN to produce energy) and builds up when there is an insufficient supply of oxygen. The muscle is unable to work properly until a period of rest and restored oxygen supply enables the lactic acid to be removed.

fatty acid one of a group of organic compounds, each consisting of a long, straight hydrocarbon chain and a terminal carboxylic acid (COOH) group. The length of the chain varies from one to nearly 30 carbon atoms, and the chains may be saturated or unsaturated. Some fatty acids can be synthesized within the body, but others, the ESSENTIAL FATTY ACIDS, must be obtained from food. Fatty acids have three major roles within the body.

1. They are components of glycolipids (lipids containing carbohydrate) and phospholipids (lipids containing phosphate). These are of major importance in the structure of TISSUES and ORGANS.

2. Fatty acids are important constituents of triglycerides (lipids that have three fatty acid molecules joined to a glycerol molecule). They are stored in the CYTOPLASM of many CELLS and are broken down when required to yield energy. They are the form in which the body stores FAT.

3. Derivatives of fatty acids function as HORMONES and intracellular messengers.

favism an inherited disorder that takes the form of severe haemolytic ANAEMIA (destruction of red blood cells), brought on by eating broad beans. A person having this disorder is sensitive to a chemical present in the beans and also to certain drugs, particularly some antimalarial drugs. It is caused by the lack of a certain ENZYME, glucose 6-phosphate dehydrogenase, which plays an important role in glucose METABOLISM. The defective GENE responsible is passed on as a SEX-LINKED dominant characteristic and appears to persist in populations in which it occurs because it also confers increased resistance to malaria.

febrile having a FEVER.

febrile convulsion see CONVULSIONS.

Fehling's test a test, now replaced by more modern methods, for detecting the presence of sugar in the URINE.

femoral the term used to describe the FEMUR or that area of the thigh, e.g. femoral artery, vein, nerve and canal.

femur the thigh BONE, which is the long bone extending from the hip to the KNEE and is the strongest bone in the body. It is the weight-bearing bone of the body and fractures are common in old people who have lost bone mass. It articulates with the PELVIC GIRDLE at the upper end, forming the HIP JOINT, and at the lower end with the PATELLA (knee cap) and TIBIA to form the knee joint.

fertilization the fusion of SPERM and OVUM to form a ZYGOTE, which then undergoes CELL division to become an EMBRYO. Fertilization in humans takes place high up in the FALLOPIAN TUBE near the OVARY, and the fertilized egg travels down and becomes implanted in the UTERUS.

fetus *see* FOETUS.

fever *or* **pyrexia** an elevation of body TEMPERATURE above the normal (37°C / 98.6°F), which accompanies many diseases and INFECTIONS. The cause of fever is the production by the body of endogenous pyrogen, which acts on the thermoregulatory centre in the HYPOTHALAMUS of the brain. This responds by promoting mechanisms that increase heat generation and lessen heat loss, leading to a rise in temperature. Fever is the main factor in many infections caused by BACTERIA or VIRUSES and is the result of TOXINS produced by the growth of these organisms. An intermittent fever describes a fluctuating body temperature, in which the temperature sometimes returns to normal. In a remittent fever there is also a fluctuating body temperature but this does not return to normal. In a relapsing fever, caused by bacteria of the genus *Borella*, transmitted by ticks or lice, there is a recurrent fever every three to 10 days following the first attack, which lasts for about one week.

Treatment of fever depends on the underlying cause. However, it may be necessary to reduce the temperature by direct methods such as sponging the body with tepid water or by giving drugs such as PARACETAMOL. As well as a rise in body temperature, symptoms of fever include HEADACHE, shivering, NAUSEA, DIARRHOEA or CONSTIPATION.

Above 41°C (105°F) there may be DELIRIUM or CONVULSIONS, especially in young children.

FH *see* **growth hormone**.

fibreoptic endoscopy a method of viewing hollow internal structures, such as the digestive tract and tracheobronchial tree, using fibreoptics. Fibreoptics uses illumination from a cold light source, which is passed down a bundle of quartz fibres. The instruments used are highly flexible compared to the older form of ENDOSCOPE and can be employed to illuminate structures that were formerly inaccessible. Using fibreoptic endoscopy, direct procedures can be carried out, such as BIOPSY and polypectomy (surgical removal of a POLYP).

fibrillation the rapid nonsynchronized contraction or TREMOR of MUSCLES in which individual bundles of fibres contract independently. It applies especially to HEART muscle and disrupts the normal beating so that the affected part is unable to pump BLOOD. Two types of fibrillation may occur, depending on which muscle is affected. Atrial fibrillation, often re-

sulting from ATHEROSCLEROSIS or rheumatic heart disease, affects the muscles of the atria and is a common type of ARRHYTHMIA. The heartbeat and pulse are very irregular and cardiac output is maintained by the contraction of the ventricles alone. With ventricular fibrillation, the heart stops pumping blood, so this is, in effect, CARDIAC ARREST. The patient requires immediate emergency resuscitation or death ensues within minutes. *See* DEFIBRILLATION; CARDIOPULMONARY RESUSCITATION.

fibrin the end product of the process of blood COAGULATION, comprising threads of insoluble PROTEIN formed from a soluble precursor, FIBRINOGEN, by the activity of the ENZYME thrombin. Fibrin forms a network that is the basis of a BLOOD CLOT.

fibrinogen a COAGULATION FACTOR present in the BLOOD, which is a soluble PROTEIN and the precursor of FIBRIN.

fibrocystic disease of the pancreas *see* CYSTIC FIBROSIS.

fibroid a type of BENIGN tumour found in the UTERUS, composed of fibrous and muscular TISSUE and varying in size from 1 or 2 mm to a mass weighing several kilograms. They more commonly occur in childless women and those over the age of 35. Fibroids may present no problems but, alternatively, can be the cause of pain, heavy and irregular menstrual bleeding, URINE retention or frequency of MICTURITION and sterility. Fibroids can be removed surgically but often the complete removal of the uterus (HYSTERECTOMY) is carried out.

fibroma a BENIGN tumour composed of FIBROUS TISSUE.

fibromyalgia *or* **fibrositis** INFLAMMATION of fibrous CONNECTIVE TISSUE, MUSCLES and muscle sheaths, particularly in the back, legs and arms, causing pain and stiffness, often accompanied by tiredness and sometimes by depression. Fibromyalgia is a chronic condition of uncertain cause. The severity of SYMPTOMS may wax and wane, but can be severely debilitating for some sufferers.

fibrosarcoma a MALIGNANT tumour of CONNECTIVE TISSUE, particularly found in the limbs, especially the legs.

fibrosis the formation of thickened CONNECTIVE TISSUE or scar tissue, usually as a result of injury or INFLAMMATION. This may affect the lining of the alveoli (*see* ALVEOLUS) of the LUNGS (pulmonary interstitial fibrosis) and causes breathlessness. *See also* CYSTIC FIBROSIS.

fibrositis see FIBROMYALGIA.

fibrous tissue a tissue type that occurs abundantly throughout the body. White fibrous tissue consists of fibres of COLLAGEN, a PROTEIN with a high tensile strength and unyielding structure, and forms ligaments, sinews and scar tissue, and occurs in the SKIN. Yellow fibrous tissue is composed of the fibres of another protein, elastin. It is very elastic and occurs in LIGAMENTS that are subjected to frequent stretching, such as those in the back of the neck. It also occurs in arterial walls and in the walls of the alveoli (*see* ALVEOLUS), and in the dermis layer of the skin.

fibula (*pl* **fibulae**) the outer, thin, long BONE that articulates with the larger TIBIA in the lower leg.

filariasis a tropical and subtropical disease caused by nematode worms in the LYMPHATIC SYS-TEM. These parasitic worms are carried to humans by mosquitoes, resulting in blockages in the lymph vessels, causing swelling (ELEPHANTIASIS).

fimbria (*pl* **fimbriae**) *see* FAL-LOPIAN TUBES.

finger *see* HAND and PHALAN-GES.

fissure a natural cleft or groove or abnormal break in the SKIN or MUCOUS MEMBRANE, e.g. an anal fissure.

fistula an abnormal opening between two hollow ORGANS or between such an organ or GLAND and the exterior. These may arise during development of the FOETUS so that a baby may be born with a fistula. Alternatively, they can be produced by injury, INFEC-TION or as a complication following surgery. A common example is an anal fistula, which may develop if an abscess present in the RECTUM bursts and produces a communication through the surface of the SKIN.

flap a section of TISSUE, usually SKIN, that is excised from the underlying tissues except for one thin strip (PEDICLE) that is left for blood and nervous supply. The flap is used to re-

pair an injury at another site in the body, the free part being sutured into place. After about three weeks, when the healing process is well under way, the remaining strip is detached and sewn into place. Flaps are commonly used in plastic surgery and also following AMPUTATION of a limb. *See* SKIN GRAFTING.

flat foot an absence of the arch of the FOOT so that the inner edge lies flat on the ground. It may occur in children in whom the LIGAMENTS of the foot are soft, or in older, obese adults or those who stand for long periods. Treatment is by means of exercises, built-up footwear and, in extreme cases, surgery.

flatulence a build-up of gas in the STOMACH or BOWELS that is released through the mouth or ANUS.

flexion bending of a JOINT or the term may also be applied to an abnormal shape in a body ORGAN.

flexor *or* **agonist** any MUSCLE that contracts to cause a LIMB or other body part to bend (*see* VOLUNTARY MUSCLE).

flutter an abnormal disturbance of heartbeat rhythm that may affect the atria or ventricles but is less severe than FIBRIL-LATION. The causes are the same, however, and the treatment is also similar.

flux an excessive and abnormal flow from any of the natural openings of the body, e.g. alvine flux, which is DIAR-RHOEA.

foetal alcohol syndrome (FAS) a wide spectrum of birth defects caused by a mother's excess consumption of alcohol during PREGNANCY. These include deformities of the face and skull, skeletal abnormalities, HEART defects, growth deficiency, global development delay, EPILEPSY and learning and behavioural difficulties.

foetus *or* **fetus** an unborn child after the eighth week of development.

foetoscope 1. a fibreoptic device used in amnnioscopy and for sugery on the foetus in utero. **2.** a conical stethoscope with a circular earpiece for listening to the heartbeat of the foetus in utero.

Foley catheter a flexible, hollow tube that is inserted through the URETHRA into the BLADDER to drain URINE. After insertion, a small balloon at the end of the catheter which is inside the bladder is inflated with water to hold it in position.

folic acid a compound that forms part of the VITAMIN B complex. It is involved in the biosynthesis of some AMINO ACIDS and is used in the treatment of ANAEMIA.

follicle any small sac, cavity or secretory GLAND. Examples are hair follicles and the Graafian follicles of the ovaries (*see* OVARY), in and from which eggs mature and are released.

follicle-stimulating hormone (FSH) *see* GONADO-TROPHINS.

fomentation *see* POULTICE.

fontanelle an opening in the SKULL of newborn and young infants in whom the BONE is not wholly formed and the SU-TURES are incompletely fused. The largest of these is the anterior fontanelle, on the top of the head, which is about 2.5 cm square at birth. The fontanelles gradually close as bone is formed and are completely covered by the age of 18 months. If a baby is unwell, e.g. with a FEVER, the fontanelle becomes tense. If an infant is suffering from DIARRHOEA and possibly DEHYDRATION, the fontanelle is abnormally depressed.

food poisoning an illness of the digestive system caused by eating food contaminated by certain BACTERIA, VIRUSes or by chemical poisons (insecticides) and metallic elements such as mercury or lead. Symptoms include VOMITING, DIARRHOEA, NAUSEA and abdominal pain, and these may arise very quickly and usually within 24 hours. In severe cases, fluid loss due to vomiting and diarrhoea, if untreated, can lead swiftly to DEHYDRATION and there can be complications such as KIDNEY failure. Bacteria are the usual cause of food poisoning and proliferate rapidly, producing TOXINs that cause the symptoms of the illness. Those involved include members of the genera *Salmonella*, *Staphylococcus*, *Campylobacter*, and also *Clostridium botulinum*, the causal organism of BOTULISM. Food poisoning may be fatal, the old and the young being especially at risk.

foot (*pl* **feet**) the part of the lower LIMB below the ankle, made up of 11 small BONES and having a structure similar to that of the HAND. The TALUS, which articulates with the leg bones, and the calcaneus, which forms the heel, are the largest of these. *See also* FLAT FOOT.

foramen a hole or opening, usually referring to those that occur in some BONES. For example, the foramen magnum is a large hole at the base of the SKULL (in the OCCIPITAL BONE) through which the SPINAL CORD passes out from the brain.

forceps a surgical instrument, of which there are many different types and sizes, that is used as pincers.

forebrain the part of the BRAIN that consists of the THALAMUS and HYPOTHALAMUS.

foreskin the prepuce, which is a fold of skin growing over the end (glans) of the PENIS.

fossa (*pl* **fossae**) a natural hollow or depression on the surface or within the body. An example is the fossae within the SKULL, which house different parts of the BRAIN.

fovea (*pl* **foveae**) any small depression, often referring to the one that occurs in the RETINA of the EYE in which a large number of the light-sensitive CELLS called CONES are situated. It is the site of greatest visual acuity, being the region in which the image is focused when the eyes are fixed on an object.

fracture any break in a BONE, which may be complete or incomplete. In a simple fracture (also called a closed fracture), the SKIN remains more or less intact, but in a compound fracture (or open fracture) there is an open wound connecting the bone with the surface. This type of fracture is more serious as it provides a greater risk of INFECTION and more blood loss. If a bone that is already diseased suffers a fracture (such as often occurs in older women who have OSTEOPOROSIS), this is known as a pathological fracture. A fatigue fracture occurs in a bone that suffers recurrent, persistent stress, e.g. the march fracture sometimes seen in the second toe of soldiers after long marches. A greenstick fracture occurs only in young children, whose bones are still soft and tend to bend. The fracture occurs on the opposite side from the causal force. A complicated fracture involves damage to surrounding soft TISSUE, including NERVES

and BLOOD VESSELS. A depressed fracture refers only to the SKULL when a piece of bone is forced inwards and may damage the BRAIN. *See also* COMMINUTED FRACTURE.

frenulum lingae *see* TONGUE.

friar's balsam a compound containing BENZOIN, which is mixed with hot water and the resulting vapour inhaled to relieve colds, etc.

Friedreich's ataxia an inherited disorder that is caused by degeneration of NERVE cells in the BRAIN and SPINAL CORD. It appears in children, usually in adolescence, and the symptoms include unsteadiness during walking and a loss of the knee-jerk REFLEX ACTION, leading progressively to tremors, speech impairment and curvature of the spine. The symptoms are increasingly disabling and may also be accompanied by heart disease. *See also* ATAXIA.

frontal lobe the anterior part of each cerebral hemisphere of the CEREBRUM of the BRAIN, extending back to a region called the central sulcus, which is a deep cleft on the upper outer surface.

frostbite damage to the SKIN and underlying TISSUES caused by extreme cold and especially affecting the 'extremities', i.e. the fingers, toes, nose and cheeks. The affected parts become white and numb and may develop BLISTERS. The skin hardens and gradually turns black, and if the frostbite is fairly superficial, this eventually peels off, exposing tender red skin underneath. In severe cases, however, deeper layers of tissue become frozen and are destroyed, and AMPUTATION may be necessary, especially where IN-FECTION has set in. *See* GANGRENE.

frozen shoulder painful stiffness of the SHOULDER joint, which limits movement and is more common in older people between the ages of 50 and 70. It may result from injury, but often there is no apparent cause. Treatment involves ANTI-INFLAMMATORY drugs, PHYSIOTHERAPY and sometimes injections of CORTICO-STEROID drugs are given, and usually there is a gradual recovery.

FSH *see* GONADOTROPHINS.

fulminant a term used to describe a pain that is sudden and sharp.

fundus (*pl* **fundi**) **1.** the enlarged base of an ORGAN farthest away from its opening. **2.** a point in the RETINA of the EYE opposite the pupil.

fungal diseases diseases or INFECTIONS caused by fungi.

fungus (*pl* **fungi**) any of a large order of single-celled plants that lack chlorophyll and reproduce by spores. Some forms are infectious, in the same way as BACTERIA, e.g. RINGWORM, and others are used in the production of ANTIBIOTICS.

furuncle *see* BOIL.

G

galactorrhoea flow of milk from the breast, not associated with childbirth or nursing. It may be a symptom of a tumour in the pituitary gland.

gall another term for bile.

gall bladder a sac-like organ, situated on the underside of the liver, that stores and concentrates bile. It is approximately 8 cm long and 2.5 cm at its widest, and its volume is a little over 30 cm^2. When fats are digested, the gall bladder contracts, sending bile into the duodenum through the common bile duct. Gallstones, the most common gall bladder disease, may form in certain circumstances.

gallstones stones of varying composition that form in the gall bladder. Their formation seems to be caused by a change in bile composition rendering cholesterol less soluble. Stones may also form around a foreign body. There are three types of stone: cholesterol, pigment and mixed, the last being the most common. Calcium salts are usually found in varying proportions. Although gallstones may be present for years without symptoms, they can cause severe pain and inflammation (cholecystitis) and may pass into the common bile duct, where the obstruction results in jaundice.

gamete a mature germ or sexual cell, male or female, that can participate in fertilization, e.g. ovum and sperm.

gamma globulin *or* **immune gamma globulin** a concentrated form of the antibody part of human blood. It is used for immunization against certain infectious diseases, e.g. MEASLES, POLIOMYELITIS, HEPATITIS A, etc. It is of no use when the disease is diagnosed but can prevent or modify it if given before. *See also* GLOBULIN.

ganglion (*pl* **ganglia**) **1.** a mass of nervous TISSUE containing nerve CELLS and SYNAPSES. Chains of ganglia are situated on each side of the SPINAL CORD while other ganglia are sited near to or in the appropriate ORGANS. Within the CENTRAL NERVOUS SYSTEM, some well-defined masses of nerve cells are called ganglia, e.g. basal ganglia (*see* BASAL GANGLION). **2.** a BENIGN swelling that often forms in the sheath of a TENDON and is fluid-filled. It occurs particularly at the wrist and may disappear quite suddenly.

gangrene death of TISSUE because of loss of BLOOD supply or bacterial INFECTION. There are two types of gangrene, dry and moist. Dry gangrene is caused purely by loss of blood supply and is a late-stage complication of DIABETES MELLITUS in which ATHEROSCLEROSIS is present. The affected part becomes cold and turns brown and black and there is an obvious line between living and dead tissue. In time the gangrenous part drops off.

Moist gangrene is the more common type and is the result

of bacterial infection which leads to putrefaction and issuing of fluids from the tissue, accompanied by an obnoxious smell. The patient may suffer from FEVER and ultimately die of blood poisoning (SEPTICAEMIA). (*See also* GAS GANGRENE.)

gaseous exchange the exchange of respiratory gases (oxygen and carbon dioxide) by diffusion across the walls of the alveoli (*see* ALVEOLUS) in the LUNGS.

gas gangrene a form of GANGRENE that occurs when wounds are infected with soil BACTERIA of the genus *Clostridium*. The bacterium produces TOXINS that cause decay and putrefaction with the generation of gas. The gas spreads into MUSCLES and CONNECTIVE TISSUE, causing swelling, pain, FEVER and possibly toxic DELIRIUM, and if untreated the condition quickly leads to death. Some of these bacteria are anaerobic (i.e. they exist without air or oxygen) hence surgery, oxidizing agents and PENICILLIN can all be used in treatment.

gastralgia a term meaning pain in the STOMACH.

gastrectomy the surgical removal of the STOMACH or, more commonly, part of it. This may be performed for stomach CANCER, severe PEPTIC ULCERS or to stop HAEMORRHAGE.

gastric a term used to describe anything relating to the STOMACH.

gastric glands GLANDS that are situated in the MUCOUS MEMBRANE of the STOMACH and secrete GASTRIC JUICE. The glands are the cardiac, pyloric and fundic.

gastric juice the secretion from the gastric GLANDS in the STOMACH. The main constituents are hydrochloric acid, rennin, mucin and pepsinogen, the last forming pepsin in the acid conditions. The acidity (which is around pH 1 to 1.5) also destroys unwanted BACTERIA.

gastric lavage a procedure for washing out the STOMACH to empty it of its contents prior to surgery, or to flush out certain POISONS or drugs after accidental ingestion or overdose. A tube is passed through the mouth or nose into the stomach via the OESOPHAGUS and the somach is washed out with water, saline or activated charcoal, depending on the reason for lavage.

gastric ulcer an erosion of the MUCOSA in the STOMACH caused by such agents as acid and BILE. It may penetrate the muscle and perforate the stomach wall (*see* PERFORATION). Typical symptoms include burning pain, belching and possibly NAUSEA when the stomach is empty or soon after eating. A bleeding ulcer can cause HAEMATEMESIS. Relief may be found with ANTACID compounds. A large percentage of gastric ulcers are caused by the bacterium HELICOBACTER PYLORI, and if this is found to be the case, ANTIBIOTIC therapy will be effective. If the ulcer perforates the stomach wall or there is excessive bleeding, surgery may be necessary.

gastrin a HORMONE that stimulates excess production of acidic GASTRIC JUICE.

gastritis INFLAMMATION of the STOMACH lining (MUCOSA). It may be caused by BACTERIA, VIRUS or excessive alcohol intake.

gastroenteritis INFLAMMATION of both the STOMACH and INTESTINES, leading to VOMITING and DIARRHOEA. It is most commonly caused by viral or bacterial INFECTION, and consequent fluid loss can be serious in children and the elderly.

gastroenterology the study of diseases that affect the gastrointestinal tract, including the PANCREAS, GALL BLADDER and BILE DUCT in addition to the STOMACH and INTESTINES.

gastroenterostomy an operation undertaken to reroute food from the STOMACH to enable an obstruction to be relieved. It consists of making an opening in the stomach and the nearby small INTESTINE and joining the two together. It is often performed with a GASTRECTOMY.

gastrointestinal tract *see* ALIMENTARY CANAL.

gastroscope a flexible instrument, comprising fibreoptics or a miniature video camera, that permits internal visual examination of the STOMACH. It is possible to see all areas of the stomach and to take specimens using special tools. The tube is introduced via the mouth and OESOPHAGUS.

gastrostomy the creation, by surgery, of an opening into the STOMACH from the outside. This permits insertion of a tube for feeding a patient who cannot swallow because of e.g. CANCER of the OESOPHAGUS, post-oesophageal surgery or who may be unconscious for a long time. A gastrostomy may also be performed to insert a tube for drainage after surgery.

gauze a material with an open weave that is used for bandages and dressings.

gavage feeding directly into the STOMACH via a tube, which may adopted when a patient is unable to feed himself or herself. *See* NASOGASTRIC TUBE.

gene the fundamental unit of genetic material found at a specific location on a CHROMOSOME. It is chemically complex and responsible for the transmission of information between older and younger generations. Each gene contributes to a particular trait or characteristic. There are more than 100,000 genes in humans, and gene size varies with the characteristic, e.g. the gene that codes for the hormone INSULIN is 1,700 base pairs long.

There are several types of gene, depending on their function, and in addition genes are said to be dominant or reces-

sive. A dominant characteristic is one that occurs whenever the gene is present while the effect of a recessive gene (e.g. a disease) requires that the gene be on both members of the chromosome pair, i.e. it must be homozygous. *See also* SEX-LINKED DISORDERS.

general paralysis of the insane *see* TABES DORSALIS.

gene therapy a form of treatment undergoing research and clinical trials in several countries whereby genetic material is introduced into a person's CELLS, using a carrier or vector (most commonly a modified VIRUS), to replace defective GENES with normal ones. It is hoped that gene therapy will improve the outlook for patients with many diseases including CYSTIC FIBROSIS and some forms of CANCER.

genetic code specific information, carried by DNA molecules, that controls the particular AMINO ACIDS and their positions in every PROTEIN and thus all the proteins synthesized within a CELL. Because there are just four NUCLEOTIDES, a unit of three bases becomes the smallest unit that can produce codes for all 20 amino acids. The transfer of information from gene to protein is based upon three consecutive nucleotides called codons. A change in the genetic code results in an amino acid being inserted incorrectly in a protein, resulting in a MUTATION.

genetic counselling the provision of advice to families about the nature and likelihood of inherited disorders and the options available in terms of testing, prevention and management. It is of value to anyone who may be concerned about personal risk of developing hereditary disease and can be particularly helpful to couples with a family history of severe hereditary disorders who are planning to have children, or to women who are already pregnant. With modern techniques of antenatal DIAGNOSIS, it is possible to identify many inherited foetal abnormalities at an early stage of a PREGNANCY. In cases where such a problem has been detected, a genetic counsellor can help parents to make informed decisions about the implications of continuing with the pregnancy. *See also* GENETIC SCREENING.

genetic engineering *or* **recombinant DNA technology** the artificial modification of an organism's genetic make-up. More specifically, for example, the insertion of GENES from a human CELL into a bacterium where they perform their usual function. Thus it is possible to produce, on a commercial scale, hormones such as INSULIN and GROWTH HORMONE by utilizing a bacterium with a human gene. The organism often used is *ESCHERICHIA coli*. The process has other applications, including production of monoclonal antibodies.

genetic fingerprinting the technique that utilizes an individual's DNA to identify that person. DNA can be extracted from body TISSUES and used in settling issues of a child's maternity or paternity. In forensic medicine, DNA testing on samples of BLOOD, hair, etc, taken at crime scenes can be compared with samples from suspects to establish whether they were present at the scene.

genetic screening the procedure whereby individuals are tested to determine whether their GENE make-up suggests they carry a particular disease or condition. If it is shown that someone carries a genetically linked disease, then decisions can be taken regarding future children. *See also* SEX-LINKED DISORDERS.

genetics the study of heredity and variation in individuals and the means whereby characteristics are passed from parent to offspring. The classical aspects of the subject were expounded by Mendel, an Austrian monk, in the early 19th century. Now there are several subdisciplines, including population genetics and molecular genetics.

genital the term used to describe anything relating to reproduction or the organs of the REPRODUCTIVE SYSTEM.

genitalia the male or female organs of the REPRODUCTIVE SYSTEM, often referring to the external parts only.

genito-urinary medicine the subdiscipline concerned with all aspects of sexually transmitted diseases.

genito-urinary tract the GENITAL and URINARY ORGANS and associated structures: KIDNEYS, URETER, BLADDER, URETHRA and GENITALIA.

genome the total genetic information stored in the CHRO-MOSOMES of an organism, the number of chromosomes being characteristic of that particular species.

genotype 1. the genetic constitution of an organism, which determines characteristics. **2.** a group of organisms that have the same genetic constitution.

genu valgum *see* KNOCK KNEE.

genu varum *see* BOW LEGS.

geriatrics the subdiscipline of medicine that deals with the diagnosis and treatment of diseases and conditions that affect the aged.

German measles *or* **rubella** a highly infectious viral disease, occurring mainly in childhood, which is mild in effect. Spread occurs through close contact with infected individuals, and there is an INCUBATION period of two to three weeks. Symptoms include headache, shivering, sore throat and a slight FE-VER. There is some swelling of the neck, and soon after the onset a RASH of pink spots appears, initially on the face and/or neck and subsequently spreading over the body. The rash disappears in roughly one week, but the condition remains infectious for three or four more days. IMMUNITY is usually conferred by the INFECTION, and although it is a mild disease it is important because an attack during the early stages of PREGNANCY may cause severe foetal abnormalities. Girls are therefore immunized around the age of 12.

germs microorganisms. The term is used particularly for microorganisms that are PATHOGENIC.

gerontology the scientific study of ageing and the diseases that affect the aged.

gestation the length of time from FERTILIZATION of the OVUM to birth (*see also* PREGNANCY).

gestational diabetes *see* DIABETES MELLITUS.

giddiness *see* VERTIGO.

gigantism *or* **giantism** excessive growth of the body, usually as a result of overproduction of GROWTH HORMONE from the PITUITARY GLAND during childhood or adolescence.

gingivitis INFLAMMATION of the gums, most commonly a symptom of bacterial INFECTION as a result of poor oral hygiene or over-vigorous tooth brushing. Symptoms include painful and bleeding gums and HALITOSIS.

gland an ORGAN or group of CELLS that secretes a specific substance or substances, e.g. HORMONES. ENDOCRINE GLANDS secrete directly into the BLOOD, while exocrine glands secrete on to an epithelial surface via a DUCT. Some glands produce fluids, for example, milk from the mammary glands, saliva from the sublingual gland. The THYROID gland is an endocrine gland that releases hormones into the bloodstream. A further system of glands, the lymphatic glands, occur throughout the body in association with the lymphatic vessels (*see* LYMPH).

glandular fever *or* **infectious mononucleosis** an infectious viral disease caused by the EPSTEIN-BARR VIRUS. It produces a sore throat and swelling in neck LYMPH NODES (also those in the armpits and groin). Other symptoms include HEADACHE, FEVER and a loss of appetite. The LIVER may be affected, and the SPLEEN may become enlarged or even ruptured, necessitating surgery. The disease is diagnosed by the large number of MONOCYTES in the blood, and although complications tend to be rare, total recovery may take many weeks.

glans the head of the PENIS, which is normally covered by the FORESKIN.

glaucoma a condition that results in loss of VISION because of high pressure in the EYE, although there is usually no associated disease of the eye. There are several types of glaucoma, which occur at differing rates but are all characterized by high intraocular pressure (because of the outflow of AQUEOUS HUMOUR being restricted), which damages nerve fibres in the RETINA and OPTIC NERVE. Treatment involves reduction of the pressure with drops and tablets (to reduce production of aqueous humour). Surgery may be undertaken to create another outlet for the aqueous humour.

gleet a discharge symptomatic of chronic GONORRHOEA.

glia *or* **neuroglia** *or* **glial cells** CONNECTIVE TISSUE in the CENTRAL NERVOUS SYSTEM composed of a variety of CELLS. The macroglia are divided into astrocytes, which surround brain capillaries, and oligodendrocytes, which form MYELIN sheaths. The microglia perform a mainly scavenging function. Glial cells are present at ten to fifty times the number of NEURONS in the nervous system.

globin *see* HAEMOGLOBIN.

globulin one of a group of globular PROTEINS that occur widely in milk, BLOOD, eggs and plants. There are four types in blood SERUM: a1, a2, b and g. The alpha and beta types are carrier proteins, like HAEMOGLOBIN, and GAMMA GLOBULINS include the IMMUNOGLOBULINS involved in the IMMUNE response.

glomerulus *see* KIDNEY; NEPHRITIS.

glottis 1. the opening between the VOCAL CHORDS. **2.** the part of the LARYNX involved with sound production.

glucagon a HORMONE important in maintaining the level of the body's BLOOD SUGAR. It works antagonistically with INSULIN, increasing the supply of blood sugar through the breakdown of GLYCOGEN to glucose in the LIVER. Glucagon is produced by the ISLETS OF LANGERHANS when blood-sugar level is low.

glucocorticosteroid *see* COR-TICOSTEROID.

glue ear *or* **secretory otitis media** a form of OTITIS, common in children, which occurs as an INFLAMMATION of the middle EAR, with the production of a persistent sticky fluid. It can cause deafness and may be associated with enlarged ADENOIDS. In treatment of the condition, the adenoids are removed and GROMMETS inserted.

gluteal the term used to describe the buttocks or the MUSCLES forming them.

gluten enteropathy *see* COELIAC DISEASE.

gluteus *or* **glutaeus** (*pl* **glutei** *or* **glutaei**) one of the three MUSCLES of each buttock. The gluteus maximus shapes the buttock and extends the thigh, the gluteus medius and gluteus minimus abduct the thigh (i.e. move the limb away from the body) while the former also rotates it.

glycerol a transparent colourless liquid with a very sweet taste, which is obtained from fats.

glygeryl trinitrate (GTN) *see* VASODILATOR.

glycogen *or* **animal starch** a CARBOHYDRATE (polysaccharide) stored mainly in the LIVER. It acts as an energy store that is liberated upon hydrolysis (*see* GLUCAGON).

glycoprotein *see* INTERFERON.

glycosuria the presence of sugar (glucose) in the URINE, which is usually because of DIABETES MELLITUS.

goitre swelling of the neck because of THYROID GLAND enlargement. The thyroid tries to counter the dietary lack of iodine necessary to produce thyroid hormone by increasing the output, thereby becoming larger. The endemic or simple goitre is the result. Other types are caused by HYPERPLASIA and AUTOIMMUNE DISEASES, e.g. when antibodies are produced against antigens in the thyroid gland.

gold salts *or* **gold compound** chemicals containing gold that are used in minute quantities to treat RHEUMATOID ARTHRITIS. They are given by injection into MUSCLES, and because SIDE EFFECTS may include skin reactions, blood disorders, mouth ULCERS and INFLAMMATION of the KIDNEYS, very careful control is kept on the DOSAGE.

gonadotrophins *or* **gonadotrophic hormone** HORMONES secreted by the anterior PITUITARY GLAND. Follicle-stimulating hormone (FSH) is produced by males and females, as is luteinizing hormone, LH, (interstitial cell-stimulating hormone, ICSH, in males). FSH controls, directly or indirectly, growth of the ova (*see* OVUM) and SPERM, while LH/ICSH stimulates reproductive activity in the GONADS.

gonads the reproductive organs that produce the GAMETES and some hormones. In the male and female, the gonads are the TESTICLES and ovaries (*see* OVARY) respectively.

gonorrhoea the most common VENEREAL DISEASE, which is spread primarily by sexual contact. The causative agent is the bacterium *Neisseria gonorrhoeae*, and it affects the MUCOUS MEMBRANE of the VAGINA or, in the male, the URETHRA. Infections can also occur in the throat or the RECTUM. Symptoms develop approximately one week after INFECTION and include pain on urinating with a discharge of PUS, although approximately 50% of women and 10% of men may have no obvious symptoms. INFLAMMATION of nearby organs may occur (TESTICLE, PROSTATE GLAND in men; UTERUS, FALLOPIAN TUBES and ovaries in women), and prolonged inflammation of the urethra may lead to formation of FIBROUS TISSUE, causing STRICTURE. JOINTS may also be affected, and later complications include ENDOCARDITIS, ARTHRITIS and CONJUNCTIVITIS. Babies born to mothers suffering from gonorrhoea can become infected during the birthing process. The resulting eye condition (ophthalmia neonatorum) can lead to blindness if not treated promptly. Gonorrhoea can be successfully treated with appropriate ANTIBIOTIC therapy. In order to prevent further spread of the disease, all known sexual contacts should be identified and treated if possible.

gout a disorder caused by an excess of URIC ACID in the bloodstream, which is deposited in JOINTS as salts (urates) of the acid. This causes INFLAMMA-

TION of the affected joints and painful gouty ARTHRITIS with destruction of the joints. The KIDNEYS may also be damaged, with formation of stones. Deposits of the salts (called tophi) may reach the stage where they prohibit further use of the joints, causing hands and feet to be set in a particular position. Treatment of gout is through drugs that increase the excretion of the urate salts or slow their formation.

Graafian follicle *see* FOLLI-CLE.

graft the removal of some TIS-SUE or an ORGAN from one person for application to or IMPLANTATION into the same person or another individual. For example, a SKIN graft involves taking healthy skin from one area of the body to heal damaged skin, and a KIDNEY (or renal) graft (or TRANSPLANT) is the removal of the ORGAN from one person (usually a recently dead individual) to another. Numerous types of graft are now feasible, including SKIN, BONE, CORNEA, CARTILAGE, NERVES and BLOOD VESSELS, and whole organs such as kidney, HEART and LUNG.

Gram's stain a technique described by H. C. J. Gram, the Danish bacteriologist, in 1884, which involves using a stain to differentiate between certain BACTERIA. Bacteria on a microscope slide are first stained with a violet dye and iodine, then rinsed in ethanol to decolourize and a second red stain added. Gram-positive bacteria keep the first stain and appear violet when examined under the microscope, while Gram-negative forms lose the first but take up the second stain, thus appearing red. The difference in staining is because of the structure of the bacteria CELL walls.

grand mal *see* TONIC-CLONIC SEIZURE.

granulocyte *see* LEUCOCYTE.

granuloma *SEE* TOXOCARIASIS.

Graves' disease a disorder typified by THYROID GLAND overactivity (*see* HYPERTHY-ROIDISM), an enlargement of the gland and protruding EYES. It is caused by antibody production and is probably an autoimmune response (*see* AU-TOIMMUNE DISEASE). Patients commonly exhibit excess ME-TABOLISM (because thyroid hormones control the body's metabolism), nervousness, TREMOR, hyperactivity, rapid HEART rate, an intolerance of heat, breathlessness, and so on. Treatment may follow one of three courses: drugs to control the thyroid's production of hormones; surgery to remove part of the thyroid; or radioactive iodine therapy.

gravid a word meaning pregnant.

graze *see* ABRASION.

greenstick fracture *see* FRACTURE.

grey matter a part of the CENTRAL NERVOUS SYSTEM comprising the central part of the SPINAL CORD and the CEREBRAL CORTEX and outer layer of the CEREBELLUM in the brain. It is brown-grey in colour and is the coordination point between the nerves of the central nervous system. It is composed of nerve CELL bodies, DENDRITES, SYNAPSES, glial cells (supporting cells, *see* GLIA) and BLOOD VESSELS.

griseofulvin *see* RINGWORM.

groin the area where the ABDOMEN joins the THIGHS.

grommet a small tube with a lip at either end that is inserted into the eardrum to permit fluid to drain from the middle EAR. It is used in the treatment of secretory otitis media (GLUE EAR).

growing pains pains similar to RHEUMATISM that occur in the JOINTS and MUSCLES of children. They are usually insignificant and may be the result of FATIGUE or bad posture but must be dealt with in case the cause is more serious, e.g. BONE disease or RHEUMATIC FEVER.

growth hormone *or* **somatotrophin** *or* **FH** a HORMONE produced and stored by the anterior PITUITARY GLAND that controls PROTEIN synthesis in MUSCLES and the growth of long BONES in legs and arms. Low levels result in DWARFISM in children. Overproduction produces GIGANTISM in children, and ACROMEGALY in adolescents.

guanine *see* NUCLEOTIDE.

gullet another term for the OESOPHAGUS.

Guthrie test *see* PHENYLKETONURIA.

gynaecology the subdiscipline of medicine that deals with diseases of women, particularly concerning sexual and reproductive function and diseases of reproductive organs (*see* REPRODUCTIVE SYSTEM).

H

haem a compound containing iron, composed of a PIGMENT, known as a porphyrin, which confers colour. It combines with a PROTEIN called globin in the BLOOD to form HAEMO-GLOBIN.

haem- a prefix that indicates anything relating to BLOOD.

haemangioma a benign TU-MOUR of the BLOOD VESSELS. It may be visible on the SKIN as a type of naevus (BIRTH-MARK), e.g. a strawberry hae-mangioma.

haemarthrosis bleeding into a JOINT, which causes swelling and pain and may be the result of injury or disease. It can be a symptom of HAEMO-PHILIA.

haematemesis VOMITING of blood, which may occur for a number of different reasons. Common causes are PEPTIC ULCERS, or GASTRITIS, especially when this is caused by irritants or poisons such as alcohol. Also, blood may be swallowed and subsequently vomited as a result of a nose-bleed.

haematinic a substance that increases the amount of HAE-MOGLOBIN in the BLOOD, e.g. ferrous sulphate. Haematinic drugs are often prescribed during PREGNANCY.

haematocoele leakage of BLOOD into a cavity, causing a swelling. A haematocoele usually forms as a result of an injury caused by the rupture of BLOOD VESSELS and the leaking of blood into a natural body cavity.

haematology the scientific study of BLOOD and its diseases.

haematoma a collection of BLOOD forming a firm swelling—a bruise. It may occur as a result of injury, a clotting disorder of the blood or if blood vessels are diseased.

haematuria the presence of BLOOD in the URINE, which may have come from the KID-NEYS, URETERS, BLADDER or URETHRA. It indicates the presence of INFLAMMATION or disease, such as a stone in the bladder or kidney.

haemodialysis the use of an artificial KIDNEY to remove waste products from a person's

BLOOD using the principle of DIALYSIS. It is carried out when a person's kidneys have ceased to function and involves passing blood from an ARTERY into the dialyser on one side of a semipermeable membrane. On the other side of the membrane, a solution of ELECTROLYTES of similar composition to the blood is circulated. Water and waste products pass through the membrane into this solution while CELLS and PROTEINS are retained within the blood. The purified blood is then returned to the patient's body through a VEIN.

haemoglobin the respiratory substance contained within the red blood cells (ERYTHROCYTES), which contains a pigment responsible for the red colour of BLOOD. It consists of the pigment HAEM and the PROTEIN globin and is responsible for the transport of oxygen around the body. Oxygen is picked up in the LUNGS by arterial blood and transported to the TISSUES, where it is released. This (venous) blood is then returned to the lungs to repeat the process (*see* OXYHAEMOGLOBIN).

haemoglobinopathy any of a number of inherited diseases in which there is an abnormality in the formation of HAEMOGLOBIN. Examples are THALASSAEMIA and SICKLE CELL ANAEMIA.

haemoglobinuria the presence of HAEMOGLOBIN in the URINE caused by disintegration of red blood cells (ERYTHROCYTES), conferring a dark red or brown colour. It can sometimes result from strenuous exercise or after exposure to cold in some people. It is also caused by the ingestion of poisons, such as arsenic, and is a symptom of some INFECTIONS, particularly BLACKWATER FEVER.

haemolysis the destruction (LYSIS) of red blood cells (ERYTHROCYTES), which may result from INFECTION, poisoning or as an antibody response (*see* ANTIBODIES).

haemolytic disease of the newborn a serious disease affecting FOETUSes and newborn babies, which is characterized by HAEMOLYSIS, leading to ANAEMIA and severe JAUNDICE. In severe cases the foetus may die because of HEART FAILURE and OEDEMA (termed hydrops foetalis). The usual cause is incompatibility between the BLOOD of the mother and that of the foetus.

Generally the foetus has Rh-positive red blood cells (i.e. they contain the rhesus factor, *see* BLOOD GROUPS) while that of the mother is Rh negative. The mother produces ANTIBODIES to the Rh factor present in the foetal blood, and these are passed to the foetus in the PLACENTAl circulation. This then produces the haemolysis of the foetal red blood cells (ERYTHROCYTES). The incidence of the disease has been greatly reduced by giving a Rh-negative mother an injection of anti-D IMMUNOGLOBULIN, following the birth of a Rh-positive baby. This prevents the formation of the antibodies that would harm a subsequent baby and is also given to Rh-negative women following MISCARRIAGES or ABORTIONS.

haemophilia an hereditary disorder of blood COAGULATION in which the blood clots very slowly. It is a SEX-LINKED DISORDER, a recessive condition carried on the X-CHROMOSOME, and hence it affects males, with females being the carriers. There are two types of haemophilia because of a deficiency of either one of two COAGULATION FACTORS in the blood. Haemophilia A is caused by deficiency of FACTOR VIII and haemophilia B by deficiency of factor IX, called Christmas factor. The severity of the disease depends on how much less of the coagulation factor than normal is present in the blood. The symptoms of haemophilia are prolonged bleeding from wounds and also into JOINTS, MUSCLES and other TISSUES. In the past, the outlook for haemophiliacs was poor, with few surviving into adult life. Now, however, the condition can be treated by injections or TRANSFUSIONS of PLASMA containing the missing coagulation factor and, with care, a sufferer can hope to lead a much more normal life.

haemopoiesis formation of BLOOD cells (particularly ERYTHROCYTES, the red blood cells) and PLATELETS, which takes place in the BONE MARROW in adults but in a FOETUS occurs in the LIVER and SPLEEN.

haemoptysis *see* HAEMORRHAGE.

haemorrhage bleeding—a flow of blood from a ruptured BLOOD VESSEL, which may occur externally or internally.

A haemorrhage is classified according to the type of vessels involved: arterial H—bright red blood spurts in pulses from an ARTERY; venous H—a darker coloured steady flow from a VEIN; CAPILLARY H—blood oozes from torn capillaries at the surface of a wound.

In addition, a haemorrhage may be primary, reactionary or secondary. Primary haemorrhage occurs at the moment of injury. It is classed as reactionary when it occurs within 24 hours of an injury and results from a rise in BLOOD PRESSURE. A secondary haemorrhage occurs after a week or ten days as a result of infection (SEPSIS). Haemorrhage from a major artery is the most serious kind as large quantities of blood are quickly lost and death can occur within minutes. Haemorrhages at specific sites within the body are designated by special names, e.g. HAEMATURIA (from the KIDNEY or URINARY TRACT), haemoptysis (from the LUNGS) and HAEMATEMESIS (from the STOMACH).

haemorrhoids *or* **piles** varicose and inflamed VEINS around the lower end of the bowel, situated in the wall of the ANUS. They are classified as internal, external and mixed, depending on whether they appear beyond the anus. They are commonly caused by CONSTIPATION or DIARRHOEA, especially in middle and older age, and may be exacerbated by a sedentary lifestyle. They may also occur as a result of childbearing. Symptoms of haemorrhoids are bleeding and pain, and treatment is by means of creams, injections and suppositories (*see* SUPPOSITORY). Attention to diet (to treat constipation) and regular exercise are important, but in severe cases, surgery to remove them (haemorrhoidectomy) may be necessary.

haemostasis 1. the natural process to arrest bleeding (*see* HAEMORRHAGE), involving blood COAGULATION and contraction of a ruptured BLOOD VESSEL. **2.** One of a number of surgical procedures designed to arrest bleeding, such as the use of LIGATURES and DIATHERMY. A haemostatic substance stops or prevents haemorrhage, e.g. phytomenadone.

haemothorax a leakage of BLOOD into the PLEURAL CAV-

ITY of the chest, usually as a result of injury.

hair a threadlike outgrowth from the epidermis layer of the SKIN, which is a dead structure consisting of KERATINIC CELLS. The part above the skin has three layers: an outer CUTICLE, a CORTEX containing PIGMENT that confers colour, and an inner core. The lower end of the hair (root) lies within the skin and is expanded to form the bulb, which contains dividing cells that are continuously pushed upwards. This is contained within a tubular structure known as the hair follicle. A small erector pili muscle, attached to the hair follicle in the dermis of the skin, operates to erect the hair. *See also* TRICHORRHOEA.

halitosis the condition of having bad breath, which may arise for a number of reasons, including the type of food recently eaten, tooth decay, gum disease or INFECTIONS of the THROAT, NOSE and LUNGS.

hallucination a false perception of something that is not there, which may involve any of the senses of sight, hearing, smell, taste and touch. They may be caused by a mental illness, e.g. SCHIZOPHRENIA, or damage to the BRAIN, and also by certain drugs. They can also be a symptom of FEVER and deprivation, such as lack of sleep.

hallucinogen a substance or drug that causes HALLUCINATIONS, e.g. mescaline and lysergic acid diethylamide (LSD).

haloperidol a major TRANQUILLIZER, widely used in the treatment of PSYCHOSIS.

hammer toe *see* CORN.

hamstring any of four TENDONs at the back of the knee, which are attached to the hamstring MUSCLES and anchor these to the TIBIA and FIBULA. The hamstring muscles are responsible for the bending of the knee JOINT.

hand the extremity of the upper limb below the wrist, which has a highly complex structure and an 'opposable' thumb, which is unique to human beings. The human hand is highly developed in terms of structure, nervous supply and function, and communicates with a large area on the surface of the BRAIN. It is capable of performing numerous functions with a high degree of precision. When there is brain damage and PA-RALYSIS, the uses of the hand tend to be lost earlier and more permanently compared to movements in the leg and face. The skeletal structure of the hand consists of eight small carpal BONES in the wrist (see CARPUS), five META-CARPAL BONES in the region of the palm and three PHA-LANGES in each finger.

haploid the description of a CELL nucleus or organism with half the normal number of CHROMOSOMES. This is the case with GAMETES and is important at FERTILIZATION to ensure that the diploid chromosome number is restored.

hare lip a CONGENITAL developmental deformity that results in the presence of a cleft in the upper lip. It is brought about by a failure in the fusion of three blocks of embryonic TISSUE and is often associated with a CLEFT PAL-ATE. It is now routinely corrected by surgery.

Hartmann's solution a solution of salts that is given to replace lost fluid in cases of DEHYDRATION, ACIDOSIS and after HAEMORRHAGE while awaiting cross-matched blood for transfusion.

Haversian canal one of numerous small channels or cylindrical tubes that run through compact BONE (the outer layer of bones) and contain BLOOD VESSELS and NERVES. They form part of the Haversian system, consisting of the canals surrounded by concentric, alternate layers of bone lamellae (thin plates) and lacunae (spaces) that house bone CELLS. These form cylindrical units in the compact bone and the lacunae are linked up by minute channels called canaliculi.

hay fever an allergic reaction to pollen, e.g. that of grasses, trees and many other plants, which affects numerous individuals. The symptoms are a blocked and runny nose, sneezing and watering eyes because of the release of HISTAMINE. Treatment is by means of AN-TIHISTAMINE drugs and, if the ALLERGEN can be identified, DESENSITIZATION may be successful. This involves injecting or exposing the individual to controlled and gradually increasing doses of the allergen until ANTIBODIES are built up.

HCG see CHORIONIC GONADO-TROPHIC HORMONE; HUMAN CHORIONIC GONADOTROPHIN.

headache pain felt within the head, which is thought to be caused by dilation of intracranial arteries (*see* ARTERY) or pressure on them. Common causes are stress, tiredness or FEVER accompanying an INFECTION, such as a cold, an excess of close work involving the eyes, DYSPEPSIA, rheumatic diseases, high BLOOD PRESSURE and URAEMIA. Headache may indicate the presence of a disease or disorder in the BRAIN, e.g. an infection such as MENINGITIS, TUMOUR or ANEURYSM, and also occurs as a result of injury and CONCUSSION. *See also* MIGRAINE.

hearing loss *see* DEAFNESS.

heart the hollow, muscular ORGAN that acts as a pump and is responsible for the CIRCULATION OF THE BLOOD. The heart is cone-shaped, with the point downwards, and is situated between the LUNGS, slightly to the left of the midline. The heart projects forwards and lies beneath the fifth rib. The wall consists mainly of CARDIAC MUSCLE, lined on the inside by a MEMBRANE known as the ENDOCARDIUM. An external membrane, known as the PERICARDIUM, surrounds the heart. A SEPTUM divides the heart into right and left halves, each of which is further divided into an upper chamber, known as an ATRIUM, and a lower one, called a VENTRICLE. Four valves control the direction of blood flow at each outlet, comprising the aortic, pulmonary, tricuspid and mitral (bicuspid). These valves prevent back flow once the blood has been forced from one chamber into the next.

heart attack *see* MYOCARDIAL INFARCTION.

heart block a condition describing a failure in the conduction of electrical impulses from the natural PACEMAKER (the SINOATRIAL NODE) through the HEART, which can lead to slowing of the pumping action. There are three types:

1. In first degree (partial or incomplete) heart block, there is a delay in conduction between atria (*see* ATRIUM) and VENTRICLES, but this does not cause slowing.

2. In second degree heart block, there is intermittent slowing because not all the impulses are conducted between atria and ventricles.

3. In third degree (or complete)

heart block, there is no electrical conduction, the heartbeats are slow, and the ventricles beat at their own intrinsic slow rhythm. This causes blackouts and can lead to HEART FAILURE.

Heart block is more common in elderly people where degenerative changes have occurred. It may, however, also be CONGENITAL or may result from other forms of heart disease, such as MYOCARDITIS, CORONARY THROMBOSIS, CARDIOMYOPATHY and VALVE DISEASE. For second and third degree heart block, treatment involves use of an artificial pacemaker.

heartburn a burning pain or discomfort felt in the region of the heart, sometimes radiating to the back and often rising upwards to the throat. It is caused by REGURGITATION of the STOMACH contents (gastro-oesophageal reflux), the burning being caused by the acid in GASTRIC JUICE or by OESOPHAGITIS. It may be aggravated by eating large meals, fatty foods and alcohol and the discomfort may be increased when bending over or lying flat. It is relieved by taking ANTACID tablets or alkaline substances such as sodium bicarbonate. Heartburn may also be a symptom of hiatus HERNIA.

heart failure the inability of the HEART to sustain effective CIRCULATION OF THE BLOOD. It is usually the result of weakness of the MYOCARDIUM or inefficiency in the rhythmical action of the heart (*see* SINOATRIAL NODE). Acute heart failure is caused most frequently by CORONARY THROMBOSIS. Chronic heart failure is a more gradual degenerative condition and is secondary to other diseases, such as ARTERIOSCLEROSIS or respiratory conditions such as EMPHYSEMA and BRONCHITIS.

heat exhaustion exhaustion and collapse as a result of overheating of the body and loss of fluid following unaccustomed or prolonged exposure to excessive heat. It is more common in hot climates and results from excessive sweating, leading to loss of fluids and salts and disturbance of the ELECTROLYTE balance in body fluids. In the mildest form, which is heat collapse, BLOOD PRESSURE and PULSE rate fall, accompanied by FATIGUE and lightheadedness, and there may be muscular CRAMPS. Treatment involves taking a salt solution, by mouth or given INTRAVENOUSLY, and avoidance by gradual acclimatization to the heat, especially if hard physical work is to be carried out.

heat rash *see* PRICKLY HEAT.

heat stroke *or* **heat hyperpyrexia** a severe condition following exposure of the body to excessive heat, characterized by a rise in temperature and failure of sweating and TEMPERATURE regulation. Untreated, it leads to loss of consciousness, followed by COMA and death, which can occur rapidly. The body must be cooled by sponging and salt solutions given either by mouth or INTRAVENOUSLY.

heel the part of the foot behind the ankle JOINT, formed by the calcaneus or heel BONE.

Heimlich's manoeuvre a procedure to dislodge a foreign body that is blocking the LARYNX and causing CHOKING. The person carrying out the procedure encircles the patient from behind with his or her arms. A fist is made with one hand slightly above the patient's navel and below the ribs. With the free hand, the fist is thrust firmly into the ABDOMEN with a rapid upward push that may need to be repeated several times. As a result of this, the foreign particle is expelled through or into the patient's mouth.

helicobacter pylori a bacterium (*see* BACTERIA) identified as a cause of a large percentage of PEPTIC ULCERS, particularly those of the DUODENUM (*see* DUODENAL ULCER). A urea breath test will identify whether the bacterium is present in the stomach. Infection with *helicobacter pylori* can be treated successfully with ANTIBIOTIC therapy.

hemiplegia *see* PARALYSIS.

Henle's loop *see* KIDNEY.

heparin an ANTICOAGULANT substance naturally present in the body and produced by LIVER and some white blood cells (LEUCOCYTES) and in some other sites. It acts by inhibiting and neutralizing the action of the ENZYME thrombin (*see* BLOOD COAGULATION) and is a polysaccharide (CARBOHYDRATE) containing sulphur and amino groups. It is used medically to prevent blood coagulation in patients with THROMBOSIS and also in blood collected for sampling.

hepatectomy surgical removal of the whole or part of the LIVER.

hepatic the term used to describe the LIVER, e.g. the hepatic VEIN, which drains BLOOD from the liver to the inferior VENA CAVA.

hepatitis INFLAMMATION of the LIVER as a result of the presence of toxic substances or INFECTION caused by VIRUSes. Acute hepatitis produces abdominal pain, JAUNDICE, itching, NAUSEA and FEVER. Chronic hepatitis has a similar range of symptoms, which may persist for years and lead eventually to CIRRHOSIS. Alcohol abuse is a common cause of hepatitis. Hepatitis may also result as a SIDE EFFECT from a number of drug treatments or from overdose. Many viral infections can cause hepatitis, such as HIV and GLANDULAR FEVER.

The so-called hepatic viruses are designated A, B, C, D, and E. Hepatitis A causes infectious hepatitis (epidemic hepatitis) and is transmitted by eating food contaminated by a person who has the virus, and it is common in conditions of poor hygiene and sanitation. Hepatitis E acts in a similar way, and both produce symptoms of FEVER, sickness and JAUNDICE. Recovery is usually complete unless the symptoms are acute, and IMMUNITY from a future attack is conferred.

Serum hepatitis is caused by viruses B, C and D, the route of infection being BLOOD or blood products. Serum hepatitis is most common where infected needles have been used among drug addicts. The infection may also be passed on by tattooing needles and also through sexual intercourse with an infected individual. The mortality rate is 5–20 per cent, but many patients make a gradual recovery from the illness, which is characterized by FEVER, chills, fatigue, headaches and jaundice. All these viruses may persist in the blood for a long time and if B is involved, the condition is known as chronic type B hepatitis. Vaccines are available for hepatitis A and hepatitis B.

hepatoma a malignant TUMOUR of the LIVER, which is rare in Western countries except among those with CIRRHOSIS. It is common in parts of the Far East and Africa, and a suspected cause is the afla-toxin, or poison, produced by a FUNGUS that contaminates stored peanuts and cereals. The CANCER often produces ALPHA FETOPROTEIN, which is detectable in the blood and is an indicator of the presence of the malignancy.

heredity the principle applied to the passing on of all bodily characteristics from parents to offspring. *See* GENETICS.

hermaphrodite *or* **intersex** an individual possessing both male and female sex organs (*see* REPRODUCTIVE SYSTEM) or in whom ovarian and tes-ticular cells are present in the GONADS (ovotestis). This con-dition is extremely rare and the individual is usually ster-ile with reduced SECONDARY SEXUAL CHARACTERISTICS.

hernia the protrusion of a part or whole of an ORGAN from out of its normal position within the body cavity. Most commonly, a hernia involves part of the INTESTINE. A CON-GENITAL hernia is present at birth, a common one being an umbilical hernia in which ab-dominal organs protrude into the UMBILICAL CORD. This is the result of a failure during development of the FOETUS and can be corrected by sur-gery. An acquired hernia occurs after birth, a com-mon example being an ingui-nal hernia, in which part of the large INTESTINE bulges through a weak part of the ab-dominal wall (known as the inguinal canal). Another com-mon type is a hiatus hernia, in which the STOMACH passes through the hiatus (a hole al-lowing passage of the OESOPH-AGUS), from the ABDOMEN into the chest cavity. A reducible hernia is freely movable and can be returned by manipula-tion into its rightful place. An irreducible hernia describes the opposite situation, and an incarcerated hernia is one that has become swollen and fixed in its position. An obstructed hernia is one involving the large intestine. The contents of the hernia are unable to pass farther down and are held up and obstructed.

The most dangerous situa-tion is a strangulated hernia, in which the BLOOD supply has been cut off because of the protrusion itself. This becomes painful and eventually gan-grenous (*see* GANGRENE) and requires immediate surgery. Strenuous physical activity can lead to a hernia, which usually develops gradually. Although short-term measures are employed to control a hernia or reduce its size, the usual treatment is by means of surgery to return and retain the protrusion in its proper pace.

hernioplasty the surgical operation to repair a HERNIA.

heroin *or* **diamorphine hydrochloride** a white crystalline powder that is derived from MORPHINE. It is a very potent ANALGESIC but is highly addictive and dangerous.

herpes infectious INFLAMMATION of the SKIN and MUCOUS MEMBRANES, characterized by the development of small BLISTERS and caused by a number of different *Herpes* VIRUSes. The *Herpes simplex* virus, types I and II, are the cause of cold sores, which usually affect the lips, mouth and face. The virus is usually acquired in childhood and, once present, persists for life. It can be contracted without causing any symptoms but tends to flare up from time to time, producing the cold sores.

Herpes simplex is also the cause of GENITAL herpes, in which the blisters affect the genital region. Herpes zoster,

or shingles, is produced by a virus that causes CHICKENPOX in children. The virus affects the course of a NERVE, producing severe pain and small yellowish blisters on the skin. Often the affected areas are the ABDOMEN, back, face and chest, and although the disease subsides after about three weeks, the blisters form SCABS that eventually drop off and the pain can persist for months. This is known as post-herpetic NEURALGIA, and pain-relieving drugs are needed to help relieve the condition. Other Herpes viruses are the cytomegalovirus and EPSTEIN-BARR virus.

hiatus hernia *see* HERNIA.

hindbrain the part of the BRAIN that consists of the MEDULLA OBLONGATA, PONS and CEREBELLUM.

hip the region on either side of the body where the FEMUR (thigh bone) articulates with the pelvis.

hip girdle *see* PELVIC GIRDLE.

hip joint a 'ball and socket' JOINT made up of the head of the FEMUR, which rests inside a deep, cup-shaped cavity (the acetabulum) in the hip BONE. The hip bone (or innominate bone) is itself made up of three fused bones: the PUBIS,

ISCHIUM and ILIUM, which form part of the PELVIS.

hirsutism the excess growth of hair. The term is most commonly used to refer to the growth of dark, coarse HAIR on the body of a female, on the face, chest, ABDOMEN and upper back. This may be because of a greater sensitivity of hair FOLLICLES to a normal level of male hormones (ANDROGENS), producing hair of a more masculine type. Or there may be an excessive production of androgens responsible for the growth of the hair. The condition may be the result of an underlying disorder, such as an ADRENAL tumour, or POLYCYSTIC OVARY SYNDROME, but there is a wide normal variation in the amount of body hair present in individuals.

histamine a substance, derived from histidine, an AMINO ACID. It is widely found throughout all the body TISSUES and is responsible for the dilation of BLOOD VESSELS (arterioles and capillaries) and the contraction of smooth MUSCLE, including that of the BRONCHI of the lungs. Histamine is released in great quantities in allergic conditions and ANAPHYLAXIS (*see* ALLERGY).

histidine *see* ESSENTIAL AMINO ACID and HISTAMINE.

histocompatible *see* HLA ANTIGENS.

histology the scientific study of TISSUES, involving such techniques as light and electron microscopy and the use of dyes and stains.

HIV the human immunodeficiency virus responsible for the condition known as AIDS. The virus affects and destroys a group of LYMPHOCYTES (T-lymphocytes), which are part of the body's natural defences (the IMMUNE system). Therapy using a combination of ANTIRETROVIRAL drugs has proved effective in helping to prevent the onset of illness in those who have been found to be HIV positive.

hives a common name for URTICARIA, or nettle rash.

HLA antigens these are the human LEUCOCYTE antigens. There are four GENES responsible for their production (A, B, C, D), which are located on CHROMOSOME 6, which makes up the HLA system. One gene or set of genes is inherited from each parent and produce the HLA ANTIGENS on the surfaces of CELLS throughout the body. These antigens are the means by which the immune system recognizes 'self' and rejects 'non-self', and this is very important in organ TRANSPLANTATION. The closer the match of HLAs between DONOR and recipient, the greater the chances of success. If two individuals share identical HLA types, they are described as histocompatible.

Hodgkin's disease *or* **Hodgkin's lymphoma** a malignant disease of unknown cause affecting the LYMPHATIC SYSTEM, in which there is a gradual and increasing enlargement of lymph glands and nodes in the body. If untreated, the disease progresses from localized involvement to more widespread involvement of lymph nodes around the body and can involve the BONE MARROW and ORGANS such as the LUNGS or LIVER. The accompanying symptoms include swollen lymph nodes, loss of weight, sweating (particularly night sweats), itching, fatigue, ANAEMIA and a characteristic type of FEVER (known as Pel-Ebstein fever). The person becomes gradually weaker and the glands may attain a very large size. Treatment involves RADIATION THERAPY and CHEMOTHERAPY. The outlook is good, especially if the disease is detected early.

holistic relating to 'wholeness'. A holistic approach to patient care does not just concentrate on the physical disease or condition but takes note of all the factors in that person's life.

homoeopathy *or* **homeopathy** a system of medicine devised by Samuel Hahnemann (1755–1843), which is part of ALTERNATIVE MEDICINE in the UK. It is based on the premise that 'like cures like', and so a patient is given minute quantities of drugs that can, in themselves, produce symptoms of the disease or malady being treated. Practitioners assess and treat their patients using a HOLISTIC approach.

homozygous *see* THALASSAEMIA.

hormone a chemical substance that is naturally produced by the body and acts as a messenger. A hormone is produced by CELLS or GLANDS in one part of the body and passes into the bloodstream. When it reaches another specific site, its 'target ORGAN', it causes a reaction there, modifying the structure or function of cells, perhaps by causing the release of another hormone. Hormones are secreted by the ENDOCRINE GLANDS, and examples are the sex hormones, e.g. TESTOSTERONE, secreted by the testes (*see* TESTICLE), and oestradiol and PROGESTERONE, secreted by the ovaries (*see* OVARY).

hormone replacement therapy (HRT) *see* MENO-PAUSE.

housemaid's knee *or* **bursitis** a painful condition resulting from a swelling of the BURSA (fluid-filled fibrous sac) in front of the kneecap.

HPV the human papilloma viruses are a group of more than 70 different types of virus, some of which can be transmitted through sexual intercourse. Some HPV viruses can cause genital warts but these are not associated with cervical cancer. Some types of HPV, however, are linked to cervical cancer and they are called high risk because just about all cervical cancers are positive for high risk HPV. Not all women infected with high risk HPVs go on to develop cervical cancer

so there are other factors involved, notably smoking. Most HPV infections do not cause any symptoms and disappear without treatment but women who test positive for a high risk strain may need treatment for abnormal cervical smears. Regular cervical smears will pick up abnormal cervical cells and these can be removed before they become cervical cancers. *See also* CERVICAL CANCER.

HRT *see* MENOPAUSE.

human chorionic gonadotrophin (HCG) a hormone secreted by the PLACENTA during early PREGNANCY, under the influence of which the CORPUS LUTEUM of the OVARY produces OESTROGEN, PROGESTERONE and relaxin. These are essential for the maintenance of pregnancy. Pregnancy can be detected early on by a laboratory procedure that tests for the presence of human chorionic gonadotrophin in the URINE. *See also* CHORIONIC GONADOTROPHIC HORMONE.

human immunodeficiency virus *see* HIV.

human T-cell lymphocytotrophic virus (HTLV) one of a group of viruses, including the HIV virus that causes AIDS (HTLV III), which are responsible for LYMPHOMAS.

humerus the BONE of the upper arm that articulates with the shoulder blade (SCAPULA) of the PECTORAL GIRDLE and the ULNA and RADIUS at the elbow.

humour a natural fluid in the body, the best-known examples being the aqueous and vitreous humours of the EYE.

Huntington's chorea *see* **chorea**.

hyaline membrane disease *see* RESPIRATORY DISTRESS SYNDROME.

hydrocephalus *or* **water on the brain** an abnormal collection of CEREBROSPINAL FLUID within the SKULL that causes, in babies and children, a great increase in the size of the head. Hydrocephalus results either from an excessive production of fluid or from a defect in the mechanism for its reabsorption or from a blockage in its circulation. The cause may be CONGENITAL, and it often accompanies SPINA BIFIDA in babies, or infection (MENINGITIS) or the presence of a TUMOUR. Hydrocephalus causes pressure on the BRAIN,

with drowsiness, irritability and mental subnormality in children.

Treatment involves surgery to redirect the fluid but is not always successful. About 50 per cent of children survive if the progress of the condition is halted, and one-third of these go on to enjoy a normal life with little or no physical or mental impairment.

hydrocortisone a STEROID glucocorticoid HORMONE produced and released by the CORTEX of the ADRENAL GLANDS (a CORTICOSTEROID). It is closely related to CORTISONE, being released in response to stress and playing a significant part in the METABOLISM of CARBOHYDRATES. Medically it has a number of uses, especially in the treatment of ADDISON'S DISEASE, inflammatory, allergic and rheumatic conditions, e.g. ECZEMA and RHEUMATOID ARTHRITIS. Hydrocortisone is contained in ointments in creams or given by mouth or injection, depending on the condition under treatment. Prolonged use may cause SIDE EFFECTS, including PEPTIC ULCERS, stunting of growth in children, CUSHING'S SYN-

DROME and damage to BONE and MUSCLE tissue.

hydrophobia *see* RABIES.

hydrops foetalis *see* HAEMO-LYTIC DISEASE OF THE NEW-BORN.

hydroxocobalamin a cobalt-containing substance (cobala-min) used in the treatment of vitamin B12 deficiencies, such as pernicious ANAEMIA.

hymen a thin MEMBRANE that covers the lower end of the VAGINA at birth and usually tears to some extent before a girl reaches PUBERTY.

hyperadrenalism a condition in which the ADRENAL GLANDS are overactive, producing the symptoms of CUSHING'S SYNDROME.

hyperalgesia an extreme sensitivity to pain.

hyperemesis VOMITING to excess. Hyperemesis gravidarum is excessive vomiting during PREGNANCY, which often begins as an exaggerated form of MORNING SICKNESS. Medical intervention is imperative in this condition to avoid complications.

hyperglycaemia the presence of excess sugar (glucose) in the BLOOD, as in DIABETES MELLITUS, caused by insufficient INSULIN to cope with CARBOHYDRATE intake. The condition can lead to a diabetic COMA.

hyperlipidaemia *or* **hyperlipaemia** the presence of an excess concentration of fat in the BLOOD. An excess of CHOLESTEROL in the blood may lead to CORONARY ARTERY DISEASE and ATHEROMA. An excess of TRIGLYCERIDES may lead to PANCREATITIS.

hyperparathyroidism *see* PARATHYROIDECTOMY.

hyperplasia increased growth in size and number of the normal CELLS of a TISSUE so that the affected part enlarges, e. g. the BREASTS during PREGNANCY. *Compare* HYPERTROPHY and NEOPLASM.

hyper-resonance *see* RESONANCE.

hypersensitivity abnormal allergic response to an ANTIGEN to which the person has previously been exposed. Hypersensitive responses vary from quite mild, such as HAY FEVER, to very severe and life-threatening, e.g. ANAPHYLACTIC SHOCK. (*See* ALLERGY.)

hypertension high BLOOD PRESSURE (in the arteries). ESSENTIAL HYPERTENSION is hypertension where the cause is uncertain, although diet and lifestyle factors may play a part. Secondary hypertension may be the result of e.g. KIDNEY disease or ENDOCRINE diseases. MALIGNANT hypertension will prove fatal if not treated. It may be a condition in itself or an end stage of essential hypertension. It tends to occur in a younger age group, and there is high diastolic blood pressure (*see* DIASTOLE) and kidney failure. ARTERIOSCLEROSIS is a complication of, and often associated with, hypertension. Other complications include cerebral HAEMORRHAGE, HEART FAILURE and kidney failure. Previously a rapidly fatal condition, antihypertensive drugs have revolutionized treatment and given sufferers a near-normal life. *See also* PULMONARY HYPERTENSION.

hyperthermia 1. extremely high and abnormal body TEMPERATURE, i.e. a FEVER. **2.** a method of treatment of certain diseases by artificially inducing a state of FEVER, achieved by a variety of techniques.

hyperthyroidism excessive activity of the THYROID GLAND—an overactive thyroid. It may be caused by increased growth of the gland, by the presence of a TUMOUR or by GRAVES' DISEASE. See also HYPOTHYROIDISM.

hypertonicity *see* SPASTICITY.

hypertrophy an increase in the size of an ORGAN because of enlargement of its CELLS (rather than in their number), often in response to a greater demand for work. An example is the increase in size of the remaining KIDNEY if the other is removed for some reason. *Compare* HYPERPLASIA.

hyperventilation breathing at an abnormally rapid rate when at rest, which may be a response to stress and, if not checked, results in unconsciousness because the concentration of carbon dioxide in the BLOOD falls. If the carbon dioxide level in the blood is abnormally high, because of impaired gas exchange in the LUNGS, e.g. in pulmonary OEDEMA and PNEUMONIA, hyperventilation may occur. (*See also* HYPOVENTILATION.)

hypnosis a state of altered attention, resembling sleep, in which the mind is more receptive to recall of memories of past events and to suggestion. The person who induces this state in another is known as a hypnotist. One of the ways of inducing hypnosis is to ask the patient to fix his or her eyes on a given point or source of light and then rhythmically to repeat soothing words in a low voice. Some people appear to be more easily hypnotized than others, and there are three merging levels of hypnosis, light, medium and deep. Hypnosis is a useful form of treatment in PSYCHIATRY and also in pain relief, e.g. during LABOUR and dental repair. It is also used in the treatment of ASTHMA and alcoholism.

hypnotic a substance or drug that induces sleep, e.g. BARBITURATES and chloral hydrate.

hypochondria an abnormal preoccupation by an individual with the state of his or her health. In its severest form, the person wrongly believes that he or she is suffering from a number of illnesses and is extremely anxious and depressed. Treatment is by means of PSYCHOTHERAPY and ANTIDEPRESSANT drugs, but the condition tends to be difficult to cure.

hypodermic literally meaning 'beneath the SKIN', the term usually used in reference to INJECTIONS given by means of a hypodermic syringe.

hypoglycaemia a lack of sugar in the blood, which occurs in starvation and also with DIABETES MELLITUS when too much INSULIN has been given and insufficient CARBOHYDRATES have been eaten. The symptoms include weakness, sweating, light-headedness and tremors, and can rapidly lead to COMA. The symptoms are alleviated by taking in glucose, either by mouth or by injection in the case of hypoglycaemic coma.

hypoparathyroidism or **tetany** see PARATHYROID GLAND.

hypophysis see PITUITARY GLAND.

hypoplasia underdevelopment of a TISSUE or ORGAN, such as can occur in the teeth as a result of illness or starvation (dental hypoplasia). It is marked by lines across the teeth of brown enamel.

hypothalamus an area of the FOREBRAIN in the floor of the third VENTRICLE, having the THALAMUS above and PITUITARY GLAND below. It contains centres controlling vital processes, e.g. fat and carbohydrate METABOLISM, thirst and water regulation, hunger and eating, thermal regulation and sexual function. It also plays a part in the emotions and in the regulation of sleep. It controls the SYMPATHETIC and PARASYMPATHETIC NERVOUS SYSTEMS and secretions from the pituitary gland.

hypothermia 1. the bodily state when the core TEMPERATURE falls below 35°C (95°F) as a result of prolonged exposure to cold. At first, shivering occurs and the HEART works harder to increase the flow of blood around the body. However, eventually shivering ceases and, with increasing chilling, the function of the body ORGANS becomes disturbed and cardiac output falls. The TISSUES require less oxygen as their functions start to fail, but eventually the heart is unable to supply even this reduced demand. The symptoms of hypothermia are fatigue and confusion followed by unconsciousness and death. The elderly are particularly at risk. **2.** A state of artificial hypothermia is occasionally induced during surgery to reduce the oxygen requirements of the tissues and enable the CIRCULATION to be briefly halted.

hypothyroidism under activity of the thyroid gland—an underactive thyroid. It occurs when the thyroid gland does not produce enough of the thyroid hormone, thyroxine. Hypothyroidism slows down the body's functions. The main symptoms are tiredness, weight gain, aches and pains, mental slowing and depression. It is more common in adult women. The main cause of hypothyroidism is autoimmune thyroidism (*see* AUTOIMMUNE DISEASE). Once diagnosed, the treatment is to take thyroxine tablets each day to replace the thyroxine that is not being produced by the thyroid gland. (See also MYXOEDEMA)

hypoventilation an abnormally slow rate of shallow breathing that may result from injury or the effects of DRUGS on the respiratory centre in the BRAIN. The effect is to increase the amount of carbon dioxide in the BLOOD and lessen that of oxygen. Eventually this leads to death from a lack of oxygen supply to CELLS and TISSUES.

hysterectomy the surgical removal of the UTERUS, either by means of an abdominal incision or through the VAGINA. It is may be carried out if FI-BROIDS are present or if the uterus is cancerous, and also if there is excessive bleeding or uterine PROLAPSE. A hysterectomy may also be necessary in some cases of CANCER of the OVARY or CERVIX. The extent of the surgery varies on the condition being treated. A subtotal hysterectomy involves excision of the FUNDUS of the uterus, leaving the cervix intact. A total hysterectomy, or panhysterectomy, involves excision of the uterus including the cervix. In a radical hysterectomy, the uterus, cervix and associated LYMPH NODES are removed, along with CONNECTIVE TISSUE adjacent to the uterus. In some cases, the ovaries and FALLOPIAN TUBES are also removed. *See* WERTHEIM'S HYSTERECTOMY.

hysteria a type of NEUROSIS that is difficult to define and in which a range of symptoms may occur. These include PARALYSIS, seizures and spasms of LIMBS, swelling of JOINTS, mental disorders and AMNESIA. The person is vulnerable to suggestion. Two types are recognized: conversion hysteria, which is characterized by physical symptoms; and disso-

ciative hysteria, in which marked mental changes occur. Mass hysteria affects a group, especially those gathered together under conditions of emotional excitement. A number of people may suffer from giddiness, VOMITING and FAINTING, which run through the whole crowd. Recovery occurs when those affected are separated from the others under calmer conditions. Treatment for hysteria is by means of PSYCHOTHERAPY, especially involving suggestion.

I

IBS *see* IRRITABLE BOWEL SYNDROME.

ibuprofen a NON-STEROIDAL ANTI-INFLAMMATORY DRUG, useful in the treatment of a number of painful conditions, including ARTHRITIS. It acts as an ANALGESIC and can also reduce FEVER.

ichthyosis a generally hereditary SKIN condition in which the skin is very dry and looks cracked, producing a resemblance to fish scales. There is no particular medication to take but vitamin A may help. The treatment is thus external and involves special baths and the application of ointments.

ICSH *see* GONADOTROPHINS.

identical twins *see* MONOZYGOTIC TWINS.

idiopathic a term to describe a disease of unknown cause.

idiot savant someone who, although suffering severe mental RETARDATION, is able to perform unusual and often astonishing mental feats or who exhibits remarkable musical ability. Examples are feats of memory, complex mental mathematical manipulations or the ability to memorize previously unheard music and then play it accurately.

ileectomy removal by surgery of all or part of the ILEUM.

ileitis INFLAMMATION of the ILEUM, with pain, bowel irregularity and loss of weight. The intestinal wall may become thickened, and if the tract becomes blocked, surgery is required immediately. The specific cause is not known, but it may occur in association with TUBERCULOSIS, bacterial INFECTION (by *Yersinia enterocolitica*), CROHN'S DISEASE and TYPHOID.

ileo-anal pouch a reservoir or pouch which is constructed surgically from the ILEUM, and is then joined to the ANUS. The procedure may be carried out as an alternative to a permanent ILEOSTOMY when the COLON and RECTUM have been removed because of FAMILIAL ADENOMATOUS POLYPOSIS or ULCERATIVE COLITIS. It is generally done in two stages. In the first operation, the colon and rectum are removed and the ileo-anal pouch is formed. A temporary (loop) ileostomy is created above the pouch to divert waste matter and allow for healing. Some weeks later, the ileostomy is closed, allowing for body waste to pass into the pouch and out through the anus.

ileostomy a surgical procedure in which an opening is made in the abdominal wall to which the ILEUM is joined. This creates a STOMA which functions as an artificial ANUS, through which the waste contents of the INTESTINES are collected in a special bag. An ileostomy may be temporary, to allow the COLON to heal after surgery, injury or COLITIS, in which case the colon will be rejoined after some time in a second operation. A permanent ileostomy may be necessary for a number of reasons, including

CANCER of the colon and rectum, CROHN'S DISEASE, ULCERATIVE COLITIS and trauma. A loop ileostomy, which is usually temporary, is formed when a loop of ileum is brought through the abdominal wall, cut and sewn into place as a stoma. An end ileostomy is created when the colon and rectum have been removed (proctocolectomy). The end of the ileum is then brought through the abdominal wall. *See also* ILEO-ANAL POUCH.

ileum the lower part of the small INTESTINE between the JEJUNUM and the CAECUM.

ileus an obstruction of the INTESTINE (often the ILEUM), which may be mechanical, as a result of worms or a gallstone from the GALL BLADDER, or because of loss of the natural movement of the INTESTINES (peristalsis). This latter condition may be caused by surgery, injury to the SPINAL COLUMN or PERITONITIS.

iliac arteries those arteries (*see* ARTERY) that supply blood to the lower limbs and pelvic region.

ilium (*pl* **ilia**) the largest of the BONES that form each half of the PELVIC GIRDLE. It has a flattened wing-like part fastening it to the SACRUM by means of LIGAMENTS.

immune the term used to mean being protected against an INFECTION by the presence of ANTIBODIES specific to the organism concerned.

immune gamma globulin *see* **gamma globulin**.

immunity the way in which the body resists INFECTION because of the presence of ANTIBODIES and white blood cells (LEUCOCYTES). Antibodies are generated in response to the presence of ANTIGENS of a disease. There are several types of immunity: active immunity is when the body produces antibodies and continues to be able to do so during the course of a disease, whether occurring naturally (also called acquired immunity) or by deliberate stimulation. Passive immunity is short-lived and is provided by the INJECTION of ready-made antibodies from someone who is already immune.

immunization the production of IMMUNITY to disease by artificial means. Injection of an ANTISERUM will produce temporary passive immunity, while active immunity is produced by making the body generate its own ANTIBODIES. This is done by the use of treated ANTIGENS (VACCINATION or INOCULATION). VACCINE is used for immunization, and it may be derived from live BACTERIA or VIRUSES or dead organisms or their products.

immunoglobulin any of a group of high molecular weight PROTEINS that act as ANTIBODIES and are present in SERUM and secretions. Designated Ig, there are five groups, each with different functions identified by a particular letter. Immunoglobulin A (Ig A) is the most common and occurs in all secretions of the body. It is the main antibody in the MUCOUS MEMBRANE of the INTESTINES, BRONCHI, saliva and tears. It defends the body against microorganisms by combining with a PROTEIN in the MUCOSA. Ig D is found in the SERUM in small amounts but increases during allergic reaction. Ig E is found primarily in the LUNGS, SKIN and mucous membrane cells and is an anaphylactic antibody (*see* ANAPHYLAXIS). Ig G is synthesized to combat BACTERIA and VIRUSES in the body. Ig M, or macroglobulin, has a very high molecular weight (about five or six times that of the others) and is the first produced by the body when ANTIGENS occur. It is also the main antibody in BLOOD GROUP incompatibilities.

immunology the study of IMMUNITY, the immune system of the body and all aspects of the body's defence mechanisms.

immunosuppression the use of drugs (immunosuppressives) that affect the body's IMMUNE system and lower its resistance to disease. These drugs are used to maintain the survival of the transplanted ORGANS in transplant surgery (*see* TRANSPLANTATION) and to treat AUTOIMMUNE DISEASES. The condition may also be produced as a side effect, e.g. after CHEMOTHERAPY treatment for CANCER. In all instances, there is an increased risk of INFECTION.

immunotherapy the largely experimental technique of developing the body's IMMUNITY to a disease by administering drugs or gradually increasing doses of the appropriate ALLERGENS, thereby modifying the immune response. The most widely studied disease is CANCER, where this forms an auxiliary treatment to drug therapy.

impacted a descriptive term for things being locked or wedged together or stuck in position. For example, a wisdom TOOTH is impacted when it cannot erupt normally because of other TISSUEs blocking it.

impetigo a staphylococcal (*see* STAPHYLOCOCCUS)and infectious SKIN disease found primarily in children. It spreads quickly over the body, starting as a red patch that forms pustules that join to create crusted yellowish sores. It is easily spread by contact or through towels, etc, and must be treated quickly otherwise it may continue to affect an individual for months. Treatment with ANTIBIOTICS is usually effective.

implant a drug, TISSUE or artificial object inserted or grafted into the SKIN or other ORGAN. Drugs are often inserted into the skin for controlled release (*see also* DOSAGE), and in RADIOTHERAPY treatment of PROSTATE TUMOURS or head/neck CANCERS can include embedding a capsule of radioactive material in the tissue. A surgical implant includes a tissue GRAFT (e.g. a BLOOD VESSEL),

insertion of a PACEMAKER or a hip PROSTHESIS.

implantation 1. the placing of an IMPLANT. **2.** the attachment of the BLASTOCYST to the UTERUS wall during the very early stages of EMBRYO development.

impotence the condition when a man is unable to have sexual intercourse because of lack of penile ERECTION or, less commonly, to ejaculate (*see* EJACULATION) having gained an erection. The cause may be organic and the result of a condition or disease (DIABETES MELLITUS, endocrine gland disorder) or, more commonly, psychogenic, i.e. caused by psychological or emotional problems such as anxiety, fear or guilt.

incision a surgical cut into TISSUE or an ORGAN and the act of making this cut.

incisor a TOOTH with a chisel edge, used for biting. The four front teeth in the jaw are incisors.

incontinence an inability to control BOWEL movements or the passage of URINE. Urinary incontinence may be caused by a lesion in the BRAIN or SPINAL CORD, injury to the SPHINCTER or damage to the nerves of the BLADDER. Stress incontinence occurs during coughing or straining and is common in women because of the weakening of MUSCLES in childbirth. There are other categories of incontinence depending on the cause or the frequency of urine passage and the stimulus causing urination.

incubation 1. the period of time between a person being exposed to an INFECTION and the appearance of the symptoms. Incubation periods for diseases tend to be quite constant, some commoner ones being: measles 10 to 15 days; German measles 14 to 21; chicken pox 14 to 21; mumps 18 to 21; and whooping cough 7 to 10 days. **2.** the time taken to start and grow microorganisms in culture media. **3.** the process of caring for and treating a premature baby in an INCUBATOR.

incubator 1. the transparent box-like container in which a premature baby is kept in controlled, INFECTION-free conditions. **2.** a heated container for growth of bacterial cultures in a laboratory.

incus (*pl* **incudes**) *see* EAR.

indigestion *see* DYSPEPSIA.

induction 1. the commencement of LABOUR by artificial means, either by administering drugs to produce uterine contractions (*see* UTERUS) or by AMNIOTOMY. **2.** in ANAESTHESIA, the process prior to the required state of anaesthesia, including PREMEDICATION with a SEDATIVE.

industrial disease *see* OCCUPATIONAL DISEASE.

infant a child from birth to 12 months.

infant mortality (rate) a statistical measure of INFANT deaths, calculated as the number of deaths of infants under one year per 1,000 live births (in any given year). The figure is regarded as a measure of social conditions in a country rather than a guide to the medical services.

infantile paralysis *see* POLIOMYELITIS.

infarction the formation of an infarct, or dead area of TISSUE, in an ORGAN or vessel because of the obstruction of the ARTERY supplying blood. The obstruction may be caused by a blood clot or an EMBOLUS.

infection the invasion of the body by PATHOGENS and the resulting condition. BACTERIA, VIRUSES, fungi (*see* FUN-

GUS), etc, are all included, and they enter the body, multiply and, after the INCUBATION period, symptoms may appear. The organisms reach the body in many ways: by airborne droplets, direct contact, sexual intercourse, or by VECTORS, from contaminated food or drink, etc.

infectious mononucleosis *see* GLANDULAR FEVER.

infertility the condition in which a person is unable to produce offspring naturally. Female infertility may be because of irregular or absence of ovulation, blocked FALLOPIAN TUBES, ENDOMETRIOSIS; while a low sperm count or other deficiency in the SPERMATOZOA can lead to male infertility. Treatment can include drug therapy, surgery or, more recently, the technique of IN VITRO FERTILIZATION.

infestation when animal parasites occur on the SKIN, in the hair or within the body (e.g. parasitic worms).

inflammation the response of the body's TISSUES to injury or infection, which involves pain, redness, heat and swelling (acute inflammation). The first sign, when the tissues are infected or injured physically or chemically, is a dilation of BLOOD VESSELS in the affected area, increasing blood flow and resulting in heat and redness. The circulation then slows a little, and white blood cells (LEUCOCYTES) migrate into the tissues producing the swelling. The white blood cells engulf invading BACTERIA, dead tissue and foreign particles. After this, either the white blood cells migrate back to the circulation or there is the production and discharge of PUS as healing commences. Chronic inflammation is when repair is not complete and there is formation of SCAR tissue.

influenza a highly infectious and sometimes fatal disease caused by a VIRUS that affects the RESPIRATORY TRACT. Symptoms include HEADACHE, weakness and FEVER, appetite loss and general aches and pains. Sometimes there is the complication of a lung INFECTION, which requires immediate treatment. There are three main strains of influenza virus, designated A, B and C. The viruses quickly produce new strains, which is why an attack of one is unlikely to provide protection against a later bout of the disease. EPI-DEMICS occur periodically, which can result in numerous deaths. A yearly injection of influenza VACCINE, which is altered annually to match circulating strains of the virus, can provide protection to those who are particularly at risk from possible complications, e.g. the elderly, people who suffer from heart and lung disorders and those with a weakend immune system.

ingestion 1. the process of chewing and swallowing food and fluid that then go into the STOMACH. **2.** the means whereby a PHAGOCYTE takes in CELL debris, foreign particales, microorganisms, etc.

inhalant a substance taken into the body by INHALATION. The substances can be in several forms: the steam of a hot solution; a pressurized AEROSOL of droplets of particles; or a powdered medication that is drawn into the body by breathing in deeply from a non-pressurized passive inhaler. Sufferers of ASTHMA use inhalers to deliver drugs to the BRONCHI (BRONCHODILATOR drugs) for relief from attacks.

inhalation 1. *or* **inspiration** the act of drawing air into the LUNGS (*see* RESPIRATION). **2.** steam, or medication, whether in gas, vapour of particulate form, that is breathed in to treat conditions of the throat, BRONCHI or LUNGS.

inhaler *see* INHALANT.

injection the means whereby a liquid (often a drug) is introduced into the body by using a syringe in cases where it would otherwise be destroyed by digestive processes or where the patient is unable to swallow. The location of the injection depends on the speed with which the drug is to be absorbed and the target site. Thus, injections may go into the SKIN (intradermal) or beneath the skin (SUBCUTANE-OUS, as with INSULIN). For slow absorption an intramuscular injection is used, and IN-TRAVENOUS for fast delivery. *See also* DOSAGE; IMPLANT.

inner ear *see* EAR.

innervation the NERVE system serving a particular ORGAN, TISSUE or area of the body that carries MOTOR impulses to the target and SENSORY impulses away from it towards the BRAIN.

innominate artery *or* **bra-chiocephalic trunk** a

branch of the AORTA. *See also* CAROTID ARTERY.

innominate bone *see* HIP JOINT.

innoculation the process whereby a small quantity of solution is injected into the body to produce or increase IMMUNITY to the disease related to the solution (*see* IMMUNIZATION; VACCINATION).

inpatient someone admitted to a hospital for a period to undergo treatment or investigation.

insemination the introduction of SEMEN into the VAGINA, whether by sexual intercourse or artificial means. *See also* ARTIFICIAL INSEMINATION.

insomnia the condition of being unable to remain asleep or to fall asleep in the first instance, resulting in debilitating tiredness. It may be caused by a painful condition but is more likely to be the result of anxiety.

inspiration *see* INHALATION and RESPIRATION.

insulin a pancreatic HORMONE, produced in the ISLETS OF LANGERHANS, that initiates uptake of glucose by body CELLS and thereby controls the level of glucose in the BLOOD. It works by stimulating PROTEINS on cell surfaces within muscles and other tissues to take up glucose for their activity. A lack of hormone results in the sugar derived from food being excreted in the URINE—the condition DIABETES MELLITUS. In such cases, insulin can be administered by injection.

intercalated disc *see* MUSCLE.

intercostal a descriptive term, meaning between the RIBS.

interferon PROTEINS released from CELLS infected with a VIRUS that restrict, or interfere with, the growth of that virus. They limit the growth of cells, hence their use in CANCER treatment (which is as yet of indeterminate value). There are three human interferons: a from white blood cells (LEUCOCYTES), β (b) from CONNECTIVE TISSUE and g from LYMPHOCYTES (*see* INTERLEUKIN). Sufficient quantities of interferon can now be produced by GENETIC ENGINEERING.

interleukin one of several cytokines (molecules secreted by a CELL to regulate other cells nearby, e.g. INTERFERON) that act between LEUCOCYTES. There are eight interleukins currently recognized, and some are involved in functions such as the recognition of ANTIGENS, enhancing the action of MACROPHAGES and the production of other cytokines. An example is interleukin 2, which promotes the production of g-INTERFERON and is used in the treatment of MELANOMA.

intersex *see* HERMAPHRODITE

interstitial cell-stimulating hormone *see* GONADOTRO-PHIN.

intervertebral disc one of the fibrous cartilaginous discs that connect adjacent VERTE-BRAE and permit rotational and bending movements. The discs make up approximately 25 per cent of the backbone length, and they act as shock absorbers, providing cushioning for the BRAIN and SPINAL CORD. With age, the discs lose their effectiveness and may be displaced (*see* PROLAPSED INTERVERTEBRAL DISC).

intestinal flora the BACTERIA usually found in the INTES-TINE, some of which synthesize VITAMIN K. Acidic surroundings are produced by the bacteria, and this helps lessen infection by PATHO-GENS unable to withstand the conditions.

intestine the part of the ALI-MENTARY CANAL or tract between STOMACH and ANUS where final digestion and absorption of food matter occur, in addition to the removal of water and production of FAE-CES. The intestine is divided into the small intestine, comprising the DUODENUM, IL-EUM and JEJUNUM, and the large intestine, which is made up of the CAECUM, vermiform APPENDIX, COLON and REC-TUM. The length of the intestine in humans is about 9 metres (30 feet).

intolerance the condition in which a patient is unable to metabolize a drug (*see* ME-TABOLISM). There is usually an associated adverse reaction.

intoxication the condition of being poisoned by drugs, alcohol or other toxic substances.

intracranial a term meaning 'within the SKULL', applied to diseases, structures, etc.

intracranial pressure the pressure within the CRANIUM; more specifically, the pressure is maintained by all tissues: BRAIN, BLOOD, CEREBROSPI-NAL FLUID, etc. An increase in the pressure can occur as a result of injury, HAEMOR-

RHAGE or TUMOUR, and treatment is necessary to restore it to normal.

intramuscular a term meaning 'within a muscle', e.g. an intramuscular INJECTION.

intrauterine device (IUD) a small plastic or metal T-shaped contraceptive device (*see* CONTRACEPTION), that is placed in the UTERUS. The device prevents CONCEPTION by preventing potential IMPLANTATION of the EMBRYO. There are sometimes SIDE EFFECTS, e.g. back pain and heavy menstrual bleeding, but it is a reasonably effective method. An intrauterine device containing PROGESTERONE for slow release, known as the intrauterine system (IUS) is also available. It works by thickening the mucous of the CERVIX, making it more difficult for sperm to enter, and by altering the lining of the uterus, making it thinner to prevent a fertilized egg from implanting. This device can reduce menstrual bleeding in the longer term and is sometimes used to treat MENORRHAGIA. All intrauterine devices have to be inserted by a doctor or trained nurse and can remain in place for a number of years.

intrauterine system (IUS) *see* INTRAUTERINE DEVICE.

intravenous a term meaning 'relating to the inside of a VEIN', hence intravenous INJECTIONS are made into a vein, as are BLOOD TRANSFUSIONS.

intubation the insertion of a tube into the body through a natural opening. It is commonly, although not exclusively, used to keep an airway open by insertion into the mouth or nose and through the LARYNX. The same technique may be adopted to enable an ANAESTHETIC gas or oxygen to be delivered.

intussusception an eventual obstruction of the BOWEL caused by one part of the bowel slipping inside another part beneath it, much as a telescope closes up. The commonest sufferers are young children, and the symptoms include pain, VOMITING and the passage of a jelly-like bloodstained MUCUS. If the condition does not right itself, corrective treatment is essential either by a barium ENEMA or surgery.

invasion 1. the state when BACTERIA enter the body. **2.** more commonly, the process whereby malignant CANCER cells move into nearby normal and deeper TISSUES and gain access to the BLOOD VESSELS.

in vitro a term used to refer to a biological or biochemical reaction or process that occurs literally 'in glassware', i.e. in a test-tube or a similar piece of laboratory apparatus.

in vitro fertilization (IVF) the process of fertilizing an OVUM outside the body. The technique is used when a woman has blocked FALLOPIAN TUBES or when there is some other reason for SPERM and ovum not uniting. The woman produces several ova (because of HORMONE therapy treatment), which are removed using LAPAROSCOPY, and these are mixed with sperm and incubated in culture medium until they are fertilized. At the BLASTOCYST stage some are implanted in the mother's UTERUS. The first successful live birth using this technique was in 1978, when the phrase 'test-tube baby' was coined.

in vivo a term used to refer to biological processes that occur in a living organism.

involuntary muscle one of two types of MUSCLE not under voluntary or conscious control, such as those in the BLOOD VESSELS, STOMACH and INTESTINES. The heart muscle is slightly different (see CARDIAC MUSCLE).

involution 1. the process whereby an ORGAN decreases in size, e.g. the return of the UTERUS to its normal size after childbirth. 2. the degeneration of organs in old age, i.e. ATROPHY.

iridectomy the surgical removal of part of the IRIS, often undertaken to correct the blockage of aqueous humour (see EYE) associated with GLAUCOMA. It may also be necessary for removal of a foreign body or as part of CATARACT surgery.

iridotomy an incision into the IRIS.

iris the part of the EYE that controls the amount of light that enters. It is, in effect, a muscular disc, and to reduce the amount of light entering, circular MUSCLEs contract, and to increase the aperture in dim light, radiating muscles contract. The varying-sized hole is the PUPIL. The iris can be seen through the CORNEA, which is transparent and is the coloured part of the eye. This latter feature is accounted for by PIGMENT cells containing melanin (blue is little; brown is more).

irradiation the use in treatment of any form of radiating energy, i.e. electromagnetic radiation in the form of X-RAYS, alpha, beta or gamma radiation and also heat and light. Some radiations are used in diagnosis or CANCER treatments, others for relief of pain (heat treatment), etc.

irrigation the washing out of a wound or body cavity with a flow of water or other fluid.

irritable bowel syndrome (IBS) an inflammatory condition affecting the function of the COLON, producing effects in the large and small INTESTINES. Symptoms include abdominal pain, bloating, wind and DIARRHOEA (which may contain MUCUS) alternating with normal bowel movements or CONSTIPATION. The specific cause is unknown and no disease is present, but symptoms are commonly aggravated by anxiety or stress and by certain foods, eating large meals, or irregular eating. Drug therapy to reduce muscle activity in the colon may relieve symptoms, along with avoidance of stress and a careful choice of diet to include a high fibre content.

irritant a general term encompassing any agent that causes irritation of a TISSUE, e.g. nettle stings, chemicals and gases, etc.

ischaemic relating to a decrease in BLOOD supply to a part of the body or an ORGAN, caused by a blockage or narrowing of the BLOOD VESSELS. It is often associated with pain.

ischium (*pl* **ischia**) one of the three BONES that comprise each half of the PELVIS. It is the most posterior of the three and supports the weight of the body when sitting.

islets of Langerhans clusters of CELLS within the PANCREAS, which are the ENDOCRINE part of the gland. There are three types of cells, termed alpha, beta and delta, the first two producing GLUCAGON and INSULIN respectively, both vital hormones in the regulation of BLOOD-SUGAR levels. The third hormone produced is somatostatin (also released by the HYPOTHALAMUS), which works antagonistically against GROWTH HORMONE by blocking its release by the PITUITARY GLAND. The islets were named after Paul Langerhans, a German pathologist.

isolation 1. the process whereby a patient with an infectious disease is kept apart from non-infected people. This often includes people who may have contracted the disease but who have yet to show any symptoms. Isolation may also be necessary to ensure a patient does not come into contact with irritating environmental factors. **2.** in surgery, when a structure or ORGAN is kept apart from all around it through the use of instruments.

isoleucine *see* ESSENTIAL AMINO ACID.

isometric a term meaning 'of equal measurement'—isometric exercises are undertaken to build up MUSCLE strength by increasing tension in the muscles without contract, e.g. by pushing against something that cannot move.

isotopes atoms that differ from other atoms of the same element because of a different number of neutrons in the nucleus. Isotopes have the same number of protons and therefore the same atomic number but a different mass number (total number of protons and neutrons). Radioactive isotopes decay into other elements or isotopes through the emission of alpha, beta or gamma radiation, and some radioactive isotopes can be produced in the laboratory. RADIOTHERAPY uses such isotopes in the treatment of cancer.

itching *or* **pruritis** a SKIN condition or sensation prompting scratching to obtain relief. The causes are numerous and include mechanical irritation, e.g. by clothing or lice, skin diseases or conditions such as ECZEMA, allergies, etc.

IUD *see* INTRAUTERINE DEVICE.

IUD *see* INTRAUTERINE DEVICE.

IVF *see* IN VITRO FERTILIZATION.

J

Japanese encephalitis *see* ENCEPHALITIS.

jaundice a condition characterized by the unusual presence of BILE pigment (BILIRUBIN) in the BLOOD. The bile produced in the LIVER passes into the blood instead of the INTESTINES, and because of this there is a yellowing of the skin and the whites of the eyes. There are several types of jaundice: obstructive jaundice, which is caused by bile not reaching the intestine as a result of an obstruction, e.g. a GALLSTONE.

haemolytic jaundice, in which red blood cells (ERYTHROCYTES) are destroyed by HAEMOLYSIS.

hepatocellular jaundice, which is caused by a liver disease such as HEPATITIS, which results in the liver being unable to use the bilirubin.

neonatal jaundice, which is quite common in newborn infants when the liver is physiologically immature but usually lasts only a few days. The infant can be exposed to blue light, which converts bilirubin to biliverdin, another (harmless) bile pigment.

jaw the term for the BONES that carry the teeth and associated soft TISSUES. More specifically, they are the upper jaw (maxilla) and the lower jaw (mandible). The maxillae are fixed, while the mandible (which is one bone after the age of about 12 months) hinges on part of the temporal bone in front of the ear.

jejunum the part of the small INTESTINE lying before the ILEUM and after the DUODENUM. Its main function is the absorption of digested food, and its lining has numerous finger-like projections (villi) that increase the surface area for absorption. The villi are longer in the jejunum than elsewhere in the small intestine.

joint a connections between BONES (and CARTILAGES). Joints can be categorized by their structure and the degree to which they permit movement:

fibrous joints are fixed by FIBROUS TISSUE binding bones together, e.g the bones of the skull.

cartilaginous joints are slightly movable. These have discs of cartilage between bones so that only limited movement is permitted over one joint but over several adjacent joints considerable flexure is achieved, as with the spine.

synovial joints can move freely. Each synovial joint comprises the bones, cartilage over the ends, then a capsule (sheath of fibrous tissue) from which the ligaments form, and a SYNOVIAL MEMBRANE containing synovia for lubrication. This type of joint then occurs in two forms: hinge joints allowing planar movement (e.g. the knee), and ball and socket joints permitting all-round movement (e.g. the hip). Joints are subject to various conditions and diseases, including SYNOVITIS, epiphysitis (inflammation of the EPIPHYSIS), GOUT, RHEUMATISM and dislocations.

jugular a general term used to describe structures in the neck.

jugular vein any of the VEINS in the neck, particularly the anterior, internal and external. The anterior jugular vein is an offshoot of the external jugular vein and runs down the front of the neck. The external jugular itself drains the scalp, face and neck, while the larger internal jugular vein drains the face, neck and BRAIN and is sited vertically down the side of the neck.

K

kala-azar *see* LEISHMANIASIS.

kaolin *or* **china clay** a white powder form of aluminium silicate used in cases of SKIN irritation and as an adsorbent taken internally to treat DIARRHOEA.

Kaposi's sarcoma a condition involving malignant SKIN tumours that form from the BLOOD vessels. Purple lumps, as a result of the tumours, form on the feet and ankles, spreading to arms and hands. The disease is common in Africa but less so in western countries, although it is associated with AIDS. RADIOTHERAPY is the primary treatment but CHEMOTHERAPY may also be required.

Kegal exercises *or* **pelvic floor exercises** exercises commonly used following childbirth to strengthen the PELVIC FLOOR MUSCLES.

keloid *or* **cheloid** SCAR tissue that forms because of the growth of FIBROUS TISSUE over a BURN or injury, creating a hard, often raised, patch with ragged edges.

keratin a fibrous, sulphur-rich PROTEIN made up of coiled polyPEPTIDE chains. It occurs in hair, fingernails and the surface layer of the skin.

keratoplasty *see* CORNEAL GRAFT.

keratosis a condition of the SKIN whereby there is a thickening and overgrowth of the horny layer (or stratum corneum) of the skin. The condition is usually induced by excessive sunlight and can occur as scales and patchy skin pigmentation (actinic keratosin) or as yellow/brown warts (seborrhoeic keratosis). It is essential to avoid overexposing the skin to sunlight if it is to be prevented or treated.

Kernig's sign the inability of someone with MENINGITIS to straighten his or her legs at the knee when the thighs are at right angles to the body. It is symptomatic of the disease.

ketoaciduria *see* **ketonuria**.

ketogenesis the normal production of KETONES in the body because of METABOLISM of fats. Excess production leads to KETOSIS.

ketone an organic compound that contains a carbonyl group $(C \neq O)$ within the compound. Ketones can be detected in the body when fat is metabolized for energy when food intake is insufficient.

ketone body one of several compounds (e.g. acetoacetic acid) produced by the LIVER as a result of METABOLISM of fat

deposits. These compounds normally provide energy, via KETOGENESIS, for the body's peripheral TISSUES. In abnormal conditions, when CARBOHYDRATE supply is reduced, ketogenesis produces excess ketone bodies in the blood (KETOSIS) which may then appear in the URINE (KETONURIA).

ketonuria *or* **acetonuria** *or* **ketoaciduria** the presence of ketone bodies (*see* KETONE and KETONE BODY) in the URINE as a result of starvation or DIABETES MELLITUS, causing excessive KETOGENESIS and KETOSIS.

ketosis the build-up of KETONES in the body and bloodstream because of a lack of CARBOHYDRATES for METABOLISM or failure fully to use the available carbohydrates, resulting in fat breakdown (*see* KETOGENESIS and KETONURIA). It is induced by starvation, DIABETES MELLITUS or any condition in which fats are metabolized quickly and excessively.

kidney one of two GLANDS/organs that remove nitrogenous wastes, mainly UREA, from the BLOOD and also adjust the concentrations of various salts. The kidney is roughly 10cm long, 6cm wide and 4cm thick, and is positioned at the back of the ABDOMEN, below the DIAPHRAGM. Blood is supplied to the kidney by the renal ARTERY and leaves via the renal VEIN. Each kidney is held in place by fat and CONNECTIVE TISSUE, and comprises an inner MEDULLA and outer CORTEX. The kidneys produce and eliminate URINE by a complex process of filtration and reabsorption. The 'active' parts are the nephrons, which filter blood under pressure, reabsorbing water and other substances. A nephron comprises a renal TUBULE and BLOOD VESSELS. The tubule expands into a cup shape (Bowman's CAPSULE) that contains a knot of capillaries (see CAPILLARY), called the glomerulus, and this brings the water, urea, salts, etc. Filtrate passes from the glomerulus through three areas of the tubule (proximal convoluted tubule; the loop of Henle, distal convoluted tubule, which together form a shape resembling a hairpin), leaving as URINE. The kidneys contain roughly two million nephrons and receive between one and two thousands litres of blood each day, processing 150 to 200 litres of filtrate, resulting in roughly 1.5 litres of urine.

kinin one of a group of polyPEPTIDES that lower BLOOD PRESSURE through dilation of the BLOOD VESSELS and cause smooth MUSCLE to contract. They are associated with INFLAMMATION, causing local increases in the permeability of TISSUE capillaries (see CAPILLARY). In addition they play some part in the allergic response and ANAPHYLAXIS. Kinins do not normally occur in the blood but form under these conditions or when the tissue is damaged (see also BRADYKININS).

Klinefelter's syndrome a genetic imbalance in males in which there are 47 rather than 46 CHROMOSOMES, the extra one being an X-CHROMOSOME, producing a genetic make-up of XXY instead of the usual XY. The physical manifestations are small testes which atrophy, resulting in a lack of sperm production, enlargement of the breasts, long thin legs and little or no facial or body hair. There may be associated learning difficulties and pulmonary disease.

knee the JOINT connecting the thigh to the lower leg and formed by the FEMUR, TIBIA and kneecap (PATELLA). It is a hinge type of synovial joint with very strong LIGAMENTS binding the BONES together. Although the knee is a strong joint, it is complex and injuries can be serious.

kneejerk *see* REFLEX ACTION.

knock-knee *or* **genu valgum** an abnormal curvature of the legs so that when the knees are touching, the ankles are spaced apart. When walking, the knees knock, and severe cases can lead to stress on the JOINTS in the legs, with AR-THRITIS. Surgery may be performed to correct the condition, which in the past was commonly a result of RICKETS but is now mainly the result of poor MUSCLES.

knuckle *see* METACARPAL BONE.

Korsakoff's syndrome a neurological disorder described by the Russian neuropsychiatrist Sergei Korsakoff (1854–1900), characterized by short-term memory loss, disorientation and confabulation (the invention and detailed description of events, situations and experiences to cover gaps in the memory). The condition is caused primarily by alcoholism and a deficiency of thiamine (VITA-MIN B, vital in converting carbohydrate to glucose).

Koplik spots *see* MEASLES.

kuru *see* SPONGIFORM ENCEPH-ALOPATHY.

kwashiorkor a type of MAL-NUTRITION seen especially among children in Africa. It is the result of a deficiency in dietary PROTEIN and foods normally eaten for energy. It occurs when a child is weaned from the breast onto an adult diet that is inadequate, so the child cannot eat enough to obtain sufficient protein. The result is appetite loss, DIAR-RHOEA, OEDEMA, ANAEMIA and other conditions caused by VITAMIN deficiencies. Initially the condition responds well to first-class protein, but it is less straightforward with more prolonged cases.

kyphosis an abnormal outward curvature of the SPINAL COL-UMN causing the back to be hunched. There is an increased curvature of the spine, which may be caused by weak musculature or bad posture (mobile kyphosis) or it may result from collapsed VERTE-BRAE (fixed kyphosis), as in OSTEOPOROSIS of the aged.

L

labia (*sing* **labium**) lips or something resembling lips, as in the folds of skin enclosing the VULVA (the labia majora and minora).

labial 1. pertaining to the lips. **2.** the TOOTH surface next to the lips.

labour the process of giving birth, from dilatation of the CERVIX to expulsion of the AF-TERBIRTH. It usually commences naturally, although some labours are induced (*see* INDUCTION). The cervix expands, and at the same time the MUSCLES of the UTERUS wall contract, pushing part of the AMNION down into the opening. The amnion ruptures, releasing the 'waters', but these two events do not necessarily occur at the same time. The second stage is the actual delivery of the child, who passes through the bony girdle of the PELVIS via the VA-GINA to the outside. Initially the head appears at the cervix,

and the uterine contractions strengthen. These contractions are augmented by abdominal muscular contractions when the baby is in the vagina. When the baby's head is clear, the whole body is helped out and the UMBILICAL CORD severed. The final stage, accomplished by some contractions, is expulsion of the PLACENTA and MEMBRANES.

On average, labour lasts 12 hours (less for subsequent pregnancies), and in the second stage an EPISIOTOMY may be necessary to facilitate the emergence of the head. In most cases, the baby lies head down at delivery, although some are delivered feet or buttocks first (BREECH PRESENTATION). Other complications tend to be rare, and maternal mortality is very low in the West.

labyrinth part of the inner EAR, consisting of canals, ducts and cavities, forming the organs of hearing and balance. There are two parts: the membranous labyrinth, comprising the semicircular canals and associated structures and the central cavity of the cochlea; and the bony labyrinth, a system of canals filled with PERILYMPH (a third) and surrounding the other parts.

laceration a WOUND with jagged edges.

lacrimal relating to, or about, tears.

lacrimal gland one of a pair of GLANDS, situated above and to the side of each EYE, that secrete saline and slightly alkaline tears that moisten the conjunctiva (the MUCOUS MEMBRANE lining the inside of the eyelid). The glands comprise part of the lacrimal apparatus, the remainder being the lacrimal ducts (or canaliculi) through which the tears drain to the lacrimal sacs and the nasal cavity.

lactase the ENZYME that acts on milk sugar (LACTOSE) to produce the simple sugars glucose and galactose.

lactation the process of milk secretion by the MAMMARY GLANDS in the breast, which begins at the end of PREGNANCY. COLOSTRUM is produced and secreted before the milk. Lactation is controlled by HORMONES and stops when the baby ceases to be breast fed.

lacteal vessels part of the LYMPHATIC SYSTEM. They occur as projections with a closed end extending into villi (*see* VILLUS) in the small INTESTINE and take up digested fats as a milky fluid called chyle.

lactic acid *see* FATIGUE.

lactose milk sugar found only in mammalian milk and produced by the MAMMARY GLANDS. It is made up of one molecule of glucose and one molecule of galactose. People with a low level of, or no, activity of the enzyme LACTASE, cannot absorb lactose, a condition called lactose intolerance.

lacuna (*pl* **lacunae**) an anatomical term meaning a small depression, cavity or pit, especially in compact BONE.

lamella (*pl* **lamellae**) a thin plate, especially of BONE. *See also* HAVERSIAN CANAL.

lamina (*pl* **laminae**) a thin plate, e.g. of BONE or MUSCLE, such as the laminae propria of MUCOUS MEMBRANE.

laminectomy the surgical procedure in which access is gained to the SPINAL CORD by the removal of the arch of one or more VERTEBRAE. It is adopted when a TUMOUR is to be removed or a slipped disc is to be treated (*see* PROLAPSED INTERVERTEBRAL DISC).

lancet a surgical knife that is small and pointed and sharp on both edges.

lanugo a fine, downy HAIR. It covers the FOETUS between the fifth and ninth months and is lost in the ninth month so is seen only on babies born prematurely. It is also a symptom of severe ANOREXIA nervosa.

laparoscope a type of ENDO-SCOPE with a light source and a means of viewing the object that is inserted into the abdominal cavity through a small incision. This allows a surgeon to view the ORGANS in the cavity and a laparoscope is also used to enable some minor operations to be performed using instruments inserted through a second incision.

laparoscopy the use of a LAP-AROSCOPE to examine the OR-GANs in the abdominal cavity. Carbon dioxide is injected into the cavity to expand it before the laparoscope is inserted. In addition to being used purely for observation, a laparoscopy is also useful for taking a BIOPSY, STERILIZA-TIONS, and for collecting ova (*see* OVUM) for IN VITRO FER-TILIZATION.

laparotomy an incision into the abdominal cavity, either for surgical treatment or to aid diagnosis. Types of laparotomy include COLOSTOMY, APPENDICECTOMY, etc.

large intestine *see* INTES-TINE.

laryngectomy surgical excision of all or part of the LAR-YNX. This procedure is adopted for CANCER of the larynx.

laryngitis INFLAMMATION of the MUCOUS MEMBRANE that lines the LARYNX and VOCAL CORDS. It is caused by viral INFECTION in the main but also by BACTERIA, chemical irritants, heavy smoking or excessive use of the voice. Acute laryngitis accompanies infections of the upper respiratory tract, and the symptoms include pain, a cough and difficulty in swallowing. Chronic laryngitis may be a recurrence of the acute form but is often attributable to excessive smoking worsened by alcohol. Changes occurring in the vocal cords are more permanent, and the symptoms are as for the acute form, but longer lasting.

laryngoscope a type of EN-DOSCOPE used to examine the LARYNX.

laryngotracheobronchitis an acute INFLAMMATION of

the major parts of the respiratory tract, causing shortness of breath, a CROUP-like cough and hoarseness. It occurs usually because of viral INFECTION and particularly in young children where there may be some obstruction of the LARYNX. The main airways, the BRONCHI, become coated with fluid generated by the inflamed TISSUES, resulting in the shortness of breath. Treatment is through INHALATIONS, ANTIBIOTICS, if appropriate, and, if the obstruction is serious, hospitalization may be necessary for INTUBATION, TRACHEOSTOMY, etc.

larynx part of the air passage connecting the PHARYNX with the TRACHEA and also the ORGAN producing vocal sounds. It is situated high up in the front of the neck and is constructed of CARTILAGES with LIGAMENTS and MUSCLES. The ligaments bind together the cartilages, and one pair of these form the VOCAL CORDS. The larynx is lined with MUCOUS MEMBRANE and in all is about 5 cm long.

laser (acronym for Light Amplification by Stimulated Emission of Radiation) a device that produces a powerful and narrow beam of light where the light is of one wavelength in phase. This produces a beam of high-energy light that can be used in surgery. Different lasers can be used for various procedures. For example, the argon laser heats and coagulates TISSUES because HAEMOGLOBIN absorbs the energy—this is therefore used to seal bleeding vessels. The carbon-dioxide laser is used to make incisions because water in CELLS absorbs the energy, thus destroying those cells. Lasers are also used in retinal (EYE) surgery and in the removal of BIRTHMARKS.

Lassa fever a highly contagious viral INFECTION (*see* VIRUS) first reported from Lassa in Nigeria. It takes from three to 21 days to incubate and results in FEVER and headache, acute muscular pains, sore throat and some difficulty in swallowing. Death often occurs because of HEART or KIDNEY failure, and pregnant women show a high mortality rate. Little can be done as it is a viral infection, but treatment with PLASMA from patients who have recovered may help.

laudanum a NARCOTIC ANAL-GESIC prepared from opium, used widely in the past.

laughing gas the common name of NITROUS OXIDE.

laxative a substance that is taken to evacuate the bowel or to soften stools (*see* FAECES). Typical laxatives include castor oil, senna and its derivatives (*see also* PURGATIVE).

l-dopa *or* **levadopa** *see* DOPA.

legionnaire's disease a bacterial INFECTION and a form of PNEUMONIA caused by *Legionella pneumophila*. It produces an illness similar to INFLUENZA with symptoms appearing after a two- to ten-day incubation period. FEVER, chills, head and muscular aches may progress to PLEURISY and chest pains. ANTIBIOTIC treatment is usually effective (e.g. ERYTHROMYCIN). The disease was named after an outbreak in America in 1976 at the American Legion convention. The bacterium is found in nature, particularly in water, and static water provides ideal conditions for multiplication. INHALATION of an AEROSOL of water is the likeliest way of becoming infected and air-conditioning cooling towers are a particular source. It is vital that infected systems be cleaned and chlorinated.

leishmaniasis a common tropical and subtropical disease (in Africa, Asia, South America and the Mediterranean) caused by the parasitic protozoa *Leishmania*, which are transmitted by the bites of sandflies. Depending on the region, it affects people of differing ages, and there are two forms, visceral and cutaneous. In the former, internal ORGANS are affected while in the latter it affects the SKIN but also the MUCOUS MEMBRANES. Visceral leishmaniasis results in FEVER, enlargement of the GLANDS, LIVER and SPLEEN, and roughly three-quarters of untreated cases result in fatalities. Cutaneous leishmaniasis produces skin ULCERS that go by various names and may include the nose and throat. The drug commonly used to treat it is a salt of sodium that contains antimony.

lens the part of the EYE that focuses incoming light onto the RETINA. It is composed of a fibrous PROTEIN, crystallin, and is enclosed in a thin CAPSULE.

leprosy a serious disease caused by the bacterium *Mycobacte-*

rium leprae that attacks the
SKIN, NERVES and MUCOUS
MEMBRANES and has an INCU-
BATION period of several
years. There are two forms of
the disease, tuberculoid and
lepromatous, depending upon
the resistance of the host (the
former occurs in those with a
higher degree of IMMUNITY).
The tuberculoid form pro-
duces discoloured patches of
skin with some numbness but
is generally BENIGN and often
heals untreated. Lepromatous
leprosy is a much more serious
and progressively destructive
form of the disease, creating
lumps, thickening of skin and
nerves, INFLAMMATION of the
IRIS, numbness with MUSCLE
weakness and PARALYSIS. The
more serious cases show
deformity and considerable
disfigurement and sometimes
blindness. There is also an
intermediate form with symptoms of both types (indeterminate leprosy).

Although many millions of
people are affected, drugs
therapy is quite effective, providing a combination of AN-
TIBIOTICS is used (because
the bacterium develops resistance to one of the SULPHON-
AMIDES commonly used).

leptomeninges *see* MENIN-
GES.

leptomeningitis INFLAMMA-
TION of two of the three
MENINGES surrounding the
BRAIN and SPINAL CORD. Specifically, the inner two (pia
mater and arachnoid) are affected.

leptospirosis an acute infectious disease caused by BAC-
TERIA of the genus *Leptospira*.
The disease varies from the
mild form of an INFLUENZA
type of illness to the more serious cases involving FEVER,
LIVER disease and therefore
JAUNDICE, and possibly KID-
NEY disease or MENINGITIS.
In such cases there may be fatalities. The organism occurs
in the URINE of rats and dogs,
and this renders workers on
farms and at sewage works,
etc, more susceptible, but it
can be contracted by bathing
or immersion in contaminated
water (e.g. canals). ANTIBIOT-
ICS can be given but are best
administered at an early stage
to be effective. One particular species *L. icterohaem-
orrhagiae*, which is transmitted by rats, is responsible for
the most severe form of
leptospirosis called Weil's
disease.

lesion 1. a WOUND or injury to body TISSUES. **2.** an area of tissue that, because of damage caused by disease or wounding, does not function fully. Thus, primary lesions include TUMOURS and ULCERS, and from primary lesions secondary lesions may form.

lethargy the state of being inactive mentally and physically and one that approaches UNCONSCIOUSNESS. The cause may be psychological or physical. The lethargy associated with the aftermath of GLANDULAR FEVER is well known, but it may also be the result of ANAEMIA, DIABETES MELLITUS or MALNUTRITION, among others.

leucine see ESSENTIAL AMINO ACID.

leucocyte or **leukocyte** a white BLOOD cell, so called because it contains no HAEMO-GLOBIN. It also differs from red blood cells (ERYTHROCYTES) in having a nucleus. Leucocytes are formed in the BONE MAR-ROW, SPLEEN, THYMUS and LYMPH NODES, and there are three types: granulocytes, comprising 70 per cent of all white blood cells, LYMPHO-CYTES (25 per cent) and MONO-CYTES (5 per cent). Granulocytes help combat bacterial and viral INFECTION and may be involved in allergies (see AL-LERGY). Lymphocytes destroy foreign bodies, either directly or through production of ANTI-BODIES, and monocytes ingest BACTERIA and foreign bodies by the process called PHAGO-CYTOSIS. In disease, immature forms of leucocytes may appear in the blood (ultimately forming both red and white blood cells).

leucocytosis except for during PREGNANCY, MENSTRUA-TION and exercise, an abnormal and temporary increase in the number of white blood cells (LEUCOCYTES) in the blood. It usually accompanies bacterial but not viral IN-FECTIONS, because the body's defence mechanism is fighting the BACTERIA by producing leucocytes. A blood sample may thus form a useful diagnostic tool for a condition that has not yet manifested any physical symptoms.

leucorrhoea a discharge of white or yellow-coloured MU-CUS from the VAGINA. It may be a normal condition, increasing before and after MENSTRU-ATION, but a large discharge probably indicates an INFEC-

TION somewhere in the genital tract. A common cause is the infection called THRUSH but it may also be a result of GONORRHOEA, in which case the treatment will differ.

leukaemia a cancerous disease in which there is an uncontrolled proliferation of LEUCOCYTES in the BONE MARROW. The cells fail to mature to adult cells and thus cannot function as part of the defence mechanism against infections. This leads to ANAEMIA, bleeding and easy bruising, with enlargement of the SPLEEN, LIVER and LYMPH NODES. Acute leukaemia has a sudden onset and development, while the chronic form may take years to develop the same symptoms. The cause of leukaemia is unknown although it has been attributed to VIRUSes, exposure to toxic chemicals or ionizing radiations. In addition to the acute and chronic forms, it is further classified by the predominant white blood cells: acute lymphoblastic leukaemia, acute myeloblastic leukaemia (myeloblast is an early form of granulocytes, see LEUCOCYTE) and chronic lymphatic leukaemia. The treatment involves RADIOTHERAPY, CHEMOTHERAPY and bone marrow TRANSPLANTS and the outlook has improved over recent years, particularly in cases of childhood leukaemia. The survival or REMISSION rate varies with the type of leukaemia, and a cure is achievable in many cases.

levodopa *or* **l-dopa** *see* DOPA.

LH *see* GONADOTROPHINS.

libido the sexual drive. Lack of libido may be the result of illness, DEPRESSION or a lack of sex HORMONES because of an ENDOCRINE disorder.

Librium chlordiazepoxide hydrochloride, a minor TRANQUILLIZER used in the treatment of anxiety. It is taken orally and relaxes MUSCLEs although there are SIDE EFFECTS such as NAUSEA and SKIN reactions.

lice (*sing* **louse**) insects parasitic on humans. Lice are wingless and attach themselves to hair or clothing by means of their legs and claws. They suck BLOOD and are particularly resistant to crushing and have to be removed using special shampoos and combs (*see also* PEDICULOSIS).

lidocaine (*formerly* **lignocaine**) a commonly used local

ANAESTHETIC. It is given by INJECTION for minor surgery and dental treatment, and it can be applied directly to the eyes, throat, etc, because it is absorbed directly through MUCOUS MEMBRANES. It is also used in the treatment of some disorders in HEART rhythm, particularly VENTRICULAR FIBRILLATION.

ligament 1. bands of fibrous CONNECTIVE TISSUE, composed chiefly of COLLAGEN, that join BONES together, restricting movement and preventing dislocation. Ligaments strengthen JOINTS, and most joints are surrounded by a capsular ligament. **2.** a layer of SEROUS MEMBRANE, e.g. the PERITONEUM, which supports or links ORGANS.

ligation 1. the procedure of tying off a DUCT or BLOOD VESSEL to prevent flow during surgery, etc. **2.** the application of a LIGATURE.

ligature material for tying firmly around a BLOOD VESSEL or DUCT to stop bleeding or prevent flow. The material may be wire, silk, catgut, etc.

lightening a sensation experienced by many pregnant women, normally towards the last month of the PREGNANCY, when the FOETUS settles lower in the PELVIS. This lessens the pressure on the DIAPHRAGM and breathing becomes easier.

light reflex the mechanism whereby the PUPIL of the EYE opens in response to direct light or consensual pupillary stimulation (i.e. stimulation of one pupil with light results in a response in the other).

lignocaine *see* LIDOCAINE.

limb 1. an appendage of a body. **2.** a branch of an internal ORGAN.

linctus a medicine, particularly to treat COUGHs, that is thick and syrup-like.

lingual a term meaning 'relating to the TONGUE', or something close to it (e.g. lingual NERVE or the lingual surface of a TOOTH).

liniment a creamy or oily substance for rubbing onto the SKIN to alleviate irritation or pain. Many of the compounds are poisonous and contain such substances as camphor, turpentine and even belladonna.

linkage the state when two or more GENES are said to be linked together if they occur close to each other on the same CHROMOSOME. The genes are thus likely to be inherited together, as will the characteristics that they represent. This is because the linked genes are more likely to be together in nuclei formed as a result of MEIOSIS (the chromosomal division that produces the GAMETES).

linoleic, linolenic *see* ESSENTIAL FATTY ACID.

lint a cotton fabric (formerly linen) used for surgical dressings, which has one fluffy side and one smooth, the latter being placed against the SKIN.

lipase *see* ENZYME; LIPOLYSIS; PANCREAS.

lipid an organic compound in fats that is soluble in organic solvents (e.g. alcohol) but insoluble in water.

lipolysis the breakdown of LIPIDS into FATTY ACIDS via the action of the ENZYME lipase.

lipoma a benign TUMOUR, made up of fat CELLS, that can occur in the FIBROUS TISSUES of the body, often beneath the SKIN. The only problem associated with such structures may be their size and position.

liposarcoma a malignant TUMOUR of fat CELLS that is very rare, particularly under the age of 30. It occurs in the buttocks or thighs.

lipoprotein a PROTEIN that has a FATTY ACID molecule attachied to it. Lipoproteins are important in certain processes, e.g. transporting CHOLESTEROL.

liposome a spherical droplet of microscopic size comprising fatty MEMBRANES around an aqueous VESICLE. Liposomes are created in the laboratory by adding an aqueous solution to a phospholipid gel (phospholipids are compounds containing FATTY ACIDS and a phosphate group). Liposomes bear some resemblance to living cell components and are studied on this basis. Additionally, they can be introduced into living CELLS and are used to transport toxic drugs to a specific treatment site. The liposomes retain the drug while in the BLOOD and on passing through the chosen ORGAN the membrane is melted by selectively heating the organ and the drug is released. This technique is used for certain forms of CANCER.

listeriosis an infectious disease caused when the Gram-positive (*see* GRAM'S STAIN) bacterium *Listeria monocytogenes*, which attacks animals, is contracted by human beings through eating infected products. It produces symptoms similar to influenza or it may cause MENINGITIS or ENCEPHALITIS. The old and frail are more susceptible, as are the newborn. It may cause ABORTION or damage the FOETUS if contracted during a PREGNANCY. ANTIBIOTICS such as PENICILLIN provide an effective treatment.

Little's disease CEREBRAL PALSY on both sides of the body that affects the legs more than the arms.

liver a very important ORGAN of the body, with many functions critical in regulating metabolic processes. The largest GLAND in the body, it occupies the top right-hand part of the abdominal cavity and is made up of four LOBES. It is fastened to the abdominal wall by LIGAMENTS and sits beneath the DIAPHRAGM and on the right KIDNEY, large INTESTINE, DUODENUM and STOMACH.

There are two BLOOD VESSELS supplying the liver: the hepatic ARTERY delivers oxygenated BLOOD, while the hepatic PORTAL VEIN conveys digested food from the stomach. Among its functions, the liver converts excess glucose to glycogen for storage as a food reserve; excess amounts of AMINO ACIDS are converted to UREA for excretion by the kidneys; BILE is produced for storage in the GALL BLADDER and LIPOLYSIS occurs; some poisons are broken down (detoxified), hence the beneficial effect of the hepatic portal vein carrying blood to the liver rather than it going around the body first.

The liver also synthesizes blood-clotting substances such as FIBRINOGEN and prothrombin and the anticoagulant HEPARIN; it breaks down red blood cells (ERYTHROCYTES) at the end of their life and processes the HAEMOGLOBIN for iron, which is stored; VITAMIN A is synthesized and stored, and it also stores VITAMINS B12, D, E and K. In the EMBRYO it forms red blood cells. Such is the chemical and biochemical activity of the liver that significant energy is generated, and this organ is a major contributor of heat to the body.

lobe certain ORGANS are divided by FISSURES into large

divisions that are called lobes, e.g. the BRAIN, LIVER and LUNGS.

lobectomy the removal of a LOBE of an ORGAN, e.g. LUNG or BRAIN. A lobe of a lung may be removed in CANCER or other disease.

lobotomy in general, cutting a LOBE. More specifically, a neurosurgical operation, rarely performed now, which involved severing the NERVE fibres in the frontal lobe of the BRAIN. It was performed to reduce severe DEPRESSION or emotional conditions but produced serious SIDE EFFECTS such as EPILEPSY and personality changes. Modern techniques permit the production of small LESIONS in specific areas and side effects are rare.

lobule a small LOBE or a subdivision of lobe in an ORGAN, e.g. the lobules of the LIVER.

lochia the material discharged through the VAGINA from the UTERUS after childbirth for a few weeks. Initially it consists mainly of BLOOD, then it contains more MUCUS but with some blood and finally a whitish mixture of CELL fragments and microbes.

lockjaw the nonmedical name for TETANUS.

locomotor ataxia an unsteady gait, which is one symptom of TABES DORSALIS, a form of SYPHILIS. The organism destroys SENSORY nerves, producing further symptoms such as pains in the legs and body, loss of BLADDER control (INCONTINENCE)and blurred vision because of OPTIC NERVE damage.

loin that area of the back between the lower RIBS and the PELVIS.

louse *see* LICE.

lumbago pain of any sort in the lower back. It can be muscular, skeletal or neurological in origin. A severe and sudden case may be caused by a strained MUSCLE or slipped disc (*see* PROLAPSED INTERVERTEBRAL DISC), and the latter is usually the cause of lumbago with SCIATICA.

lumbar a general term for anything relating to the LOINS, e. g. LUMBAR VERTEBRAE.

lumbar puncture the procedure wherein a hollow needle is inserted into the spinal canal in the lumbar region (usually between the third and fourth LUMBAR VERTEBRAE) to obtain a sample of CEREBROSPINAL FLUID. The fluid is used in diagnosis of diseases of the NERVOUS SYSTEM or to introduce drugs, ANAESTHETICS, etc.

lumbar vertebrae the five vertebrae between the SACRUM and the thoracic VERTEBRAe at the lowest part of the back. The lumbar vertebrae are not fused and have strong attachments points (PROCESSes) for the MUSCLES of the lower back.

lumpectomy the surgical removal of a TUMOUR with the tissue immediately around it but leaving intact the bulk of the tissue and the LYMPH NODES. This applies particularly to BREAST CANCER, when the procedure is often followed by RADIOTHERAPY and is undertaken for patients with a small tumour (less than 2 cm) and no metastases (see METASTASIS) to nearby lymph nodes or ORGANS elsewhere in the body.

lungs the sac-like, paired ORGANS of RESPIRATION, situated with their base on the DIAPHRAGM and the top projecting into the neck. Each lung consists of fibrous, elastic sacs that are convoluted to provide a large surface area for gaseous exchange. Air enters the body through the windpipe or TRACHEA, which branches into two BRONCHI, one to each lung. Further branching then occurs into numerous BRONCHIOLES. The bronchioles divide further and then end in alveoli (see ALVEOLUS), which are tiny sac-like structures where the gaseous exchange occurs. The exchange of oxygen and carbon dioxide occurs between the many blood capillaries (see CAPILLARY) on one side of the MEMBRANE and the air on the other. The lungs are served by the pulmonary arteries (see ARTERY) and pulmonary VEINS. The total lung capacity of an adult male is five to six litres although only about half a litre (500 ml) is exchanged in normal breathing (called the tidal volume).

lunula (*pl* **lunulae**) *see* NAIL.

lupus any of a number of skin diseases, of which lupus vulgaris and lupus erythematosus are the two main types. Lupus vulgaris is characterized by small yellow transparent nodules that, if left unreated, will ulcerate and thicken, causing scars. Lupus erythematosus is thought to be an AUTOIMMUNE response to INFECTION, sunlight or some other cause. It is characterized by red raised patches on the SKIN which may merge at the edges ('butterfly lesions'). *See also* SYSTEMIC LUPUS ERYTHEMATOSUS.

lutienizing hormone *see* GONADOTROPHINS; PROGESTERONE.

Lyme disease an arthritic disease with RASHES, FEVER and possibly carditis (INFLAMMATION of the heart) and ENCEPHALITIS. It is caused by a spirochaete (a type of BACTERIUM) that is transmitted by a tick bite. Symptoms may not appear until some time after the bite but ANTIBIOTICS can be used in treatment.

lymph a colourless, watery fluid that surrounds the body TISSUES and circulates in the LYMPHATIC SYSTEM. It is derived from BLOOD and is similar to PLASMA, comprising 95 per cent water with PROTEIN, sugar, salts and LYMPHOCYTES. The lymph is circulated by muscular action, and passes through LYMPH NODES, which act as filters, and is eventually returned to the BLOOD via the thoracic duct (one of the two main vessels of the lymphatic system).

lymphadenectomy removal of LYMPH NODES, e.g. when a node has become cancerous and drains the area around an ORGAN with a malignancy.

lymphadenitis INFLAMMATION of the LYMPH NODES, which become enlarged, hard and tender. The neck lymph nodes are commonly affected in association with another inflammatory condition.

lymphadenoma *see* HODGKIN'S DISEASE.

lymphangiography the technique of injecting a radio-opaque substance into the LYMPHATIC SYSTEM to render it visible on an X-RAY, used primarily in investigating the spread of CANCER.

lymphatic gland *see* GLAND.

lymphatic system *or* **lymphatics** the network of vessels, valves, nodes, etc, that carry LYMPH from the tissues to the bloodstream and help maintain the internal fluid environment of the body. Lymph drains into capillaries and larger vessels, passing through nodes and eventually into two large vessels (the thoracic duct and right lymphatic duct), which return it to the bloodstream by means of the innominate VEINS.

lymph node any of numerous small oval structures that occur at various points in the LYMPHATIC SYSTEM. They are found grouped in several parts of the body, including the neck, groin and armpit, and their main functions are to remove foreign particles and produce LYMPHOCYTES, important in the IMMUNE response.

lymphocyte a type of white blood cell (LEUCOCYTE) produced in the BONE MARROW and also present in the SPLEEN, THYMUS GLAND and LYMPH NODES, which forms a vital component of the IMMUNE system. There are two types: B-cells or B-lymphocyte and T-cells or T-lymphocyte. B-cells produce ANTIBODIES and search out and bind with particular ANTIGENS. T-cells circulate through the thymus gland, where they differentiate. When they contact an antigen, large numbers of T-cells are generated, which secrete chemical compounds to assist the B-cells in destroying foreign bodies, e.g. BACTERIA.

lymphocytosis when the BLOOD contains an increased number of LYMPHOCYTES, as during many diseases or in lymphocytic LEUKAEMIA.

lymphoedema the build-up of LYMPH in soft tissues, causing swelling. It may be the result of obstruction of the vessels by PARASITES, TUMOUR or INFLAMMATION. A secondary form of lymphoedema may occur after removal of lymph vessels in surgery or by blocking. The condition occurs most often in the legs, and treatment comprises use of elastic bandages and DIURETIC drugs.

lymphography see LYMPHANGIOGRAPHY.

lymphoid tissue tissues that are involved in the formation of LYMPH, LYMPHOCYTES and ANTIBODIES, such as the SPLEEN, THYMUS and lymph nodes.

lymphoma a TUMOUR, usually MALIGNANT, of the LYMPH NODES. Often several lymph nodes become enlarged and subsequent symptoms include FEVER, ANAEMIA, weakness and weight loss. If much of the lymphoid tissue is involved, there may be enlargement of the LIVER and SPLEEN. Life expectancy is often very low although treatment with drugs usually produces a marked response. RADIO-THERAPY may be used for localized varieties (*see also* HODGKIN'S DISEASE).

lymphosarcoma a TUMOUR of the LYMPHATIC SYSTEM resulting in enlargement of the GLANDS, SPLEEN and LIVER. In general an older term applied to LYMPHOMAS other than HODGKIN'S DISEASE.

lysin *see* LYSIS.

lysine *see* ESSENTIAL AMINO ACID.

lysis 1. the destruction of CELLS by ANTIBODIES called lysins. Thus, HAEMOLYSIS is the break-up of red blood cells (ERYTHROCYTES) by haemolysin. **2.** more generally, the destruction of cells or TISSUES because of breakdown of the cell MEMBRANES.

lysozyme an ENZYME, present in tears, nasal secretions and on the SKIN, that has an ANTI-BACTERIAL action (by breaking the CELL wall of the bacterium). Lysozyme also occurs in egg white.

M

macrocephaly an abnormal enlargement of the head when compared with the rest of the body, *see* MICROCEPHALY, HYDROCEPHALUS.

macrocyte a red blood cell (ERYTHROCYTE) that is abnormally large. Macrocytes are characteristic of PERNICIOUS ANAEMIA.

macrocytosis the condition in which abnormally large red blood cells (ERYTHROCYTES) are present in the blood. It is characteristic of macrocytic ANAEMIAS such as those caused by the deficiency of VITAMIN B12 (cyanocobalamin, *see also* PERNICIOUS ANAEMIA) and FOLIC ACID. Macrocytes are also produced in those anaemias in which there is an increased rate of production of erythrocytes.

macroglia *see* GLIA.

macroglobulin *see* IMMUNO-GLOBULIN.

macrophage a large scavenger CELL (phagocyte), numbers of which are found in various TISSUES and ORGANS including the LIVER, SPLEEN, BONE MARROW, LYMPH NODES, CONNECTIVE TISSUE and the microglia of the CENTRAL NERVOUS SYSTEM. They remove foreign bodies such as BACTERIA from blood and tissues. Fixed macrophages remain in one place in the connective tissue; free microphages are able to migrate between cells and gather at sites of infection to remove bacteria and other foreign material.

macula (*pl* **maculae**) *or* **macule 1.** a small area or spot of tissue that is distinct from the surrounding region, e.g. the yellow spot in the retina of the EYE. **2.** a spot of small pigmented area in the SKIN, which may be thickened. They appear as a result of PREGNANCY, SUNBURN, ECZEMA or PSORIASIS and may be symptomatic of other diseases such as SYPHILIS and those affecting internal organs.

mad cow disease an informal name for BOVINE SPONGIFORM ENCEPHALOPATHY (BSE).

magnetic resonance imaging (MRI) a scanning technique using NUCLEAR MAGNETIC RESONANCE instead of X-RAYS to visualize internal body structures. It is used in the investigation of a variety of disorders, particularly those involving the BRAIN, HEART, soft TISSUES or SPINAL CORD.

major histocompatibility complex *see* MHC.

malabsorption syndrome a group of diseases in which there is a reduction in the normal absorption of digested food materials in the small INTESTINE. The food materials involved are commonly fats, vitamins, minerals, aminoacids and iron. The diseases include COELIAC DISEASE, PANCREATITIS, CYSTIC FIBROSIS, SPRUE and STAGNANT LOOP SYNDROME and also surgical removal of a part of the small intestine.

malaria an infectious disease caused by the presence of minute parasitic organisms of the genus *Plasmodium* in the BLOOD. The disease is characterized by recurrent bouts of FEVER and ANAEMIA, the interval between the attacks depending upon the species . The PARASITE is transmitted to humans by the *Anopheles* mosquito (common in subtropical and tropical regions) being present in the SALIVARY GLANDS and passed into the bloodstream of a person when the insect bites. Similarly, the parasite is ingested by the mosquito when it takes a blood meal from an infected person. Efforts to control malaria have centred on destruction of the mosquito and its breeding sites. Once they have been injected into the blood, the organisms concentrate in the LIVER, where they multiply, and then re-enter the bloodstream destroying red blood cells (ERYTHROCYTES). This releases the parasites, causing shivering, fever, sweating and anaemia. The process is then repeated, with hours or days between attacks. Drugs are used both to prevent INFECTION, although these may not be totally effective, and to cure the disease once present.

malignant a term used in several ways **1.** to describe a TUMOUR that proliferates rapidly and destroys surrounding healthy TISSUE and can spread via the LYMPHATIC SYSTEM and bloodstream to other parts of the body. **2.** to describe a form of a disease that is more serious than the usual one and is life-threatening, such as malignant HYPERTENSION.

malignant pustule see ANTHRAX.

malleus see EAR; TYMPANIC MEMBRANE.

malnutrition a condition caused either by an unbalanced diet, i.e. too much of one type of food at the expense of others, or by an inadequate food intake (subnutrition), which can lead to starvation. The condition may also arise because of internal dysfunction, e.g. MALABSORPTION SYNDROME or other metabolic disturbance within the body. It may also arise as a result of ANOREXIA NERVOSA.

Malpighian layer see EPIDERMIS; SKIN.

malposition and **malpresentation** the situation in which the head of an unborn baby before and near delivery is not in the usual (occipitoanterior) position. In malposition the baby is head down but a wider part of the skull is presented to the opening of the PELVIS because of the angle of the head. In malpresentation the baby is not head down. Both these conditions prolong and complicate LABOUR and, in the latter case especially, are likely to require delivery by CAESAREAN SECTION.

mammary gland a GLAND present in the female BREAST that produces milk after childbirth.

mammography a special X-ray technique used to determine

the structure of the BREAST. It is useful in the early detection of TUMOURS and in distinguishing between BENIGN and MALIGNANT tumours.

mammoplasty PLASTIC SURGERY of the BREASTS to decrease or increase size and alter shape.

mammothermography *see* THERMOGRAPHY.

mandible *see* JAW.

mandibular nerve *see* TRIGEMINAL NERVE.

mania a mental illness characterized by great excitement and euphoria (which then gives way to irritability) and sometimes violent and destructive behaviour. Alternating with depression, it is a phase of BIPOLAR DISORDER.

manic depressive psychosis *see* BIPOLAR DISORDER.

Mantoux test a test for the presence of a measure of IMMUNITY to TUBERCULOSIS. A PROTEIN called tuberculin, extracted from the TUBERCLE bacilli (BACTERIA), is injected in a small quantity beneath the skin of the forearm. If an inflamed patch appears within 18 to 24 hours, it indicates that a measure of immunity is present and that the person has been exposed to tuberculosis. The size of the reaction indicates the severity of the original tuberculosis infection, although it does not mean that the person is actively suffering from the disease at that time.

marasmus a wasting condition in infants usually caused by defective feeding. The child has a low body weight (less than 75 per cent of normal), lacks skin fat and is pale and apathetic. Various disorders and diseases can bring this about, including prolonged VOMITING and DIARRHOEA, organ disease, e.g. of the HEART, KIDNEYS and LUNGS; INFECTIONS and parasitic diseases and MALABSORPTION. Treatment depends on the cause but the provision and gradual increase of nourishment and fluids is always of primary importance.

Marfan's syndrome an inherited disease of the CONNECTIVE TISSUE, producing defects in the SKELETON, HEART and EYES. The person is abnormally tall and thin, has spindly, elongated fingers and toes (arachnodactyly), deformities of the spine and CHEST and weak LIGAMENTS. HEART defects include a hole in the septum separating the right and left atrium (ATRIAL SEPTAL DEFECT) and narrowing of the AORTA (coarctation of the aorta). The lenses of the eyes are partially dislocated.

mastalgia pain in the BREAST.

mast cell a large CELL, many of which are found in loose CONNECTIVE TISSUE. The CYTOPLASM contains numerous granules with chemicals important in the body, including HISTAMINE, SEROTONIN, HEPARIN and the antibody IMMUNOGLOBULIN E. All are important in allergic and inflammatory responses.

mastectomy surgical removal of the BREAST, usually performed because of the presence of a TUMOUR. Mastectomy may be simple, leaving the skin (and possibly the nipple) so that an artificial breast (PROSTHESIS) can be inserted. Or it may be radical, in which case the whole breast, the pectoral MUSCLES and the LYMPH NODES beneath the armpit are all removed, generally performed because a CANCER has spread.

mastication the chewing of food in the MOUTH, the first stage in the digestive process (*see* DIGESTION).

mastitis INFLAMMATION of the BREAST, usually caused by bacterial INFECTION during breast-feeding, the organisms responsible gaining access through cracked nipples. Cystic mastitis does not involve INFLAMMATION, but the presence of CYSTS (thought to be caused by hormonal factors) causes the breast(s) to be lumpy.

mastoid *see* MASTOID PROCESS.

mastoidectomy surgical removal of the inflamed CELLS in (and drainage of) the MASTOID PROCESS of the TEMPORAL bone of the SKULL, which is situated behind the ear, when these have become very severely infected. *See also* MASTOIDITIS.

mastoiditis INFLAMMATION of the mastoid cells and mastoid ANTRUM, usually caused by bacterial INFECTION that spreads from the middle EAR. Treatment is by means of ANTIBIOTIC drugs and sometimes surgery. *See* MASTOID PROCESS and MASTOIDECTOMY.

mastoid process *or* **mastoid** a projection of the TEMPORAL bone of the SKULL, which contains numerous air spaces (mastoid cells) and is situated behind the ear. It provides a point of attachment for some of the neck muscles and communicates with the middle EAR through an air-filled channel called the mastoid ANTRUM. *See* MASTOIDITIS.

maxilla (*pl* **maxillae**) *see* JAW.

maxillary nerve *see* TRIGEMINAL NERVE.

ME *see* MYALGIC ENCEPHALOMYELITIS.

measles an extremely infectious disease of children caused by a VIRUS and characterized by the presence of a RASH. It occurs in EPIDEMICS every two or three years. After an INCUBATION period of 10–15 days, the initial symptoms are those of a COMMON COLD, with coughing, sneezing and high FEVER. It is at this stage that the disease is most infectious and spreads from one child to another in airborne droplets before measles has been diagnosed. This is the main factor responsible for the epidemic nature of the disease. Small red spots with a white centre (known as Koplik spots) may appear in the mouth on the inside of the cheeks. Then a characteristic rash develops on the skin, spreading from behind the ears and across the face and also affecting other areas. The small red spots may be grouped together in patches, and the child's fever is usually at its height while these are developing. The spots and fever gradually decline and no marks are left on the skin, most children making a good recovery. However, complications can occur and include PNEUMONIA, middle EAR infections, deafness, ENCEPHALITIS, MENINGITIS and BRAIN damage. A VACCINE now available has reduced the incidence and severity of measles in the UK.

meatus a passage or opening, e.g. the external auditory meatus linking the pinna of the outer EAR to the eardrum.

meconium the first stools (*see* FAECES) of a newborn baby which are dark green and slimy and contain BILE pigments, MUCUS and debris from CELLS and passed during the first two days after birth.

media (*pl* **mediae**) the middle layer of a TISSUE or ORGAN. Usually it is applied to the middle layer of the wall of a VEIN or ARTERY, comprising alternating sheaths of smooth MUSCLE and elastic fibres.

mediastinum the space in the CHEST cavity between the two LUNGS, which contains the HEART, AORTA, OESOPHAGUS, TRACHEA, THYMUS GLAND and PHRENIC NERVES.

medication any substance introduced into or on the body for the purposes of medical treatment, e.g. drugs and medicated dressings.

medulla the inner portion of a TISSUE or ORGAN when there are two distinct parts. Examples include the ADRENAL medulla and the medulla of the KIDNEYS. *Compare* CORTEX.

medulla oblongata the lowest part of the BRAIN stem, which extends through the FORAMEN magnum to become the upper part of the SPINAL CORD. It contains important centres that govern RESPIRATION, CIRCULATION, swallowing and salivation.

megaloblast an abnormally large form of any of the CELLS that go on to produce ERYTHROCYTES (red blood cells). In certain forms of ANAEMIA (megaloblastic anaemias), they are found in the BONE MARROW, and their presence is the result of a deficiency of VITAMIN B12 or of FOLIC ACID. They indicate a failure in the maturation process of erythrocytes, which results in anaemia.

megalomania a psychiatric disorder in which a person suffers from delusions of grandeur about his or her greatness and power. It can accompany certain mental illnesses, such as SCHIZOPHRENIA.

meiosis a type of CELL division that occurs in the maturation process of the GAMETES (sperm and ova) so that the sex cells eventually contain only half the number of CHROMOSOMES of the parent cells from which they are derived. The daughter cells also have genetic variation from the parent cell, brought about by a process known as 'crossing over', which occurs during meiosis. When sperm and ovum fuse at FERTILIZATION, the full chromosome number is restored in a unique combination in the EMBRYO. There are two phases of division in meiosis each of which is divided into four stages, namely prophase, metaphase, anaphase and telophase.

melanin a dark brown PIGMENT found in the SKIN and HAIR and also in the choroid layer of the EYE. Melanin is contained and produced

within CELLS, known as melanocytes, in the dermis layer
of the skin. When the skin is
exposed to hot sunshine,
more melanin is produced,
giving a suntan. In dark-
skinned races, more melanin
is produced by greater activity of the melanocytes, and it
helps to protect the skin from
harmful ultraviolet radiation.

melanocyte *see* MELANIN;
MELANOMA.

melanoma an extremely malignant TUMOUR of the melanocytes, the cells in the SKIN
that produce MELANIN. Mel-
anomas are also found, although less commonly, in the
MUCOUS MEMBRANES and in
the EYE. There is a link between the occurrence of melanoma of the skin and exposure
to harmful ultraviolet light
during sunbathing. A highly
malignant form can also arise
from the pigmented CELLS of
MOLES. Melanoma can be successfully treated by surgery if
it is superficial and caught at
an early stage. It commonly
spreads, however, especially
to the LIVER and LYMPH
NODES, in which case the outlook is poor. The incidence of
MALIGNANT melanoma is in-
creasing and has attracted

much attention in connection
with the formation of holes
in the ozone layer, which
screens the earth from harmful
UV radiation. Experts recom-
mend that people should
cover exposed skin, use high
protection-factor sunscreens
and avoid the sun at the hot-
test part of the day.

membrane 1. a thin composite layer of LIPOPROTEIN surrounding an individual CELL.
2. a thin layer of tissue surrounding an organ, lining a
cavity or tube or separating
tissues and organs within the
body.

memory the function of the
BRAIN that enables past events
to be stored and remembered.
It is a highly complex function, which probably involves
many areas of the brain, including the TEMPORAL lobes.
Memory involves three stages
comprising registration, storage and recall (of information). Information is committed
either to the short-term or
long-term memory. Most for-
getfulness involves the re-
trieval of information, and
memory of a particular item is
improved if the context in
which it was registered and
stored can be recreated. This

technique is used by the police when trying to gain information from witnesses in the field of reconstruction of a crime.

Ménière's disease a disease first described by the French physician Prosper Ménière in 1861, which affects the inner EAR, causing deafness and TINNITUS (ringing in the ears), VERTIGO, VOMITING and sweating. The disease is most common in middle-aged men, with severe attacks of VERTIGO followed by VOMITING. The time interval between attacks varies from one week to several months, but the deafness gradually becomes more pronounced. The symptoms are caused by an over-accumulation of fluid in the LABYRINTHS of the inner ears, but the reason for this is not known. Treatment is by a variety of drugs and surgery, neither of which is completely successful.

meningeal sarcoma see ME-NINGIOMA.

meninges (sing **meninx**) the three CONNECTIVE TISSUE membranes that surround the SPINAL CORD and BRAIN. The outermost layer, or meninx, is called the dura mater, which is fibrous, tough and inelastic, and also called the pachyme-ninx, closely lining the inside of the SKULL and helping to protect the brain. It is thicker than the middle layer, the arachnoid mater, which surrounds the brain. The innermost layer, the pia mater, is thin and delicate and lines the brain. CEREBROSPINAL FLUID circulates between it and the arachnoid mater, and both these inner layers are richly supplied with BLOOD VESSELS that supply the surface of the brain and skull. These two inner membranes are sometimes collectively called the pia-arachnoid or leptomeninges.

meningioma a slow-growing TUMOUR affecting the ME-NINGES of the BRAIN or SPI-NAL CORD that exerts pressure on the underlying nervous TISSUE. It may cause PARA-PLEGIA or other losses of sensation if present in the spinal cord. In the brain it causes increasing neurological disability. A meningioma can be present for many years without being detected. The usual treatment is surgical removal if the tumour is accessible. MALIGNANT meningiomas, known as meningeal sarcomas, can invade surrounding tissues. These are treated by means of surgery and also RADIOTHERAPY.

meningitis INFLAMMATION of the MENINGES (membranes) of the BRAIN (cerebral meningitis) or SPINAL CORD (spinal meningitis), or the disease may affect both regions. Meningitis may affect the dura mater membrane, in which case it is known as pachymeningitis, although this is relatively uncommon. It often results as a secondary infection because of the presence of disease elsewhere, as in the case of syphilitic meningitis and tuberculous meningitis (*see* SYPHILIS; TUBERCULOSIS). Meningitis that affects the other two membranes (the pia-arachnoid membranes) is known as leptomeningitis and is more common, and it may be either a primary or secondary INFECTION. Meningitis is also classified according to its causal organism and may be either viral or bacterial. Viral meningitis is fairly mild and, as it does not respond to drugs, treatment is by means of bed rest until recovery takes place. Bacterial meningitis is much more common and is caused by the organisms responsible for TUBERCULOSIS, PNEUMO-

NIA and SYPHILIS. Also, the *meningococcus* type of BACTERIA causes one of the commonest forms of the disease, meningococcal meningitis. The symptoms are a severe headache, sensitivity to light and sound, muscle rigidity especially affecting the neck, KERNIG'S SIGN, VOMITING, PARALYSIS, COMA and death. These are caused by inflammation of the meninges and by a rise in INTRACRANIAL PRESSURE. One of the features of meningitis is that there is a change in the constituents and appearance of the CEREBROSPINAL FLUID, and the infective organism can usually be isolated from it and identified. The onset of the symptoms can be very rapid and death can also follow swiftly. Treatment is by means of ANTIBIOTIC drugs and SULPHONAMIDES.

menopause *or* **climacteric** the time in a woman's life when the ovaries (*see* OVARY) no longer release an egg CELL every month and MENSTRUATION ceases. The woman is normally no longer able to bear a child. The age at which the menopause occurs is usually between 45 and 55. The menopause may be marked by a gradual decline in menstruation or in its frequency, or menstruation may cease abruptly. There is a disturbance in the balance of SEX HORMONES, and this causes a number of physical symptoms, including palpitations, hot flushes, sweats, vaginal dryness, loss of LIBIDO and DEPRESSION. In the long term, there is a gradual loss of BONE (OSTEOPOROSIS) in postmenopausal women, which leads to greater risk of FRACTURES, especially of the FEMUR in the elderly. All these symptoms are relieved by hormone replacement therapy (HRT), involving OESTROGEN and PROGESTERONE, or oestrogen only, but there are associated risks, particularly with long-term use.

menorrhagia abnormally heavy menstrual bleeding.

menstrual cycle *and* **menstruation** the cyclical nature of the reproductive life of a sexually mature female. One OVUM develops and matures within a Graafian FOLLICLE in one of the ovaries (*see* OVARY). When mature, the follicle ruptures to release the egg, which passes down the FALLOPIAN TUBE to the UTERUS. The ruptured follicle becomes a temporary ENDOCRINE GLAND, called the CORPUS LUTEUM which secretes the hormone PROGESTERONE. Under the influence of progesterone, the uterus wall (ENDOMETRIUM) thickens and its blood supply increases in readiness for the implantation of a fertilized egg. If the egg is not fertilized and there is no PREGNANCY, the thickened endometrium is shed along with a flow of blood through the VAGINA (menstruation). The usual age at which menstruation starts is 12 to 15 but it can be as early as 10 or as late as 20. The duration varies and can be anything from 2 to 8 days, the whole cycle usually occupying about 29 to 30 days.

mercaptopurine a type of ANTIMETABOLITE, CYTOTOXIC drug that prevents the proliferation of malignant CANCER cells and is used in the treatment of certain kinds of LEUKAEMIA and CROHN'S DISEASE (a disease of the digestive tract).

metronidazole *see* TRICHOMONIASIS.

mesencephalon *or* **midbrain** the part of the BRAIN

that connects the PONS and CEREBELLUM with the CEREBRUM.

mesentery a double layer of the peritoneal MEMBRANE (PERITONEUM), which is attached to the back wall of the ABDOMEN. It supports a number of abdominal ORGANS, including the STOMACH, small INTESTINE, SPLEEN and PANCREAS, and contains associated NERVES, LYMPH and BLOOD VESSELS.

mesothelioma a malignant TUMOUR of the PLEURA of the chest cavity and also of the PERICARDIUM or PERITONEUM. It is usually associated with exposure to asbestos dust but may arise independently with no known cause. Most mesotheliomas are in sites that render them inoperable, and CHEMOTHERAPY and RADIOTHERAPY are used but often with limited success.

metabolism the sum of all the physical and chemical changes within CELLS and tissues that maintain life and growth. The breakdown processes that occur are known as catabolic (CATABOLISM), and those that build materials up are called anabolic (anabolism). The term may also be

applied to describe one particular set of changes, e.g. PROTEIN metabolism. Basal metabolism is the minimum amount of energy required to maintain the body's vital processes, e.g. heartbeat and RESPIRATION, and is usually assessed by means of various measurements taken while a person is at rest.

metabolite see ANTIMETABOLITE; DRUG METABOLISM.

metacarpal bone one of the five BONES of the middle of the HAND, between the PHALANGES of the fingers and the carpal bones of the wrist (see CARPUS) forming the metacarpus. The heads of the metacarpal bones form the knuckles.

metaphase see MEIOSIS.

metaplasia an abnormal change that has taken place within a TISSUE e.g. myeloid metaplasia, where elements of BONE MARROW develop within the SPLEEN and LIVER. Also squamous metaplasia, which involves a change in the EPITHELIUM lining the BRONCHI of the LUNGS.

metastasis the process by which a malignant TUMOUR spreads to a distant part of the body and also the secondary growth that results from this.

The spread is accomplished by means of three routes: the blood CIRCULATION, LYMPHATIC SYSTEM and across body cavities.

metatarsal bone one of the five BONES in the FOOT, lying between the toes and the TARSAL bones of the ankle, together forming the metatarsus. The metatarsal bones are equivalent to the METACARPAL BONES in the HAND.

methadone a strong ANALGESIC and narcotic drug, resembling MORPHINE, that is used in pain relief and as a COUGH suppressant. In addition, it is used as a HEROIN substitute in the treatment of addiction.

methicillin resistant staphylococcus aureus (MRSA) a strain of *staphylococcus aureus* that has developed resistance to many ANTIBIOTICS. INFECTION with MRSA occurs most frequently in hospitals, particularly among patients with open wounds, patients who have undergone antibiotic therapy, patients requiring intensive care and the elderly, but it can also occur elsewhere. It can be treated with antibiotics but infections may be very severe and recovery is often slow. It can be fatal.

methionine *see* ESSENTIAL AMINO ACID.

methyldopa a drug that is used to reduce high BLOOD PRESSURE, especially in PREGNANCY.

metritis inflammation of the UTERUS.

MHC (major histocompatibility complex) a group of GENES located on CHROMOSOME 6, which code for the HLA ANTIGENS.

microbe a microscopic organism such as a BACILLUS or bacterium (*see* BACTERIA).

microbiology the scientific study of microorganisms, i.e. those that are too small to be studied with the naked eye. They include VIRUSES and BACTERIA, some of which are major causes of disease in humans and animals.

microcephaly the condition in which there is abnormal smallness of the head compared to the rest of the body. *See also* MACROCEPHALY.

microglia *see* MACROPHAGE.

microorganism *see* MICROBIOLOGY.

microsurgery surgery performed with the aid of an operating microscope using high precision, miniaturized instruments. It is routine for some operations on the EYE, LARYNX and EAR and increasingly in areas inaccessible to normal surgery, e.g. parts of the BRAIN and SPINAL CORD. Microsurgery is also performed in the rejoining of severed limbs, fingers, toes, etc, where very fine suturing of minute BLOOD VESSELS and NERVES is required.

microwave therapy the use of very short wavelength electromagnetic waves in the procedure known as DIATHERMY.

micturition the act of URINATION.

mid-brain *see* MESENCEPHALON.

middle ear *see* EAR.

midwifery a specialised branch of the nursing profession devoted to the care of mothers during PREGNANCY and childbirth and of mothers and babies during the period after delivery. A member of the profession is known as a midwife.

migraine a very severe throbbing HEADACHE, usually on one side of the head, which is often accompanied by disturbances in vision, NAUSEA and VOMITING. Migraine is a common condition and seems to be triggered by any one or several of a number of factors. These include anxiety, FATIGUE, watching television or video screens, loud noises, flickering lights (e.g. strobe lights) and certain foods such as cheese and chocolate or alcoholic drinks. The cause is unknown but thought to involve constriction followed by dilation of BLOOD VESSELS in the BRAIN and an outpouring of fluid into surrounding TISSUES. Attacks can last up to 24 hours. Treatment is by means of bed rest in a darkened, quiet room and pain-relieving drugs.

miliaria *see* PRICKLY HEAT.

miliary a term meaning 'resembling tiny seeds', used to describe a disease or condition of the skin that is characterized by small LESIONS that look like seeds, e.g. miliary TUBERCULOSIS.

mineralocorticosteroid *see* CORTICOSTEROID.

miscarriage *or* **spontaneous abortion** the premature, spontaneous ending of a PREGNANCY, resulting in the expulsion of a FOETUS which is not VIABLE. Most miscarriages occur in the first trimester of pregnancy.

mitobronitol a type of drug, used in the treatment of LEU-KAEMIA, that prevents the growth of CANCER cells.

mitochondrion (*pl* **mito-chondria**) a tiny rodlike structure, numbers of which are present in the CYTOPLASM of every CELL. Mitochondria contain ENZYMES and ATP involved in cell METABOLISM.

mitosis the type of CELL division undergone by most body cells by means of which the growth and repair of tissues can take place. Mitosis involves the division of a single cell to produce two genetically identical daughter cells, each with the full number of CHRO-MOSOMES. *Compare* MEIOSIS.

mitral incompetence *or* **mi-tral regurgitation** a condition in which the MITRAL VALVE of the HEART is defective and allows BLOOD to leak back from the left VENTRICLE into the left ATRIUM. It is often caused by RHEUMATIC FE-VER or can be a congenital defect or the result of MYO-CARDIAL INFARCTION. The left ventricle is forced to work harder and enlarges but eventually may be unable to cope, and this can result in left-sided HEART FAILURE. Other symptoms include atrial FI-BRILLATION, BREATHLESS-NESS and EMBOLISM. Drug treatment and/or surgery to replace the defective valve may be required (mitral pros-thesis, *see* MITRAL STENOSIS).

mitral stenosis a condition in which the opening between the left ATRIUM and left VENTRICLE is narrowed because of scarring and adhesion of the MITRAL VALVE. This scarring is often caused by RHEUMATIC FEVER, and the symptoms are similar to those of MITRAL INCOMPE-TENCE, accompanied also by a diastolic MURMUR. It is treated surgically by widening the STE-NOSIS (mitral VALVOTOMY) or by valve replacement—mitral PROSTHESIS.

mitral valve (formerly known as the bicuspid valve) a VALVE that is located between the ATRIUM and VENTRICLE of the left side of the HEART, attached to the walls at the opening be-tween the two. It has two cusps or flaps and normally allows BLOOD to pass into the ventri-cle from the atrium but pre-vents any back flow.

MMR vaccine a VACCINE, in-troduced in 1988, that protects against MEASLES, MUMPS and GERMAN MEASLES (rubella). It is normally given to children during their second year.

molar *see* TOOTH.

mole a dark-coloured PIG-MENTED spot in the SKIN, which is usually brown. It may be flat or raised and may have hair protruding from it. Some types can become MA-LIGNANT (*see* MELANOMA).

monocyte the largest type of white blood cell (LEUCOCYTE) with a kidney-shaped nucleus and found in the blood and LYMPH. It ingests foreign bodies such as BACTERIA and TIS-SUE particles.

mononucleosis *see* GLANDU-LAR FEVER.

monozygotic twins *or* **identical twins** twin children who are derived from a single fertilized egg which then divides into two separate EM-BRYOS.

morbidity the state of being diseased, the morbidity rate being expressed as the number of cases of a disease occurring within a particular number of the population.

moribund a term meaning dying.

morning sickness VOMITING and NAUSEA, most common during the first three months of PREGNANCY. Although the symptoms are commonly present on waking, they may also persist throughout the day. *See also* HYPEREMESIS.

morphine a NARCOTIC and very strong ANALGESIC drug that is an alkaloid derived from OPIUM. It is used for the relief of severe pain but tolerance and dependence may occur, leading to ADDIC-TION.

motility the ability to move without outside aid.

motion sickness *or* **travel sickness** symptoms of VOM-ITING, NAUSEA and HEAD-ACHE caused by travel via car, boat or aeroplane. The symptoms are caused by over-stimulation of the balance mechanism in the inner EAR because of numerous changes in position and an inability to adjust to them rapidly. Although unpleasant, the symptoms are generally not serious and a number of drugs are used to alleviate the condition or to prevent its onset.

motor nerve a nerve, containing MOTOR NEURONE fibres, that carries electrical impulses outwards from the CENTRAL NERVOUS SYSTEM to a MUSCLE or GLAND to bring about a response there.

motor neuron one of the units or fibres of a MOTOR NERVE. An upper motor neuron is contained entirely within the CENTRAL NERVOUS SYSTEM, having its CELL body in the BRAIN and its AXON (a long process) extending into the SPINAL CORD where it SYNAPSES with other neurons. A lower motor neuron has its cell body in the spinal cord or BRAIN stem and an axon that runs outwards via a spinal or cranial motor nerve to an effector MUSCLE or GLAND.

motor neurone disease a disease of unknown cause that most commonly occurs in middle age and is a degenerative condition affecting elements of the CENTRAL NERVOUS SYSTEM (i.e. the fibres of the CEREBRAL CORTEX and SPINAL CORD, motor nuclei in the BRAIN stem and the cells of the anterior horn of the spinal cord). It causes increasing PARALYSIS involving NERVES and MUSCLES and is ultimately fatal.

mouth the opening that forms the beginning of the ALIMENTARY CANAL and through which food enters the digestive process. The entrance is guarded by the lips, behind which lie the upper and lower sets of teeth (*see* TOOTH) embedded in the JAW. The roof of the mouth is called the PALATE, the front part being hard and immobile while behind lies the mobile soft palate. The TONGUE is situated behind the lower teeth, and SALIVARY GLANDS which are present secrete saliva into the mouth through small ducts. Saliva contains the ENZYME ptyalin, which begins the breakdown of starch while the chewing action of the teeth and manipulation with the tongue reduce the food to a more manageable size so that it can be swallowed.

MRI *see* MAGNETIC RESONANCE IMAGING.

MRSA *see* METHICILLIN RESISTANT STAPHYLOCOCCUS AUREUS.

mucosa another term for MUCOUS MEMBRANE.

mucous membrane a moist MEMBRANE that lines many tubes and cavities within the body and is lubricated with MUCUS. The structure of a mucous membrane varies according to its site, and they are found, for example, lining the mouth, respiratory, urinary and digestive tracts. Each has a surface EPITHELIUM, a layer containing various cells and glands that secrete mucus. Beneath this lie CONNECTIVE TISSUE and MUSCLE layers, the laminae propria and muscularis mucosa respectively, the whole forming a pliable layer.

mucus a slimy substance secreted by MUCOUS MEMBRANES as a lubricant. It is a clear viscous fluid that may contain ENZYMES and has a protective function. It is normally present in small amounts but the quantity increases if INFLAMMATION or INFECTION is present.

multiple births twins, triplets, quadruplets, quintuplets and sextuplets born to one mother. While naturally-occurring twins are relatively common, other multiple births are normally rare. Their incidence has increased with the advent of fertility drugs although often some of the infants do not survive.

multiple sclerosis a disease of the BRAIN and SPINAL CORD that affects the MYELIN sheaths of NERVES and disrupts their function. It usually affects people below the age of 40, and its cause is unknown but is the subject of much research. The disease is characterized by the presence of patches of hardened (sclerotic) CONNECTIVE TISSUE irregularly scattered through the brain and spinal cord. At first the fatty part of the nerve sheaths breaks down and is absorbed, leaving bare nerve fibres, and then connective tissue is laid down. Symptoms depend on the site of the patches in the CENTRAL NERVOUS SYSTEM, and the disease is characterized by periods of progression and REMISSION. However, they include unsteady gait and apparent clumsiness, tremor of the limbs, involuntary eye movements, speech disorders, bladder dysfunction and PARALYSIS. The disease can progress very slowly, but generally there is a tendency for the paralysis to become more marked.

mumps an infectious disease of childhood, usually occurring in those between the ages of five to 15 and caused by a virus that produces INFLAMMATION of the PAROTID GLANDS. The INCUBATION period is two to three weeks, followed by symptoms including FEVER, headache, sore THROAT and VOMITING, before or along with a swelling of the parotid gland on one side of the face. The swelling may be confined to one side or spread to the other side of the face and also may go on to include the submaxillary and sublingual SALIVARY GLANDS beneath the jaw. Generally, after a few days the swelling subsides and the child recovers but remains infectious until the glands have returned to normal. The infection may spread to the PANCREAS and, in 15–30 per cent of males, to the TESTICLES. In adult men this can cause sterility. More rarely, inflammation in females can affect the ovaries and breasts, and MENINGITIS is another occasional complication, especially in adults. A protective vaccine is now available (*see* MMR VACCINE).

Munchausen's syndrome a rare mental disorder in which a person tries to obtain hospital treatment for a nonexistent illness. The person is adept at simulating symptoms and may self-induce these or cause self-inflicted injury to add authenticity. The person may end up having unnecessary treatment and operations and is resistant to psychotherapy. Munchausen's Syndrome by Proxy is a related syndrome whereby the sufferer tries to produce the symptoms of illness in another person. It is most commonly manifest in parents, particularly mothers, who try to make their children appear sick and may cause significant harm in doing so.

murmur a characteristic sound, which can be heard using a STETHOSCOPE, caused by uneven blood flow through the HEART or BLOOD VESSELS when these are diseased or damaged. Heart murmurs can also be present in normal individuals, especially children, without indicating disease. Murmurs are classified as diastolic, when the VENTRICLES are relaxed and filling with blood, or systolic, when they are contracting.

muscle the contractile TISSUE of the body, which produces movements of various structures both internally and externally. There are three types of muscle:

1. striated or VOLUNTARY MUSCLE, which has a striped appearance when viewed under a microscope and is attached to the SKELETON. It is called 'voluntary' because it is under the

control of the will and produces movements, e.g. in the limbs.

2. smooth or INVOLUNTARY MUSCLE, which has a plain appearance when viewed microscopically and is not under conscious control but is supplied by the AUTONOMIC NERVOUS SYSTEM. Examples are the muscles that supply the digestive and respiratory tracts.

3. CARDIAC MUSCLE, the specialized muscle of the walls of the HEART, which is composed of a network of branching, elongated fibres that rejoin and interlock, each having a nucleus. It has a somewhat striated appearance, and where there are junctions between fibres, irregular transverse bands occur, known as intercalated discs. This muscle is involuntary, and contracts and expands rhythmically throughout an individual's life. However, rate of heartbeat is influenced by activity within the VAGUS NERVE.

muscle cramp *see* CRAMP.

muscle relaxant a substance or drug that causes MUSCLES to relax. They are mainly used in ANAESTHESIA to produce relaxation or PARALYSIS of muscles while surgery is being carried out, e.g. tubocurarine and gallamine. Others are administered to counteract muscular spasms, which are a feature of spastic conditions such as PARKINSONISM, e.g. DIAZEPAM.

muscular dystrophy *or* **myopathy** any of a group of diseases that involve wasting of MUSCLES and in which an hereditary factor is involved. The disease is classified according to the groups of muscles that it affects and the age of the person involved. The disease usually appears in childhood and causes muscle fibres to degenerate and to be replaced by fatty and FIBROUS TISSUE. The affected muscles eventually lose all power of contraction, causing great disability, and affected children are prone to chest and other INFECTIONS, which may prove fatal in their weakened state. The cause of the disease is not entirely understood but the commonest form, Duchenne muscular dystrophy, is a SEX-LINKED DISORDER and recessive, so it nearly always affects boys, with the mother as a carrier, and appears in very early childhood.

muscularis mucosa *see* MU-COUS MEMBRANE.

mutagen any substance or agent that increases the rate of MUTATION in body CELLS, examples being various chemicals, viruses and radiation. Mutagens increase the number, rather than the range, of mutations beyond what might be expected.

mutation a change that takes place in the DNA (the genetic material) of the CHROMO-SOMES of a cell, which is normally a rare event. The change may involve the structure or number of whole chromosomes or take place at one GENE site. Mutations are caused by faulty replication of the cell's genetic material at cell division. If normal body (somatic) cells are involved, there may be a growth of altered cells or a TUMOUR, or these may be attacked and destroyed by the IMMUNE system. In any event, this type of mutation cannot be passed on. If the sex cells (ova or sperm) are involved in the mutation, the alteration may be passed on to the offspring, producing a changed characteristic.

mutism the refusal or inability to speak, which may result from BRAIN damage or psychological factors. Speechlessness is most common in those who have been born deaf (deaf-mutism).

myalgia pain in a MUSCLE.

myalgic encephalomyelitis (ME) *or* **post-viral fatigue syndrome** a disorder characterized by muscular pain, FATIGUE, general DEPRESSION and loss of memory and concentration. The cause is not understood but seems to follow on from viral infections such as INFLUENZA, hence its alternative name. Recovery may be prolonged and there is no specific treatment.

myasthenia gravis a serious and chronic condition of uncertain cause, which may be an AUTOIMMUNE DISEASE. It is more common among young people, especially women (men tend to be affected over 40). Rest and avoidance of unnecessary exertion is essential to conserve MUSCLE strength as there is a reduction in the ability of the neurotransmitter, ACETYLCHOLINE, to effect muscle contraction. There is a weakening that affects skeletal muscles and those for breathing and swallowing, etc. However, there is little wasting of the muscles themselves. It seems the body produces ANTIBODIES that interfere with the acetylcholine receptors in the muscle and that the THYMUS GLAND may be the original source of these receptors. Surgical removal of the THYMUS GLAND is one treatment. Other treatment is by means of drugs that inhibit the activity of the ENZYME cholinesterase, which destroys excess acetylcholine. Other IMMUNOSUPPRESSIVE drugs are used to suppress production of the antibodies that interfere with the receptors.

mycoplasma a microorganism of the *Mycoplasma* genus, several species of which cause disease.

mycosis any disease caused by a FUNGUS, e.g. THRUSH.

myelin a sheath of phospholipid (*see* LIPOSOME) and PROTEIN that surrounds the axons of some NEURONS. It is formed by specialized CELLS known as Schwann cells, each of which encloses the axon in concentric folds of its cell MEMBRANE. These folds then condense to form myelin, the neuron then being described as myelinated. Schwann cells produce myelin at regular intervals along the length of the axon, and electrical impulses pass more rapidly along myelinated nerve fibres than along non-myelinated ones.

myelitis 1. any inflammatory condition of the SPINAL CORD such as often occurs in MULTIPLE SCLEROSIS. **2.** inflammation of BONE MARROW, *see* OSTEOMYELITIS.

myeloblast *see* LEUKAEMIA.

myelocyte a CELL that is an immature type of granulocyte (*see* LEUCOCYTE) responsible for the production of white blood cells.

myelofibrosis a disease, the cause of which is unknown, in which FIBROSIS takes place within the BONE MARROW, and many immature red and white blood cells (*see* ERYTHROCYTE, LEUCOCYTE) appear in the circulation because of the resultant ANAEMIA. There is an enlargement of the SPLEEN, and blood-producing (MYELOID) tissue is abnormally found both here and in the LIVER.

myelography a specialized X-RAY technique involving the injection of a radio-opaque dye into the central canal of the SPINAL CORD in order to distinguish the presence of disease. The X-rays are called myelograms.

myeloid a term meaning like or relating to BONE MARROW or like a MYELOCYTE.

myeloma a MALIGNANT disease of the BONE MARROW in which TUMOURS are present in more than one bone at the same time. The bones may show 'holes' when X-rayed because of typical deposits, and certain abnormal PROTEINS may be present in the blood and urine. Treatment is by chemotherapy and radiotherapy. Myelomatosis is the production of myeloma, which is usually fatal.

myocardial infarction NECROSIS of part of the MYOCARDIUM, usually as a result of a CORONARY THROMBOSIS.

myocarditis INFLAMMATION of the MUSCLE in the wall of the HEART.

myocardium the middle of the three layers of the HEART wall, which is the thick, muscular area. The outer layer is the epicardium (forming part of the PERICARDIUM) and the inner the ENDOCARDIUM.

myoglobin an iron-containing PIGMENT that is similar to HAEMOGLOBIN and occurs in MUSCLE cells. It binds oxygen from haemoglobin and releases it in the muscle cells.

myoma a benign TUMOUR in MUSCLE, often in the UTERUS (womb).

myomectomy surgical removal of FIBROIDS from the muscular wall of the UTERUS.

myometrium the muscular TISSUE of the UTERUS, composed of smooth MUSCLE and surrounding the ENDOMETRIUM. Its contractions are influenced by the presence of certain HORMONES and are especially strong during LABOUR.

myopathy see MUSCULAR DYSTROPHY.

myofibril see VOLUNTARY MUSCLE.

myopia short-sightedness, which is corrected by wearing spectacles with concave lenses.

myxoedema a disease caused by underactivity of the THYROID gland (HYPOTHYROIDISM). There is a characteristic development of a dry, coarse SKIN and swelling of SUBCUTANEOUS tissue. There is intellectual impairment, with slow speech and mental dullness, lethargy, MUSCLE pain, weight gain and constipation. The hair thins and there may be increased sensitivity to cold. As the symptoms are caused by the deficiency of thyroid HORMONES, treatment consists of giving THYROXINE in suitable amounts.

N

naevus see BIRTHMARK.

nail the horny structure at the end of a finger or toe. It is formed of KERATIN, which is derived from the EPIDERMIS (superficial layer of the SKIN made up from an outer dead part and a living cellular part beneath). The body is the part of the nail showing, while the root is beneath the skin. The pale crescent is called the lunula.

narcolepsy a condition wherein a person has a tendency to fall asleep a few times per day for several minutes or hours. The attacks may occur when in quiet surroundings or may be induced by laughter and the person may be woken easily. It is thought that it may be an IMMUNE-related disease and lasts for life. Drugs (AMFETAMINE type)

may be taken to ensure attacks do not occur at certain times, but regular doses are considered ill-advised in view of possible mental effects.

narcosis a state induced by NARCOTIC drugs in which a person is completely unconscious or nearly so but can respond a little to stimuli. It is the result of the depressant action of the drugs on the body.

narcotic a drug that leads to a stupor and complete loss of awareness. In particular, OPIATES derived from MORPHINE or produced synthetically induce various conditions: deep sleep, euphoria, mood changes and mental confusion. In addition, RESPIRATION and the cough reflex are depressed and MUSCLE spasms may be produced. Because of the dependence resulting from the use of morphine-like compounds, they have largely been replaced as sleeping drugs.

nasal cavity one of two cavities in the NOSE, divided by a SEPTUM, which lie between the roof of the MOUTH and the floor of the CRANIUM.

nasogastric tube a tube of small diameter that is passed through the NOSE into the STOMACH for purposes of introducing food or drugs or removing fluid (ASPIRATION).

nausea a feeling of being about to VOMIT. It may be caused by MIGRAINE, MOTION SICKNESS, early PREGNANCY, pain, FOOD POISONING or a VIRUS.

navel *see* UMBILICAL CORD.

nebula (*pl* **nebulae**) **1.** a slight opacity or SCAR of the CORNEA that does not obstruct VISION but may create haziness. **2.** an oily substance applied in a fine spray.

nebulizer a device for producing a fine spray. Many inhaled drugs are administered in this way, and it is an effective method of delivering a concentrated form of medication, e.g. BRONCHODILATORS.

neck 1. the part of the body between the head and the trunk. **2.** the narrow part of a BONE or organ.

necropsy an autopsy (POST-MORTEM) that results in little disfigurement.

necrosis death of TISSUE in a localized area or ORGAN, caused by disease, injury or loss or interruption of BLOOD supply.

necrotizing fasciitis a progressive INFECTION that causes the destruction of soft TISSUE just below the SKIN. There are two types: type 1 is caused by a mixture of BACTERIA, including *E. coli* (*see* ESCHERICHIA); type 2 includes bacteria of the *Streptococcus pyogenes* strain (*see* STREPTOCOCCUS).

neomycin an ANTIBIOTIC, usually applied as a cream, that is effective against a wide spectrum of BACTERIA. Its main use is as a SKIN treatment.

neonatal a term meaning 'relating to the first 28 days of life'.

neonatal abstinence syndrome (NAS) *or* **neonatal withdrawal syndrome** a condition in newborn infants that is caused by a mother's dependence on drugs during PREGNANCY. Symptoms develop within two to seven days after birth, the time taken for them to appear varying with the drug (or drugs) of dependency. Typical symptoms include irritability and poor sleep patterns, a loud, high-pitched crying, sweating, sneezing, yawning, fever, DIARRHOEA and feeding difficulties. The condition is associated with premature births and low birth weight. If the mother has drunk excessive quantities of alcohol during pregnancy, there are likely to be physical signs of FOETAL ALCOHOL SYNDROME. There is evidence that the risk of SUDDEN INFANT DEATH SYNDROME is increased in infants with neonatal abstinence syndrome.

neoplasm a new and abnormal growth of CELLS, i.e. a TUMOUR, which may be BENIGN or MALIGNANT.

nephrectomy surgical removal of the KIDNEY (radical) or part of the kidney (partial). It may be necessary to remove a TUMOUR (when the surrounding fat and ADRENAL GLAND will probably also be excised) or to drain an ABSCESS.

nephritis INFLAMMATION of the KIDNEY, which may be the result of one of several causes. Types of nephritis include glomerulonephritis (when the glomerulus is affected), acute nephritis, hereditary nephritis, etc.

nephroblastoma *see* WILM'S TUMOUR.

nephron *see* KIDNEY.

nerve a bundle of fibres comprising NEURONS and glial (supporting) CELLS (*see* GLIA),

all contained in a fibrous sheath, the epineurium. MOTOR NERVES carry (efferent) impulses in motor neurons from the BRAIN (or SPINAL CORD) to MUSCLES or GLANDS, and a SENSORY nerve carries (afferent) impulses in sensory neurons from sensory organs to the brain or spinal cord. Most large nerves are mixed nerves containing both motor and sensory nerves.

nerve block *or* **conduction anaesthesia** the technique of blocking SENSORY nerves sending pain impulses to the brain, thus creating ANAESTHESIA in that part of the body. It is achieved by injecting the TISSUE around a nerve with local ANAESTHETIC (e.g. LIDOCAINE) to permit minor operations.

nerve impulse the transmission of information along a NERVE fibre by electrical activity, which has its basis in the formation of chemical substances and the generation of the action potential. This is a change in electrical potential across the cell MEMBRANE (between inside and outside) of an AXON (nerve CELL) as an impulse moves along. It is a temporary and localized occurrence caused by a stimulus that travels down the axon, and the voltage is caused by sodium ions (Na+) entering the axon and changing the potential across the cell membrane from −65mV to +45mV (millivolts). When the stimulus has passed, the membrane is restored to its resting potential. When a stimulus is continually received, several hundred pulses travel along the nerve per second.

nerve injury a NERVE may be injured by being severed; pressure may damage a nerve directly or push it against a BONE. Damage to a SENSORY nerve results in a lack of, or lessening in, sensation, while PARALYSIS of MUSCLES will result from damage to the associated MOTOR NERVE.

nervous system the complete system of TISSUES and CELLS, including NERVES, NEURONS, SYNAPSES and RECEPTORS (a special cell sensitive to a particular stimulus which then sends an impulse through the nervous system). The nervous system operates through the transmission of NERVE IMPULSES that are conducted rapidly to and from MUSCLES, ORGANS, etc. It consists of the CENTRAL NERVOUS SYSTEM (brain and spinal cord) and the PERIPHERAL NERVOUS SYSTEM, which includes the CRANIAL NERVES and spinal nerves (*see* AUTONOMIC NERVOUS SYSTEM).

nettle rash *see* URTICARIA.

neuralgia strictly, pain in some part or the whole of a NERVE (without any physical change in the nerve) but used more widely to encompass pain following the course of a nerve or its branches, whatever the cause. Neuralgia often occurs at the same time each day and is frequently an agonizing pain. It occurs in several forms and is named accordingly, e.g. SCIATICA, trigeminal neuralgia (affecting the face, *see* TRIGEMINAL NERVE) and intercostal neuralgia (affecting the RIBS). Treatment often involves the application of ointments and the taking of painkilling drugs. If such treatments do not bring relief, it is possible to freeze the nerve or destroy part of it by surgery.

neuritis INFLAMMATION of a NERVE or nerves, which may be the result of inflammation from nearby TISSUES or a more general condition in which the nerve fibres degenerate. This latter condition (polyneuritis) is caused by a systemic poison such as alcohol or long-term exposure to solvents such as naphtha.

neuroendocrine system one of a number of dual control systems regulating bodily functions through the action of NERVES and HORMONES.

neurofibromatosis *see* VON RECKLINGHAUSEN'S DISEASE.

neuroglia the fine web of tissues that support nerve fibres (*see* GLIA).

neurohormone a HORMONE that is secreted by the NERVE endings of specialized nerve CELLS (i.e. neurosecretory cells) and not by an ENDOCRINE GLAND. They are secreted into the bloodstream or directly into the target tissue. Included are NORADRENALINE and VASOPRESSIN (produced in the HYPOTHALAMUS and secreted by the PITUITARY GLAND—active in the control of water reabsorption in the KIDNEYS).

neurohypophysis *see* PITUITARY GLAND.

neuroleptic any drug that induces neurolepsis, i.e. reduced activity, some indifference to the surroundings and possibly sleep. They are used to quieten disturbed patients suffering from DELIRIUM, BRAIN damage or behavioural disturbances.

neurology the subdiscipline of medicine that involves the study of the BRAIN, SPINAL CORD and peripheral NERVES, their diseases and the treatment of those conditions.

neuromuscular blockade the blocking of impulses at the NEUROMUSCULAR JUNCTION to paralyse a part of the body for surgery (*see also* NERVE BLOCK).

neuromuscular junction the area of MEMBRANE between a MUSCLE cell and a MOTOR NEURON, forming a SYNAPSE between the two. NERVE IMPULSES travel down the neuron, and each releases ACETYLCHOLINE, which slightly depolarizes the enlarged end of the neuron (the motor end plate). These small depolarizations are totaled until a threshold of -50mV is reached, and this results in the production of an 'action potential' that crosses the synapse into the muscle fibre, thereby producing a muscle contraction.

neuron a NERVE cell, vital in the transmission of NERVE IMPULSES. Each CELL has an enlarged portion (the cell body) from which extends the long, thin AXON for carrying impulses away. Shorter, more numerous DENDRITES receive impulses. The transmission of impulses is faster in axons that are covered in a sheath of MYELIN.

neuropathy any disease that affects the peripheral NERVES, whether singly (mononeuropathy) or more generally (polyneuropathy). The SYMPTOMS depend on the type of nerves affected.

neurosecretory cell *see* NEUROHORMONE.

neurosis (*pl* **neuroses**) a mental disorder but one in which the patient retains a grasp on reality (unlike PSYCHOSIS). Neuroses may be caused by DEPRESSION, PHOBIA, HYSTERIA or HYPOCHRONDRIA. Anxiety is the commonest version, although this does respond to treatment. In practice, the boundary between neurosis and psychosis is vague.

neurosurgery surgical treatment of the BRAIN, SPINAL CORD or NERVES, including dealing with head injuries, intracranial pressure, HAEMORRHAGES, INFECTIONS and TUMOURS.

neurotic someone afflicted with a NEUROSIS. More generally, a nervous person who acts on emotions more than reason.

neurotransmitter one of several chemical substances released in minute quantities by axon tips into the SYNAPSE to enable a NERVE IMPULSE to cross. It diffuses across the space and may depolarize the opposite MEMBRANE, allowing the production of an action potential. Outside the central nervous system, ACETYLCHOLINE is a major neurotransmitter, and NORADRENALINE is released in the SYMPATHETIC NERVOUS SYSTEM. Acetylcholine and noradrenaline also operate within the CENTRAL NERVOUS SYSTEM, as does DOPAMINE, amongst others.

new variant CJD (vCJD) a rare degenerative brain disorder that is inevitably fatal. Symptoms are similar to those of classic CREUTZFELDT JACOB DISEASE but differ in order of presentation. The age of victims is typically younger than that of those who develop classic CJD. The disease is now thought to be transmissible in two ways: 1. through consumption of beef infected with BOVINE SPONGIFORM ENCEPHALOPATHY and 2. through transfusion of blood products from an infected DONOR. The incubation period of the disease is not known but is thought to be a number of years. The disease progresses rapidly after the appearance of the first symptoms. DIAGNOSIS is made on assessment of symptoms and is finally confirmed by post mortem examination of the BRAIN.

nicotinic acid *see* PELLAGRA.

nifedipine a drug used in the treatment of ANGINA and high BLOOD PRESSURE.

night blindness *or* **nyctalopia** poor vision in dim light or at night because of a deficiency within the CELLS responsible for such vision (*see* ROD). The cause may be a lack of VITAMIN A in the diet or a CONGENITAL defect.

nitroglycerine *see* VASODILATOR.

nitrous oxide (formerly called laughing gas) a colourless gas used for ANAESTHESIA over short periods. Longer effects require its use with oxygen and it may be used as a 'carrier' for stronger ANAESTHETICS.

non-steroidal anti-inflammatory drugs (**NSAID**) a large group of drugs used to relieve pain and also inhibit INFLAMMATION. They are used for conditions such as RHEUMATOID ARTHRITIS, sprains, etc, and include ASPIRIN and IBUPROFEN. Possible side effects with long-term use include GASTRIC ULCER and HAEMORRHAGE, but the synthesis of new compounds has led to the availability of NSAID's with milder side effects.

noradrenaline *or* **norepinephrine** (US) a NEUROTRANSMITTER of the SYMPATHETIC NERVOUS SYSTEM secreted by nerve endings and also the ADRENAL GLANDS. It is similar to ADRENALINE in structure and function. It increases BLOOD PRESSURE by constricting the vessel, slowing heartbeat and increasing breathing both in rate and depth.

nose the olfactory ORGAN and also a pathway for air entering the body, by which route it is warmed, filtered and moistened before passing into the LUNGS. The 'external' nose leads to the NASAL CAVITY, which has a MUCOUS MEMBRANE with olfactory (smell) CELLS.

notifiable diseases diseases that must be reported to the health authorities to enable rapid control and monitoring to be undertaken. The list varies between countries, but in the UK includes acute POLIOMYELITIS, AIDS, CHOLERA, DYSENTERY, FOOD POISONING, MEASLES, MENINGITIS, RABIES, GERMAN MEASLES (RUBELLA), SCARLET FEVER, SMALLPOX, TETANUS, TYPHOID, viral HEPATITIS and WHOOPING COUGH.

NSAID *see* NON-STEROIDAL ANTI-INFLAMMATORY DRUGS.

nuclear magnetic resonance an analytical technique based upon the absorption of electromagnetic radiation over specific frequencies for those nuclei that spin about their own axes. The result is a change in orientation of the nuclei and certain elements are particularly susceptible (hydrogen, fluorine and phosphorus). The technique has been developed into a medical imaging tool (*see* MAGNETIC RESONANCE IMAGING) that can create an image of soft TISSUES in any part of the body.

nucleic acid a linear molecule that occurs in two forms: DNA (deoxyribonucleic acid) and RNA (ribonucleic acid), composed of four NUCLEOTIDES. DNA is the major part of CHROMOSOMES in the cell nucleus while RNA is also found outside the nucleus and is involved in PROTEIN synthesis.

nucleotide the basic molecular building block of the nucleic acids RNA and DNA. A nucleotide comprises a five-carbon sugar molecule with a phosphate group and an organic base. The organic base can be a purine, e.g. adenine and guanine, or a pyrimidine, e.g. cytosine and thymine as in DNA. In RNA uracil replaces thymine.

nucleus the large ORGANELLE in a MEMBRANE-bounded CELL that contains the DNA. Unless it is dividing, a nucleolus with RNA is present. During cell division, the DNA, which is normally dispersed with PROTEIN (as chromatin), forms visible CHROMOSOMES.

nyctalopia *see* NIGHT BLIND-
NESS.

O

obesity the accumulation of
excess fat in the body, mainly
in the SUBCUTANEOUS tissues,
caused by eating more food
than is necessary to produce
the required energy for each
day's activity. The effects of
obesity are serious, being associated with increased mortality or a cause of illness,
e.g. cardiovascular disease,
DIABETES MELLITUS, GALL
BLADDER complaints, HERNIA
and many others. Following a
medically approved diet and
taking more exercise will
achieve weight loss but in severe cases more drastic measures (e.g. stapling of the
STOMACH) may be necessary.

obstetrics the subdiscipline of
medicine that deals with
PREGNANCY and childbirth
and the period immediately
after birth (*see* MIDWIFERY).

occipital bone a BONE of the
SKULL, which is shaped like a
saucer and forms the back of
the CRANIUM and part of its
base. Arising from the base
of this bone are two occipital

CONDYLES, which articulate
with the first cervical VERTE-
BRA (the atlas) of the SPINAL
COLUMN.

occipitoanterior *see* MALPO-
SITION.

occlusion 1. the closing or
blocking of an organ or duct.
2. in dentistry, the way the
teeth meet when the jaws are
closed.

occult a term meaning 'not
easily seen', 'not visible to the
naked eye'.

occupational disease *or* **industrial disease** a disease
that is specific to a particular
occupation and to which
workers are prone. There are
many lung conditions, including PNEUMOCONIOSIS (from
coal mining), SILICOSIS (from
mining, stone dressing, etc),
ASBESTOSIS, FARMER'S LUNG
(from fungal spores), and so
on. In addition there are dan-
gers from excessive noise, irritant chemicals, occupations
resulting in musculo-skeletal
disorders, decompression
sickness (*see* BENDS), radiation and INFECTIONS from either animals or humans.

occupational therapy the
treatment of both psychiatric
and physical conditions by
encouraging patients to un-

dertake activities to enable them to develop skills and to achieve greater independence and self-confidence. The activities may vary enormously, from activities of daily living to arts and crafts and social and community activities.

oculomotor nerve either of a pair of CRANIAL NERVES that are involved in EYE movements, including movement of the eyeball and alterations in the size of the PUPIL and LENS.

odontoblast *see* DENTINE.

oedema an accumulation of fluid in the body, possibly beneath the skin or in cavities or ORGANS. With an injury the swelling may be localized, or it can be more general, as in cases of KIDNEY or HEART failure. Fluid can collect in the chest cavity, ABDOMEN or lung (PULMONARY OEDEMA). The causes are numerous, e.g. CIRRHOSIS of the liver, heart or kidney failure, starvation, acute NEPHRITIS, allergies or drugs. To alleviate the symptom, the root cause has to be removed. Subcutaneous oedema commonly occurs in women before MENSTRUATION, as swollen legs or ankles, but subsides if the legs

are rested in a raised position.

oesophagitis INFLAMMATION of the OESOPHAGUS. *See also* HEARTBURN.

oesophagoscope an instrument for inspecting the OESOPHAGUS. It has a light source and can be used to open the tube if narrowed, remove material for BIOPSY or clear an obstruction.

oesophagus the first part of the ALIMENTARY CANAL, lying between the PHARYNX and STOMACH. The MUCOUS MEMBRANE lining produces secretions to lubricate food as it passes, and the movement of the food to the STOMACH is achieved by waves of muscular contractions called peristalsis.

oestradiol the major female SEX HORMONE. It is produced by the OVARY and is responsible for development of the BREASTS, sexual characteristics and premenstrual uterine changes.

oestrogen one of a group of STEROID hormones secreted mainly by the ovaries (*see* OVARY)and, to a lesser extent, by the ADRENAL CORTEX and PLACENTA. (The TESTICLES also produce small amounts.) Oestrogens control the female

SECONDARY SEXUAL CHARAC-
TERISTICS, i.e. enlargement of
the breasts, change in the pro-
file of the PELVIC GIRDLE, pubic hair growth and deposition
of body fat. High levels are
produced at ovulation and,
with PROGESTERONE, they
regulate the female reproductive cycle. Naturally occurring oestrogens include
OESTRADIOL, oestriol and
oestrone. Synthetic varieties
are used in the contraceptive
pill and to treat gynaecological disorders.

olfaction the sense of smell,
see NOSE.

olfactory nerve one of a pair
of SENSORY nerves for smell.
It is the first CRANIAL NERVE
and comprises many fine
threads connecting RECEP-
TORS in the MUCOUS MEM-
BRANE of the olfactory area
of the NOSE, which pass
through holes in the SKULL,
fuse to form one fibre and
then pass back to the BRAIN.

oncogene any GENE directly
involved in CANCER, whether
in VIRUSES or in the individual.

oncogenic any factor that
gives rise to TUMOURS. This
may be an organism, a chemical or some environmental
condition. Some VIRUSES are

oncogenic and have the result
of making a normal CELL
cancerous.

oncology the subdiscipline of
medicine concerned with the
study and treatment of
TUMOURS, including medical
and surgical aspects and
treatment with radiation.

oocyte a cell in the OVARY that
undergoes MEIOSIS to produce
an OVUM, the female reproductive CELL. A newborn female already has numerous
primary oocytes, of which
only a small number survive
to PUBERTY and only a frac-
tion are ovulated (*see* OVULA-
TION).

operculum (*pl* **opercula**) a
term meaning a lid, plug or
flap that is used in several areas of medicine. For example,
it is a plug of MUCUS blocking
the CERVIX in a pregnant
woman. It is also used in
NEUROLOGY and dentistry.

ophthalmic nerve *see* TRI-
GEMINAL NERVE.

ophthalmology the branch of
medicine dealing with the
structure of the EYE, its function, associated diseases and
treatment.

ophthalmoplegia PARALYSIS
of the MUSCLES serving the
EYE, which may be internal

(affecting the IRIS and ciliary muscle) or external (those muscles moving the eye itself).

ophthalmoscope an instrument with a light source, used to examine the interior of the EYE. Some opthalmoscopes focus a fine beam of light into the eye so that the point upon which it falls can be seen, while others form an image of the inside of the eye, which can be studied.

opiate one of several drugs derived from OPIUM and including MORPHINE and CODEINE. They act by depressing the CENTRAL NERVOUS SYSTEM, thus relieving pain and suppressing coughing. Morphine and HEROIN, synthetic derivatives of opium, are NARCOTICS.

opium a milky liquid extracted from the unripe seed capsules of the poppy *Papaver somniferum*, which has almost 10 per cent of anhydrous (i.e. containing no water) MORPHINE. Opium is a NARCOTIC and ANALGESIC.

opportunistic a term used to describe an INFECTION that is contracted by someone with a lowered RESISTANCE. This may be because of drugs or disease, such as DIABETES MELLITUS, CANCER or AIDS. In normal circumstances, in a healthy person, the infecting organism would not cause the disease.

optic atrophy a deterioration and wasting of the OPTIC DISC as a result of degeneration of fibres in the OPTIC NERVE. It may accompany numerous conditions, including DIABETES MELLITUS, ARTERIOSCLEROSIS or GLAUCOMA, or may be because of a CONGENITAL defect, INFLAMMATION or injury, or toxic poisoning from alcohol, lead, etc.

optic chiasma *or* **optic commissure** the cross-shaped structure formed from a crossing over of the OPTIC NERVE running back from the eyeballs to meet beneath the BRAIN in the midline.

optic disc an oval area on the RETINA of the EYE where the OPTIC NERVE enters the eyeball.

optic nerve the second CRANIAL NERVE. It is a SENSORY nerve, sending messages from the RETINA to the BRAIN. *See also* OPTIC CHIASMA.

orchidectomy removal of one or both TESTICLES (castration), usually to treat a MALIGNANT growth.

orchidopexy the operation performed to bring an undescended TESTICLE into the SCROTUM. It is undertaken well before PUBERTY to ensure subsequent normal development.

organ any distinct and recognizable unit within the body that is composed of two or more types of TISSUE and is responsible for a particular function or functions. Examples are the LIVER, KIDNEY, HEART and BRAIN.

organelle a functional entity that is bound by a MEMBRANE to separate it from other CELL constituents, e.g. a MITOCHONDRION.

orgasm the climax of sexual arousal which, in men, coincides with EJACULATION and comprises a series of involuntary MUSCLE contractions. In women there are irregular contractions of the VAGINAl walls.

orthodontics a part of dentistry dealing with development of the teeth and the treatment of (or prevention of) any disorders.

orthopaedics the subdiscipline of medicine concerned with the study of the skeletal system and the JOINTS, MUS-CLEs, etc. It also covers the treatment of BONE damage or disease, whether CONGENITAL or ACQUIRED.

orthopnoea a severe difficulty in breathing that is so bad that a patient cannot lie down and has to sleep in a sitting position. It usually occurs only with serious conditions of the HEART and LUNGS.

osmosis the process whereby solvent molecules (usually water) move through a semipermeable MEMBRANE to a more concentrated solution. CELL membranes function as semipermeable membranes, and osmosis is important in regulating water content in living systems.

ossicle the term for a small BONE, often applied to those of the middle EAR, e.g. the auditory ossicles that transmit sound to the inner ear from the eardrum.

ossification or **osteogenesis** BONE formation, which occurs in several stages via special CELLS called OSTEOBLASTS. COLLAGEN fibres form a network in CONNECTIVE TISSUE and then a cement of polysaccharide is laid down. Finally, CALCIUM salts are distributed among the cement as tiny crystals. The osteoblasts are enclosed as bone cells (OSTEOCYTES).

osteitis INFLAMMATION of BONE, 2caused by damage, INFECTION or bodily disorder. Symptoms include swelling, tenderness, a dull aching SKIN and pain and redness of the affected area.

osteitis deformans *see* PAGET'S DISEASE OF BONE.

osteoarthritis a form of ARTHRITIS involving degeneration of the joint CARTILAGE with accompanying changes in the associated BONE. It usually involves the loss of cartilage and the development of OSTEOPHYTES at the bone margins. The function of the JOINT (most often the thumb, knee and hip) is affected and it becomes painful. The condition may be caused by overuse and affects those past middle age. It also may complicate other joint diseases. Treatment usually involves administering ANALGESICS, possibly ANTI-INFLAMMATORY drugs and the use of corrective or replacement surgery.

osteoblast a specialized CELL responsible for the formation of BONE.

osteochondritis INFLAMMATION of BONE and CARTILAGE.

osteochondrosis a disease affecting the OSSIFICATION centres of BONE in children. It begins with degeneration and NECROSIS, but the bone regenerates and calcifies again.

osteoclast *see* OSTEOSCLEROSIS.

osteocyte a bone CELL formed from an OSTEOBLAST that is no longer active and has become embedded in the matrix of the BONE.

osteogenesis *see* OSSIFICATION.

osteogenesis imperfecta *or* **brittle bone disease** an hereditary disease that results in the BONES being unusually fragile and brittle. It may have associated symptoms, namely transparent teeth, unusually mobile JOINTS, DWARFISM, etc. It may be caused by a disorder involving COLLAGEN, but there is little that can be done in treatment.

osteomalacia a softening of the BONES and the adult equivalent of RICKETS, which is caused by a lack of VITAMIN D. This vitamin is obtained from the diet and is produced on exposure to sunlight, and it is necessary for the uptake of CALCIUM from food.

osteomyelitis INFLAMMATION of BONE MARROW caused by INFECTION. This may happen after a compound FRACTURE or during bone surgery. It produces pain, swelling and FEVER, and high doses of ANTIBIOTICS are necessary.

osteopathy

osteophyte a bony projection that occurs near a joint or intervertebral disc where CARTILAGE has degenerated or been destroyed (*see* OSTEOARTHRITIS). Osteophytes may, in any case, occur with increasing age, with or without loss of cartilage.

osteoporosis a loss of BONE tissue because of its being resorbed, resulting in bones that become brittle and likely to fracture. It is common in menopausal women and can also be a result of long-term STEROID therapy. Hormone replacement therapy is one treatment available to women (*see* MENOPAUSE), but there associated risks.

osteosarcoma the commonest and most malignant TUMOUR of the BONE found most commonly in older children. The FEMUR is usually affected but metastases (*see* METASTASIS) are common. It produces pain and swelling, and although AMPUTATION used to be the standard treatment, surgery is now possible, with replacement of the diseased bone and associated CHEMOTHERAPY and/or RADIOTHERAPY. It remains, nevertheless, a serious CANCER with a relatively poor survival rate.

osteosclerosis a condition in which the density of BONE tissue increases abnormally. It is caused by TUMOUR, INFECTION or poor BLOOD supply and may be the result of an abnormality involving osteoclasts, CELLS that resorb calcified bone.

otitis INFLAMMATION of the EAR. This may take several forms, depending on the exact location, which produce diverse symptoms. For example, inflammation of the inner ear (otitis interna) affects balance, causing VERTIGO and VOMITING, while otitis media is usually a bacterial INFECTION of the middle ear, resulting in severe pain and a fever requiring immediate ANTIBIOTIC treatment. Secretory otitis media is otherwise known as GLUE EAR.

otology the subdiscipline of medicine concerned with the EAR, its disorders, diseases and their treatment.

otosclerosis an hereditary condition in which there is overgrowth of BONE in the inner EAR, which restricts and then stops sound being conducted to the inner ear from the middle ear. The person affected becomes progressively more deaf, often beginning with TINNITUS, but surgery is effective.

outpatient a person whose condition requires hospital treatment but is not sufficiently serious to merit admission as an INPATIENT.

ovarian cyst a sac filled with fluid that develops in the OVARY. Most are benign but their size may cause swelling and pressure on other ORGANS. For those CYSTS that do become MALIGNANT, it is possible that its discovery comes too late to allow successful treatment. ULTRASOUND scanning can be adopted to detect TUMOURS at an early stage.

ovariotomy literally cutting into an OVARY, but more generally used for surgical removal of an ovary or an ovarian tumour.

ovary the reproductive organ of females, which produces eggs (ova) and hormones (mainly OESTROGEN and PROGESTERONE). There are two ovaries, each the size of an almond, on either side of the UTERUS, and each contains numerous Graafian FOLLICLES in which the eggs develop. At OVULATION an egg is released from a follicle. The follicles secrete oestrogen and progesterone, which regulate the MENSTRUAL CYCLE and the UTERUS during PREGNANCY.

ovotestis (*pl* **ovotestes**) *see* HERMAPHRODITE.

ovulation the release of an egg from an OVARY (i.e. from a mature Graafian FOLLICLE), which then moves down the FALLOPIAN TUBE to the UTERUS. Ovulation is brought about by secretion of luteinizing hormone secreted by the anterior PITUITARY GLAND.

ovum (*pl* **ova**) the mature, unfertilized female reproductive CELL, which is roughly spherical with an outer MEMBRANE and a single nucleus.

oxytocin a HORMONE from the PITUITARY GLAND that causes the UTERUS to contract during LABOUR and prompts

LACTATION because of contraction of muscle fibres in the milk ducts of the BREASTS.

P

pacemaker 1. the part of the HEART that regulates the beat, the SINOATRIAL NODE. **2.** in patients with a HEART BLOCK, a device inserted into the body to maintain a normal heart rate. There are different types of pacemaker, some being permanent, others temporary; some stimulate the beat while others are activated only when the natural rate of the heart falls below a certain level.

pachymeningitis *see* MENINGITIS.

pachymeninx *see* MENINGES.

paediatrics the branch of medicine that deals with the development and care of children and diseases that affect them.

paedophilia an abnormal sexual attraction to children.

Paget's disease of bone *or* **osteitis deformans** a chronic BONE disease, particularly of the long bones (e.g. the FEMUR), SKULL and SPINE, that results in them becoming thickened, disorganized and

soft, causing them to bend. The cause is unknown, and although there is no cure, good results are being obtained with calcitonin, which is a HORMONE produced by the THYROID GLAND that regulates levels of CALCIUM in the BLOOD. The main symptom is pain.

palate the roof of the MOUTH, which separates the cavity of the mouth below from that of the NOSE above. It consists of the hard and soft palate. The hard palate is located at the front of the mouth and is a bony plate covered by MUCOUS MEMBRANE. The soft palate is a muscular layer also covered by mucous membrane. The movable soft palate is important in the production of sounds and speech.

palliative a medicine or treatment that is given to effect some relief from symptoms, if only temporarily, but does not cure the ailment. This is often the case in the treatment of CANCER.

pallor abnormal paleness of the SKIN because of a reduced BLOOD flow or a lack of the normal PIGMENTS. It may be a direct result of ANAEMIA or

SHOCK or spending an excessive amount of time indoors.

palpation examination of the surface of the body by carefully feeling with hands and fingertips. By doing this, it is often possible to distinguish between solid lumps or swelling and cystic structures.

palpitation when the HEART beats noticeably or irregularly and the person becomes aware of it. The heartbeat is not normally noticed but, with fear, emotion or exercise, it may be felt, unpleasantly so. Palpitations may also be caused by neuroses (*see* NEUROSIS), ARRHYTHMIA or heart disease, and a common cause is too much tea, coffee, alcohol or smoking. Where an excess is the cause (tea, coffee, etc) this can be eliminated. For disease-associated palpitations, drugs can be used for control.

palsy the term used formerly for PARALYSIS and retained for the names of some conditions, e.g. BELL'S PALSY.

pancreas a GLAND with both ENDOCRINE and EXOCRINE functions. It is located between the DUODENUM and SPLEEN, behind the STOMACH, and is about 15 cm long. There are two types of CELLS producing secretions. The acini produce pancreatic juice that goes to the INTESTINE via a system of DUCTS. This contains an alkaline mixture of salt and ENZYMES—TRYPSIN and chymotrypsin to digest PROTEINS, amylase to break down starch and lipase to aid digestion of fats. The second cell types are in the ISLETS OF LANGERHANS, and these produce two hormones, INSULIN and GLUCAGON, secreted directly into the BLOOD for control of sugar levels (*see also* DIABETES MELLITUS, HYPO-GLYCAEMIA and HYPERGLY-CAEMIA).

pancreatectomy surgical removal of the PANCREAS (or part of it) to deal with TUMOURS or chronic PANCREATITIS. After total or subtotal pancreatectomy (where all or almost all is removed), the pancreatic secretions to aid DIGESTION and control BLOOD SUGAR have to be administered.

pancreatitis INFLAMMATION of the PANCREAS, occurring in several forms but often associated with GALLSTONES or alcoholism. Any bout of the condition that interferes with the function of the pancreas may lead to DIABETES MELLITUS and MALABSORPTION.

pandemic an EPIDEMIC that is so widely spread that it affects large numbers of people in a country or countries or even on a global scale.

pantothenic acid *see* VITAMIN B3.

Papanicolaou test *or* **Pap test** another name for a CERVICAL SMEAR.

papilla (*pl* **papillae**) any small protuberance, such as the papillae on the TONGUE.

papilloma (*pl* **papillomata**) a usually BENIGN growth on the SKIN surface or MUCOUS MEMBRANE, e.g. WARTS.

Pap test *see* PAPANICOLAOU TEST.

papule *see* PIMPLE.

paracentesis the procedure of tapping or taking off (excess) fluid from the body by means of a hollow needle or CANNULA.

paracetamol a drug that has ANALGESIC effects and also reduces FEVER. It is taken for mild pain (HEADACHE, etc). It may cause digestive problems, and large doses are very dangerous. Excessive doses can produce LIVER failure, causing progressive NECROSIS in a matter of days,

and can be fatal. Treatment of paracetamol overdose includes GASTRIC LAVAGE with activated charcoal and administration of an antidote, N-acetylcystene.

parainfluenza viruses a group of VIRUSES that cause respiratory tract INFECTIONS with usually mild INFLUENZA-like symptoms. Infants and young children seem to be affected most. There are four types of the virus, virulent at different times of the year.

paralysis MUSCLE weakness or total loss of MUSCLE movement, depending on the causal disease and its effect on the BRAIN. Various descriptive terms are used to qualify the parts of the body affected. Thus, hemiplegia affects one side of the body (*see also* DIPLEGIA, MONOPLEGIA, PARAPLEGIA, QUADRIPLEGIA). Paralysis is really a symptom of another condition or disease, e.g. BRAIN disease such as a cerebral HAEMORRHAGE or THROMBOSIS causing hemiplegia; disease or injury of the SPINAL CORD leading to paraplegia; and POLIOMYELITIS (infantile paralysis). In addition, there is the paralysis associated with MOTOR-NEURONE DISEASE.

paramedic a health professional trained in emergency care who works with the ambulance service.

paramedical a term for professionals working closely with medics, e.g. nurses, radiographers and dietitians.

paranoia an abnormal mental condition typified by DELUSIONS associated with a certain complicated system that usually involves feelings of persecution or grandeur. The complex web of delusion may develop with time, and with some logic, so that it may appear plausible and the person seems normal in other aspects of behaviour, except for that involving the delusions. Paranoia is a common symptom of PSYCHOSIS.

paraphimosis constriction of the PENIS because of retraction of an abnormally tight FORESKIN, which contracts on the penis behind the GLANS and cannot be easily moved. Swelling and pain may be caused and usually CIRCUMCISION is necessary to prevent a recurrence. *See also* PHIMOSIS.

paraplegia PARALYSIS of the legs. It may be caused by in-

jury or disease of the SPINAL CORD, and often the BLADDER and RECTUM are also affected.

parasite any organism that obtains its nutrients by living in or on the body of another organism (the host). The extent to which the host is damaged by the parasite ranges from virtually no effect to, in extreme cases, death. Parasites in humans include worms, VIRUSES, fungi (*see* FUNGUS), etc.

parasympathetic nervous system one of the two parts of the AUTONOMIC NERVOUS SYSTEM, which acts antagonistically with the SYMPATHETIC NERVOUS SYSTEM. The parasympathetic nerves originate from the BRAIN and lower portion of the SPINAL CORD (sacral region). The AXONS of this system tend to be longer than sympathetic nerves, and SYNAPSES with other neurons are close to the target ORGAN. The parasympathetic system contracts the BLADDER, decreases HEART rate, stimulates the sex organs, promotes DIGESTION, etc.

parathyroidectomy removal of the PARATHYROID GLANDS, usually in treatment of hyperparathyroidism (hyper-activity of one or all of the glands).

parathyroid gland one of four small GLANDS, located behind or within the THYROID GLAND, that control the METABOLISM of CALCIUM and phosphorus (as phosphate) in the body. The HORMONE responsible, parathormone (or simply parathyroid hormone), is produced and released by the glands. A deficiency of the hormone leads to lower levels of calcium in the BLOOD, with a relative increase in phosphorus. This produces tetany, a condition involving muscular spasms that can be treated by injection. This is also known as hypoparathyroidism and is often caused by the removal or injury of the glands during THYROIDECTOMY. If the hormone is at high levels, calcium is transferred from bones to the blood, causing weakness and susceptibility to breaks.

paratyphoid fever a bacterial INFECTION caused by *Salmonella paratyphi* A, B or C. Symptoms resemble those of TYPHOID FEVER and include DIARRHOEA, a rash and mild fever. It can be treated with ANTIBIOTICS and temporary IMMUNITY against the A and B form is gained by VACCINATION with TAB vaccine.

parenteral nutrition provision of nutrition by any means other than by the mouth. For patients with burns, RENAL failure, etc, or after major surgery, this mode of feeding may be necessary and is accomplished INTRAVENOUSLY. PROTEIN, fat and CARBOHYDRATE can all be delivered as special solutions containing all the essential compounds. The main hazard of such a system is the risk of INFECTION and reactions to the solutions introduced, e.g. HYPERGLYCAEMIA can result.

parietal 1. pertaining to the walls of a CAVITY of the body. **2.** pertaining to the BONES that form the sides and upper part of the SKULL.

Parkinsonism symptoms similar to those of PARKINSON'S DISEASE, which may be caused by other factors, e.g. neurological disorders (*see* NEUROLOGY) or PSYCHOTROPIC DRUGS.

Parkinson's disease a progressive condition, occurring in mid to late life, that results in a rigidity of MUSCLES affecting the voice, FACE and limbs. A TREMOR also develops, possibly in one hand initially and then spreading to other limbs, and it appears most pronounced when sitting. Mobility becomes progressively slower (BRADYKINESIA) and more severely impaired as limbs become more rigid, and balance is also affected. The disease is caused by a deficiency in the DOPAMINE (a NUEROTRANSMITTER) because of degeneration of the basal ganglia of the brain (*see* BASAL GANGLION). There is no cure, but a number of drugs are able, in varying degrees, to control the condition (*see* DOPA).

parotid gland one of a pair of SALIVARY GLANDS situated in front of each EAR and opening inside on the cheek near the second-last molar of the upper JAW.

parotitis INFLAMMATION of the PAROTID GLAND, which, as EPIDEMIC or infectious parotitis, is called MUMPS.

paroxysm 'a sudden attack', a term used especially about CONVULSIONS.

parturition *see* LABOUR.

pasteurization the STERILIZATION of food by heating it to a certain TEMPERATURE to destroy potentially harmful BACTERIA. Milk, for example, is heated to 62–65°C for 30 minutes, followed by rapid cooling. INFECTIONS avoided by this process include TUBERCULOSIS and TYPHOID, SCARLET FEVER, DIPHTHERIA and FOOD POISONING.

patch test a test undertaken to identify the substances causing a person's ALLERGY. Different ALLERGENS are placed in very small amounts on the SKIN. A red flare with swelling will develop if the person is allergic. This commonly happens within 15 minutes but may take up to 72 hours.

patella (*pl* **patellae**) the kneecap, an almost flat BONE, shaped somewhat like an oyster shell, that lies in front of the knee in the TENDON of the thigh MUSCLE.

patellar reflex *see* REFLEX ACTION.

pathogen an organism that causes disease. Most pathogens affecting humans are BACTERIA and VIRUSES.

pathology the study of the causes, characteristics and effects of disease on the body by examining samples of body fluids and products whether from a living patient or at AUTOPSY.

PCOS *see* POLYCYSTOC OVARY SYNDROME.

pectoral the descriptive term for anything relating to the CHEST.

pectoral girdle *or* **shoulder girdle** the skeletal structure to which the BONES of the upper limbs are attached. It is composed of two shoulder blades (SCAPULAE) and two collar bones (CLAVICLES) attached to the vertebral column and breastbone (STERNUM) respectively.

pedicle 1. a narrow roll of SKIN by which a piece of skin for grafting is attached. It is used when it is not possible to place an independent GRAFT on the site, perhaps because of poor blood supply. **2.** a narrow neck of TISSUE connecting a TUMOUR to its tissue of origin.

pediculosis parasitic infestation with LICE. Head lice are a common problem in school-age children. Pubic lice infest the pubic hair and are generally less common, except in conditions of poor hygiene. Both can be cleared with insecticide preparations.

Pel-Epstein fever *see* HODGKIN'S DISEASE.

pellagra a DEFICIENCY DISEASE caused by a lack of nicotinic acid, part of the VITAMIN B complex. It occurs when the diet is based on maize (rather than wheat) with an associated lack of first-class PROTEIN (meat and milk). The reason is that although maize contains nicotinic acid it is in an unusable form and also it does not contain the AMINO ACID tryptophan, which the body can use to produce nicotinic acid. The symptoms are DERMATITIS, DIARRHOEA and DEPRESSION.

pelvic floor exercises see **Kegal exercises.**

pelvic floor muscles the MUSCLES that form a hammock across the lower entrance of the PELVIS, supporting the BLADDER, RECTUM, UTERUS and VAGINA. The pelvic floor muscles may become damaged or weakened during childbirth, leading to problems such as urinary INCONTINENCE or uterine PROLAPSE.

pelvic floor repair surgery to strengthen the MUSCLES of the pelvic floor which have become weakened. Pelvic floor repair may be used to correct CYSTOCELE, ENTEROCELE, RECTOCELE or uterine PRO-

LAPSE. A HYSTERECTOMY may also be necessary.

pelvic girdle *or* **hip girdle** the skeletal structure to which the bones of the lower limbs are attached. It is made up of the two HIP bones, each comprising the ILIUM, PUBIS and ISCHIUM, fused together.

pelvic inflammatory disease (PID) an acute or chronic INFECTION of the UTERUS, ovaries (*see* OVARY) or FALLOPIAN TUBES. It is the result of infection elsewhere, e.g. in the APPENDIX, which spreads, or one that is carried by the BLOOD. It produces severe abdominal pain, which usually responds to ANTIBIOTICS but surgery may sometimes be necessary to remove diseased tissue.

pelvis 1. the skeletal structure that is formed by the HIP bones, SACRUM and COCCYX and connects with the SPINAL COLUMN and legs. The female pelvis is shallower and the ilia (*see* ILIUM) are wider apart and there are certain angular differences from the male pelvis, all of which relate to childbearing. The pelvis is a point of contact for the MUSCLES of the legs, and it partially envelops the BLAD-DER and RECTUM. In males it also houses the PROSTATE GLAND and seminal vesicles while in females it contains the UTERUS and ovaries (*see* OVARY). **2.** a basin-shaped cavity in the body, e.g. the renal pelvis, the hollow interior of the KIDNEY that opens out into the URETER, into which URINE is drained.

penicillin the ANTIBIOTIC, derived from the mould *Penicillium notatum*, that grows naturally on decaying fruit, bread or cheese. The genus used for production of the drug is *P. chrysogenum*. Penicillin is active against a large range of BACTERIA and it is nontoxic. It is usually given by INJECTION but can be taken orally. There are many semisynthetic penicillins acting in different ways, including AMPICILLIN and propicillin. Some patients are allergic to penicillin but there tend to be very few serious SIDE EFFECTS.

penis the male organ through which the URETHRA passes, carrying URINE or SEMEN. It is made up of TISSUE that is filled with blood during sexual arousal, producing an erection that enables penetration of the VAGINA and EJACULATION of semen. The GLANS is the end part, normally covered by the FORESKIN (prepuce).

pepsin a digestive ENZYME that acts on PROTEINS contained in GASTRIC JUICE.

peptic ulcer an ULCER in the STOMACH (GASTRIC ULCER), OESOPHAGUS, DUODENUM (DUODENAL ULCER) or JEJUNUM. It is caused by a break in the mucosal lining as a result of the action of acid and pepsin (an enzyme active in PROTEIN breakdown), either because of their high concentrations or other factors affecting the mucosal protective mechanisms, e.g bacterial INFECTION. *See* HELICOBACTER PYLORI.

peptide an organic compound made up of two or more AMINO ACIDS and collectively named by the number of amino acids. A dipeptide therefore contains two, and a polypeptide many.

percussion the diagnostic aid that involves tapping parts of the body (particularly on the back or CHEST) with the fingers to produce a vibration and a note-like sound. The sound produced gives an indication of abnormal enlargement of ORGANS and the presence of fluid in the LUNGS.

perforation a hole that forms in a hollow ORGAN, TISSUE or tube, e.g. the STOMACH, eardrum, etc. In particular, it is a serious development of an ULCER in the STOMACH or bowels because, on perforation, the INTESTINE contents, with BACTERIA, enter the peritoneal cavity (*see* PERITONEUM), causing PERITONITIS. This is accompanied by severe pain and SHOCK, and usually corrective surgery is required.

pericarditis INFLAMMATION of the PERICARDIUM. It may be a result of URAEMIA, CANCER or viral INFECTION and produces FEVER, chest pain and possible accumulation of fluid.

pericardium the smooth MEMBRANE surrounding the HEART. The outer fibrous part covers the heart and is connected to the large vessels coming out of it. The inner serous part is a closed SEROUS MEMBRANE attached both to the fibrous part and the heart wall. Some fluid in the resulting SAC enables smooth movement as the heart beats.

pericranium see SCALP.

perilymph the fluid that separates the bony LABYRINTH and the membranous labyrinth of the EAR.

perinatal mortality foetal deaths after week 28 of PREGNANCY and newborn deaths during the first week or two of life. The main causes of perinatal mortality are CONGENITAL defects, complications involving the PLACENTA, lack of oxygen in the final stages of pregnancy (called antepartum anoxia), BRAIN injuries during birth and birth ASPHYXIA.

perineum the area of the body between the ANUS and the opening of the URETHRA.

periodontal a descriptive term relating to the TISSUES surrounding the teeth (see TOOTH).

periosteum see BONE.

peripheral nervous system those parts of the NERVOUS SYSTEM excluding the CENTRAL NERVOUS SYSTEM (BRAIN and SPINAL CORD). It comprises the afferent (SENSORY) and EFFERENT (motor) nerves, which include 12 pairs of CRANIAL NERVES and 31 pairs of spinal nerves. The motor nervous system then comprises the SOMATIC NERVOUS SYSTEM, carrying impulses to the skeletal MUSCLES, and the AUTONOMIC NERVOUS SYSTEM, which is further divided into the SYMPATHETIC and the PARASYMPATHETIC NERVOUS SYSTEMS.

peripheral neuritis inflammation of the nerves of the PERIPHERAL NERVOUS SYSTEM.

peristalsis the wave-like contraction and relaxation of MUSCLES in the OESOPHAGUS and INTESTINES that move ingested food gradually along the ALIMENTARY CANAL.

peritonsillar abscess see QUINSY.

peritoneum the SEROUS MEMBRANE that lines the abdominal cavity. That lining the abdominal walls is the parietal peritoneum, while the visceral peritoneum covers the ORGANS. The folds of peritoneum from one organ to another are given special names, e.g. MESENTERY. Both are continuous and form a closed sac at the back of the ABDOMEN in the male, while in the female there is an opening for the FALLOPIAN TUBE on either side.

peritonitis INFLAMMATION of the PERITONEUM. It may be caused by a primary INFECTION caused by BACTERIA in the bloodstream (e.g. tuberculous peritonitis), resulting in pain and swelling, FEVER and weight loss. Secondary infection results from entry into the abdominal cavity of bacteria (e.g. from APPENDICITIS) and irritants (e.g. digestive juices) from a perforated or ruptured organ, e.g. DUODENUM or STOMACH. This produces severe pain and SHOCK, and surgery is often necessary.

pernicious anaemia a type of ANAEMIA caused by VITAMIN B12 deficiency, which results from dietary lack or the failure to produce the substance that enables B12 to be absorbed from the bowel. This in turn results in a lack of red blood cell (ERYTHROCYTE) production and MEGALOBLASTS in the BONE MARROW. The condition is easily treated by regular injections of the vitamin.

perspiration *or* **sweat** the excretion from millions of tiny SWEAT GLANDS in the skin. Sweat that evaporates from the skin immediately is insensible perspiration, while that forming drops is sensible perspiration. Sweat is produced in two types of sweat glands. The EXOCRINE GLANDS are found mainly on the soles of the feet and palms of the hands. The APOCRINE glands are in the armpits and around the ANUS and GENITALIA. Sweat is produced in response to stimuli such as fear and sexual arousal, but the major function of sweating is the regulation of body TEMPERATURE.

Perthes' disease a hip condition in children between the ages of four and ten, which is self-healing. Because of OSTEOCHONDROSIS of the EPIPHYSIS of the FEMUR, a limp is developed with associated pain. Rest is essential, as is TRACTION, until the pain subsides, and then a special SPLINT is fitted to permit walking until the condition is fully healed.

pertussis *see* WHOOPING COUGH.

pessary 1. an instrument that fits into the VAGINA to treat a PROLAPSE. **2.** a soft solid substance that is shaped for insertion into the vagina and contains drugs for some gynaecological disorder (also used for inducing LABOUR).

pethidine a drug with ANAL-GESIC and mild sedative action for relief of moderate pain. It may be given by mouth or injection but SIDE EFFECTS include nausea, dizziness and a dry mouth. Prolonged use may create dependence.

petit mal see ABSENCE SEIZURE.

Petri dish a round, shallow, flat-bottomed dish used to produce cultures of microorganisms in a laboratory. It often has a fitted cover.

PG see PROSTAGLANDIN.

phage a short form of BACTERIOPHAGE.

phagocyte any of various CELLS able to absorb and digest BACTERIA and dead or harmful matter, such phagocytic cells including white blood cells (LEUCOCYTES). See also INGESTION; MACROPHAGE.

phagocytosis the process by which a phagocytes, e.g. LEUCOCYTES, engulfing microorganisms and cell debris to remove them from the body.

phalanges (sing **phalanx**) the BONES of the digits (fingers and toes) which number 14 in each hand and foot. The thumb and big toe comprise two while all the other digits have three phalanges.

phallus 1. the PENIS or a penis-like object. **2.** the term used for the embryonic penis before the final development of the URETHRA.

phantom limb the feeling that a LIMB or part of a limb is still attached to the body after it has been amputated. This is probably because of stimulation of the severed NERVES and usually wears off with time.

pharmaceutical relating to PHARMACY or drugs.

pharmacist a trained, qualified and registered person who is authorized to keep and dispense medicines.

pharmacology the branch of medicine concerning the preparation, properties, uses and effects of DRUGS.

pharmacy the preparation of DRUGS (and their dispensing); or the place where this function is undertaken.

pharyngectomy surgical EXCISION of part of the PHARYNX.

pharyngitis INFLAMMATION of the PHARYNX and therefore the throat, commonly caused by a VIRUS and resulting in a sore throat. It is often associated with TONSILLITIS.

pharynx the region extending from the beginning of the OESOPHAGUS up to the base of the SKULL at the cavity into which the NOSE and MOUTH open. It is muscular, with a MUCOUS MEMBRANE, and acts as the route for both food (to the oesophagus) and air (to the LARYNX). The EUSTACHIAN TUBES open from the upper part of the pharynx.

phenobarbital (*formerly* **phenobarbitone**) a very widely used BARBITURATE. It can be given orally or by injection and is taken as an anticonvulsant in epilepsy and to treat INSOMNIA or anxiety. It may produce drowsiness and some skin reactions, and continued use should be avoided in case dependence ensues.

phenotype the detectable, observable characteristics of an individual, which are determined by the interaction of his or her GENES (genotype) and the environment in which he or she develops. The expression of the dominant gene masks the presence of a recessive one, as only the expressed gene affects the phenotype.

phenylalanine *see* ESSENTIAL AMINO ACID.

phenylketonuria a genetic disorder that results in the deficiency of an ENZYME that converts phenylalanine, an ESSENTIAL AMINO ACID, to tyrosine. Children can be severely mentally retarded by an excess of phenylalanine in the BLOOD, damaging the NERVOUS SYSTEM. The responsible GENE is recessive, so the condition occurs only if both parents are carriers. However, there is a test for newborn infants (the Guthrie test) that ensures the condition can be detected and the diet can be modified to avoid phenylalanine and thus any brain damage.

phial a small, glass, bottle-like receptacle for storing medicines.

phimosis a condition in which the edge of the FORESKIN is narrowed and cannot be drawn back over the GLANS of the PENIS. To avoid INFLAMMATION and an exacerbation of the problem, CIRCUMCISION may be necessary. *See also* PARAPHIMOSIS.

phlebectomy removal of a VEIN, or part of a vein, sometimes undertaken in the treatment of VARICOSE VEINS.

phlebitis inflammation of a VEIN. This commonly occurs as a complication of VARICOSE VEINS, producing pain and a hot feeling around the vein, with possible THROMBOSIS development. Drugs and elastic support are used in treatment.

phlebography *see* VENOGRAPHY.

phlebothrombosis the obstruction of a VEIN by a BLOOD CLOT, common in the deep veins of the leg (in particular the calf). The condition may result from HEART failure, PREGNANCY, injury or surgery, which may change the clotting factors in the blood. The affected leg may swell, and there is the danger that the clot may move, creating a PULMONARY EMBOLISM. Large clots may be removed surgically, otherwise the treatment involves ANTICOAGULANT drugs and exercise.

phlebotomy the opening of a VEIN, or its puncture, to remove blood or to infuse fluids.

phlegm a general term (nonmedical) for SPUTUM, MUCUS.

phobia an anxiety disorder and irrational fear of certain objects, animals, situations, events, etc. Avoiding the situation can lead to significant disruption, restriction of normal life or even suffering. There are a variety of phobias, including animal and specific and social, and treatment often involves behavioural therapy.

phonation the production of speech sounds.

phospholipid *see* LIPOSOME.

photophobia an atypical sensitivity to light. Exposure produces discomfort and actions to evade the light source. The condition may be associated with medication or MIGRAINE, MENINGITIS, etc.

photoreceptor *see* CONE.

phrenic nerve the NERVE to the muscles of the DIAPHRAGM, arising from the 3rd, 4th and 5th cervical spinal nerves.

phthisis *see* TUBERCULOSIS.

physical the term used to describe the material part or structure of the body, as opposed to the mind.

physician a registered medical practitioner who deals with non-surgical practice.

physiology the study of the functions of and processes within the body and its various ORGANS.

physiotherapy the use of physical methods to help

healing. It may involve exercise, massage and manipulation, heat treatment and the use of light and ultraviolet radiation, etc.

pia-arachnoid *see* MENINGES.

pia mater *see* BRAIN; MENINGES.

pica an abnormal desire to eat non-food substances such as soap, chalk, glue, clay, etc. The disorder may arise during early childhood or in mental illness. Although it also occurs during PREGNANCY, the desire is more often for unusual foods and an excess of ordinary foods.

pigment an organic colouring agent, e.g. the blood pigment HAEMOGLOBIN, BILE pigments, rhodopsin (found in the RODS of the RETINA) and MELANIN.

piles *see* HAEMORRHOIDS.

pilus (*pl* **pili**) a HAIR or a structure like a hair.

pimple *or* **papule** a small swelling on the SKIN that is inflamed and may contain PUS. The cause is often INFECTION of a PORE that is blocked with fatty secretions from the SEBACEOUS GLANDS. On the face, the condition is called ACNE.

pinna *see* EAR.

pituitary gland *or* **hypophysis** a small, but very important ENDOCRINE GLAND at the base of the HYPOTHALAMUS. It has two LOBES, the anterior adenohypophysis and the posterior neurohypophysis. The pituitary secretes HORMONES that control many functions and is itself controlled by hormonal secretions from the hypothalamus. The neurohypophysis stores and releases PEPTIDE hormones produced in the hypothalamus, namely OXYTOCIN and VASOPRESSIN. The adenohypophysis secretes GROWTH HORMONE, GONADOTROPHIN, prolactin (involved in stimulating LACTATION), ACTH and THYROID-stimulating hormones.

placebo an inactive substance, taken as medication, that nevertheless may help to relieve a condition. The change occurs because the patient expects some treatment (even if nothing need, in reality, be done) and an improvement reflects the expectations of the patient. New drugs are tested in trials against placebos, when the effect of the drug is measured against the placebo response, which happens even when there is no active ingredient.

placenta the organ attaching the EMBRYO to the UTERUS. It is a temporary feature, comprising maternal and embryonic TISSUES, and it allows oxygen and nutrients to pass from the mother's BLOOD to that of the embryo. There is, however, no direct contact of blood supplies. The embryo also receives salt, glucose, AMINO ACIDS, some PEPTIDES and ANTIBODIES, fats and VITAMINS. Waste molecules from the embryo are removed by diffusion into the maternal circulation. It also stores GLYCOGEN for conversion to glucose, if required, and secretes HORMONES to regulate the PREGNANCY. It is expelled after birth. *See also* UMBILICAL CORD.

placenta praevia the condition when the PLACENTA is situated in the bottom part of the UTERUS next to or over the CERVIX. In the later stages of PREGNANCY there may be placental separation (ABRUPTIO PLACENTAE), causing bleeding that will require attention. In the more extreme cases, a CAESAREAN SECTION is necessary for delivery.

plague any EPIDEMIC disease that results in a high death rate and specifically the bubonic plague, which is transmitted to humans from infected rats by the rat flea. After an INCUBATION period of two to six days, the symptoms occur as headache, weakness, FEVER, aches in the LIMBS and delirium. The LYMPH NODES (especially in the groin) swell and become painful (buboes— hence 'bubonic') and may burst, releasing PUS. In other cases, the infective fluid may not be released and there may be SUBCUTANEOUS bleeding with creation of black patches (gangrenous) on the skin, leading to ULCERS (hence the old term, black death). If the BACTERIA enter the BLOOD (septicaemic plague), death follows rapidly, but the most serious is pneumonic plague, when the LUNGS are affected. Preventive actions are very important in such cases, particularly to eliminate the carriers. However, the disease can be treated effectively with ANTIBIOTICS and SULPHONAMIDES.

plantar a descriptive term meaning 'relating to the sole of the foot'.

plaque a surface layer on teeth formed from BACTERIA and food debris and, later, calcium salts.

plasma a light-coloured fluid component of BLOOD in which the various CELLS are suspended. It contains inorganic salts with PROTEIN and some trace substances. One protein present is FIBRINOGEN.

plaster of Paris a type of calcium sulphate (gypsum) used to make plaster models in dentistry and plaster casts in ORTHOPAEDICS. When mixed with water, it sets firmly, and in the preparation of a SPLINT for FRACTURES, bandages impregnated with the plaster are used. These are easily applied and moulded to the shape of the LIMB.

plastic surgery a branch of surgery that deals with the repair or rebuilding of damaged, deformed or missing parts of the body. Cosmetic plastic surgery is merely for the improvement of appearance but most plastic surgery is to repair burns, accident damage or congenital defects.

platelet *or* **thrombocyte** a disc-like structure in the BLOOD involved in the halting of bleeding.

plegmasia alba dolens *see* THROMBOPHLEBITIS.

pleura (*pl* **pleurae**) the SEROUS MEMBRANE that covers the LUNGS (visceral) and the inside of the CHEST wall (parietal). The membranes have a smooth surface that is moistened to allow them to slide over each other.

pleural cavity the small space between the PLEURAe when they slide over each other as a person breathes in and out. Should gas or fluid enter the cavity because of INFECTION or injury, the space increases and may hinder breathing.

pleurectomy removal, by surgery, of part of the PLEURA to overcome PNEUMOTHORAX or to excise diseased areas.

pleurisy *or* **pleuritis** INFLAMMATION of the PLEURA, resulting in pain from deep breathing and shortness of breath. There is a typical frictional rub heard through a STETHOSCOPE. Pleurisy is often caused by PNEUMONIA in the adjacent lung and is always associated with disease in the lung, DIAPHRAGM, chest wall or ABDOMEN, e.g. TUBERCULOSIS, ABSCESSes, bronchial CARCINOMA, etc.

pleurocentesis *see* THORACOCENTESIS.

plexus a network formed from intersecting NERVES and/or BLOOD VESSELS or lymphatic vessels.

PMS, PMT *see* PREMENSTRUAL TENSION.

pneumoconiosis a general term for a chronic form of LUNG disease caused by inhaling dust while working. Most of the cases are anthracosis (coal miner's pneumoconiosis), SILICOSIS and ASBESTOSIS.

pneumocystis a severe lung infection that commonly infects people suffering from AIDS.

pneumonectomy the surgical removal of a LUNG, performed mainly for CANCER but also for TUBERCULOSIS.

pneumonia INFECTION of the LUNGS resulting in INFLAMMATION and filling of the ALVEOLI (*see* ALVEOLUS) with PUS and fluid. As a result, the lung becomes solid and air cannot enter. The symptoms vary, depending on how much of the lung is unavailable for RESPIRATION, but commonly there will be chest pain, coughing, BREATHLESSNESS, FEVER and possibly CYANOSIS. Pneumonia may be caused by several BACTERIA, VIRUSes or FUNGI, but bacterial infection is commonest. Bronchopneumonia affects the BRONCHI and BRONCHIOLES; lobar pneumonia the whole LOBES of the lung(s). ANTIBIOTIC treatment is usually effective, although it helps to know which is the infecting organism to provide the most specific treatment. (*See also* VIRAL PNEUMONIA).

pneumonitis INFLAMMATION of the LUNGS by chemical or physical agents.

pneumothorax air in the PLEURAL CAVITY, which enters via a wound in the chest wall or lung. When this happens, the lung collapses, but if the air is absorbed from the pleural cavity the lung reinflates.

pock a small eruption on the SKIN, which may contain PUS, typical of CHICKENPOX and SMALLPOX.

polio the short term for POLIOMYELITIS.

poliomyelitis *or* **infantile paralysis** an infectious disease caused by a VIRUS that attacks the CENTRAL NERVOUS SYSTEM. The virus is taken in by mouth, passes through the ALIMENTARY CANAL and is excreted with the FAECES. The hands may be contaminated, leading to further spread. The INCUBATION period is seven to 12 days, and there are several types of condition, depending on the severity of the attack. In some cases the symptoms resemble a stomach upset or INFLUENZA; in others there is, in addition, some stiffness of MUSCLES. Paralytic poliomyelitis is less common, resulting in muscle weakness and PARALYSIS, while the most serious cases involve breathing, when the DIAPHRAGM and related muscles are affected (bulbar poliomyelitis). IMMUNIZATION is highly effective, and the disease has almost been eradicated in most countries. However, booster doses are advisable when visiting countries with a high incidence of the disease.

polycystic ovary syndrome (PCOS) a common endocrine disorder among women, in which the ovaries (*see* OVARY) have several fluid-filled cysts on the surface and become enlarged. Symptoms of the disorder include irregular or absent MENSTRUATION, obesity, HIRSUTISM, ACNE and infertility.

polydactyly the condition in which there are extra fingers or toes.

polydipsia an intense abnormal thirst. It is a characteristic symptom of DIABETES MELLITUS and certain other diseases.

polyneuritis *see* NEURITIS.

polyp a growth from a MUCOUS MEMBRANE and attached to it by a stalk. Most are BENIGN but may cause obstructions or INFECTIONS. They commonly occur in the SINUSES, nose or possibly the BLADDER or bowels. Their removal is usually straightforward, unless a more extensive operation proves necessary to reach the affected ORGAN.

polypeptide *see* PEPTIDE.

polyuria the passing of a larger than normal quantity of URINE, which is also usually pale in colour. It may be the result merely of a large fluid intake or of a condition such as DIABETES INSIPIDUS, DIABETES MELLITUS or a KIDNEY disorder.

pons (*pl* **pontes**) TISSUE that joins parts of an ORGAN, e.g. the pons Varolii, a part of the BRAIN stem that links various parts of the brain stem, including the MEDULLA OBLONGATA, and THALAMUS.

pore a small opening, especially one of the minute openings in the SKIN through which fluids and minute substances are excreted or exhaled or by which they are absorbed.

porphyrin *see* HAEM.

portal vein a VEIN within the hepatic portal system that carries BLOOD to the LIVER from other abdominal organs (STOMACH, SPLEEN, INTESTINE, etc). It is atypical in that it does not take blood directly to the HEART but ends in a CAPILLARY network.

possetting the term for the normal habit of some quite healthy babies to regurgitate small amounts of a recently eaten meal.

posterior a term meaning 'situated towards the back or at the back', the opposite of ANTERIOR.

post mortem examination an examination of a corpse to determine the cause of death, an AUTOPSY. *See also* NECROPSY.

postpartum the term meaning 'relating to the first few days after birth'.

post-viral fatigue syndrome *see* MYALGIC ENCEPHALOMYELITIS.

poultice *or* **fomentation** hot, moist material applied to the body to soften the SKIN, soothe irritations, ease pain or increase the circulation locally.

pox 1.pus-filled PIMPLES, as in CHICKENPOX or SMALLPOX. **2.** the small pit-like depressions that are SCARS of smallpox.

precancerous a term to describe any condition that is not MALIGNANT but may become so if left untreated.

pre-eclampsia the development of high BLOOD PRESSURE in the later stages of PREGNANCY (and sometimes immediately after delivery), which, unless treated, may result in ECLAMPSIA. Signs of pre-eclampsia include raised blood pressure, PROTEINURIA and OEDEMA and the FOETUS may be growth retarded. If the condition progresses the mother may experience headaches, blurred vision, dizziness and abdominal pain which precede the CONVULSIONS of eclampsia. The condition is potentially threatening to the lives of both mother and baby and an early induced labour (*see* INDUCTION) or CAESAREAN SECTION may be necessary. The risk of pre-eclampsia is greater for mothers under the age of twenty or over the age of forty, during first pregnancies and for those who have suffered from pre-eclampsia in previous pregnancies or have a family history of pre-clampsia.

pregnancy the period of time, lasting approximately 280 days from the first day of the last menstrual period, during which a woman carries a developing FOETUS. Signs of a pregnancy include cessation of MENSTRUATION, increase in size of the BREASTS, MORNING SICKNESS and, later, the obvious sign of enlargement of the ABDOMEN. A foetal heartbeat and movements can also be detected. Many of these changes are HORMONE-controlled, by PROGESTERONE (from the OVARY and PLACENTA).

pregnancy test any of various tests used to check for PREGNANCY, most of which are based on the presence of CHORIONIC GONADOTROPHIC HORMONE in the URINE.

premature birth a birth occurring before the end of the normal full term of PREGNANCY. The definition refers to babies weighing less than 2.5 kg. In many cases the cause is unknown, but in some it may be because of PRE-ECLAMPSIA, KIDNEY or HEART disease or multiple pregnancy. Premature babies often require INCUBATOR care.

premedication a drug given to a patient before an operation in which an ANAESTHETIC will be used. It is usually a SEDATIVE and a drug to reduce secretions of the LUNGS, which could otherwise be inhaled.

premenstrual tension (PMT) *or* **premenstrual syndrome (PMS)** the occurrence for up to ten days before MENSTRUATION of such symptoms as headache, nervousness and irritability, emotional disturbance, DEPRESSION, fatigue with other physical manifestations such as swelling of legs and breasts, and CONSTIPATION. The condition usually disappears soon after menstruation begins. The cause is not known, although the hormone PROGESTERONE is probably involved in some way.

premolar one of two teeth between the canines and molars on each side of the jaw.

prenatal diagnosis *see* AMNIOCENTESIS.

prepuce *see* FORESKIN.

presbyopia difficulty in focusing on objects a short distance from the EYES. Presbyopia is associated with advancing age.

presentation the point, during LABOUR, at which some part of the FOETUS lies at the mouth of the UTERUS. In most cases the head presents but *see also* BREECH PRESENTATION.

pressure sores *see* BED SORES.

preventive medicine the branch of medicine that seeks to prolong life by PROPHYLAXISIS, by early diagnosis (e.g. CERVICAL SMEAR) or to prevent the occurence of a disease by encouraging a healthy lifestyle.

prickly heat *or* **heat rash** *or* **miliaria** an itchy RASH of small red spots that are minute blisters caused by the blocking of SWEAT GLANDS or SEBACEOUS GLANDS in the SKIN. Scratching may produce INFECTION, but the condition itself is not serious.

prima gravida *or* **primigravida** the technical term for a woman in her first PREGNANCY.

process an anatomical term for a protuberance or projecting part of a BONE or other part.

proctocolectomy the surgical operation to remove the COLON and RECTUM. *See* ILEO-ANAL POUCH; ILEOSTOMY.

progesterone a steroid HORMONE that is vital in PREGNANCY. It is produced by the CORPUS LUTEUM of the OVARY when the lining of the UTERUS is prepared for the implanting of an egg cell. Progesterone is secreted under the control of other hormones (prolactin from the anterior PITUITARY GLAND and luteinizing hormone also from the pituitary, which stimulates ovulation and formation of the corpus luteum) until the PLACENTA adopts this role later in the pregnancy. The function of progesterone is to maintain the uterus and ensure that no further eggs are produced. Small amounts of this hormone are also produced by the testes (*see* TESTICLE).

prognosis (*pl* **prognoses**) a forecast of the likely outcome of a disease, based on the patient's condition and the course of the disease in other known patients.

prolactin *see* PITUITARY GLAND; PROGESTERONE.

prolapse a moving down of an ORGAN or TISSUE from its normal position because of weakening of the supporting tissues. This may happen to the lower end of the bowel (in children) or the UTERUS and VAGINA in women who have sustained some sort of injury during childbirth. In the latter case, prolapse may result in the uterus itself showing on the outside. Surgery can shorten the supporting LIGAMENTS and narrow the vaginal opening.

prolapsed intervertebral disc *or* **slipped disc** the INTERVERTEBRAL DISCS provide cushioning for the BRAIN and SPINAL CORD and each is composed of an outer fibrous layer over a pulpy centre. A slipped disc is caused by the inner layer being pushed through the fibrous layer to impinge upon NERVES, causing pain (commonly LUMBAGO or SCIATICA). The PROLAPSE usually occurs during sudden twisting or bending of the SPINAL COLUMN and is more likely to occur during middle age. Treatment

involves a short period of rest followed by gentle mobilization, possibly with manipulation and PHYSIOTHERAPY. Pain can be relieved with NON-STEROIDAL INFLAMMATORY DRUGS. Surgical treatment may be necessary in severe cases, where there is a danger of nerve damage. *See* LAMINECTOMY.

prone a term meaning 'lying face downwards'.

prophase *see* MEIOSIS.

prophylaxis a treatment or action that is taken to avoid disease or a condition, e.g. taking a prophylactic medication to prevent ANGINA.

propicillin *see* PENICILLIN.

prostaglandin (**PG**) any of a group of compounds, derived from ESSENTIAL FATTY ACIDS, that act in a way that is similar to HORMONES. They are found in most body TISSUES (but especially SEMEN), where they are released as local regulators (in the UTERUS, BRAIN, LUNGS, etc). A number have been identified, two of which act antagonistically on BLOOD VESSELS, PGE causing dilation, PGF constriction. Certain prostaglandins cause contraction of the UTERUS in LABOUR, and others are involved in the body's defence mechanisms.

prostatectomy surgical excision of the PROSTATE GLAND, performed to relieve URINE retention caused by enlargement of the prostate. It is also done to counter poor flow of urine or frequent urination. The operation can be undertaken from several approaches: via the URETHRA, from the BLADDER, or from the PERINEUM (for a BIOPSY).

prostate gland a GLAND in the male reproductive system that is located below the BLADDER, opening into the URETHRA. Upon EJACULATION, it secretes an alkaline fluid into the SEMEN, which aids sperm motility. In older men, the gland may become enlarged, causing problems with urination (*see* PROSTATECTOMY).

prostatitis INFLAMMATION of the PROSTATE GLAND as a result of bacterial INFECTION. The symptoms tend to be similar to a urinary infection although in the chronic form obstructions may form, necessitating PROSTATECTOMY.

prosthesis (*pl* **prostheses**) an artificial device fitted to the body, ranging from dentures to hearing aids, pacemakers and artificial limbs.

protein a large group of organic compounds containing carbon, hydrogen, oxygen, sulphur and nitrogen, with individual molecules built up of AMINO ACIDS in long polyPEPTIDE chains. Globular protein includes ENZYMES, ANTIBODIES, carrier proteins (e.g. HAEMOGLOBIN) some HORMONES, etc. Fibrous proteins have elasticity and strength and are found in MUSCLE, CONNECTIVE TISSUE and also CHROMOSOMES. Proteins are thus vital to the body and are synthesized from their constituent AMINO ACIDS, which are obtained from DIGESTION of dietary protein.

proteinuria the condition in which PROTEIN (usually ALBUMIN) is found in the URINE. It is important because it may signify HEART or KIDNEY disease. Proteinuria may also occur with FEVER, severe ANAEMIA and intake of certain drugs or poisons.

prothrombin *see* COAGULATION; THROMBIN; VITAMIN K.

pruritus another term for ITCHING, of whatever origin.

psilosis *see* SPRUE.

psittacosis a bacterial INFECTION of parrots and budgerigars that can be transmitted to humans. It causes headache, shivering, nosebleeds, FEVER and lung problems. It is treatable with ANTIBIOTICS.

psoriasis a chronic SKIN disease, the cause of which is unknown and the treatment for which is PALLIATIVE. The affected skin appears as itchy, scaly red areas, starting usually around the elbows and knees. It often runs in families and may be associated with anxiety, commencing usually in childhood or adolescence. Treatment involves the use of ointments and creams with some drugs and VITAMIN A.

psychedelic drugs drugs that affect the mind and consciousness and are often HALLUCINOGENIC.

psychiatrist a qualified physician who deals with mental disorders including emotional and behavioural problems.

psychiatry the study of mental disorders, their diagnosis, treatment/management and prevention.

psychoanalysis a method of treating mental ill-health by uncovering repressed fears and dealing with them in the conscious mind. This school of psychology began at the end of the 19th century with the work of Sigmund Freud.

psychogeriatrics the branch of PSYCHIATRY dealing with mental ill-health in old people.

psychology the study of the mind, its working and resulting behaviour patterns. There are many schools of psychology, experimental (laboratory experiments to study topics such as learning), PSYCHOANALYSIS, ethology (study of animal behaviour in the natural environment) and behaviourism. Clinical psychology involves the study and treatment of behavioural and emotional disorders.

psychopathic a term used to describe a person who has a personality disorder resulting in antisocial and sometimes perverted and violent behaviour with little or no guilt for any such acts committed. In addition, psychopaths do not possess any ability for showing real sympathy or love to others and punishment does not deter a repeat of any criminal act.

psychosis (*pl* **psychoses**) a very serious state of mental ill-health. The sufferer loses touch with reality and may suffer disordered thoughts, delusions and hallucinations. SCHIZOPHRENIA and manic depressive psychosis (*see* BIPOLAR DISORDER) are two important psychoses.

psychosomatic a term meaning 'relating to both mind and body' and used most often for illnesses and conditions that result from the effects of excessive emotional stress upon the body. Numerous physical ailments can be triggered in this way, from NAUSEA, abdominal pains, ULCERS and ASTHMA to dizziness, INSOMNIA and ARRHYTHMIA. The causes of the stress may be even more numerous but essentially fall into categories such as personal/marital, occupational and social. Although psychological treatment may help, attention to the physical symptoms is more effective.

psychotherapy the treatment of mental disorders or the mental part of an ailment by psychological means, i.e. by concentrating upon and working through the mind. There are several approaches to this method of treatment, including PSYCHOANALYSIS, group therapy and behavioural therapy.

psychotropic drugs DRUGS that affect the mind and its moods, e.g. ANTIDEPRESSANTS, SEDATIVES and STIMULANTS.

ptyalin *see* MOUTH; SALIVA.

puberty the changes that occur in boys and girls around the age of 10 to 14, which signify the beginnings of sexual maturity and the subsequent functioning of reproductive organs (*see* REPRODUCTIVE SYSTEM). It is apparent through the appearance of SECONDARY SEXUAL CHARACTERISTICS, such as a deepening of the voice in boys and growth of BREASTS in girls. In addition, girls commence MENSTRUATION and in boys the size of TESTICLES increases. In both sexes body shape changes noticeably and body hair grows. The changes are initiated by PITUITARY GLAND hormones acting on the ovaries (*see* OVARY) and testes.

pubic pertaining to the pubes (*see* PUBIS), e.g. pubic hair.

pubis (*pl* **pubes**) one of the three BONES, and the most anterior, that make up each half of the PELVIC GIRDLE.

puerperal fever an INFECTION, now rare in developed countries, that occurs within two or three days of childbirth when a mother is susceptible to disease. Because the body's resources are low and the genital tract after childbirth provides ready access for BACTERIA, it is essential that clean conditions are maintained to avoid INFECTION. A mild infection of the genital tract may cause high temperature and raised pulse rate. INFLAMMATION, and possibly PERITONITIS, may result from infection of local LYMPH and BLOOD VESSELS while access to the general circulation can cause SEPTICAEMIA. Serious cases are, however, rare. Preventive measures are vital, but infections respond to ANTIBIOTIC treatment.

pulmonary relating to the LUNGS.

pulmonary embolism a condition involving the blocking of the pulmonary ARTERY or a branch of it by an EMBOLUS (usually a blood CLOT). The clot usually originates from PHLEBOTHROMBOSIS of the leg.

The seriousness of the attack relates to the size of the clot. Large pulmonary emboli can be immediately fatal. Smaller ones may cause death of parts of the lung, PLEURISY and the coughing up of blood. ANTICOAGULANT drugs are used in minor cases; STREPTOKINASE may be used to dissolve the clot, or immediate surgery may be necessary. Several embolisms may produce PULMONARY HYPERTENSION.

pulmonary hypertension an increase in BLOOD PRESSURE in the pulmonary ARTERY because of increased resistance to the flow of blood. The cause is usually disease of the lung (such as BRONCHITIS, EMPHYSEMA, *see also* PULMONARY EMBOLISM), and the result is that the pressure increases in the right VENTRICLE, enlarging it, producing pain with the possibility of HEART failure.

pulmonary oedema gathering of fluid in the LUNGS, caused by, for example, MITRAL STENOSIS.

pulmonary stenosis a narrowing of the outlet from the HEART to the pulmonary ARTERY via the right VENTRICLE, which may be CONGENITAL or, more rarely, as a result of

RHEUMATIC FEVER. Severe cases can produce ANGINA, fainting and enlargement of the HEART with eventual HEART FAILURE. Surgery is necessary to clear the obstruction.

pulp *see* TOOTH.

pulse the regular expansion and contraction of an ARTERY as a fluid wave of BLOOD passes along, originating with the contraction of the HEART muscle and blood leaving the left VENTRICLE. It is detected in arteries near the surface, e.g. the radial artery in the wrist or the brachial artery at the inner side of the upper arm, and decreases with a reduction in size so that the capillaries are under a steady pressure (hence the reason why venous flow is also steady).

pulse oximeter a monitoring device to measure PULSE rate and oxygen saturation in the HAEMOGLOBIN. A probe is attached to the patient's finger or ear and linked to a computerized unit, giving a constant reading.

pump oxygenator *or* **heart-lung machine** *see* CARDIO-PULMONARY BYPASS.

puncture a small hole in the skin made by a sharp object such as a needle, prickle or sting.

pupil the circular opening in the IRIS which permits light into the LENS in the EYE. *See also* LIGHT REFLEX.

purgative a drug or other treatment taken to evacuate the bowels. They may be grouped by their mode of action, LAXATIVES providing a gentle effect. Purgatives work by increasing the muscular contractions of the INTESTINE or by increasing the fluid content.

purine *see* NUCLEOTIDE.

pus the liquid found at an infected site (ABSCESS, ULCER, etc). It is coloured white, yellow or greenish and consists of dead white blood cells (LEUCOCYTES), living and dead BACTERIA and dead TISSUE.

pustule an inflamed elevation of the SKIN, containing PUS.

putrid fever a former name for typhus fever (*see* RICKETTSIAE).

pyelitis INFLAMMATION of part of the KIDNEY, the renal PELVIS. The cause is usually a bacterial INFECTION (commonly *E. coli, see* ESCHERIA) and sometimes it occurs as a complication of PREGNANCY. Symptoms include pain in the loins, high temperature, loss of weight, but it does respond to ANTIBIOTICS. Usually the infection is not limited to the pelvis but all the kidney is involved, hence a more accurate term is pyelonephritis.

pyelonephritis *see* PYELITIS.

pyloric stenosis a narrowing of the PYLORUS, which limits the movement of food from the STOMACH to the DUODENUM, resulting in VOMITING. It may be accompanied by distension and PERISTALSIS of the stomach, visible through the abdominal wall. A continuation of the condition causes weight loss and dehydration. The condition may be congenital, caused by hypertrophy of the muscles surrounding the pylorus. In this case surgery will be required in early infancy. In adults it may be caused by an ULCER or CANCER near the pylorus.

pylorus the lower end of the STOMACH where food passes into the DUODENUM and at which there is a ring of MUSCLE, the pyloric SPHINCTER.

pyrexia another term for FEVER.

pyridoxine *see* VITAMIN B6.

pyrimethamine *see* TOXOPLASMOSIS.

pyrimidine *see* NUCLEOTIDE.

pyrogen any substance that causes a rise in TEMPERATURE of the body. *See also* FEVER.

Q

Q fever an infectious disease that produces symptoms resembling PNEUMONIA, including a severe headache, high FEVER and breathing problems. It is caused by the organism *Coxiella burnetti* and is a disease of sheep, goats and cattle that can be passed to humans, mainly through unpasteurized milk (*see* PASTEURIZATION). The disease is treated with drugs and lasts about two weeks.

quadriceps the large thigh MUSCLE, which is divided into four distinct parts and is responsible for movements of the KNEE joint.

quadriplegia paralysis of all four limbs of the body.

quarantine a period of time in which a person (or animal) who has, or is suspected of having, an infectious disease is isolated from others to prevent the spread of the INFECTION.

quartan fever the recurrent FEVER, which usually occurs

every fourth day, associated with MALARIA.

quickening the first movements of a baby in the womb (UTERUS), which are perceived by the mother usually around the fourth month of PREGNANCY.

quinine a colourless alkaloid, derived from the bark of certain (cinchona) trees, which is a strong ANTISEPTIC and especially effective against the malarial parasite. It was formerly widely used in the treatment of MALARIA but has now been replaced because it is toxic in larger doses. In small amounts it has a stimulating effect and is used in tonic water.

quinsy *or* **peritonsillar abscess** a complication of TONSILLITIS, when a pus-filled ABSCESS occurs near the tonsil, causing great difficulty in swallowing. In addition to treatment with ANTIBIOTICS, the abscess may require surgical lancing.

R

rabies *or* **hydrophobia** a very severe and fatal disease affecting the CENTRAL NERVOUS SYSTEM, which occurs in dogs, wolves, cats and other animals. Human beings are infected through the bite of a rabid animal, usually a dog. The onset of symptoms varies from 10 days to up to a year from the time of being bitten. Characteristically, the person becomes irritable and depressed, swallowing and breathing difficulties develop, there are periods of great mental excitement, increased salivation and muscular SPASMS of the throat. Eventually, even the sight of water causes severe muscular spasms, CONVULSIONS and PARALYSIS, and death follows within about four days. Treatment consists of thorough cleansing of the bite and injections of rabies vaccine, ANTISERUM and IMMUNO-GLOBULIN. As the UK is currently free of rabies, vigilant QUARANTINE and other regulations involving the movement of animals, are in force.

radial a term meaning 'pertaining to the RADIUS'.

radiation sickness any illness that is caused by harmful radiation from radioactive substances. This may be a complication of RADIOTHERAPY for CANCER and produces symptoms of NAUSEA, VOMITING and sometimes itchiness of the skin. ANTIHISTAMINE drugs and TRANQUILLIZERS such as CHLORPROMAZINE are used to alleviate the condition.

radical hysterectomy *see* HYSTERECTOMY.

radical treatment treatment aimed at the complete cure of a condition (i.e. 'to the root'), rather than the alleviation of SYMPTOMS. In contrast, conservative treatment is directed towards the minimum interference necessary to keep a condition under control.

radiograph an image produced by X-RAYS on a film.

radiography the diagnostic technique used to examine the body using X-RAYS.

radiologist a doctor specialized in the interpretation of X-RAYS and other diagnostic records.

radiology the branch of medicine concerned with the use of X-RAYS.

radiotherapy the therapeutic use of penetrating radiation, including X-RAYS, beta rays and gamma rays. These may be derived from X-ray machines or radioactive isotopes and are especially employed in the treatment of CANCER.

The main disadvantages of radiotherapy is that there may be damage to normal, healthy surrounding TISSUES.

radium a radioactive metallic element that occurs naturally and emits alpha, beta and gamma rays as it decays. The gamma rays derived from radium are used in the treatment of CANCER.

radius (*pl* **radii**) the shorter outer bone of the forearm, the other being the ULNA.

radon a radioactive gas produced when RADIUM decays. Radon seeds are small, sealed capsules that are used in RADIOTHERAPY for CANCER.

rapid eye movement sleep *see* REM SLEEP.

rash an eruption of the SKIN, which is usually short-lived and consists of a reddened, perhaps itchy, area or raised red spots.

rat-bite fever two types of infectious disease that are contracted following the bite of a rat. The first type is caused by either of two kinds of BACTERIA and produces symptoms of FEVER, skin RASH and JOINT and MUSCLE pains. The second type is caused by a FUNGUS and produces similar symptoms and VOMITING.

Both diseases are treated with PENICILLIN.

receptor a SENSORY nerve ending that changes stimuli into NERVE IMPULSES to the brain. *See also* NERVOUS SYSTEM.

recessive gene a GENE the character of which will only be expressed if paired with a similar gene (ALLELE).

recombinant DNA DNA (deoxyribonucleic acid) containing GENES that have been artificially combined by the techniques of GENETIC ENGINEERING. Recombinant DNA technology has become synonymous with genetic engineering.

recrudescent a term used to describe a disease (e.g. HEPATITIS) that appears again after a period of abatement.

rectocele bulging of the RECTUM through the posterior wall of the VAGINA, which has become weakened.

rectum the final portion of the large INTESTINE between the SIGMOID COLON and anal canal in which FAECES are stored prior to elimination.

red blood cell *see* ERYTHROCYTE.

referred pain *or* **synalgia** pain felt in another part of the body at a distance from the site at which it might be expected, e.g. certain HEART conditions cause pain in the left arm and fingers. The condition arises because some SENSORY nerves share common routes in the CENTRAL NERVOUS SYSTEM, hence stimulation of one causes an effect in another.

reflex action an unconscious movement that is brought about by relatively simple nervous circuits in the CENTRAL NERVOUS SYSTEM. In its simplest form it involves a single reflex arc of one RECEPTOR and SENSORY nerve, which forms a SYNAPSE in the BRAIN or SPINAL CORD with a MOTOR NERVE, which then transmits the impulse to a MUSCLE or GLAND to bring about a response. However some reflex actions are more complicated than this, involving several NEURONS. Examples are the plantar reflex of the toes when the sole of the foot is stroked, the knee-jerk reflex and the reflex PUPIL of the EYE, which contracts suddenly when a light is directed on its surface. The presence or absence of reflexes gives an indication of the condition of the nervous system and is a pointer to the presence or absence of disease or damage.

refractory a term used to describe a condition that does not respond to treatment.

refractory period the time taken for a NERVE or MUSCLE cell to recover after an electrical impulse has passed along or following contraction. During this time, the nerve or muscle cell is unable to respond to a further stimulus.

regimen a course of treatment that usually involves several elements, including drugs, diet and lifestyle (such as the taking of exercise), aimed at curing a disease or promoting good health.

regression 1. in medicine, the term for the stage in the course of a disease when symptoms cease and the patient recovers. **2.** in PSYCHIATRY, a reversion to a more immature form of behaviour.

regurgitation 1. the bringing up of swallowed undigested food from the STOMACH to the mouth (*see also* POSSETTING). **2.** the backward flow of BLOOD in the HEART if one or more VALVES is diseased and defective, e.g. MITRAL REGURGITATION.

rehabilitation the process of restoring (as far as possible) back to normal life a person who has been disabled by injury or physical and/or mental illness. Rehabilitation usually involves various different kinds of therapy and retraining, including OCCUPATIONAL THERAPY, PHYSIOTHERAPY and SPEECH THERAPY.

Reiter's syndrome a disease of unknown cause that affects men and produces symptoms of URETHRITIS, CONJUNCTIVITIS and ARTHRITIS. It may also produce other symptoms, including FEVER and DIARRHOEA, and it is suspected that the cause may be a VIRUS.

rejection in TRANSPLANTATION, the situation in which the IMMUNE system of the recipient individual rejects and destroys an organ or tissue grafted from a donor. Various drugs are given to the recipient to dampen down the immune system and reduce the risk of rejection.

relapse the return of the symptoms of a disease from which a person had apparently recovered or was in the process of recovering.

relapsing fever a disease caused by spirochaete BACTE-

RIA of the genus *Borrelia*, which is transmitted to humans by lice and ticks. The disease is characterized by recurrent bouts of FEVER accompanied by headache, JOINT and MUSCLE pains and nosebleeds. The first attack lasts for about two to eight days and further milder bouts occur after three to ten days. Treatment is by means of bed rest and with ERYTHROMYCIN and TETRACYCLINE drugs.

remission a period during the course of a disease when symptoms have lessened or disappeared.

REM sleep (Rapid Eye Movement SLEEP) a phase of sleep when the eyeballs move rapidly behind closed eyelids. This appears to be the phase during which dreaming occurs.

renal describing or relating to the KIDNEYS.

renal calculus *or* **kidney stone** a hard deposit in the KIDNEY, formed from crystallised waste products in the URINE. Calculi may travel into the URETER, causing pain, SPASM (RENAL COLIC) and occasionally blockage. Small kidney stones may be passed in the urine, but larger

ones may require surgical treatment.

renal colic acute, severe, one-sided pain in the the lower back, which can radiate outwards to the side and downwards to the groin. The pain is sudden in onset and increases to a peak level after a period of one or two hours. Renal colic occurs when a kidney stone (*see* RENAL CALCULUS) has moved into the URETER, causing SPASM.

repetitive strain injury (RSI) *see* TENDINITIS.

reproductive system the name given to all the organs involved in reproduction. In males these comprise the TESTICLES, VASA deferentia, PROSTATE GLAND, seminal vesicles, URETHRA and PENIS. In females, the reproductive system consists of the ovaries (*see* OVARY), FALLOPIAN TUBES, UTERUS, VAGINA and VULVA.

resection a surgical operation in which part of an ORGAN, or any body part, is removed.

resistance 1. the degree of natural IMMUNITY that an individual possesses against a certain disease or diseases. **2.** the degree to which a disease or disease-causing organism can withstand treatment with drugs, such as a course of ANTIBIOTICS.

resonance the quality and increase of sound produced by striking the body over an air-filled structure. If resonance is decreased compared to normal, this is termed dullness and if increased hyperresonance. Tapping the body, often the chest, to determine the degree of resonance, is called PERCUSSION. An opinion may be formed about the condition of underlying ORGANS, i. e. the amount of air present or fluid (e.g. in the lungs) or if there is any enlargement.

respiration the whole process by which air is drawn into and out of the LUNGS, during which oxygen is absorbed into the bloodstream and carbon dioxide and water are given off. External respiration is the actual process of breathing and the exchange of gases that takes place in the lungs. Internal respiration is the process by which oxygen is given up from the blood CIRCULATION to the tissues, in all parts of the body, and carbon dioxide is taken up to be transported back to the lungs and eliminated. The process of drawing air into the lungs is known as inhalation or inspiration and expelling it out is exhalation or expiration. The rate at which this occurs is known as the respiratory rate, and it is about 18 times a minute in a static healthy adult.

respirator or **ventilator** a machine used to provide an air supply to the LUNGS of patients who cannot breathe normally for themselves. Blood gases and other body functions can be monitored at the same time. A respirator takes over RESPIRATION, especially when the MUSCLES that should normally be involved are paralysed, as in some forms of POLIOMYELITIS.

respiratory distress syndrome or **hyaline membrane disease** a condition usually arising in newborn babies, especially those who are PREMATURE, being particularly common in infants born between 32 and 37 weeks' GESTATION. It is characterized by rapid shallow laboured breathing. It arises because the LUNGS are not properly expanded and lack a substance (known as a surfactant) necessary to bring their expansion about. Adults may suffer from adult respiratory distress syndrome in which there is PULMONARY OEDEMA and a high mortality rate.

respiratory syncitial virus *or* **RS virus** the main cause of BRONCHIOLITIS and PNEUMONIA in babies under the age of six months.

respiratory system *or* **respiratory tract** all the ORGANS and TISSUES involved in RESPIRATION, including the NOSE, PHARYNX, LARYNX, TRACHEA, BRONCHI, BRONCHIOLES, LUNGS and DIAPHRAGM, along with the MUSCLES that bring about respiratory movements.

resuscitation the reviving of a person in whom heartbeat and breathing have ceased. *See* CARDIOPULMONARY RESUSCITATION.

retardation the slowing down of an activity or a process, often referring to delayed or slow mental development.

retina the layer that lines the interior of the EYE. The retina itself consists of two layers. The inner layer, next to the cavity of the eyeball, contains the light-sensitive CELLS, the RODS and CONES, and also NERVE fibres. This layer receives light directed on to its surface by the LENS. The

outer layer of the retina, next to the choroid (MEMBRANE), contains pigmented cells that prevent the passage of light.

retinol *see* VITAMIN A.

retractor one of a number of different surgical instruments designed to pull apart the cut edges of an incision to allow greater operating access.

retroflexion the bending backwards of a part of an ORGAN, particularly the upper portion of the UTERUS (*compare* RETROVERSION).

retroversion an abnormal position of the UTERUS in which the whole organ is tilted backwards instead of forwards, as is normally the case. A retroverted uterus occurs in about 20 per cent of women (*see* RETROFLEXION).

Retrovir *see* AZT.

retrovirus a type of VIRUS containing RNA (ribonucleic acid), which is able to introduce its genetic material into the DNA of body cells. These viruses are suspected as causal agents in the development of certain CANCERS.

Reye's syndrome a rare disorder, of unknown cause, that affects children and seems to follow on from a viral infection such as CHICKENPOX, often manifesting itself during the recovery phase. The symptoms include vomiting, high FEVER, DELIRIUM, CONVULSIONS, leading to COMA and death, the mortality rate being about 25 per cent. Among those who survive, about half suffer some brain damage. It has been suggested that ASPIRIN may be implicated in the development of this condition, and this drug is not now recommended for children under the age of 12.

rhesus factor *or* **Rh factor** *see* BLOOD GROUP.

rheumatic fever a severe disease, affecting children and young adults, which is a complication of upper RESPIRATORY TRACT infection with BACTERIA known as *Haemolytic streptococci*. The symptoms include FEVER, JOINT pain and ARTHRITIS that progresses from joint to joint, a characteristic red rash, known as ERYTHEMA marginatum, and also painless nodules that develop beneath the skin over bony protuberances such as the elbow, knee and back of the wrist. In addition there is CHOREA and INFLAMMATION of the HEART, including the muscle, valves and membranes. The condition may lead to rheumatic heart disease in which there is scarring and inflammation of heart structures. The initial treatment consists of destroying the streptococci that cause the disease with ANTIBIOTIC drugs such as PENICILLIN. Other drugs are also used, such as non-steroidal anti-inflammatory drugs (*see* NSAID) and CORTICOSTEROIDS. Surgery may be required later in life to replaced damaged heart valves.

rheumatism a general term used to describe aches and pains in JOINTS and MUSCLES.

rheumatoid arthritis the second most common form of JOINT disease, after OSTEOARTHRITIS, which usually affects the feet, ankles, fingers and wrists. The condition is diagnosed by means of X-RAYS, which show a typical pattern of changes around the inflamed joints, known as rheumatoid erosions. At first there is swelling of the joint and INFLAMMATION of the SYNOVIAL MEMBRANE (the membraneous sac that surrounds the joint), followed by erosion and loss of CARTILAGE and BONE.

In addition, a blood test reveals the presence of serum rheumatoid factor antibody, which is characteristic of this condition. The condition varies greatly in its degree of severity, but at its worst can be progressive and seriously disabling. In other people, after an initial active phase, there may be a long period of REMISSION. A number of different drugs are used to treat the disease, including ANALGESICS and ANTI-INFLAMMATORY agents.

rheumatology the branch of medicine concerned with diseases of the JOINTS and associated TISSUES and structures. The medical specialist in this field is known as a rheumatologist.

Rh factor *or* **rhesus factor** *see* BLOOD GROUP.

rhinitis INFLAMMATION of the MUCOUS MEMBRANE of the NOSE, such as occurs with colds and allergic reactions.

rhinophyma *see* ROSACEA.

rhinoplasty PLASTIC SURGERY performed to reconstruct the NOSE following accidental injury or for cosmetic reasons.

rhodopsin *see* PIGMENT; ROD.

rib *see* RIBS.

riboflavin *see* VITAMIN B2.

ribonucleic acid *see* RNA.

ribs 12 pairs of thin, slightly twisted and curved BONES that form the thoracic rib cage, which protects the LUNGS and HEART. The true ribs are the first seven pairs, which are each connected to the STERNUM at the front by a COSTAL CARTILAGE. The false ribs are the next three pairs and are indirectly connected to the sternum as each is attached by its cartilage to the rib above. The floating ribs are the last two pairs, which are unattached and end freely in the muscle of the thoracic wall. At the backbone, the head of each rib articulates with one of the 12 thoracic VERTEBRAE.

rickets a disease affecting children that involves a deficiency of VITAMIN D. Vitamin D can be manufactured in the SKIN in the presence of sunlight, but dietary sources are important especially where sunlight is lacking. The disease is characterized by soft BONES that bend out of shape and cause deformities. Bones are hardened by the deposition of calcium salts and this cannot happen in the absence of vitamin D. Treatment consists of giving vitamin D, usually in the form of

CALCIFEROL, and ensuring that there is an adequate amount in the child's future diet. Vitamin D deficiency in adults causes the condition called OSTEOMALACIA.

rickettsiae (*sing* **rickettsia**) a group of microorganisms that share characteristics in common with both BACTERIA and VIRUSES and are parasites that occur in lice, fleas and ticks and other arthropods. They can be passed to humans by the bites of these animals and are the cause of several serious diseases including TYPHUS, ROCKY MOUNTAIN SPOTTED FEVER and Q FEVER.

Rift Valley fever a disease, caused by a VIRUS, that formerly mainly affected domestic animals and rarely human beings in sub-Saharan Africa. A widespread outbreak in Egypt in 1977, however, caused many fatalities, and it now poses a threat to people throughout the Middle East. A new strain of virus of a more virulent type is thought to be responsible, and the infection is characterized by FEVER, MUSCLE and JOINT pains, HAEMORRHAGES, headache, PHOTOPHOBIA and loss of appetite. The virus is transmitted to humans by mosquitoes or by direct contact with the carcases of heavily infected animals. An effective VACCINE is available.

rigidity stiffness in a limb, especially one that is being moved passively, which is a symptom of PARKINSON'S DISEASE.

rigor a sudden bout of shivering and feeling of coldness that often accompanies the start of a FEVER.

rigor mortis the stiffening of the body that occurs usually within eight hours of death as a result of chemical and enzyme reactions in the MUSCLES. It generally passes off after about 24 hours.

Ringer's solution a physiological solution containing sodium chloride (salt), potassium chloride and calcium chloride and some other minerals, in the same proportions as in blood SERUM. It is injected intravenously in people suffering from DEHYDRATION and is used to bathe and maintain ORGANS that have been removed for TRANSPLANTATION operations.

ringworm an infection caused by various species of fungi (*see* FUNGUS) and known medically as tinea. It is classified according to the area affected, e.g. tinea capitis, which is ringworm of the scalp. Other areas affected are the beard, groin (tinea cruris or dhobie itch), nails and feet (ATHLETE'S FOOT). The infection is slightly raised, itchy and has a ring-like appearance. It is highly contagious, and the commonest form is athlete's foot. The ANTIBIOTIC drug griseofulvin, taken by mouth, is the normal treatment for ringworm and also antifungal creams applied to the affected areas.

Rinne's test a hearing test that uses a vibrating tuning fork and helps to determine whether DEAFNESS is perceptive (nervous) or conductive (indicating an obstruction within the ear).

RNA *or* **ribonucleic acid** a complex nucleic acid present mainly in the CYTOPLASM of cells but also in the NUCLEUS. It is involved in the production of PROTEINS and exists in three forms, ribosomal (r), transfer (t) and messenger (m) RNA. In some viruses it forms the genetic material (*see also* DNA).

rod one of the two types of light-sensitive CELL present in the RETINA of the EYE. The rods enable vision in dim light because of a PIGMENT called rhodopsin (visual purple). This pigment degenerates or bleaches when light is present and regenerates during darkness. In bright light all the pigment bleaches and the rods cannot function. Bleaching of the pigment gives rise to NERVE IMPULSES that are sent to the BRAIN and interpreted.

rodent ulcer a slow-growing malignant ULCER that occurs on the face in elderly people, usually near the lips, nostrils or eyelids. SKIN and underlying TISSUES and BONE are destroyed if the ulcer is untreated. Normally, treatment is by means of surgery and possibly RADIOTHERAPY.

rosacea a disease of the SKIN of the face characterized by a red, flushed appearance and enlargement of the SEBACEOUS GLANDS in the skin. The nose may also enlarge and look red and lumpy (rhinophyma). The cause is unknown but may be aggravated by certain foods or drinks, such as an excess of alcohol. Treatment is by means of tetracycline drugs.

roseola any rose-coloured RASH such as accompanies

various infectious diseases, e.g. MEASLES.

Rose-Waaler test a diagnostic BLOOD test that is used to detect RHEUMATOID ARTHRITIS.

rotavirus one of a number of VIRUSES that commonly cause GASTROENTERITIS and DIARRHOEA in children under the age of six. They infect the lining cells of the small INTESTINE.

roughage dietary fibre, which is necessary to maintain the healthy function of the bowels and helps to prevent constipation and DIVERTICULOSIS. The eating of sufficient dietary fibre is though to be important in the prevention of CANCER of the COLON.

RSI *see* TENDINITIS.

RS virus *see* RESPIRATORY SYNCITIAL VIRUS.

rubella *see* GERMAN MEASLES.

rupture 1. the bursting open of an ORGAN, TISSUE or structure, e.g. ruptured APPENDIX. **2.** a popular name for a HERNIA.

S

Sabin vaccine an oral VACCINE for POLIOMYELITIS. The appropriate VIRUS is cultured but rendered nonviolent while retaining its ability to stimulate production of ANTIBODIES.

sac a structure resembling a bag, e.g. the ALVEOLUS.

sacral nerves NERVES that serve the legs, anal and genital region and originate from the sacral area (SACRUM) of the SPINAL COLUMN. There are five pairs of sacral nerves.

sacral vertebrae the five VERTEBRAE that are fused together to form the SACRUM.

sacrum the lower part of the SPINAL COLUMN, comprising five fused vertebrae (SACRAL VERTEBRAE) in a triangular shape. The sacrum forms the back wall of the PELVIS and articulates with the COCCYX below, LUMBAR VERTEBRAE above and the HIPS to the sides.

SAD *see* SEASONAL AFFECTIVE DISORDER.

safe period the days in a woman's MENSTRUAL CYCLE when conception is least likely. OVULATION usually occurs midway through the cycle, about 15 days before onset of menstruation, and the fertile period is about 5 days before and 5 after ovulation. Providing periods are regular, it can be calculated when intercourse is unlikely to result in PREGNANCY but it is an unreliable method of CONTRACEPTION.

safe sex sexual activity using precautionary measures to avoid the transmission of sexually transmitted disease, for example, sexual intercourse using a condom.

Saint Vitus' dance the former name for Sydenham's CHOREA.

saliva an alkaline liquid present in the MOUTH to keep the mouth moist, aid swallowing of food and, through the presence of amylase ENZYMES (ptyalin), to digest starch. It is secreted by the SALIVARY GLANDS, and, in addition to ptyalin, contains water, MUCUS and buffers (to minimize changes in acidity).

salivary glands three pairs of glands—parotid, submandibular and sublingual—that produce SALIVA. The stimulus to produce saliva can be the taste, smell, sight or even thought of food.

Salk vaccine a VACCINE against POLIOMYELITIS administered by INJECTION. The VIRUS is treated to render it unable to cause the disease but it still prompts the production of ANTIBODIES.

salmonella infections FOOD POISONING caused by *Salmonella*, a genus of Gramnegative (*see* GRAM'S STAIN) rod-like BACTERIA.

salpingectomy the surgical excision of a FALLOPIAN TUBE. The removal of both produces STERILIZATION.

salpingitis INFLAMMATION of a tube, usually the FALLOPIAN TUBE, by bacterial INFECTION. It may originate in the VAGINA or UTERUS, or be carried in the BLOOD. PERITONITIS can ensue. Severe cases may cause a blockage of the Fallopian tubes, *de facto* STERILIZATION.

salpingostomy the clearing of a blocked FALLOPIAN TUBE in which the blocked part is removed surgically.

sanatorium a hospital or similar insitution for CONVALESCENCE or REHABILITATION.

sandfly fever *or* **bartonellosis** a viral INFECTION passed to humans through the bite of a sandfly. It occurs in much of the tropics and subtropics during the warmer months. It is a short-lived infection that resembles INFLUENZA in its symptoms.

sanguineous a term meaning containing BLOOD, covered or stained with blood.

sarcoma *see* CANCER.

sarcomere *see* VOLUNTARY MUSCLE.

SARS *see* SEVERE ACUTE RESPIRATORY SYNDROME.

scab a crust that forms over an injury (scratch, sore, etc) during the body's healing processes. The scab consists of FIBRIN, dried BLOOD, SERUM or PUS and epithelial cells (*see* EPITHELIUM). Healing occurs beneath the protective scab, which falls off when the process is complete. Scabs caused by INFECTIONS occur, e.g. on the face, with no previous sign.

scabies a skin INFECTION causing severe itching. It is caused by the mite *Sarcoptes scabiei*, which burrows into the SKIN and lays eggs, the resulting larvae causing the itching. The areas of the body commonly affected are the skin between fingers, wrists, buttocks and genitals.

scalds *see* BURNS.

scalp the covering of the SKULL around the top of the head, which comprises several layers, from the SKIN with HAIR on the outside through fat and FIBROUS TISSUE to another fibrous layer (the pericranium) that is attached closely to the skull.

scalpel a small surgical knife with renewable blades, used for cutting body TISSUES.

scan examination of the body using one of a number of techniques, such as COMPUTERIZED TOMOGRAPHY and ultrasonography (*see* ULTRASOUND).

scaphoid bone a BONE of the WRIST, the outside one on the thumb side of the HAND.

scapula (*pl* **scapulae**) *or* **shoulder blade** a triangular BONE and one of a pair forming the PECTORAL GIRDLE.

scar the mark left after a wound heals. It is the result of damaged TISSUES not repairing completely and being replaced by a fibrous CONNECTIVE TISSUE.

scarlet fever an infectious disease, mainly of childhood, caused by the bacterium *Streptococcus*. Symptoms show after a few days and include sickness, sore throat, FEVER and a scarlet RASH that may be widespread. ANTIBIOTICS are effective and also prevent any complications, e.g. inflammation of the kidneys.

schistosomiasis *or* **bilharziasis** a parasitic INFECTION caused by blood flukes (*Schistosoma*). Human beings are infected with the larvae of the fluke, which enter through the skin from infected water in tropical regions. The adults then settle in BLOOD VESSELS of the INTESTINE or BLADDER. Subsequent release of eggs causes ANAEMIA, DIARRHOEA, DYSENTERY, enlargement of the SPLEEN and LIVER and CIRRHOSIS of the liver. The disease can be treated with drugs but preventative measures are preferable. Schistosomiasis affects millions of people worldwide, particularly in the Far and Middle East, South America and Africa.

schizophrenia any one of a large group of severe mental disorders typified by gross distortion of reality, disturbance in language and breakdown of thought processes, perceptions and emotions. Delusions and HALLUCINATIONS are usual, and other signs of the disorder include apathy, confusion, incontinence and strange behaviour.

No single cause is known but genetic factors are probably important. Drug therapy has improved the outlook markedly over recent years.

Schwann cell *see* MYELIN.

sciatic pertaining to the HIP.

sciatica pain in the SCIATIC NERVE and therefore felt in the back of the thigh, leg and foot. The commonest cause is a PROLAPSED INTERVERTEBRAL DISC pressing on a nerve root, but it may also result from ankylosing SPONDYLITIS and other conditions.

sciatic nerve the major NERVE in the leg, passing down the back of the thigh from the base of the SPINAL COLUMN.

sclera the outer layer of the eyeballs, which is seen as white and fibrous except at the front of the EYE when it becomes the transparent CORNEA.

scleritis INFLAMMATION of the white of the eye (SCLERA).

scleroderma a condition in which CONNECTIVE TISSUE hardens and contracts. The tissue may be the SKIN, HEART, KIDNEY, LUNG, etc, and the condition may be localized or it may spread throughout the body, eventually being fatal. If the skin is affected, it becomes tough and patchily pigmented and may lead to stiff joints and wasting MUSCLES.

sclerosis hardening of TISSUE, usually after INFLAMMATION, leading to parts of ORGANS being hard and of no use. It is applied commonly to such changes in the NERVOUS SYSTEM (MULTIPLE SCLEROSIS); in other organs it is termed FIBROSIS or CIRRHOSIS.

sclerotherapy a treatment for VARICOSE VEINS. An irritant solution is injected, causing FIBROSIS of the vein lining and its eventual removal by THROMBOSIS and scarring.

screening test a programme of tests carried out on a large number of apparently healthy people to find those who may have a particular disease, e.g. CERVICAL SMEARS to detect the precancerous stage of cervical cancer.

scrofula TUBERCULOSIS of the LYMPH NODES in the neck, which form sores and SCARS after healing. It is now an uncommon condition, but drug treatment is effective.

scrotum the SAC that contains the TESTICLES and holds them outside the body to permit production and storage of sperm at a temperature lower than that of the abdomen.

scrub typhus a disease prevalent in Southeast Asia, caused by a parasitic microorganism, *Rickettsia*, which is transmitted from rodents to humans by the bite of mites. It causes chills, headaches, high temperatures, RASHES and possibly DELIRIUM. An ULCER develops at the site of the initial bite. The condition can be treated with ANTIBIOTICS.

scrum-pox a bacterial (IMPETIGO) or viral (HERPES simplex) infection of the face that is common in rugby players, occurring probably through facial contact in the scrum or communal changing facilities.

scurvy a deficiency disease caused by a lack of VITAMIN C (ascorbic acid) as a result of a dietary lack of fruit and vegetables. Symptoms begin with swollen, bleeding gums and then SUBCUTANEOUS bleeding, bleeding into joints, ULCERS, ANAEMIA and fainting, DIARRHOEA and trouble with major organs. Untreated, it is fatal, but nowadays it is easily prevented, or cured should it arise, through correct diet or administration of the vitamin.

seasonal affective disorder (SAD) a recurring form of DEPRESSION, sometimes severe, which sufferers experience during the winter months. The condition is associated with reduced hours of daylight. Light therapy may be effective in reducing the symptoms, which include low mood, carbohydrate cravings, irritability and disturbed sleep patterns. Symptoms disappear in the spring and summer months.

sebaceous cyst *or* **wen** a CYST formed in the duct of a SEBACEOUS GLAND of the skin.

sebaceous gland any of the minute GLANDS in the skin that secrete an oily substance called SEBUM. The glands open into hair FOLLICLES. Activity of the glands varies with age, PUBERTY being the most active period.

seborrhoea excessive production of SEBUM by the SEBACEOUS GLANDS, producing either a build-up of dry skin scales or oily deposits on the skin. The condition often leads to the development of ACNE.

sebum the secretion, formed by the SEBACEOUS GLANDS, that forms as a thin oily film on the skin, preventing excessive dryness. It also has an antibacterial action.

secondary sexual characteristics the physical features that develop at PUBERTY. In girls, the BREASTS and genitals increase in size and PUBIC hair grows. Boys grow pubic hair and facial hair, the voice breaks and the genitals become adult size.

secretin a polyPEPTIDE hormone produced by the lining of the DUODENUM and JEJUNUM in response to acid from the stomach. It stimulates production of alkaline pancreatic juice, and BILE secretion by the LIVER.

secretion the material produced by a GLAND.

secretory otitis media *see* GLUE EAR.

section 1. in surgery, cutting, e.g. an abdominal section. **2.** in microscopy, a thin slice of a specimen as examined under a microscope.

sedative a drug that lessens tension and anxiety. Sedatives are hypnotic drugs, e.g. BARBITURATES, given in doses lower than would bring on sleep. They may be used to combat pain, sleeplessness, spasms, etc.

seizure the accepted term for any form of epileptic attack, whether convulsive or otherwise. *See* CONVULSIONS; EPILEPSY.

semen the fluid that contains the SPERM, which is ejaculated (*see* EJACULATION) from the PENIS during copulation.

seminiferous tubule *see* TESTICLE.

senile dementia an organic mental disorder of the elderly involving generalized ATROPHY of the BRAIN. The result is a gradual deterioration with loss of memory (particularly short-term memory), impaired judgement, confusion, emotional outbursts and irritability. The condition is progressive.

sensation a feeling, the result of stimulation of a SENSORY receptor that produces a NERVE IMPULSE that travels along an AFFERENT fibre to the BRAIN.

sense organ a bodily structure that reacts to stimuli and transmits them to the brain as NERVE IMPULSES.

sensitivity in a SCREENING TEST, the proportion of people with the disease who are identified by the test.

sensitization a change in the body's response to foreign substances. With the development of an ALLERGY, a person becomes sensitized to a certain ALLERGEN and then becomes hypersensitive. Similarly, it may be an acquired reaction when ANTIBODIES develop in response to an ANTIGEN.

sensory 1. of or relating to the senses, sensation or the SENSE ORGANS. **2.** of a NERVE, conveying NERVE IMPULSES to the BRAIN.

sepsis the destruction of TISSUES through putrefaction by BACTERIA-causing disease or TOXINS produced by bacteria.

septal defect a hole in the SEPTUM or partition between the left and right sides of the HEART, whether in the atria (*see* ATRIUM) or VENTRICLES. This condition is a CONGENITAL disorder caused by an abnormal development of the foetal heart. Whether the defect is atrial or ventricular, it allows incorrect CIRCULATION of the blood from left to right, from higher pressure to lower. This is called a shunt and results in too much blood flowing through the LUNGS. PULMONARY HYPERTENSION results, and a large shunt may cause HEART FAILURE. Surgery can correct the defect, although a small one may not require any treatment.

septic affected with SEPSIS.

septicaemia 1. a term used loosely for any type of blood poisoning. **2.** a systemic infection with PATHOGENs from an infected part of the body circulating in the bloodstream.

septic shock a form of shock that occurs because of SEPTI-CAEMIA. The toxins cause a drastic fall in BLOOD PRESSURE as a result of TISSUE damage and blood clotting. Kidneys, heart and lungs are affected, and related symptoms include FEVER, TACHYCARDIA or even COMA. The condition occurs most in those who already have a serious disease, such as CANCER, DIABETES MELLITUS or CIRRHOSIS. Urgent treatment is vital, with ANTIBIOTICS, oxygen and fluids given intravenously.

septum (*pl* **septa**) a planar dividing feature within a structure of the body; a partition, e.g. the nasal septum.

serology a laboratory medical subdiscipline involving the study of blood SERUM and its consitutuents, including ANTIGEN-ANTIBODY reactions.

serositis INFLAMMATION of a SEROUS MEMBRANE.

serotonin an AMINE that acts as a vasoconstrictor (*see* VASOCONSTRICTION). It is present in the CENTRAL NERVOUS SYSTEM, blood PLATELETS and the INTESTINE. *See also* MAST CELL.

serous of or producing SERUM.

serous membrane a MEMBRANE lining a large CAVITY in the body. The membranes are smooth and transparent and the surfaces are moistened by fluid derived from BLOOD or LYMPH serum (hence the name). Examples are the PERITONEUM and the PERICARDIUM. Each consists of two layers: the visceral, which surrounds the ORGANS, and the parietal, which lines the cavity. The two portions are continuous and the surfaces are close together, separated by fluid that permits free movement of the organs.

sertoli cells *see* TESTICLE.

serum 1. the clear, sticky fluid that separates from BLOOD and LYMPH when blood clotting occurs. In addition to water, serum contains ALBUMIN and GLOBULIN with salts, fat, sugar, UREA and other compounds important in disease prevention. **2.** a VACCINE prepared from the serum of a hyperIMMUNE donor for use in protection against a particular infection.

serum sickness a hypersensitive reaction that occasionally occurs several days after INJECTION of foreign SERUM, producing RASHES, JOINT pains, FEVER and swelling of the LYMPH NODES. It is the result of circulating ANTIGEN material to which the body responds. It is not a serious condition.

sessile in the description of a TUMOUR or growth, one HAVING no stalk.

Severe acute respiratory syndrome (SARS) a strain of coronavirus which originated in China in 2002. Symptoms are similar to those of INFLUENZA, accompanied by shortness of breath and PNEUMONIA. The disease may be severe and is fatal in some cases. The VIRUS mutates rapidly, making development of an effective vaccine difficult.

sex chromosomes CHROMOSOMES that play a major role in determining the sex of the bearer. Sex chromosomes contain GENES that control the characteristics of the individual, e.g. TESTICLES in males, ovaries (*see* OVARY) in

females. Women have two X-CHROMOSOMES while men have one X-chromsome and one Y-CHROMOSOME.

sex hormones steroid HORMONES responsible for the control of sexual development (primary and SECONDARY SEXUAL CHARACTERISTICS) and reproductive function. The ovaries (*see* OVARY) and TESTICLES are the organs primarily involved in hormone production, of which there are three main types: ANDROGENS, the male sex hormones; OESTROGENS and PROGESTERONE, the female sex hormones.

sex-linked disorders conditions produced because the GENES controlling certain characteristics are carried on the SEX CHROMOSOMES, usually the X-CHROMOSOME. Some result from an abnormal number of chromosomes, e.g. KLINEFELTER'S SYNDROME affecting only men, and TURNER'S SYNDROME affecting only women. Other disorders, such as HAEMOPHILIA, are carried on the X-chromosome and these manifest themselves in men because, although the genes are RECESSIVE, there is no other X-chromosome to mask the recessive type, as is the case with women.

sexually transmitted diseases *see* VENEREAL DISEASES.

shin bone *see* TIBIA.

shingles *see* HERPES.

shock acute circulatory failure when the arterial BLOOD PRESSURE is too low to provide the normal blood supply to the body. The signs are a cold, clammy skin, PALLOR, CYANOSIS, weak rapid PULSE, irregular breathing and dilated pupils. There may also be a reduced flow of URINE and confusion or LETHARGY. There are numerous causes of shock, from a reduction in blood volume following a burn, external bleeding, DEHYDRATION, etc, to reduced heart activity, as in CORONARY THROMBOSIS, PULMONARY EMBOLISM, etc.

Certain other circumstances may produce shock, including severe allergic reactions (anaphylactic shock, *see* ANAPHYLAXIS), drugs overdose, emotional shock, etc.

short sight *see* MYOPIA.

shoulder the JOINT formed by the shoulder blade (SCAPULA) and the upper end of the HUMERUS. It is a ball-and-socket joint surrounded by a fibrous CAPSULE strengthened with bands of LIGAMENT. The strength of the joint is derived from the associated MUSCLES.

shoulder blade *see* SCAPULA.

shoulder girdle *see* PECTORAL GIRDLE.

shunt *see* SEPTAL DEFECT.

Siamese twins *see* CONJOINED TWINS.

sickle-cell anaemia a type of inherited, haemolytic ANAEMIA (*see* HAEMOLYSIS) that is genetically determined and is the most common hereditary disease in the world. It is caused by a RECESSIVE GENE and is manifested when this GENE is inherited from both parents. One AMINO ACID in the HAEMOGLOBIN molecule is substituted, causing the disease, which results in an abnormal type of haemoglobin being precipitated in the red blood CELLS (ERYTHROCYTES) during deprivation of oxygen. This produces the distortion of the cells, which are removed from the circulation, causing anaemia and JAUNDICE. Many people are carriers as a result of inheritance of just one defective gene and because this confers increased resistance to MALARIA, this gene remains at a high level.

side effect an additional and unwanted effect of a DRUG above the intended action. Sometimes side effects are harmful and may be the stronger than anticipated results of a drug or something quite different.

sigmoid colon the end part of the COLON, which is S-shaped.

sigmoidectomy surgical EXCISION of the SIGMOID COLON, performed usually for TUMOURS, diverticular disease (*see* DIVERTICULITIS, DIVERTICULOSIS) or a long and twisted sigmoid colon.

sigmoidoscopy the examination of the SIGMOID COLON and RECTUM with a special viewing device. The instrument is tubular, with illumination, although modern forms use fibreoptics, which are flexible. *See also* FIBREOPTIC ENDOSCOPY.

sildenafil citrate a drug (trade name Viagra) used in the treatment of IMPOTENCE. It increases blood flow to erectile tissue in the PENIS, thereby promoting full erection in response to penile stimulation.

silicosis a type of PNEUMOCONIOSIS caused by the inhalation of silica as particles of dust. The silica promotes FIBROSIS of the lung tissue, resulting in BREATHLESSNESS and a greater likelihood to contract TUBERCULOSIS. Workers in quarrying, mineral mining, sand-blasting, etc, are most susceptible.

sinew the TENDON of a MUSCLE.

sinoatrial node the natural HEART pacemaker, which consists of specialized MUSCLE cells in the right ATRIUM. These cells generate electrical impulses, contract and initiate contractions in the muscles of the heart. The AUTONOMIC NERVOUS SYSTEM supplies the node, and certain HORMONES also have an effect.

sinus 1. in general terms a cavity or channel. **2.** an air cavity in BONE, as in the bones of the FACE and SKULL. **3.** a channel, as in the dura mater, which drains venous BLOOD from the BRAIN (*see also* MENINGES).

sinusitis INFLAMMATION of a SINUS, usually referring to the sinuses in the face that link with the nose and may therefore be caused by a spread of INFECTION from the nose. Headaches and a tenderness over the affected sinus are typical symptoms, with a PUS-containing discharge from the nose. Persistent infection may necessitate surgery to drain the sinus.

Sjögren's syndrome dryness of the mouth and eyes, associated with RHEUMATOID ARTHRITIS. The syndrome is the result of the destruction of the SALIVARY GLANDS (and LACRIMAL GLANDS).

skeleton the rigid, supporting framework of the body that protects ORGANS and TISSUES, provides MUSCLE attachments, facilitates movement, and produces red blood cells (ERYTHROCYTES). There are 206 BONES, divided into the axial skeleton (head and trunk) and the appendicular skeleton (limbs). The types of bone are: long (e.g. HUMERUS), short (e.g. carpals, *see* CARPUS), flat (parts of the CRANIUM) and irregular (e.g. the VERTEBRAE).

skin the outer layer of the body, comprising an external EPIDERMIS, itself made up of a stratum corneum (horny layer) formed of flat cells that rub off, being replaced from below. Beneath this are two more layers (stratum lucidum and stratum granulosum), which act as intermediate stages between the stratum corneum and a still lower layer, the Malpighian layer. The Malpighian layer is where the epidermis is produced. The dermis lies beneath the epidermis, and there is subcutaneous tissue, composed mainly of fat. The SUBCUTANEOUS tissue contains glands (SWEAT, SEBACEOUS, etc), SENSORY receptors for pain, pressure and TEMPERATURE, NERVES, MUSCLES and blood capillaries. The skin is a protective layer against injury and parasites, and it moderates water loss. It is a medium of temperature control by means of the SWEAT GLANDS and blood capillaries and also the HAIRS (which provide insulation).

skin graft a piece of skin taken from another site on the body to cover an injured area, commonly the result of BURNS. The GRAFT is normally taken from elsewhere on the patient's body (autograft) but occasionally from someone else (homograft). A variety of thicknesses and graft types are used, depending on the WOUND.

skull the part of the SKELETON that forms the head and encloses the BRAIN. It is made up of 22 BONES, forming the CRANIUM (eight bones) and 14 in the FACE, and all except the mandible (lower JAW) are fused along SUTURES, creating immovable JOINTS. The mandible articulates close to the ears. A large opening at the base of the skull (FORAMEN magnum) allows the SPINAL CORD to pass from the brain to the trunk of the body.

sleep a state of lower awareness accompanied by reduced metabolic activity and physical relaxation. When falling asleep, there is a change in the brain's electrical activity, which can be recorded by an ELECTROENCEPHALOGRAM (EEG). There are high amplitude, low frequency waves (slow-wave sleep) interrupted by short periods of low amplitude, high frequency waves. The periods of high frequency waves are typified by restless sleep with dreams and rapid eye movements, hence the name REM SLEEP, and the EEG is similar to that of a waking person. REM sleep comprises about 25 per cent of the time asleep.

sleep apnoea see APNOEA.

sleeping sickness or **African trypanosomiasis** a parasitic disease found in tropical Africa which is spread through the bite of tsetse flies. Initially the symptoms consist of a recurring FEVER, a slight RASH, headache and chills. Then follows ANAEMIA, enlarged LYMPH NODES and pain in JOINTS and limbs. Then after some time (possibly years), sleeping sickness itself develops. This is because of the parasites occupying minute blood vessels in the brain, resulting in damage and symptoms of drowsiness and lethargy. Death may follow from weakness or an associated disease.

sleepwalking see SOMNAMBULISM.

sling a BANDAGE so arranged as to support an injured limb, usually an arm.

slipped disc see PROLAPSED INTERVERTEBRAL DISC.

slough dead TISSUE, usually of limited extent, that, after INFECTION, separates from the healthy tissue of the rest of the body. In cases of GANGRENE it is possible for limbs to be lost.

slow virus one of several VIRUSES that show their effects some time after INFECTION, by which time considerable damage of NERVE tissue has occurred, resulting ultimately in death. Such a virus was found to cause scrapie in sheep and recently BOVINE SPONGIFORM ENCEPHALOPATHY in cows. In humans, a slow virus is thought to be the cause of CREUTZFELDT-JAKOB DISEASE and a type of MENINGITIS.

small intestine *see* INTESTINE.

smallpox a highly infectious, frequently fatal viral disease, eradicated after a global programme of vaccination. Initial symptoms of INFECTION are high FEVER, head and body aches and vomiting. Eventually red spots appear, which change to water and then pus-filled vesicles that, on drying out, leave SCABS. The person stays infectious until all scabs are shed. Complications include PNEUMONIA.

smooth muscle *see* INVOLUNTARY MUSCLE.

sneezing the involuntary REFLEX expulsion of air via the NOSE and MOUTH caused by irritating particles in the nose, e.g. pollen. It is also symptomatic of the COMMON COLD, MEASLES, HAY FEVER, etc.

One sneeze can project many thousands of drops over several metres at great speed (>60 km/hour) and is therefore instrumental in the spread of INFECTIONS.

Snellen chart the chart commonly used for testing distant VISION. It comprises rows of capital letters that become progressively smaller.

snoring a vibration of the soft PALATE that produces a hoarse sound. Although breathing through the mouth is essential for snoring, not all those who breathe through the mouth snore. The main cause is blockage of the NOSE and OBESTITY can aggravate the problem. *See also* APNOEA.

snow blindness a disorder of the EYE caused by excessive exposure to ultraviolet light, e.g. as reflected from a snow field, resulting in temporary loss of vision. Covering the eyes for 24 hours is usually an effective treatment.

solar plexus a network of sympathetic NERVES and ganglia (*see* GANGLION) behind the STOMACH. It is a major autonomic PLEXUS of the body where nerves of the SYMPATHETIC and PARASYMPATHETIC NERVOUS SYSTEM combine.

somatic 1. a descriptive term meaning 'relating to the body', as opposed to the mind. **2.** more specifically, concerning the nonreproductive parts of the body.

somatostatin *see* ISLETS OF LANGERHANS.

somatotrophin *see* GROWTH HORMONE.

somnambulism *or* **sleep-walking** walking and performing other functions during sleep without recollection upon waking. It is thought that it may occur in HYSTERIA and if episodes continue medical advice should be sought.

soporific sleep-inducing. *See also* HYPNOTICS.

sore a common term for an ULCER or open skin WOUND.

sound an instrument that resembles a rod with a curved end used to explore a body cavity, e.g. the bladder, or to dilate STRICTURES.

Southey's tubes very fine tubes for drawing off fluid, e.g. from subcutaneous TISSUE. They are rarely used today.

spasm a muscular contraction that is involuntary. Spasms may be part of a more major disorder (e.g. SPASTIC PARALYSIS, CONVULSIONS) or they may be specific, such as in CRAMP, COLIC, etc. A HEART spasm is known as ANGINA.

spasmolytic a drug that reduces SPASMS (in smooth MUSCLE) in a number of ways. It may generally depress the CENTRAL NERVOUS SYSTEM, act directly on the muscles in question, or modify the NERVE IMPULSES causing the spasm. Spasmolytics are used in the treatment of ANGINA, COLIC and as BRONCHODILATORS.

spastic colon *see* IRRITABLE BOWEL SYNDROME.

spasticity muscular hypertonicity (i.e. an increase in the state of readiness of MUSCLE fibres to contract; an increase in the normal partial contraction) with an increased resistance to stretch. Moderate cases show movement requiring great effort and a lack of normal coordination while slight cases show exaggerated movements that are coordinated.

spastic paralysis weakness of a limb characterized by involuntary muscular contraction and loss of muscular function. As with SPASTICITY, it is caused by disease of the NERVE fibres that usually control movement and REFLEXES.

spatula a knife-like instrument with a flat, blunt blade used for spreading or mixing ointments and materials. Also used to hold down the tongue when the throat is being examined.

speculum (*pl* **specula**) an instrument for use in examination of an opening in the body. The speculum holds open the cavity and may also provide illumination.

speech therapy treatment of patients who are unable to speak coherently. Such patients may have congenital conditions or may have suffered an accident or illness producing a condition requiring therapy.

sperm the mature male reproductive CELL or GAMETE. It has a head with the HAPLOID nucleus containing half the CHROMOSOME number and an acrosome (a structure that aids penetration of the egg). Behind the head comes a midpiece with energy-producing MITOCHONDRIA, and then a long tail that propels it forward. A few millilitres of SEMEN is ejaculated during intercourse, containing many millions of sperm.

spermatic the term given to any vessel or structure associated with the TESTICLE.

spermatozoon (*pl* **spermatozoa**) the scientific name for SPERM.

spermicide a cream, foam, jelly, etc, that kills SPERM and is commonly used in conjunction with a DIAPHRAGM as a CONTRACEPTIVE.

sphenoid bone a BONE in the SKULL that lies behind the eyes.

sphincter a circular MUSCLE around an opening. The opening is closed totally or partially by contraction of the muscle, e.g. the anal SPHINCTER around the ANUS.

sphygmomanometer the instrument used to measure arterial BLOOD PRESSURE. An inflatable rubber tube is put around the arm and inflated until the blood flow in a large ARTERY stops. This pressure is taken as the systolic pressure (i.e. the pressure at each heart beat). The pressure is then released slowly and the point at which the sound heard in the artery changes suddenly is taken as the diastolic pressure (*see* DIASTOLE).

spina bifida a CONGENITAL malformation in newborn babies in which part of the SPINAL CORD is exposed by a gap in the backbone. Many cases are also affected with

HYDROCEPHALUS. The symptoms usually include PARALYSIS, INCONTINENCE, a high risk of MENINGITIS and mental RETARDATION. There is usually an abnormally high level of ALPHA FETOPROTEIN in the AMNIOTIC FLUID and since this can be diagnosed and then confirmed by AMNIOCENTESIS, it is possible to terminate these pregnancies.

spinal anaesthesia 1. the generation of ANAESTHESIA by injecting the CEREBROSPINAL FLUID around the SPINAL CORD. Of the two types, the epidural (*see* EPIDURAL ANAESTHESIA) involves injecting into the outer lining of the spinal cord, while subarachnoid anaesthesia is produced by injecting between vertebrae in the LUMBAR region of the vertebral column. Spinal anaesthesia is useful for patients who have a condition that precludes a general ANAESTHETIC (e.g. a chest infection or heart disease). **2.** the loss of sensation in a part of the body as a result of spinal injury.

spinal column *or* **spine** *or* **backbone** *or* **vertebral column** the bony and slightly flexible column that forms a vital part of the SKEL-ETON. It encloses the SPINAL CORD, articulates with other BONES, e.g. the SKULL and RIBS, and provides attachments for MUSCLES. It consists of bones, the VERTEBRAE, between which are discs of fibrocartilage (the INTERVERTEBRAL DISCS). From the top, the column comprises 7 cervical, 12 thoracic, 5 lumbar, 5 sacral and 4 coccygeal vertebrae. In adults the last two groups are fused to from the SACRUM and COCCYX respectively.

spinal cord the part of the CENTRAL NERVOUS SYSTEM that runs from the BRAIN, through the SPINAL COLUMN. Both GREY and WHITE MATTER are present, the former as an H-shaped core within the latter. A hollow core in the grey matter forms the central canal, which contains the CEREBROSPINAL FLUID. The cord is covered by MENINGES, and it contains both SENSORY and MOTOR NEURONS. Thirty-one pairs of spinal nerves arise from the cord, passing out between the arches of the VERTEBRAE.

spine the SPINAL COLUMN.

spirochaete any of a group of spiral shaped BACTERIA that are the causal organisms of

LYME DISEASE; RELAPSING FEVER and YAWS.

spirometer an instrument used to test how the LUNGS are working by recording the volume of air inhaled and exhaled.

spleen a roughly ovoid (egg-shaped) ORGAN, coloured a deep purple, that is situated on the left of the body, behind and below the STOMACH. It is surrounded by a peritoneal MEMBRANE and contains a mass of lymphoid TISSUE. MACROPHAGES in the spleen destroy microorganisms by PHAGOCYTOSIS. The spleen produces LYMPHOCYTES, LEUCOCYTES, PLASMA cells and blood PLATELETS. It also stores red blood cells (ERYTHROCYTES) for use in emergencies. Release of red blood cells is facilitated by smooth MUSCLE under the control of the SYMPATHETIC NERVOUS SYSTEM, and when this occurs, the familiar pain called STITCH may be experienced. The spleen removes worn-out red blood cells, conserving the iron for further production in the BONE MARROW. Although the spleen performs many functions, it can be removed without detriment and as a result there is an increase in size of the lymphatic GLANDS.

splenectomy removal of the SPLEEN, possibly because of rupture and bleeding.

splenomegaly an abnormal enlargement of the SPLEEN, which occurs commonly with blood disorders and parasitic infections.

splint a support that holds a broken BONE in the correct and stable position until healing is complete.

spondylitis INFLAMMATION of the spinal VERTEBRAE—ARTHRITIS of the spine. Ankylosing spondylitis is a rheumatic disease of the SPINAL COLUMN and sacroiliac JOINTS (i.e. those of the SACRUM and ILIUM), causing pain and stiffness in the hip and shoulder. It may result in the spine becoming rigid (*see* KYPHOSIS).

spondylosis degeneration of JOINTS and the INTERVERTEBRAL DISCS of the spine, producing pain in the neck and LUMBAR region where the joints may actually restrict movement. OSTEOPHYTES are commonly formed and the space occupied by the discs reduced. PHYSIOTHERAPY may help sufferers, and collars or surgical belts can prevent movement and give support. Surgery may be required occasionally to relieve pressure on NERVES or to fuse joints.

spongiform encephalopathy a neurological disease that is caused by a SLOW VIRUS and results in a spongy degeneration of the BRAIN with progressive DEMENTIA. Examples are CREUTZFELDT-JAKOB DISEASE and kuru (a progressive and fatal viral INFECTION seen in New Guinea Highland peoples, the incidence of which has decreased with the decline in cannibalism).

sprain an injury to LIGAMENTS (or MUSCLES or TENDONS) around a JOINT, caused by a sudden overstretching. Pain and swelling may occur, and treatment comprises, in the main, avoiding use of the affected joint.

sprue *or* **psilosis** essentially a composite DEFICIENCY DISEASE because of lack of food being absorbed as a result of a disease of the INTESTINE or a metabolic disorder that means fats cannot be absorbed. The symptoms include DIARRHOEA, inflamed TONGUE, ANAEMIA and weight loss. The condition was considered a disease of tropical climates but other versions have been seen. Treatment involves ANTIBIOTICS, folic acid (to combat the ANAEMIA), vitamins and a high-PROTEIN diet. There may be an immediate improvement on returning to a temperate climate.

sputum SALIVA and MUCUS from the respiratory tract.

squint *or* **strabismus** an abnormal condition which the prevents the EYES from focusing together and which may be the result of muscular or neurological malfunction. Some squints can be corrected by surgery.

stagnant loop syndrome the condition when a segment of the small INTESTINE is discontinuous with the rest or when there is an obstruction, either of which causes slow movement through the intestines. The result is bacterial growth with malabsorption (*see* MALABSORPTION SYNDROME) and steatorrhoea (passage of fatty stools).

stammering *or* **stuttering** when normal speech falters with a repetition of the initial consonant of words. Usually it appears first in childhood but often responds to speech therapy.

stapes *see* EAR.

staphylococcus (*pl* **staphylococci**) any of a group of minute spherical Gram-positive (*see* GRAM'S STAIN) BACTERIA of the genus *Staphylococcus* that are normally present on SKIN and MUCOUS MEMBRANES. *S. albus* may be found in superficial skin IN-FECTIONS. *S. aureus* is a more invasive, and therefore harmful, species and is a common cause of ABSCESSES.

starvation *see* MALNUTRITION.

status epilepticus a term used to describe a prolonged epileptic SEIZURE, or a series of seizures with no intervening recovery period. It is treated as a medical emergency. If a person experiences a seizure lasting more than five minutes, or has more than two seizures in rapid succession, medical help should be sought immediately.

steatorrhoea *see* STAGNANT LOOP SYNDROME.

stem cells *see* THYMUS GLAND.

stenosis (*pl* **stenoses**) the abnormal narrowing of a BLOOD VESSEL, heart VALVE or similar structure.

stent a device used in surgery to help the healing of two structures, such as a tube inserted into a BLOOD VESSEL which has been cut, to support the place where the two ends have been rejoined.

sterilization 1. the process of destroying all microorganisms on instruments and other objects by means of heat, radiation, etc. **2.** a surgical operation to render someone incapable of producing children. Men usually undergo a VASECTOMY while in women sterilization can be achieved by cutting and tying the FAL-LOPIAN TUBES or removing them. The latter operation is performed via an INCISION in the abdominal wall or through the VAGINA.

sternum (*pl* **sterna**) *or* **breastbone** the long flat narrow vertical BONE situated in the centre of the anterior wall of the CHEST, extending from the neck to the ABDO-MEN. The CLAVICLE and the first seven pairs of RIBS are attached to it.

steroid one of a group of compounds, resembling CHOLES-TEROL, that are made up of four carbon rings fused together. The group includes the sterols (e.g. cholesterol), BILE acids, some HORMONES, and VITAMIN D. Synthetic versions act like steroid hormones and include derivatives of the glucocorticoids used as anti-inflammatory agents for RHEUMATOID ARTHRITIS; oral contraceptives, usually OESTROGEN and PROGESTERONE derivatives; and anabolic steroids, such as testosterone, used to treat OSTEOPOROSIS and wasting.

sterol *see* CHOLESTEROL; STEROID.

stertor noisy breathing, similar to SNORING, often heard in patients who are deeply unconscious.

stethoscope an instrument used to listen to sounds within the body, particularly the LUNGS and HEART. The simplest type consists of earpieces for the examiner, leading via a tube to a diaphragm placed on the body.

Stevens-Johnsonsyndrome a common HYPERSENSITIVITY reaction to SULPHONAMIDE antibiotics, and a form of ERYTHEMA. It produces skin lesions and the eyes and mucosa may ulcerate.

stiffness a condition with numerous causes that results in a reduced movement in JOINTS

and MUSCLES. The cause may be quite straightforward, e.g. physical injury, or it may be caused by disease, such as RHEUMATISM, MENINGITIS, or CENTRAL NERVOUS SYSTEM disorders.

stigma (*pl* **stigmata**) a mark or impression upon the SKIN, possibly one that is typical of a particular disease.

stilboestrol a synthetic OESTROGEN (female SEX HORMONE) with several uses. It relieves menstrual disorders and menopausal symptoms. It also proves helpful in treating CANCERS of the BREAST and PROSTATE.

stillbirth the birth of any child that provides no evidence of life.

Still's disease a chronic ARTHRITIS affecting children and affecting several JOINTS, with FEVER and a red RASH. Some cases develop into ankylosing SPONDYLITIS and there is often MUSCLE wasting. The illness may affect the whole body, complicated by other conditions, e.g. enlargement of the SPLEEN and PERICARDITIS.

stimulus (*pl* **stimuli**) an agent that arouses or provokes a response in a SENSE ORGAN.

stimulant any drug or other agent that increases the rate of activity of an organ or system within the body. This assumes that the target organ is capable of increased activity and merely requires the necessary stimulus.

stitch a sharp pain in the side, often caused by CRAMP after hard exertion (*see also* SPLEEN).

stoma (*pl* **stomata**) an opening made in the abdominal surface to accommodate a tube from the COLON or ILEUM. This operation is undertaken because of malignancy or inflammatory bowel diseases, e.g. CROHN'S DISEASE. *See also* COLOSTOMY, ILEOSTOMY.

stomach an expansion of the ALIMENTARY CANAL that lies between the OESOPHAGUS and the DUODENUM. It has thick walls of smooth MUSCLE that contract to manipulate the food, and its exits are controlled by SPHINCTERS, the cardiac anteriorly and the pyloric at the junction with the duodenum (*see* PYLORUS). Mucosal CELLS in the lining secrete GASTRIC JUICE. The food is reduced to an acidic semi-liquid that is moved on to the duodenum. The stomach varies in size but its greatest length is roughly 30 cm and the breadth 10 to 12 cm. Its capacity is approximately 1 to 1½ litres.

stools *see* FAECES.

strabismus *see* SQUINT.

strangulation the constriction or closure of a passage or vessel. This may be because of INTESTINE twisting or herniation (*see* HERNIA) of the intestine. Strangulation of a BLOOD VESSEL and/or airway affects the ORGANS being supplied and, if vital organs are affected, can prove fatal.

strangury the desire to pass water, which can be done only in a few drops and with accompanying pain. It is symptomatic of an irritation of the base of the BLADDER by a stone, CANCER at this site or CYSTITIS or PROSTATITIS.

strapping the application of layers of adhesive plaster to cover part of the body and maintain moderate pressure so as to prevent too much movement and provide rest, as with fractured 9.

stratum (*pl* **strata**) a layer, especially of the SKIN or MUCOUS MEMBRANE, e.g. the stratum corneum and stratum germiativum of the EPIDERMIS.

streptococcus (*pl* **streptococci**) a spherical bacterium (*see* BACTERIA) of the genus *Streptococcus*, which is Gram-positive (*see* GRAM'S STAIN) and forms chains. Many species are responsible for a variety of INFECTIONS, including SCARLET FEVER, ENDOCARDITIS and PNEUMONIA.

streptokinase an ENZYME that is produced by streptococci and causes FIBRIN to undergo LYSIS.

streptomycin an ANTIBIOTIC that is used in the treatment of TUBERCULOSIS and bacterial INFECTIONS.

stress fracture a FRACTURE created by making excessive demands on the body, as commonly happens in sport. Treatment involves rest and ANALGESICS for the pain.

striated marked with small channels running parallel to each other, e.g. striated muscle (*see* VOLUNTARY MUSCLE).

stricture a narrowing of a passage in the body, e.g. the URETHRA, OESOPHAGUS, or URETER. It may result from INFLAMMATION, a SPASM, growth of a TUMOUR or pressure from surrounding ORGANS. In many cases it is caused by ulceration and contraction of the subsequent SCAR tissue. With a urethral stricture, it becomes increasingly difficult to pass URINE.

stridor the noise created on breathing in when there is a narrowing of the upper RESPIRATORY TRACT, especially the LARYNX.

stroke *or* **cerebrovascular accident (CVA)** *or* **apoplexy** the physical effects, involving some form of PARALYSIS, that result from an interruption to the BRAIN'S BLOOD supply. The effect in the brain is secondary, and the cause lies in the HEART or BLOOD VESSELS and may be a THROMBOSIS, EMBOLUS or HAEMORRHAGE. The severity of a stroke varies greatly, from a temporary weakness in a limb, or tingling, to paralysis, COMA and death. The extent of recovery also varies considerably.

stuttering *see* STAMMERING.

stye a bacterial INFECTION and INFLAMMATION of a GLAND at the base of an eyelash, resulting in a pus-filled CYST.

subarachnoid anaesthesia
see SPINAL ANAESTHESIA.

subarachnoid haemorrhage bleeding into the SUBARACHNOID SPACE, often because of a ruptured cerebral ANEURYSM. Initial symptoms are a severe headache, stiff neck, followed by VOMITING and drowsiness, and there may be a brief period of unconsciousness after the event. BRAIN damage is possible and severe haemorrhages may result in death.

subarachnoid space the space between the arachnoid and pia mater MENINGES covering the BRAIN and SPINAL CORD. It contains CEREBROSPINAL FLUID and BLOOD VESSELS.

subcutaneous a general term meaning 'beneath the SKIN'.

subdural a term meaning 'below the dura mater' and referring to the space between this and the arachnoid MENINGES around the BRAIN.

sublingual gland *see* SALIVARY GLAND.

submandibular gland *see* SALIVARY GLAND.

subnutrition *see* MALNUTRITION.

subphrenic abscess an ABSCESS occurring beneath the DIAPHRAGM and commonly on the right side. It may be caused by INFECTION after an operation or PERFORATION of an ORGAN, e.g. a PEPTIC ULCER. Surgery is usually necessary although ANTIBIOTICS may be effective.

succus entericus *see* DIGESTION.

sudden infant death syndrome *or* **cot death** the sudden death of a baby, often occurring overnight, from unknown causes. A significant proportion of infant deaths occur in this way. Although the cause is unknown, numerous suggestions have been put forward, including viral INFECTION, allergic reaction, poor breathing and overheating. It is now accepted that babies born to mothers who smoke are more at risk. A campaign to encourage the practice of positioning young babies on their backs to sleep has proved successful in reducing the number of incidences. Research continues.

sulcus (*pl* **sulci**) *see* FRONTAL LOBE; TEMPORAL LOBE.

sulphonamide one of a group of drugs containing the chemical group -SO$_2$NH$_2$. These drugs do not kill BACTERIA but prevent bacterial growth and are thus very useful in controlling INFECTIONS. Some SIDE EFFECTS may occur but in general these are outweighed by the benefits.

sunburn damage to the SKIN caused by exposure to the ultraviolet rays in sunlight. This may vary from a reddening of the skin and itching to the formation of BLISTERS that can cause shock if a large area is affected. Fair-skinned people are more susceptible than others, and it is advisable to adapt to the sun in gradual stages.

sunstroke *see* HEATSTROKE.

supine the term used to describe the position in which someone is lying on his or her back, face upwards.

suppository medication prepared in a form that enables it to be inserted into the RECTUM (or VAGINA). It may be a lubricant, contain drugs for treatment in the area of the rectum or ANUS or for absorption. The suppository has to be inserted beyond the SPHINCTER muscle to ensure retention.

suppuration PUS formation, whether on the surface (ulceration) or more deep-seated (as with an ABSCESS).

suprarenal gland *see* ADRENAL GLAND.

surfactant *see* RESPIRATORY DISTRESS SYNDROME.

surgeon a qualified practitioner specializing in SURGERY.

surgery the branch of medicine in which operations on the body are performed to treat disease and injuries or deformities.

susceptibility the condition in which there is a lack of RESISTANCE to disease because of either poor general health or a deficiency in the defence mechanism because of another condition, e.g. AIDS. Susceptibility can be decreased by VACCINATION, etc.

suture 1. in surgery, the means whereby a WOUND or INCISION is closed, using threads of silk or catgut. There are several types of suture to deal with different situations. **2.** a type of JOINT across which there is no movement, e.g. in the SKULL, where there are several sutures.

swab a general term applied to a pad of material used in various ways. It can be used to clean wounds, apply medication, remove BLOOD during operations and to obtain samples from infected areas, e.g. the THROAT, for further examination.

sweat *see* PERSPIRATION.

sweat glands the GLANDS in the EPIDERMIS of SKIN that project into the dermis and are under the control of the SYMPATHETIC NERVOUS SYSTEM. The glands occur over most of the body but are especially abundant on the forehead, palms of the hands and soles of the feet and under the arms. *See also* PERSPIRATION.

Sydenham's chorea *see* CHOREA.

sympathetic the term used to describe a symptom or disease that occurs as a result of disease elsewhere in the body, e.g. injury of one EYE and a related INFLAMMATION in the other, both being connected by the LYMPHATIC SYSTEM.

sympathetic nervous system with the PARASYMPATHETIC NERVOUS SYSTEM (and acting in opposition to it), this makes up the AUTONOMIC NERVOUS SYSTEM. NORADRENALINE and ADRENALINE are the main NEUROTRANSMITTERS released by its nerve endings. Its functions include raising the heartbeat rate, constricting BLOOD VESSELS and inhibiting secretion of SALIVA.

symptom any evidence of a disease or disorder.

synalgia *see* REFERRED PAIN.

synapse the junction between two NERVE cells at which there is a minute gap. A NERVE IMPULSE bridges the gap via a NEUROTRANSMITTER (*see also* ACETYLCHOLINE). The chemical diffuses across the gap that connects the AXON of one nerve CELL to the DENDRITES of the next. Some BRAIN cells have many thousand synapses.

syncope *or* **fainting** a temporary loss of consciousness because of a fall in BLOOD PRESSURE and a reduced supply of blood to the BRAIN. It may occur after standing for a long time (particularly in hot weather) or after shock or injury. Typical signs that occur before an attack are sweating and a feeling of light-headedness.

syndactyly a fusion of fingers or toes, which is a CONGENITAL effect. It may affect two or more fingers through webbing or result in complete fusion of all digits.

syndrome a number of SYMP-
TOMS and signs that in combination together constitute a
particular condition.

synovia *see* SYNOVIAL MEM-
BRANE.

synovial membrane *or*
synovium the inner MEM-
BRANE of a capsule that encloses a JOINT that moves
freely. It secretes into the joint
a thick lubricating fluid (synovia), which may build up after
injury to cause pain.

synovitis INFLAMMATION of
the SYNOVIAL MEMBRANE that
lines a JOINT capsule. The result is swelling with pain. It is
associated with RHEUMATIC
DISEASE, injury or INFECTION
(e.g. chronic TUBERCULOSIS).
The treatment depends on the
cause of the condition, and often a sample of the synovia is
taken for examination.

synovium *see* SYNOVIAL MEM-
BRANE.

syphilis an infectious, sexually
transmitted disease (*see* VE-
NEREAL DISEASE) caused by
the bacterium *Treponema pal-
lidum*, which shows symptoms
in three stages. BACTERIA enter the body through MUCOUS
MEMBRANES during sexual intercourse and an ULCER appears in the first instance.

Within a short time the LYMPH
NODES locally and then all
over the body enlarge and
harden and this lasts several
weeks. Secondary symptoms
appear about two months after
INFECTION and include FEVER,
pains, enlarged lymph nodes
and a faint RASH, which is usually noticed on the chest. The
bacterium is found in enormous numbers in the primary
sores and any skin lesions of
the secondary stage. The final
stage may not appear until
many months or years after
infection and comprises the
formation of numerous TU-
MOUR-like masses throughout
the body (in SKIN, MUSCLE,
BONE, BRAIN, SPINAL CORD
and other ORGANS such as the
LIVER, STOMACH, etc). This
stage can cause serious damage to the heart, brain or spinal cord, resulting in blindness,
TABES DORSALIS and mental
disability. CONGENITAL syphilis is much rarer than the former, ACQUIRED, type. It is
contracted by a developing
FOETUS from the mother and
symptoms show a few weeks
after birth. Treatment of syphilis is with PENICILLIN early in
the development of the disease.

syringe an instrument used for injecting fluids into the body or for the removal of body fluids for examination. In such cases, it comprises a hollow needle connected to a piston within a tube. Larger metal syringes are used to wash the outer EAR and remove wax.

syrup a mixture of sugar, water and drug, used for the easy administration of medications that may taste unpleasant. It also provides a means of delivering drugs that would otherwise deteriorate when exposed to air.

systemic a general term used to refer to the body as a whole.

systemic lupus erythematosus a chronic inflammatory disease of CONNECTIVE TISSUES, believed to be an AUTOIMMUNE DISEASE. Symptoms of the condition vary but generally include malaise, JOINT pain, red raised patches of SKIN and the involvement of internal ORGANS as the disease progresses (including PULMONARY HYPERTENSION and haemolytic OEDEMA). Treatment is aimed at symptomatic relief as the disease itself cannot be cured. ANTI-INFLAMMATORY drugs and immunosuppressives (*see* IMMUNOSUPRESSION) are used in conjunction with ANTIBIOTICS to treat any INFECTIONS that may arise. *See also* LUPUS.

systole the contraction of the HEART that alternates with the resting phase (DIASTOLE). It usually refers to ventricular systole (*see* VENTRICLE), which, at 0.3 seconds, is three times longer than atrial systole (*see* ATRIUM).

systolic pressure *see* BLOOD PRESSURE.

T

TAB (typhoid-paratyphoid A and B) a VACCINE obtained from SALMONELLA bacteria and used in the treatment of TYPHOID and the A and B strains of PARATYPHOID. If administered before a person is at risk, it can provide IMMUNITY for a year.

tabes dorsalis *or* **locomotor ataxia** a complication of SYPHILIS, occuring five to 20 years after the initial infection. It affects the SENSORY nerves, especially of the trunk and legs, causing stabbing pains and unsteadiness in walking. There is often loss of BLADDER control and disturbance of vision if the the optic NERVES are involved. Treatment is by means of PENICILLIN, and the condition may be associated with taboparesis, which is also called general paralysis of the insane.

taboparesis *see* TABES DORSALIS.

tachycardia increased rate of heartbeat, which may be caused naturally, as with exercise, or be symptomatic of disease.

talus (*pl* **tali**) the ankle bone, which articulates with the lower leg bones (TIBIA and FIBULA) above and also with the heel bone (calcaneus) below (*see* TARSUS).

tamoxifen a drug used in the treatment of certain CANCERS of the BREAST.

tampon a plug of compressed gauze inserted into a wound or cavity to absorb BLOOD.

target cell an abnormal form of ERYTHROCYTE (red blood cell), which is large and has a ringed appearance when stained and viewed microscopically, resembling a target. These cells are present in several kinds of ANAEMIA, including those caused by iron deficiency. They are also found when there is LIVER disease, a small SPLEEN, HAEMOGLOBIN abnormalities (haemoglobinopathies) and THALASSAEMIA.

tarsus (*pl* **tarsi**) a part of the foot in the region of the instep, consisting of seven BONES, chiefly the TALUS and the calcaneus (heel bone) and also the cuboid, navicular (boat-shaped) and three cuneiform (wedge-shaped) bones.

taste the perception of flavour brought about by CHEMORECEPTORS (the TASTE BUDS) situated on the TONGUE.

taste buds the SENSORY receptors responsible for the perception of TASTE, located in the grooves around the PAPILLAE of the TONGUE, in the EPIGLOTTIS, parts of the PHARYNX and the soft PALATE. The taste buds are stimulated by the presence of dissolved food in the SALIVA, and messages are sent via NERVES to the BRAIN where the information is interpreted and perceived.

taxis the returning to their normal position of displaced ORGANS, parts of organs or BONES by manipulation (*see* HERNIA).

T-cell *see* LYMPHOCYTE.

teeth *see* TOOTH.

telophase *see* MEIOSIS.

temperature (of the body) the normal body temperature is around 37°C (98.4°F), but it varies considerably both between individuals and in one person throughout the day. In addition, temperature differences occur between various areas of the body, being lower in the SKIN than internally.

temple the side of the head above the level of the eye and the ear.

temporal the term used to describe the TEMPLE, e.g. temporal ARTERY.

temporal lobe one of the main areas of the CEREBRAL CORTEX in each of the CEREBRAL HEMISPHERES of the BRAIN, occurring in the TEMPORAL region of the SKULL. A cleft known as the lateral sulcus separates it from the FRONTAL LOBE.

temporal lobe seizure a common type of simple partial epileptic seizure (*see* EPILEPSY). A seizure which originates in the temporal lobe can be characterized by a number of symptoms, including feelings of intense emotion, feelings of déjà vu and sensory disturbances, e.g. strange smells or tastes. A person experiencing a seizure of this nature will remain conscious.

tendinitis inflammation of a TENDON, which often results from excessive or unaccustomed exercise but may also result from INFECTION. Treatment involves rest, possibly splinting of an affected JOINT and CORTICOSTEROID injections and the taking of ANALGESIC drugs.

tendon a tough and inelastic white cord, composed of bundles of COLLAGEN fibres, that attaches a MUSCLE to a BONE. A tendon concentrates the pull of the muscle onto one point on the bone, and the length and thickness vary considerably. The fibres of a tendon pass into, and become continuous with, those of the bone it serves. Many tendons are enclosed in tendon sheaths lined with SYNOVIAL MEMBRANE containing synovia, which reduces friction and enables easy movement to occur.

tennis elbow a form of TENDINITIS affecting the TENDON at the outer part of the elbow, which becomes inflamed and painful. It is caused by hard and excessive use of the arm, and treatment involves rest and CORTICOSTEROID injections.

TENS transcutaneous electrical nerve stimulation. A method of pain relief whereby an intermittent current produced by a small machine is delivered through the SKIN via electrodes, to stimulate surface NERVES and block the transmission of pain signals to the brain. TENS is non-invasive and can be used by patients without medical supervision. It is widely used to relieve the pains of LABOUR and in physiotherapy.

teratogen a substance or disease or any other factor that causes the production of abnormalities in a FOETUS. The drugs in this category include THALIDOMIDE and alcohol. GERMAN MEASLES is among the INFECTIONS.

teratogenesis the processes that result in the development of physical abnormalities in a FOETUS.

teratoma a TUMOUR that is composed of unusual TISSUES not normally found at that site and derived from partially developed embryological CELLS. Teratomas are most common in the OVARY and TESTICLE (particularly if the latter is undescended).

testicle or **testis** (*pl* **testes**) one of the pair of male sex ORGANS that are situated within the SCROTUM and produce SPERM and secrete the hormone TESTOSTERONE. The testicles develop within the ABDOMEN of the FOETUS but descend around the time of birth into the SCROTUM. Each testicle has an outer double MEMBRANE layer, known as the tunica vaginalis. The tunica vaginalis contains an inner fibrous layer, called the tunica albuginea, which protects the testicle. The bulk of the testicle consists of numerous fine, convoluted tubules called seminiferous tubules, which are lined with CELLS that produce the sperm. In addition, other cells, known as sertoli cells, occur, which provide support and possibly nourishment for the developing sperm. The tubules are supported by CONNECTIVE TISSUE containing NERVES and BLOOD VESSELS and also the cells of Leydig, which are responsible for HORMONE production. The tubules connect with another highly folded tube, called the epididymis, which is about 7m long and connects with the VAS DEFERENS, which leads to the URETHRA. The spermatozoa are passed by passive movement along the epididymis, completing their development as they go, and are stored in the lower part until EJACULATION.

testis (*pl* **testes**) *see* TESTICLE.

testosterone the male SEX HORMONE secreted by the testes (*see* TESTICLE). *See also* ANDROGEN.

test-tube baby *see* IN VITRO FERTILIZATION.

tetanus *or* **lockjaw** a very serious and sometimes fatal infectious disease that is caused by the bacterium *Clostridium tetani*, spores of which enter through a WOUND. Rapid multiplication of the BACTERIA produces a TOXIN that affects the NERVES, resulting in rigidity and SPASM of MUSCLES (hence its nonmedical alternative name). Often there is high FEVER and the spasms cause extreme agony. If respiratory MUSCLES are involved, death may occur by ASPHYXIA. Effective ANTITOXIN is available, although its effects are not permanent and it needs to be regularly maintained. ANTIBIOTICS such as PENICILLIN are also effective against the bacteria.

tetany *see* PARATHYROID GLAND.

tetracyline an ANTIBIOTIC that is obtained both naturally and synethically and is used to treat rickettsial, viral and bacterial INFECTIONS (e.g. RELAPSING FEVER).

thalamus (*pl* **thalami**) one of a pair of masses of GREY MATTER located within each side of the FOREBRAIN. Each is a centre for coordinating and relaying the SENSORY information concerned with all the senses, apart from that of smell.

thalassaemia *or* **Cooley's anaemia** an inherited form of ANAEMIA in which there is an abnormality in the HAEMOGLOBIN. There is a continuation in the production of foetal haemoglobin, and two forms of the disorder are recognized: thalassaemia major, in which the disorder is inherited from both parents (homozygous), and thalassaemia minor. The minor form is usually symptomless, but the major type causes, in addition to the severe anaemia, BONE MARROW abnormalities and enlargement of the SPLEEN. Treatment is by means of repeated BLOOD TRANSFUSIONS. The disease is wide-spread throughout the Mediterranean, Asia and Africa.

thalidomide a TERATOGENIC drug that was formerly prescribed for treatment of MORNING SICKNESS in PREGNANCY. It was withdrawn when it was discovered that it caused developmental damage to the FOETUS, particularly malformation of limbs.

therapeutics the area of medicine concerned with the various methods of healing and treatment.

therapy the treatment of physical or mental illness.

thermography a method of recording the heat produced by different areas of the body, using photographic film sensitive to infrared radiation. Areas with good blood CIRCULATION produce more heat, and this can occur abnormally if a TUMOUR is present. The record thus obtained is a thermogram, and this is one of the techniques used to detect BREAST tumours (mammothermography).

thiabendazole see TOXOCARIASIS.

thiamine see VITAMIN B.

Thiersch's graft a type of skin GRAFT in which thin strips of SKIN, involving the EPIDERMIS and the upper layer of the dermis, are taken from one part of the body and placed on the WOUND that is required to be healed.

thigh the part of the leg above the knee.

thoracentesis see THORACOCENTESIS.

thoracic pertaining to the CHEST, e.g. the thoracic duct (see LYMPH).

thoracocentesis or **thoracentesis** or **pleurocentesis** the withdrawal, by means of a hollow needle inserted through the CHEST wall, of fluid from the PLEURAL CAVITY.

thorax the CHEST, the cavity of the body formed by the SPINAL COLUMN, RIBS and STERNUM and containing the LUNGS, HEART, etc.

threonine see ESSENTIAL AMINO ACID.

throat the part of the digestive and respiratory tracts in the anterior part of the neck, which contains the OESOPHAGUS, TRACHEA and PHARYNX and also the LARYNX.

thrombin an ENZYME derived from prothrombin, its inactive precursor, which is formed and is active during the final stages of blood clotting (*see* COAGULATION).

thrombocyte *see* PLATELET.

thromboembolism the situation in which a blood CLOT (THROMBUS) forms in one part of the CIRCULATION, usually a deep VEIN in the leg (PHLEBO-THROMBOSIS), and a portion breaks off and becomes lodged elsewhere, causing a total blockage (EMBOLISM). The embolism often involves the pulmonary ARTERY or one of its branches, and this is known as PULMONARY EMBOLISM.

thrombolysis the dissolving of BLOOD CLOTS by ENZYME activity. Natural enzymes produced within the body have this effect but drug treatment, especially involving STREPTOKINASE, may be used to break up clots following PULMONARY EMBOLISM, COR-ONARY THROMBOSIS and PHLEBOTHROMBOSIS.

thrombophlebitis INFLAM-MATION of the wall of a VEIN along with CLOT formation in the affected section of the vessel. This is a complication of PREGNANCY and may be dangerous, involving a deep vein THROMBOSIS that can re-sult in PULMONARY EMBOLISM. The condition known as white leg (plegmasia alba dolens) is thrombophlebitis, especially of the FEMORAL vein, which can occur after childbirth.

thrombosis (*pl* **thromboses**) the process of CLOTting within a BLOOD VESSEL, producing a THROMBUS. It may occur within an ARTERY or VEIN, often one that is diseased or damaged, and can be very serious or even fatal, e.g. STROKE, CORONARY THROMBOSIS.

thrombus (*pl* **thrombi**) a BLOOD CLOT within a vessel that partially or totally obstructs the CIRCULATION.

thrush an INFECTION caused by the FUNGUS *Candida albicans*, which affects the MUCOUS MEMBRANES of the MOUTH and VAGINA, producing white patches. It is a popular name given to a group of infections known as candidiasis.

thumb the short, thick digit of the HAND. *See* PHALANGES.

thymine *see* NUCLEOTIDE.

thymus gland a GLAND, divided into two lobes, that is present in the neck and forms a vital part of the body's response to INFECTION. It is especially large in children and important in the development of the IMMUNE response and the production of lymphoid TISSUE. After PUBERTY, it gradually begins to shrink. BONE MARROW CELLS, known as stem cells, undergo maturation within the thymus, and one group, the T-LYMPHOCYTES, are dependent on the gland. These are very important cells in the body that produce ANTIBODIES.

thyroidectomy surgical removal of the THYROID GLAND.

thyroid gland a bilobed ENDOCRINE GLAND situated at the base and front of the neck. It is enclosed by FIBROUS TISSUE and well supplied with BLOOD, and internally consists of numerous VESICLES containing a jelly-like colloidal substance. These vesicles produce thyroid HORMONE, which is rich in iodine, under the control of thyroid-stimulating hormone (THYROTROPHIN STIMULATING HORMONE) released from the PITUITARY GLAND. Two hormones are produced by the gland, THYROXINE and triiodothyronine, which are essential for the regulation of METABOLISM and growth. See

also CRETINISM, MYXOEDEMA and HYPERTHYROIDISM.

thyrotoxic adenoma a form of thyrotoxicosis or GRAVES' DISEASE.

thyrotoxicosis *see* GRAVES' DISEASE.

thyrotrophin-releasing hormone a HORMONE produced and released from the HYPOTHALAMUS that acts on the anterior lobe of the PITUITARY GLAND, which then releases THYROTROPHIN-STIMULATING HORMONE (*see also* THYROID GLAND).

thyrotrophin-stimulating hormone a HORMONE produced and released by the anterior PITUITARY GLAND, which stimulates the THYROID GLAND to produce its hormones (*see also* THYROID GLAND).

thyroxine an important HORMONE produced by the THYROID GLAND and used medically to treat conditions resulting from underactivity of this gland, e.g. CRETINISM and MYXOEDEMA (HYPOTHYROIDISM).

tibia (*pl* **tibiae**) *or* **shin bone** the larger of the two BONES in the lower leg, articulating above with the FEMUR and with the TALUS of the ankle below.

tic douloureux see TRIGEMI-
NAL NEURALGIA.

tidal volume see LUNGS.

tinea see RINGWORM.

tinnitus any ringing or buzzing
sound in the EAR that does not
have a real external cause.
Many disorders of the ear can
cause this, e.g. hardened wax
or MÉNIÈRE'S DISEASE, and
also drugs, including ASPIRIN
and QUININE, and there can
be damage to the auditory
NERVE. In many cases no underlying cause is found.

tissue one of the primary layers
composing any of the parts of
the body, consisting of a large
number of CELLS with a similar structure and function, e.g.
CONNECTIVE TISSUE.

T-lymphocyte see LYMPHO-
CYTE; THYMUS.

toe one of the five small digits
at the extremity of the FOOT.
See PHALANGES.

tocopherol see VITAMIN E.

tolerance the adaptation of the
body to a particular DRUG or
substance so that over a period
of time there is a reduction in
the response to a particular
dose. Usually a larger dose
must then be given to produce
the same effect as before.

tomography a particular technique using X-RAYS or ULTRA-
SOUND so that structures at a
given depth are brought into
sharp focus while those at
other levels are deliberately
blurred. In this way, pictures of
slices of the body are obtained
at different levels to build up a
three-dimensional image. The
image obtained is called a to-
mogram. See CAT SCAN.

tongue the muscular and highly
mobile ORGAN attached to the
floor of the MOUTH, the three
main functions of which are
manipulation of food during
chewing prior to swallowing,
taste and production of speech.
The three areas of the tongue
are the tip, body and root, and
it is covered with a MUCOUS
MEMBRANE that unites with
that of the mouth and PHAR-
YNX. The tongue is anchored
at the root by various muscles
that attach it to the back of the
mouth. In addition, the under-
surface of the tongue is attached in the midline to the
floor of the mouth by a fold of
mucous membrane, called the
frenulum lingae. The tongue
has a furred appearance because its surface is covered
with minute projections called
PAPILLAe, of which there are
three different kinds: filiform,
fungiform and circumvallate.

There are grooves surrounding the papillae in which the TASTE BUDS occur. The tongue is well supplied with BLOOD and receives branches from five different NERVES on each side.

tonic-clonic seizure formerly known as a grand mal SEIZURE, a generalized, convulsive epileptic seizure (*see* EPILEPSY) that occurs in two phases. In the tonic phase, all the MUSCLES of the body contract. The person goes rigid and falls to the ground, unconscious. Breathing stops for a short period and the person's lips and skin may turn blue. The clonic phase then begins. The limbs and body jerk as muscles contract and relax alternately. After a period of one or two minutes, the person's body relaxes, but they remain unconscious for a short period. On regaining consciousness, the person is unlikely to have any memory of the event. Possible after-effects include a brief period of confusion and head and muscle aches. Tonic-clonic seizures generally last for only a few minutes. If the seizure lasts for more than five minutes, medical help should be sought. *See* STATUS EPILEPTICUS.

tonsillectomy surgical removal of the TONSILS.

tonsillitis INFLAMMATION of the TONSILS caused by bacterial or viral INFECTION. The symptoms include a severe sore throat, causing painful swallowing, accompanied by FEVER and earache, especially in children. The tonsils are swollen and white in appearance because of infected material exuded from them, and GLANDS in the neck are enlarged. Treatment is by means of ANTIBIOTICS, especially PENICILLIN and ERYTHROMYCIN, along with ANALGESICS for pain relief.

tonsils usually the two small masses of LYMPHOID TISSUE situated on either side at the back of the mouth (the palatine tonsils). However, another pair occur below the TONGUE, which are the lingual tonsils, while the ADENOIDS are the pharyngeal tonsils. All are part of the body's protective mechanism against INFECTION.

tooth (*pl* **teeth**) a hard structure used for biting and chewing. Each tooth consists of a root embedded in a socket within the jawbone to which it is attached by the fibrous periodontal membrane. The projecting part of the tooth, called the crown, is covered with a hard resistant layer of enamel (composed primarily of calcium phosphate and calcium carbonate). The root is covered with a thin hard layer of CEMENTUM. Most of the interior of the tooth consists of DENTINE, a hard ivory-like substance that surrounds the inner core or pulp. The pulp contains blood vessels and nerve fibres and is connected with the dentine by means of fine cellular processes. There are four different types of teeth: canine, INCISOR, premolar and MOLAR.

tophi (*sing* **tophus**) see GOUT.

torpor a state of physical and mental sluggishness that accompanies various mental disorders and some kinds of poisoning and may also be present in elderly people with arterial disease.

torsion a twisting, particularly an abnormal state of the whole or part of an organ that impairs the NERVE and BLOOD supply. Examples are a torsion of a loop of bowel or of the spermatic cord of the TESTICLE. Surgery is usually required to correct a torsion.

torticollis see WRYNECK.

total hysterectomy see HYSTERECTOMY.

touch the sense that is conferred by specialized SENSORY receptors present in the SKIN (and also in MUSCLES and other areas of the body), which enable sensations of pain, temperature, pressure and touch to be perceived. The SENSE ORGANS involved are specially adapted to respond to particular sensations conveying their messages to the brain along different NERVE pathways.

tourniquet a device used to arrest bleeding, usually from an ARTERY in a limb, which may be a length of bandage, rubber tube or cord tied tightly around the limb, generally as an emergency measure. Direct pressure on a WOUND is now considered to be preferable as a first aid measure, because a tourniquet can deprive all the TISSUES of oxygen by arresting the CIRCULATION and there is a risk of damage and of GANGRENE.

toxaemia blood poisoning resulting from the TOXINS produced by rapidly multiplying BACTERIA at a localized site of INFECTION, such as an ABSCESS. Symptoms are varied, including FEVER, VOMITING and DIARRHOEA and a general feeling of being unwell. The source of the infection has to be treated with ANTIBIOTIC drugs. Toxaemia of PREGNANCY involves two relatively rare conditions known as ECLAMPSIA and PRE-ECLAMPSIA.

toxicology the scientific study of poisons and their effects.

toxic shock syndrome a state of acute SHOCK as a result of SEPTICAEMIA and caused by TOXINS produced by staphylococcal BACTERIA (*see* STAPHYLOCOCCUS). The symptoms include high FEVER, skin RASH and DIARRHOEA and can prove rapidly fatal if not adequately treated with ANTIBIOTICS, especially PENICILLIN and CEPHALOSPORIN, along with fluid and salt replacement. The syndrome is associated with the use of TAMPONS by women during MENSTRUATION, particularly if a tampon is left in place too long, but can also occur in other people and is in all cases rare.

toxin a poison produced by BACTERIA and by many species of plant and also present in snake VENOM. In the body, a toxin acts as an ANTIGEN and provokes the production of special ANTIBODIES, called antitoxins. The antitoxins produced may be used in IMMUNIZATION to protect against the disease, as with TETANUS and DIPHTHERIA. An endotoxin is contained within the bacterial CELL and released only when the organism dies and decays. Endotoxins do not provoke antitoxin production (*see* TOXOID).

toxocariasis a disease caused by the larvae of roundworms, which normally infect the domestic dog (*Toxicara canis*) and cat (*Toxicara cati*) but can be passed to humans if they swallow material contaminated with eggs in infected faeces. Those most at risk are children, especially at a young age when hands may become infected while playing. Once swallowed, the larvae, which hatch from the eggs, travel around the body in the circulation and can cause considerable damage to, for example, the LUNGS and LIVER. Also, the larvae may lodge in the RETINA of the EYE, causing INFLAMMATION and the production of abnormal granulated TISSUE called granuloma. Symptoms of the INFECTION include muscular pain, FEVER, skin RASH, respiratory problems, VOMITING and CONVULSIONS. Treatment is with drugs, such as diethylcarbamazine and thiabendazole.

toxoid a preparation of TOXIN that has been treated with chemicals so that it cannot cause disease but is able to provoke the production of antitoxin. This is the basis of VACCINES against DIPHTHERIA and TETANUS.

toxoplasmosis an infectious disease caused by a protozoan organism known as *Toxoplasma*. The INFECTION is either transmitted by eating undercooked meat or through direct contact with contaminated soil or, especially, with infected cats. This form of the infection is mild and causes few ill effects. However, a much more serious form of the disease can be passed from a mother infected during PREGNANCY to her unborn baby. The newborn infant may suffer from HYDROCEPHALUS, mental RETARDATION, blindness or may even be stillborn. Treatment is by means of SULPHONAMIDE drugs and pyrimethamine.

tracer a substance that is marked so that when it is introduced into the body its progress can be followed, e.g. radioactive tracers used in the detection of brain TUMOURS and thyroid disease.

trachea the windpipe, the part of the air passage that is situated between the LARYNX and the BRONCHI.

tracheitis INFLAMMATION of the TRACHEA, often accompanying a viral INFECTION of the upper respiratory tract. The symptoms include a persistent painful COUGH and sore chest, and it often accompanies BRONCHITIS and also DIPHTHERIA.

tracheostomy *or* **tracheotomy** a surgical procedure in which a hole is made in the TRACHEA to allow direct access of air to the lower respiratory passages. This may be performed in an emergency if there is an obstruction in breathing. However, usually this operation is carried out in hospital, especially on patients in intensive therapy who require long-term artificial VENTILATION. This is to avoid the damage to the trachea that is caused by the long-term use of an ENDOTRACHEAL TUBE (inserted through the nose or mouth) which would normally be used first. Once the opening has been made, a double tube is inserted and held in place by tapes around the neck. The inner tube can be freely withdrawn and replaced and needs to be kept scrupulously clean and free from any obstruction.

traction the use of weights and pulleys to apply a pulling force on a broken BONE to ensure that it is kept correctly aligned while healing takes place.

trance a sleep-like state in which a person ceases to react normally to the environment and loses the power of voluntary movement but remains aware. It can be induced by HYPNOSIS, meditation, HYSTERIA, CATATONIA and drug abuse.

tranquillizer a drug that has a soothing and calming effect, relieving stress and anxiety. Minor tranquillizers such as diazepam and chlordiazepoxide (LIBRIUM) are widely used to relieve these symptoms, which may arise from a variety of causes. There is a danger of dependence with long-term use. Major tranquillizers, e.g. CHLORPROMAZINE and HALOPERIDOL, are used

to treat severe mental illnesses such as SCHIZOPHRENIA.

transcutaneous electrical nerve stimulation *see* TENS.

transdermal drug *see* DOSAGE.

transfusion *see* BLOOD TRANSFUSION.

transplantation the transfer of an ORGAN or TISSUE from one person to another (allotransplant) or within the body of an individual (autotransplant), i.e. SKIN and BONE grafting. The person from whom the organ is obtained is known as the DONOR and the one who receives it is known as the recipient. Organ transplants involving the KIDNEY, HEART, BONE MARROW, CORNEA, LUNGS and LIVER have all become more common. Success varies but is improving in all areas, especially with the advent of immunosuppressive drugs to prevent organ rejection by the recipient's immune system. *See also* IMMUNOSUPPRESSION and GRAFT.

trauma 1. an event that causes physical damage, such as a FRACTURE. **2.** an emotional shock brought about by a harmful and upsetting circumstance.

travel sickness *see* MOTION SICKNESS.

tremor an involuntary movement that may involve the whole of a MUSCLE or only part of it and produce fine trembling or more pronounced shaking. Tremors are classified according to the type of movement produced and are a symptom of many diseases, including CHOREA, MULTIPLE SCLEROSIS and PARKINSONISM.

trench fever an infectious disease caused by *Rickettsia quintana*, which was epidemic among troops in the First World War and still occurs in Mexico. It is transmitted to humans by the body louse and causes FEVER, rash, leg aches and general weakness.

triceps a three-headed MUSCLE, present in the upper arm, that extends the forearm.

trichomoniasis either of two types of INFECTION caused by a protozoan organism that either attacks the digestive system, causing DYSENTERY (*Trichomonas hominis*), or causes vaginal INFLAMMATION and discharge (*Trichomonas vaginalis*). In the latter case the infection can be transmitted to a male sexual partner. The ANTIBIOTIC drug metronidazole is highly effective.

trichorrhoea the medical name for the falling out of HAIR, which may be caused by disease, such as TYPHOID FEVER or SCARLET FEVER, or has no apparent cause.

tricuspid valve a VALVE that has three flaps or cusps and controls the passage of BLOOD from the right ATRIUM to the right VENTRICLE of the HEART and normally prevents back flow.

trigeminal nerve the fifth and largest of the CRANIAL NERVES, which has three divisions: the mandibular, maxillary and ophthalmic nerves. The ophthalmic and maxillary are SENSORY nerves and the mandibular has both sensory and MOTOR functions. Hence the trigeminal nerve is involved in the relaying and perception of sensations (temperature, touch, pain, etc) from the whole of the FACE and MOUTH and also in controlling the MUSCLES involved in chewing.

trigeminal neuralgia *or* **tic douloureux** a severe form of NEURALGIA that can affect all the divisions of the TRIGEMINAL NERVE. It affects women more commonly than men, especially those over the age of 50. It causes severe pain of a burning or cutting nature, which can be constant or spasmodic and may be provoked by simple actions such as eating or by heat or cold. The SKIN of the face may be inflamed and the eye red and watery and the neuralgia is usually confined to one side. The condition is debilitating in that the pain is intense and interferes with sleeping and eating, but the ANTICONVULSANT drug carbamazepine is proving to be highly beneficial.

triglycerides fats consisting of three FATTY ACID molecules combined with GLYCEROL, which are the form in which the body stores fat. Triglycerides are derived from the DIGESTION of fats in food.

trihexyphenidyl a drug prescribed in the treatment of PARKINSON'S DISEASE.

triiodothyronine *see* THYROID GLAND.

trophic a term used to describe nutrition. For example, trophic FRACTURE occurs when the BONE is weakened as a result of poor nourishment in the person concerned.

truss a device that consists of a pad attached to a belt with spring straps to maintain its position, worn under clothing to support a HERNIA.

trypanosomiasis *see* SLEEPING SICKNESS.

trypsin an important ENZYME involved in the DIGESTION of PROTEINS. Its inactive precursor, trypsinogen, is secreted by the PANCREAS and converted to trypsin in the DUODENUM by the action of another enzyme, called enteropeptidase.

tryptophan *see* ESSENTIAL AMINO ACID; PELLAGRA.

tubercle 1. a small rounded knob on a BONE, e.g. on the RIBS. **2.** a minute nodular TISSUE mass (LESION) that is characteristic of TUBERCULOSIS.

tuberculin *see* MANTOUX TEST.

tuberculosis a group of INFECTIONS caused by the BACILLUS *Mycobacterium tuberculosis*, of which PULMONARY tuberculosis of the LUNGS (consumption or phthisis) is the best-known form. The pulmonary disease is acquired by inhalation of air containing the organism from an infected person or dust laden with BACTERIA. People infected in this way can show no symptoms but still be carriers. In the lungs, the infection causes formation of a primary TUBERCLE, which spreads to LYMPH NODES to form the primary complex. The disease may wax and wane for years as the body's natural IMMUNE system acts against the infection. If the infection is severe, symptoms include FEVER, wasting, night sweats and the coughing up of BLOOD. The bacteria may enter the bloodstream and spread throughout the body, setting up numerous tubercles in other TISSUES (MILIARY tuberculosis). The organism may also be acquired by eating contaminated food, especially milk, in which case the production of a primary complex in abdominal lymph nodes can lead to PERITONITIS. Tuberculosis affects people throughout the world (about 6,000 new cases each year in England and Wales). Many people acquire the infection and recover without suspecting its presence, and the disease is curable with ANTIBIOTICS, e.g. STREPTOMYCIN. In addition, BCG VACCINATION as a preventative measure is given to children in the UK, in addition to X-RAY screening to detect carriers.

tubule a small tube-like structure in the body, as in the KIDNEY, testis (*see* TESTICLE), etc.

tumour an abnormal swelling in any part of the body, which consists of an unusual growth of TISSUE and may be MALIGNANT or BENIGN. Tumours tend to be classified according to the tissue of which they are composed, e.g. FIBROMA (mainly FIBROUS TISSUE) and MYOMA (largely MUSCLE fibres).

tunica (*pl* **tunicae**) *see* TESTICLE.

turgor a state of being distended, engorged or swollen.

Turner's syndrome a genetic disorder affecting females in which there is only one X-CHROMOSOME instead of the usual two. Those affected therefore have 45 instead of 46 CHROMOSOMES, are infertile (as the ovaries are absent), MENSTRUATION is absent and BREASTS and body hair do not develop. Those affected are short in stature, may have webbing of the neck and other developmental defects. The HEART may be affected and there can be deafness and intellectual impairment. In a less severe form of the disorder, the second X-chromosome is present but abnormal, lacking in normal genetic material.

turning *see* VERSION.

tympanic membrane the eardrum, which separates the middle and outer EARS and vibrates in response to sound waves, transmitting the vibrations to one of the ear OSSICLES (the malleus).

typhoid fever a severe infectious disease of the digestive system that is caused by the bacterium *Salmonella typhi* and causes symptoms including a rise in TEMPERATURE, a rash on the ABDOMEN and chest, headache and nosebleeds. The temperature rise occurs in a characteristic fashion known as a step-ladder temperature. In severe cases there may be ulceration of the intestinal wall, leading to PERITONITIS if an ULCER bursts or HAEMORRHAGE from the bowels and INFLAMMATION of the LUNGS, SPLEEN and BONES. In these cases the disease can prove to be fatal. The INFECTION is acquired through ingesting contaminated food or water, so preventative measures involving high standards of hygiene and sanitation are important. Drug treatment is by means of ANTIBIOTICS such as chloramphenicol and AMPICILLIN. Inoculation with TAB VACCINE confers temporary IMMUNITY.

typhus fever a disease that is characterized by FEVER, debility and RASH and is spread by body lice (*see* RICKETTSIAE).

tyrosine *see* DOPA; PHENYLKETONURIA.

U

ulcer a break on the SKIN surface or on the MUCOUS MEMBRANE lining within the body cavities that may be inflamed and fails to heal. Ulcers of the skin include BED SORES and VARICOSE ULCERS (which are caused by defective CIRCULATION). For ulcers of the alimentary tract, *see* DUODENAL ULCER, GASTRIC ULCER and PEPTIC ULCER.

ulcerative colitis *see* COLITIS.

ulna (*pl* **ulnae**) one of the two BONES making up the forearm. It is the inner and longer of the two bones (the other being the RADIUS). It articulates with the radius at both

ends and also with the HU-
MERUS above and indirectly
with the wrist below.

ultrasonography *see* ECHOG-
RAPHY.

ultrasound *or* **ultrasonic
waves** high frequency sound
waves (above 20kHz), beyond
the range of the human ear.
Ultrasound is used to examine
the body's ORGANS, DUCTS,
etc, in addition to assessing
the progress of a developing
FOETUS. The patient is not
submitted to harmful radiation as with other techniques
and no contrast medium is required. It can be used to examine the LIVER, KIDNEY,
BLADDER, PANCREAS and ovaries (*see* OVARY) and is used in
diagnosing brain TUMOURS.
The vibrations of the sound
waves can be used in other
ways, e.g. breaking up kidney
stones (*see* RENAL CALCULUS).

umbilical cord the cord connecting the FOETUS to the
PLACENTA, containing two
arteries (*see* ARTERY) and one
VEIN. It is approximately
60cm long, and after birth it
is severed and the stump
shrivels to leave a scar, the
navel or umbilicus.

umbilicus the navel (*see* UM-
BILICAL CORD).

unconsciousness the state of
being partially or totally un-
aware of one's surroundings
and lacking in response to
stimuli. SLEEP is a natural
form of unconsciousness.
Unnatural states of unconsciousness can have numerous
causes, including injuries to
the BRAIN, resulting in compression or CONCUSSION, fainting because of insufficient
blood supply to the brain, EPI-
LEPSY, poisoning and various
diseases, e.g. DIABETES MEL-
LITUS.

undulant fever *see* BRUCEL-
LOSIS.

ungual a term meaning relating to the fingernails or toe-
nails.

unguent the term in pharmacy
for an ointment.

unguis a fingernail or toenail.

uracil *see* NUCLEOTIDE.

uraemia a condition in which
there is excess UREA in the
blood because of KIDNEY disease or failure. Waste products are usually excreted by
the kidneys, but accumulation
in the blood leads to headaches, drowsiness and lethargy, nausea and vomiting
and diarrhoea. Eventually,
without treatment, death follows. HAEMODIALYSIS on a

kidney machine may be necessary or even renal TRANSPLANTATION.

urataemia the presence in the blood of urate compounds (*see* URIC ACID), associated with GOUT, when urates are deposited in the body.

urate *see* GOUT; URIC ACID.

urea a metabolic byproduct of the chemical breakdown of PROTEIN and the form in which excess nitrogen is removed from the body in URINE. It is formed in the LIVER and taken in the blood to the KIDNEYS. The amount excreted daily is 30–35 g. Although urea is not poisonous in itself, an excess in the BLOOD (URAEMIA) implies a defective kidney, which will cause an excess of other waste products that may be poisonous.

ureaplasma microorganisms responsible for diseases such as PROSTATITIS, nonspecific URETHRITIS, infertility and NEONATAL death. The latter can be associated with INFECTION of the PLACENTA by *Ureaplasma urealyticum.*

ureter one of the two tubes joining the KIDNEYS to the BLADDER, through which URINE passes. The muscular ureter walls contract to force URINE into the bladder.

ureterectomy surgical EXCISION of the URETER, usually with the removal of the associated KIDNEY.

ureteritis INFLAMMATION of the URETER, which usually occurs with BLADDER inflammations.

ureteroenterostomy the creation by surgery of a link between the URETER and the bowel, thus bypassing the BLADDER. The join is made at the SIGMOID COLON and done so to bypass a diseased bladder. The URINE is then passed with the FAECES, thus avoiding an external opening for collection of urine.

ureteroplasty reconstruction of a damaged or diseased URETER by surgery, using TISSUE from the bowel or from the BLADDER.

ureteroscope an instrument introduced into a dilated URETER often to locate a stone or remove stone fragments created by ultrasonic destruction of a larger stone.

ureterostomy the creation of an external opening to the URETER whereby the ureter is brought to the surface to permit drainage.

ureterotomy an incision into the URETER, commonly to remove a stone . *See* RENAL CALCULUS.

urethra the duct carrying URINE from the BLADDER out of the body. It is about 3.5 cm long in women and 20 cm in men. The male urethra runs through the PENIS and also forms the ejaculatory duct (*see* EJACULATION).

urethritis INFLAMMATION of the mucous lining of the URE-THRA, which may be associated with CYSTITIS, often being the cause of the latter. The commonest cause of urethritis is GONORRHOEA (specific urethritis). Alternatively, it may be caused by INFECTION with microorganisms (nonspecific urethritis). The symptoms include pain on passing URINE and a discharge, and inflammations in other organs such as the BLADDER and TESTICLE are possible. SULPHONAMIDE and ANTIBIOTIC drugs are effective once the infecting organism is identified.

uric acid an organic acid that contains nitrogen and is the end-product of the METABO-LISM of PROTEIN. It occurs in the URINE but in small amounts (less than 1 gram). It is formed in the LIVER and ex-creted by the KIDNEYs, but in excess, salts (urates) form and occur as stone in the urinary tract. Deposits of urates in JOINTS is a feature of GOUT.

urinary organs the system responsible for the extraction of components from the BLOOD to form URINE, its storage and periodic discharge from the body. The organs are the KID-NEYs, URETERS, BLADDER and URETHRA.

urinary tract the system of ducts that permits movement of URINE out of the body from the KIDNEYs, i.e. the URETERS, BLADDER and URETHRA.

urination *or* **micturition** the discharge of URINE from the body via the URETHRA. It is begun by a voluntary relaxation of the SPHINCTER muscle below the BLADDER.

urine the body's fluid waste excreted by the KIDNEYs. The waste products include UREA, URIC ACID and creatinine (produced by muscles), with salt, phosphates and sulphates and ammonia also present. In a solution with about 95–96 per cent water, there may be 100 or more compounds but the vast majority occur only in trace amounts. Many diseases alter the quantity and composition of urine, and its analysis is standard procedure to assist DIAGNOSIS of diseases.

urine retention the condition when URINE is produced by the KIDNEYS but it is retained in the BLADDER. This may be because of an obstruction or a weakness in the bladder (less common). Enlargement of the PROSTATE GLAND is a common cause of blockage in men. It may also be caused by a STRICTURE caused by an injury SCAR or ulceration.

urinogenital a collective term describing all organs and tissues involved in excretion and reproduction because they are closely linked anatomically and functionally.

urology the subdiscipline of medicine dealing with diseases of the URINARY TRACT, from the KIDNEY to the URETHRA.

urticaria *or* **nettle rash** an allergic reaction in an individual exposed to a substance to which he or she is hypersensitive, in which the response is manifested on the SKIN. Raised red patches develop, which may last for hours or days. There is intense itching. The sensitivity may be to certain foods, e.g. shellfish, and the effect may occur anywhere on the body but commonly erupts on the face and trunk. If it also affects the tongue or throat, there is danger of a blockage of the airway, which needs urgent attention.

uterine relating to the UTERUS.

uterus *or* **womb** a roughly pear-shaped ORGAN within the cavity of the PELVIS that is specialized for the growth and nourishment of a FOETUS. FALLOPIAN TUBES connect to the upper part and the lower part joins the VAGINA at the CERVIX. It has a plentiful blood supply along with lymphatic VESSELS and NERVES. During PREGNANCY it enlarges considerably and the smooth MUSCLE walls thicken. Contractions of the muscular wall push the foetus out via the vagina at childbirth. If there is no PREGNANCY, the lining undergoes periodic changes (MENSTRUATION).

uvea the middle pigmented layer of the EYE, consisting of the IRIS, choroid and ciliary body.

uveitis INFLAMMATION of any part of the UVEA of the EYE. The IRIS and ciliary body are often both inflamed (anterior uveitis), producing a painful condition, unlike posterior uveitis (when the choroid is affected). The cause of both types is usually different and may follow from affected areas elsewhere in the eye. All types lead to visual impairment, and symptoms may include blurred vision with discomfort or pain, and diseases or conditions with which it is known to be linked are ARTHRITIS, TUBERCULOSIS, SYPHILIS, and viral and parasitic INFECTIONS.

V

vaccination the production of IMMUNITY to a disease by INOCULATION with a VACCINE or a specially prepared material that stimulates the production of ANTIBODIES. It was used initially to refer only to cowpox VIRUS (which also protected against SMALLPOX) but now is synonymous with INOCULATION in immunizing against disease.

vaccine a modified preparation of a bacterium (*see* BACTERIA) or VIRUS that is no longer dangerous but will stimulate development of ANTIBODIES and therefore confer IMMUNITY against actual INFECTION with the disease. Other vaccines consist of specific TOXINS (e.g. TETANUS) or dead bacteria (e.g. CHOLERA and TYPHOID). Live but weakened organisms are used against SMALLPOX and TUBERCULOSIS.

vacuum extractor *see* VENTOUSE.

vagina the lower part of the female reproductive tract that leads from the UTERUS to the outside. It receives the erect PENIS during sexual intercourse, the SEMEN being ejaculated into the upper part from where the SPERM pass through the CERVIX and UTERUS to the FALLOPIAN TUBES. The vagina is essentially a muscular tube lined with MUCOUS MEMBRANE.

vaginismus a sudden and painful contraction of MUSCLES surrounding the VAGINA in response to contact of the vagina or VULVA, e.g. an attempted intercourse. It may be caused by a fear of intercourse or by an INFLAMMATION.

vaginitis INFLAMMATION of the VAGINA as a result of infection or deficiency in diet or poor hygiene. There may be itching, a discharge and pain on urination.

vagotomy the cutting of fibres of the VAGUS nerve to the STOMACH. The operation can be performed to reduce the STOMACH's acid and pepsin secretion in treatment of a PEPTIC ULCER.

vagus nerve the tenth CRANIAL NERVE, which comprises MOTOR, SENSORY, VASODILATOR and secretory fibres. It supplies the MUSCLES for swallowing, and fibres go to the HEART, throat, LUNGS and STOMACH and other ORGANS in the abdomen. It also carries the taste sensation from the mouth.

valine *see* ESSENTIAL AMINO ACID.

valve a structure within an ORGAN or VESSEL that restricts flow to one direction, whether the fluid be BLOOD or LYMPH. The valves comprise cusps on the vessel wall. The cusp is like a membranous pocket that fills with blood and prevents backward flow by distending and closing the valve.

valvotomy an operation undertaken to open a stenosed HEART valve (*see* STENOSIS) and render it functional. Several techniques are available, including surgery, an inflating balloon or a dilating instrument.

valvular heart disease a disease that affects mainly the AORTIC VALVE and MITRAL VALVE, which may narrow (*see* AORTIC STENOSIS and STENOSIS) or weaken. Aortic valve disease is associated more with old age while mitral valve disease is rheumatic in origin. *See also* MITRAL INCOMPETENCE.

valvulitis INFLAMMATION of a VALVE, particularly in the HEART. It is commonly caused by RHEUMATIC FEVER.

vaporizer a device that produces a mist of liquid medication for INHALATION. It is commonly used to treat ASTHMA.

varicose ulcer an ULCER on the lower leg that is difficult to heal because of poor CIRCULATION.

varicose veins VEINS that have become stretched, distended and twisted. The saphenous veins (superficial veins in the legs) are often affected, although it may occur elsewhere. Causes include congenitally defective VALVES, OBESITY, PREGNANCY and THROMBOPHLEBITIS (INFLAMMATION of the wall of a vein with secondary THROMBOSIS in the affected part of the vein). Elastic support is a common treatment, although alternatives are SCLEROTHERAPY and PHLEBECTOMY.

variola a name for SMALLPOX.

vas (*pl* **vasa**) a VESSEL or DUCT, especially one carrying BLOOD, LYMPH or SPERM.

vascular relating to BLOOD VESSELS; supplied with blood vessels.

vasculitis INFLAMMATION of the BLOOD VESSELS, which may cause damage to the linings and narrowing. It may result from several conditions, including acute NEPHRITIS and SERUM SICKNESS.

vas deferens (*pl* **vasa deferentia**) one of the two tubes that join the testes (*see* TESTICLE) to the ejaculatory duct via the PROSTATE GLAND. It carries SPERM to the URETHRA on EJACULATION, aided by contraction of its muscular wall.

vasectomy the cutting of the VAS DEFERENS, which is performed on both ducts, causing sterility, although the effect is not immediate.

vasoconstriction the narrowing of BLOOD VESSELS with a consequent reduction in blood supply to the TISSUES. A variety of circumstances can cause vasoconstriction, including cold and shock.

vasodilation *or* **vasodilation** the increase in diameter of BLOOD VESSELS, producing a lowering of BLOOD PRESSURE and increased flow.

vasodilator a body mechanism, substance or drug that causes BLOOD VESSELS to relax. Nitroglycerine, or glyceryl trinitrate (GTN) is commonly used as a coronary vasodilator in the treatment of ANGINA.

vasopressin *or* **antidiuretic hormone** a HORMONE of the PITUITARY GLAND that constricts BLOOD VESSELS and reduces URINE secretion by increasing the quantity of water reabsorbed by the KIDNEY.

vasovagal attack fainting, precipitated by a slowing of the HEART and a fall in BLOOD PRESSURE. This may be as a result of SHOCK, severe pain, fear, etc, and is caused by excessive stimulation of the VAGUS NERVE, which participates in the control of breathing and the circulation.

vasovasostomy the reversal of VASECTOMY.

vCJD *see* NEW VARIANT CJD.

vector commonly, an insect that carries parasitic microorganisms between people or from animals to people, e.g. mosquitoes carrying MALARIA.

vein one of the numerous BLOOD VESSELS carrying deoxygenated blood to the right ATRIUM of the HEART (the one exception is the PULMONARY vein). Each vein has three TISSUE layers, similar to the layers of the heart. Veins are less elastic than arteries and collapse when cut. They also contain VALVES to prevent back flow.

vena cava (*pl* **venae cavae**) either of two major VEINS carrying blood from other veins to the right ATRIUM of the HEART. The inferior vena cava takes blood from the body below the DIAPHRAGM, and the superior vena cava takes blood from the head, neck, arms and thorax.

venereal diseases *or* **sexually transmitted diseases** diseases transmitted by sexual intercourse. These include AIDS, SYPHILIS, GONORRHOEA, nonspecific URETHRITIS, HPV etc.

venography *or* **phlebography** examination of VEINS using X-RAYS after INJECTION of a radio-opaque substance. This enables leaks, blockages or other abnormalities to be identified.

venom the poisonous substance produced by snakes, scorpions, etc, that in humans may produce only localized pain and swelling, or in serious cases cause more general effects and even death.

venous pertaining to a VEIN or containing veins, e.g. venous BLOOD, which is distinguishable from arterial blood by its darker colour.

ventilation the means whereby air passes into and out of the LUNGS, aided by movement of the DIAPHRAGM. Artificial ventilation is the use of a machine (RESPIRATOR) to regulate and perform a person's breathing. This may be during an operation. Also, damage to the relevant part of the BRAIN, chest injury, lung disease or NERVE and MUSCLE disorders may all necessitate the use of artificial ventilation.

ventilator *see* RESPIRATOR.

ventouse *or* **vacuum extractor** a machine used in childbirth, comprising a suction cup attached to the head of the FOETUS enabling it to be gently pulled out of the UTERUS. It is an alternative to the use of FORCEPS.

ventral the term used to describe anything relating to the front, abdominal part of the body or a hollow structure.

ventricle 1. one of the two major chambers within the HEART. They are thick-walled and muscular and form the main pumping chamber. The right ventricle receives BLOOD from the right ATRIUM and the VENAE CAVAE, and its outflow is the pulmonary ARTERY. The left ventricle takes blood from the pulmonary VEIN via the left atrium, and its outflow is the AORTA. **2.** cavities within the BRAIN, filled with CEREBROSPINAL FLUID.

ventricular fibrillation a rapid ARRHYTHMIA of the VENTRICLE, which is dangerous.

venule a tiny VEIN that collects blood from the capillaries (*see* CAPILLARY).

vermiform appendix *see* APPENDIX.

verruca a term for WART.

verrucose covered with WARTS.

version *or* **turning** the procedure to move a FOETUS in the UTERUS to a more normal position to make delivery easier.

vertebra (*pl* **vertebrae**) any of the bones making up the SPINAL COLUMN. Each has a cavity (the vertebral canal or FORAMEN) and various PRO-CESSES for attachment of MUSCLES or articulation of adjacent vertebrae. The SPINAL CORD passes through the vertebral canal. *See also* INTERVERTEBRAL DISC.

vertebral canal *see* VERTEBRA.

vertebral column *see* SPINAL COLUMN.

vertigo a condition in which a person has a false sensation of imbalance and of the surroundings moving. It is commonly a sensation of spinning but may be as if the ground is tilting. The semicircular canals of the EAR are fundamental in the maintenance of balance, and vertigo is generally the result of some problem with this mechanism or with the appropriate centres in the BRAIN.

vesicle 1. a small bladder-like structure, cavity or CELL, etc, in the body, usually containing fluid. **2.** a little SAC or CYST. **3.** a small BLISTER or PUSTULE on the SKIN.

vesicular breathing soft, normal sounds of breathing heard in the LUNGS by means of a stethoscope. The sounds change when the lungs are diseased, and the different sounds help a doctor diagnose the condition.

vessel any tube that carries fluid, particularly BLOOD or LYMPH.

vestigial the term applied to an ORGAN that has progressively, over a long time, lost its function and structure to become rudimentary.

viable able to live separately.

Viagra *see* SILDENAFIL CITRATE.

villi (*sing* **villus**) *see* JEJUNUM.

Vincent's angina a former name for ulcerative GINGIVITIS and ulcerative INFLAMMATION of the throat, caused by BACTERIA.

viral haemorrhagic fever a viral disease with a high mortality rate. After the INCUBATION period there is HEADACHE, FEVER, severe internal bleeding, DIARRHOEA and VOMITING. Death may follow, usually eight or nine days later. SERUM taken from someone recovering from the disease is a useful source of ANTIBODIES.

viral pneumonia an acute lung INFECTION caused by one of a number of VIRUSES. The symptoms include FEVER, headache, MUSCLE pains and a thick SPUTUM associated with a cough. It often occurs after a viral infection, and

treatment, in the main, deals with the symptoms only.

virology the study of VIRUSES.

virulence the ability of BACTERIA or VIRUSES to cause disease, measured by the number of people infected, the speed with which they spread through the body, etc.

virus the smallest microbe that is completely parasitic because it is capable only of replication within the CELLS of its host. Viruses infect animals, plants and microorganisms. Viruses are classified according to their nucleic acids and can contain double or single-stranded DNA or RNA. In an INFECTION, the virus binds to the host cells and then penetrates to release the viral DNA or RNA, which controls the cell's METABOLISM. It then replicates itself and forms new viruses. Viruses cause many diseases, including INFLUENZA (single-stranded RNA), HERPES (double-stranded DNA), AIDS (a RETROVIRUS, single-stranded RNA) and also MUMPS, CHICKENPOX and POLIOMYELITIS.

viscera (*sing* **viscus**) the term for organs within the body cavity, usually the ABDOMEN.

visceral pertaining to the VIS-CERA.

vision the capacity for sight. Light enters the EYE through the CORNEA and the aqueous HUMOUR. Next, it passes through the PUPIL, LENS and VITREOUS HUMOUR to impinge upon the RETINA. There the ROD and CONE cells detect light and send impulses to the nerve fibres, which are relayed to the visual cortex in the BRAIN via the optic nerve. Visual acuity is the sharpness of vision, dependent on a healthy retina and accurate lens. *See also* SNELLEN CHART.

vital capacity the largest volume of air that can be exhaled after breathing in deeply.

vitamin any of a group of organic compounds required in very small amounts in the diet to maintain good health. Deficiencies lead to specific diseases. Vitamins are divided into two groups: vitamins A, D, E and K are fat-soluble, while C and B are water-soluble.

vitamin A *or* **retinol** a fat-soluble VITAMIN that must be in the diet as it cannot be synthesized in the body. It is essential for vision in dim light,
growth and the maintenance of mucous tissue.

vitamin B a group of VITAMINS that, although they are not related chemically, are often found in the same types of food. *See also* FOLIC ACID.

vitamin B1 *or* **thiamine** a VITAMIN active in the form thiamine pyrophosphate, a deficiency of which leads to BERI-BERI.

vitamin B2 *or* **riboflavin** a VITAMIN important in tissue respiration (ENZYME reactions in CELLS) although a deficiency is not serious.

vitamin B3 *or* **pantothenic acid** a VITAMIN that occurs widely in foods and is therefore unlikely to be lacking in the diet.

vitamin B6 *or* **pyridoxine** a VITAMIN that is important in the METABOLISM of several amino acids.

vitamin B12 *or* **cyanocobalamin** an important VITAMIN in the synthesis of NUCLEIC ACIDS, maintenance of MYELIN surrounding nerve fibres and in the production of red blood cells (ERYTHROCYTES). A deficiency produces ANAEMIA and degeneration of the NERVOUS SYSTEM.

vitamin C *or* **ascorbic acid** a VITAMIN that is essential in maintaining CELL walls and CONNECTIVE TISSUE and a deficiency of which leads to fragility of TENDONS, BLOOD VESSELS and SKIN, all characteristic of SCURVY. The presence of ascorbic acid is believed to assist the uptake of iron during DIGESTION.

vitamin D a VITAMIN that occurs as two STEROID derivations: D2 or CALCIFEROL in yeast, and D3 or cholecalciferol, which is produced by the action of sunlight on the SKIN. It is vital in the control of blood calcium levels. It prompts an increase in calcium takeup in the intestine, increasing the supply for the production of BONE. It also affects phosphorus uptake. A deficiency leads to RICKETS and OSTEOMALACIA.

vitamin E a group of compounds (tocopherols) thought to prevent damage to CELL membranes. A deficiency is unusual because of its widespread occurrence in foods.

vitamin H *see* BIOTIN.

vitamin K a VITAMIN that is essential for the clotting of blood as it is involved in the formation of prothrombin (the inactive precursor of THROMBIN) in the LIVER. A deficiency rarely occurs because the vitamin is synthesized by BACTERIA in the large INTESTINE.

vitreous humour the jelly-like substance occurring between the LENS and the RETINA in the EYE.

vocal cords two MEMBRANES in the LARYNX that vibrate to produce sound when air is expelled over them. Tension in the cords is controlled by MUSCLES and TENDONS, thus changing the sound generated.

Volkmann's contracture a condition often caused by pressure from a cast (*see* PLASTER OF PARIS) or tight BANDAGE on the arm. The result is persistent contraction (FLEXION) of forearm MUSCLES and decreased BLOOD supply to hand and arm. The muscles then swell and become fibrosed (*see* FIBROSIS).

voluntary muscle *or* **striated muscle** MUSCLE that is under conscious control, e.g. those operating the skeleton. It consists of bundles of elongated fibres surrounded by CONNECTIVE TISSUE. A TENDON at the end of the muscle attaches it to the BONE. Each muscle fibre comprises smaller fibres (myofibrils) with alternating dark and light bands (sarcomeres), which produce the striated appearance and provide the contractile function. A flexor (or agonist) muscle contracts, becoming shorter and thus moving bones closer to each other. An extensor or antagonist muscle works in the opposite way.

volvulus a twisting of part of the INTESTINE, which usually results in some obstruction that may reduce the BLOOD supply, ending in GANGRENE. It may right itself spontaneously or may be righted by manipulation. However, surgery is often necessary.

vomiting *or* **emesis** the RE-FLEX ACTION wherein the contents of the STOMACH are expelled through the mouth because of the contraction of the DIAPHRAGM and abdominal wall MUSCLES. Vomiting is caused by stimulus of the appropriate centre in the BRAIN, but the primary agent is usually a sensation from the stomach itself, e.g. a gastric disease or some irritant. Other causes may be the action of drugs, some effect on the inner EAR (e.g. MOTION SICKNESS), MIGRAINES, etc.

von Recklinghausen's disease a CONGENITAL disorder, neurofibromatosis, in which soft tissue TUMOURS form along NERVES and beneath the SKIN. There are often other anomalies, such as decalcification of BONES, FIBROSIS of the LUNGS and formation of KIDNEY stones (renal calculi).

vulva (*pl* **vulvae**) the external female GENITALIA, comprising two pairs of fleshy folds (LABIA) surrounding the opening of the VAGINA. Below them is the CLITORIS.

vulvectomy surgical removal of the VULVA. The extent of the operation depends on whether there is a MALIGNANT or non-malignant growth.

vulvitis INFLAMMATION of the VULVA.

vulvovaginitis INFLAMMATION of both the VULVA and VAGINA.

W

warfarin an ANTICOAGULANT given to reduce the risk of EMBOLISM. It may be administered orally or by INJECTION, and the significant SIDE EFFECT is bleeding, usually from the gums and other MU-COUS MEMBRANES.

wart *or* **verruca** a solid, BE-NIGN growth in the skin caused by a VIRUS. They are infectious and spread rapidly in schools, etc. There are several types: plantar, on the foot; juvenile in children; and venereal, on the genitals. Warts often disappear spontaneously but can be dealt with in several ways, e.g. CRYOSURGERY (freezing), LASER treatment and ELECTROCAUTERY.

water bed a bed with a water-containing mattress that readily accommodates a patient's posture. It is useful to avoid BED SORES.

water on the brain *see* HY-DROCEPHALUS.

weal *or* **wheal** an area of the skin that is temporarily raised and coloured red, or pale with red margins. It may be caused by an ALLERGY, nettle rash (*see* URTICARIA) or a sharp blow, and in the former cases may be accompanied by itching.

webbed fingers *see* SYNDAC-TYLY.

Weber's test the assessment of a person's DEAFNESS by using a tuning fork. The stem of a vibrating fork is placed on the forehead or maxillary IN-CISORS and if the hearing is normal, the sound is equal in both EARS. It helps to diagnose whether hearing loss is caused by a middle ear disorder or a neurosensory loss.

Weil's disease *see* LEPTOSPI-ROSIS.

wen *see* SEBACEOUS CYST.

Wertheim's hysterectomy a major form of HYSTEREC-TOMY undertaken to deal with uterine or ovarian CANCER. It involves the removal of the UTERUS, ovaries (*see* OVARY), FALLOPIAN TUBES, upper part of the VAGINA and the surrounding LYMPH NODES.

wheal *see* WEAL.

wheeze the sound produced by the long-drawn-out breathing associated with ASTHMA. It also occurs when bronchial tubes are narrowed, e.g. as in BRONCHITIS.

whiplash injury damage caused by the sudden jerking backwards of the head and neck, as in a road accident. A severe whiplash can cause death, but injury is the usual outcome. The VERTEBRAe, spinal cord, LIGAMENTS and NERVES in the neck may all be damaged. Treatment usually involves wearing a special collar to immobilize the affected area.

Whipple's disease a rare disease of the INTESTINES, resulting in malabsorption of food (*see* MALABSORPTION SYNDROME). Symptoms include ANAEMIA, weight loss, ARTHRITIS, skin pigmentation, chest pain and a nonproductive COUGH. It seems to be caused by microorganisms in the MUCOSA. It responds to extensive ANTIBIOTIC treatment.

white leg *see* THROMBOPHLEBITIS.

white matter nerve TISSUE in the CENTRAL NERVOUS SYSTEM, composed primarily of NERVE fibres in light-coloured MYELIN sheaths. In the BRAIN it occupies the central part of the CEREBRAL CORTEX.

whitlow INFLAMMATION in the finger tip and usually an ABSCESS affecting the fat and FIBROUS TISSUES that comprise the pulp of the finger.

whoop the noisy and characteristic drawing in of breath following a coughing attack in WHOOPING COUGH.

whooping cough *or* **pertussis** an infectious disease caused by the bacterium *Bordetella pertussis*. The MUCOUS MEMBRANES lining the air passages are affected, and after a one to two week INCU-BATION period, fever, CATARRH and a cough develop. The cough then becomes paroxysmal, with a number of short coughs punctuated with the 'whooping' drawing in of breath. Nosebleeds and VOMITING may follow a paroxysm. After about two weeks the symptoms abate, but a cough may continue for some weeks. Whooping cough is not usually serious, and IMMUNIZATION reduces the severity of an attack. However, a child may be susceptible to PNEUMONIA and TUBERCULOSIS during the disease.

Wilm's tumour a TUMOUR of the KIDNEY (nephroblastoma) in infancy. Early removal of the kidney, with RADIOTHERAPY and CHEMOTHERAPY, confers a high survival rate.

windpipe *see* TRACHEA.

wisdom tooth the last (third) molar TOOTH on each side of either JAW. The wisdom teeth normally erupt last, around the age of 20 to 25, although some remain IMPACTED in the jaw bone.

withdrawal symptoms a characteristic feature when someone stops using a DRUG upon which he or she is dependent. Hard drugs such as

HEROIN and COCAINE induce dependence, as do alcohol, nicotine and amfetamines. Symptoms include shivering, tremors, VOMITING and sweating.

womb *see* UTERUS.

woolsorter's disease *see* ANTHRAX.

wound a sudden break in the body TISSUES and/or ORGANS caused by an external agent. There are four types based on the result of the injury: INCISIONS, punctures, LACERATIONS and CONTUSIONS.

wrist the JOINT between the HAND and forearm. The wrist region comprises eight carpal BONES and five metacarpal bones joined by strong LIGAMENTS. The wrist joint then articulates with the RADIUS and ULNA. The joint can move in all directions with little risk of DISLOCATION.

writer's cramp an involuntary contraction of the HAND muscles when writing but not when using those muscles to undertake other functions. A similar condition may arise with musicians (guitarists and pianists), typists and computer operators.

wryneck *or* **torticollis** the condition when the head is twisted to one side because of a SCAR contracting or, more commonly, excessive MUSCLE contraction.

XYZ

xanthelasma yellow fatty deposits in the eyelids and SKIN around the eyes. It often occurs in elderly people, when it is insignificant, but a severe case may be caused by a fat METABOLISM disorder.

xanthochromia a yellow colouring, e.g. the SKIN in JAUNDICE or the CEREBROSPINAL FLUID when it contains HAEMOGLOBIN breakdown products.

X-chromosome the SEX CHROMOSOME present in males and females, although women have a pair and men just one (with one Y-CHROMOSOME). Certain disorders, such as HAEMOPHILIA, are carried as GENES on the X-chromosome.

xenophobia an abnormal condition in which there is dislike and fear of foreigners.

xeroderma a condition of the skin that manifests itself as a dryness and roughness with the formation of scales. It is a mild form of ICHTHYOSIS.

xiphoid process *or* **xiphoid cartilage** the lowest part of the STERNUM. It is a flat CARTILAGE that is progressively replaced by BONE, a process completed sometime after middle age.

X-rays the part of the electromagnetic spectrum with waves of wavelength 10^{-12} to 10^{-9}m and frequencies of 10^{17} to 10^{21}Hz. They are produced when high-velocity electrons strike a target. The rays penetrate solids to a depth that depends on the density of the solid. X-rays of certain wavelengths will penetrate flesh but not BONE. They are therefore useful in therapy and DIAGNOSIS within medicine.

yawning a REFLEX ACTION when the mouth is opened wide and air is drawn into the lungs and slowly released. It is usually, although not exclusively, associated with tiredness or boredom.

yaws an infectious disease of the tropics caused by a SPIROCHAETE, *Treponema pertenue*, usually in unhygienic conditions. The bacteria enter through ABRASIONS, and after about two weeks, during which time there is FEVER, pain and itching, small TUMOURS appear, each with a yellow crust of dried SERUM. These may eventually form deep ULCERS. The final stages may not appear until several years later and include LESIONS of skin and bone. Fortunately, PENICILLIN works dramatically and effectively in this disease.

Y-chromosome the small SEX CHROMOSOME that carries a dominant GENE conferring maleness. Normal males have 22 matched CHROMOSOME pairs and one unmatched pair, comprising one X-CHROMOSOME and one Y-chromosome. During sexual reproduction, the mother contributes an X-chromosome, but the father contributes an X or Y-chromosome. XX produces a female offspring and XY a male.

yellow fever an infectious viral disease in tropical Africa and South America. Transmitted by mosquitoes, it causes TISSUE degeneration in the LIVER and KIDNEYS. Symptoms include headache, back pains, FEVER, VOMITING, JAUNDICE, etc, and an attack can prove fatal. VACCINATION will prove effective and anyone recovering from an attack has IMMUNITY conferred.

zidovudine *see* AZT.

Zollinger-Ellison syndrome an uncommon disorder resulting in DIARRHOEA and multiple PEPTIC ULCERS. The cause is a pancreatic TUMOUR or enlarged PANCREAS, which in turn leads to high levels of the HORMONE gastrin, which stimulates excess production of acidic GASTRIC JUICE, causing the ulceration. Surgery is usually effective.

zoonosis (*pl* **zoonoses**) an infectious animal disease that can be transmitted to humans. Some of the 150 or so diseases are: ANTHRAX, BRUCELLOSIS, BOVINE TUBERCULOSIS, RIFT VALLEY FEVER, RABIES, LEPTOSPIROSIS and TYPHUS.

zoophobia an unnatural and strong fear of animals.

zygomatic arch the arch of BONE on either side of the FACE, below the eyes.

zygomatic bone a facial BONE and one of a pair of bones that form the prominence of the cheeks.

zygote the CELL produced by the fusion of male and female germ cells (GAMETES) during the early stage of FERTILIZATION, i.e. an OVUM fertilized by a SPERM. After passing down the FALLOPIAN TUBE, it implants in the UTERUS, forming the EMBRYO.